THE ANZACS

Patsy Adam-Smith is one of Australia's best-known and best-loved authors. Awarded the OBE in 1980 for services to literature and an AO in 1993 for services to recording oral history, she has had thirty books published, all of which have either topped or been featured on the best-seller lists of their time. Among her most popular books are *Hear the Train Blow*, *The Shearers*, *Australian Women at War*, *Heart of Exile*, *There Was a Ship*, *Outback Heroes*, *Romance of the Australian Railways*, *The Anzacs*, which was joint winner of the Age Book of the Year award in 1978, and *Prisoners of War*, which won the prestigious triennial Order of Australia Association Book Prize in 1993. *Goodbye Girlie*, which follows on from the autobiographical *Hear the Train Blow*, was published in 1994.

PATSY ADAM-SMITH
the ANZACS

PENGUIN BOOKS

Penguin Books Australia Ltd
487 Maroondah Highway, PO Box 257
Ringwood, Victoria 3134, Australia
Penguin Books Ltd
Harmondsworth, Middlesex, England
Penguin Putnam Inc.
375 Hudson Street, New York, New York 10014, USA
Penguin Books Canada Limited
10 Alcorn Avenue, Toronto, Ontario, Canada M4V 3B2
Penguin Books (N.Z.) Ltd
Cnr Rosedale and Airborne Roads, Albany, Auckland, New Zealand
Penguin Books (South Africa) (Pty) Ltd
5 Watkins Street, Denver Ext 4, 2094, South Africa
Penguin Books India (P) Ltd
11, Community Centre, Panchsheel Park, New Delhi 110 017, India

First published in hardback by Thomas Nelson Australia 1978
Reprinted 1979 (three times), 1982, 1983, 1985
Paperback edition published by Sphere Books 1981
Reprinted 1982, 1985
Large-format illustrated paperback edition published by
    Thomas Nelson Australia 1985
This edition published by Penguin Books Australia Ltd 1991

16 15 14 13 12 11 10 9 8

Cover designed by Karen Trump
Printed in Australia by Australian Print Group, Maryborough, Victoria

National Library of Australia
Cataloguing-in-Publication data:

Adam-Smith, Patsy.
    The Anzacs.

    Bibliography.
    Includes index.
    ISBN 0 14 016539 8.

    1. World War, 1914–1918 – Personal narratives, Australian.
    2. World War, 1914–1918 – Campaigns. I. Title

940.48194

Contents

Acknowledgements   vi

Preface   viii

Part One: The Beginning
 1 Why Did You Go To the
    Great War, Daddy?   2
 2 Moulding the Lads   12
 3 The First Man, the First
    Shilling   17
 4 Goodbye to *AE1*   31
 5 The Great Adventure   38
 6 What Price Me Now?   49
 7 Painting Egypt Red   63
 8 The Battle of the
    Wazzir   71
 9 The Arena   77
10 All Those Empty
    Pages   83
11 The White Ships   108
12 The Lonesome Pine   113
13 Fight I Must   135
14 The Face of a Hero   157
15 T.P. (The Padre)   165
16 What, Gone? The
    Australians Gone!   178
17 The Tap Root   186

Part Two: After Gallipoli
18 Run For Your
    Life, Dig!   194
19 The 'Fair Dinkums'   208
20 The Station Hands   224
21 Somewhere in
    France   229
22 Fromelles   236

23 Beaucoup Australie,
    Fini Pozières   249
24 Blighty   271
25 One In Every Ten   281
26 The Rose of No Man's
    Land   290
27 Kangaroo Feathers   302
28 The Shellal Mosaic   316
29 The Boys in Blue   319
30 The Circus   328
31 The Red Baron   346
32 The Butchers' Picnic   352
33 Wipers   368
34 The Dinki-dis   384
35 Keep the Home Fires
    Burning   388
36 I Want To Go Home   397
37 Never Forget
    Australia   404
38 The Mutinies   418
39 The New Never-Never
    Land   423
40 Boys, You've Lost
    Your Jobs   430
41 Part of the Price   441
42 Good-bye-ee   445
43 So Ends the Bloody
    Business of the Day   454

Appendix I:
  C. E. W. Bean   472
Appendix II: Tables   475
Bibliography   477
Sources of
  Illustrations   482
Index   484

Acknowledgements

This book was written while survivors who had returned from World War I were still alive and alert. Names of many of these men (and women) appear in the text. To these, and the others whose stories do not appear but who helped make the book, and all the wives, widows and sisters who aided me, I owe a great deal, as I do to Dan Webb of TV Channel 7 who broadcast encouragement to these men to come to me.

The men and women wrote about the war as they saw it. They were not always accurate because of the turmoil surrounding them. However, I have indicated inaccuracies where it is relevant in the text.

I used both spoken impressions, and written material, most of the latter being drawn from contemporary diaries and letters. These I researched in the John Oxley Memorial Library, Brisbane, the Mitchell Library, Sydney, the Tasmanian State Archives, Hobart, the South Australian Archives, Adelaide, and the Battye Library, Perth. At the Australian War Memorial Library, Canberra, Mr N. J. Flanagan, Director, and staff including Mrs M. Price, Librarian-in-charge of films and photographs, and Mr P. Burness, curator of relics, gave generously of their time, as did Miss P. Reynolds and the staff of the La Trobe Library in the State Library of Victoria, Melbourne. Miss Leonie Mills, in charge of the photographic section, gave me the advice I often sought.

Mr N. Drummond and Mrs P. Heywood of the Education Department, Victoria, cheerfully and ably researched the material for use in the chapter 'Moulding the Lads'. Miss Lyn Kolodji and Mrs Beryl Baldwin typed the long manuscript and Mrs Nancy Robertson and my daughter Cate Adam-Smith came to my rescue at the end when I needed help to assemble the work. I will remember with pleasure and appreciation the hours spent with Sue Ebury who edited the finished manuscript with patience and felicitous skill. During the four years the book was being written my mother and father gave me constant encouragement, advice and meals.

In England, Mr David Lance, oral historian at the British War Museum spent many hours with me discussing the recording on tape of these usually reticent subjects; my guide on the Gallipoli Peninsula, Mr Sureyya Dilman, and in France, Mr W. H. Dunkow ('Bill of Arras' as he is known to the British Legion), both walked – and climbed – many miles with me and gave unstintingly of their time and unique knowledge as did M. Jacques de Vos, Ypres, Belgium, and M. Andre Coilliot, Beaurains, France.

I am grateful to my translators, Professor I. Giritli, Mr D. Nelson and Mr C. Tomadin. Other assistance is acknowledged in the text.

I am grateful to the *Bulletin* for permission to reproduce 'Anzac Ghosts' by Nora McAuliffe and Angus & Robertson for 'War' by Dame Mary Gilmore. Every effort has been made to trace copyright holders. If any infringement has occurred, I apologise.

The book was written with the assistance of the Literature Board of the Australia Council.

Preface

'War is Hell!'
General Sherman

It is time to strip the film from honour-dimmed eyes and face the uncomfortable, terrible facts as well as the emotion-stirring flutter of pennants and silvery cries of trumpets and beating of drums. War *is* hell. But in our attempt to denigrate it, to outlaw it, we must remember not to castigate the victims of war – and every man who fights is a victim. We must remember that the hand that holds the weapon is not he who plans or benefits from the battle.

Many of the old men who took part in World War I have been hurt too long, sometimes purposely, sometimes thoughtlessly, but when I wrote this book I was never thoughtless and I am sorry if anything I wrote hurts or embarrasses them. Aware that figures and details of venereal disease might distress the survivors and their families, I nevertheless felt it necessary to include them. Chroniclers of that period have habitually ignored this subject, as though to write of it might in some way lessen the immortality that the men's endurance made legendary. In my opinion this merely perpetuates the hypocrisy that made these facts appear an aberration rather than an unavoidable hazard of war. It is a damnable man or woman who would use these facts against them. War is not pleasant, and those who wish to write of pleasant things should avoid it as a subject.

Travelling anywhere outside Australia at that time would have been a sexual revelation, but they went to Egypt, where a trade in titillation of the senses has been practised in all degrees since the days of the Old Testament. This

viii

trade has thrived and perfected its skill on the armies that have marched across the land from pre-history to Napoleon's time and our own.

Sometimes, when reading the diaries of the Australian troops, one longs for a boy-diarist to have experienced any and all delights and thrills that might have comforted him or brought him the soothing waters of Lethe in that most awful time. On Gallipoli I sought the grave of one of the diarists: from his diary I had realised that he took part in the 'Battle of the Wazzir' when 2000 troops ransacked and set fire to the brothels in the best known street in Cairo. On the little flat stone with his name soberly printed on it, one longed to record 'He had one rip-roaring "bosker" night out'. He was aged twenty.

Perhaps some of the old men may wish I had not written of John Simpson Kirkpatrick as a boozer, a brawler, a rowdy stoker-type larrikin. But that is what he was. He was never the delicate, aesthetic visionary the artists and eulogists have recorded. He was tough, so tough that when he saw the men drop and disappear in the reddening water on that morning of 25 April 1915, he waded ashore and stalked straight up the beach – forgetting military etiquette – and set off as a one-man unit to bring the wounded down to where the hospital ships awaited them. None of your men who 'walk down Piccadilly with a poppy or a lily' could have done what Simpson did. I was sick at heart at the proliferation of simpering words for school children about this delightful man's man. I was reminded of the affected paintings in churches of Saint Thérèse, a graceful, cool beauty with an elegant bouquet tastefully laid across her arms, her gown and veil arranged meticulously to suggest unassailed and unassailable virginity, while her eyes stared out as a visionary, but accusingly at we other, weaker, vessels. In more recent years Thérèse's diaries have been cleared by the Vatican for publication and we learn that she was as frail in spirit as any of us, as fierce as an unbroken filly and as ashamed of her shortcomings as we are. Like 'Simpson', something happened in her life, an

opportunity a more delicate nature might not even notice
but, because of the make-up of these individuals who take
life at the full, each walked straight off into immortality.

I do not write about strategy, nor about generals and the
games they play. 'Games' is not a sardonic term of dis-
approval, but the actual name: war games. These games
are played in various ways but usually on a large table set
with topographical details of the proposed battlefield. Metal
blocks of varying colours represent Divisions, Brigades,
Battalions – of men. In this way generals can anticipate
losses their strategy and planning will entail, they can
decide how many men they can 'afford' to lose; with their
knowledge they can arrange to have in reserve the numbers
of reinforcements they will need as each of the metal blocks
are removed; they decide how many hospital ships, field
abulances, stretcher bearers and burial parties will be
required. We learn that it is such a fascinating game that
the men who play it find actual war rather aggravating in
comparison because of the untidiness of the field once the
metal blocks are replaced by groups of real men. These
groups are apt to fall down dead at the unexpected blast of
a field gun or the tap-tap-tapping of a nest of concealed
machine guns. Sometimes in that war of 1914–18, eighty
per cent of a battalion's men were casualties and these
dead, dying and wounded cluttered up the trenches and the
lines of command as well as the generals' neatly printed
plans. Playing these games many miles from the battlefields
the generals could be as courageous as they wished, they
could sacrifice as many men as they liked without the sight
of the gobbets of flesh on tangled barbed wire to trouble
them. The blocks they moved across painted fields and up
precipitous cliff-faces never cried out, 'Dear God, what is to
become of us?'

I have consulted numerous manuscripts, and read some
7 820 separate letters and diaries. In writing about the
events of such a fierce, crowded five years, one can use only
some of the hundreds of facets, and doubtless an author's
personal predeliction may be blamed for omission – or

inclusion – of material others would have preferred to excise. It was not possible to use excerpts from all the diaries and letters I read and all the words on tape. Eventually, after reading some six, seven and even eight times in an effort more clearly to appreciate the men and their era, the book was formed, every man being a part of the whole. When I travelled in their footsteps to Albany, Egypt, Jordan, Alexandria, across the Aegean Sea to Gallipoli and back to Lemnos, I remembered every one of them. Sometimes, standing with my feet crushing the sweet-scented thyme on the slopes at Anzac Beach Cemetery or along Shrapnel Gully, I've seen the grave of a diarist, or the little marker of a boy who wrote, 'I don't know how I've been able to keep going mother'.

When I walked sixty miles along the Somme, which was the extent of our operations in France, those writers whose works have been largely ignored – the young dead – were there. There is an indescribable feeling about these 'Silent Cities of the Dead', as Byron called them. Many are larger than provincial cities back home in Australia, and each is peopled by boys, every one of them young. A young reporter from the Melbourne *Age* told me he had been to the cemetery at Villers-Bretonneux. 'I never felt so Australian before,' he said. 'I don't think I even *felt* I was Australian until I walked through those cities where every man was my age and had come from where I came. I can tell you I wept tears, and I don't care who knows it.'

From the many men and women who had been 'over there' not once did I meet with a refusal to answer my questions or requests to tape record or take notes. Their families were urgent in their desire to have the record made while there was still time. 'These are the dying years', one old lady said as we watched the ones and twos representing whole battalions march by on Anzac Day 1977.

So, to you old men, who have spent so much of the last of your time with me ensuring that I knew how you felt, why you went – and stayed – what you did and how you came home again, I dedicate this book. You had the greatest number of casualties per men on the field of all the Allied armies; you travelled furthest, were away the longest. You were the only volunteers. You came from a newer land, were a younger race than any who entered that awful arena. When time has removed this age to a distance, our descendants will speak of you as we now speak of the three hundred at Thermopylae – but I have had the rare, and peerless, privilege of knowing you.

Part One:
The Beginning

1
Why Did You Go To the Great War, Daddy?

We children of the nineteen-twenties and thirties didn't need to be told by our parents that the angel of death had been abroad throughout the land: we had almost heard the beating of his wings. We were the generation whose fathers, uncles, and sometimes elder brothers were either dead, or 'returned' men: not 'returned' in the sense of the English and Germans coming home from battle as they had done since time immemorial; the Australians – and the New Zealanders – had not before been to a war. For this country, the Boer War was a skirmish to which we sent a few men, and even these went without an invitation. This was the *real* thing. 'The people didn't know what to do,' my father answered when, as a child, I questioned him about the ill-treatment of a German in his town. 'We hadn't had a war before this.'

If there was no precedent for the returning men themselves, there was none for the people at home who waited for the heroes to come back, and none for the children who followed. We grew up in a wrenching dichotomy of deep pride and bewildering discomfort; we lived in a world of proud April days when we wore our fathers' medals to school, in moments of thrilling, chilling excitement as the Last Post died away, the bugle silenced, and we stood with bowed heads beneath our family names on the ugly stone memorial in our little towns. We were children who *saw* those daunting cliffs, actually saw them in our minds' eye, because the men who had been at the Landing, having no need to boast, spoke rarely, and then only in grudging monosyllables; through their brevity we toiled up Shrapnel Gully, over Rhododendron Ridge, along Dead Man's, and attempted to force a way across to the Dardanelles; we knew the Somme because we saw the long, shapeless, faceless bundle in a hospital bed when we were taken to visit.

The reputation of the men who lived in our world, their endurance, the buoyancy of their spirits, shrouded us with an aura, a legend, a heritage that every Australian since that day has been born with, like it or not. 'It is part of the inheritance that my father did bequeath unto me', Shakespeare said, as did Sophocles' Antigone. There was no denying it: we could ridicule it − and many of us later did so − but we could not rid ourselves of it. So we grew up in an ordinary world shot across with mysterious, disturbing spectres.

We lived in a world where men were called 'Hoppy', 'Wingy', 'Shifty', 'Gunner', 'Stumpy', 'Deafy', 'Hooky', according to whether they lost a leg, an arm (or part of one), an eye, their hearing, or had a disfigured face drawn by rough surgery into a leer. A world where the smell of suppurating sores (we called them 'running') and Rexona ointment was not unknown; where our parents' friends or relatives graduated from crutches to squeaky 'wooden' legs. We watched the blind man beg outside Sydney's Central Station with a plaque around his neck that said *Help a Blinded Digger*; we saw the unemployed men pack Martin Place, carrying placards that read 'We Were Good Enough to Fight For You, Surely We're Good Enough to Work For You'. And we listened through the thin walls when our parents came home from visiting a 'returned' uncle in hospital: 'I can't stand it. I can't go again.' It is mother. Your father's voice comes, strangled, like hers. 'You'll be alright.' 'No, but the smell. When he coughs . . . and breathes out . . . it's . . . oh, I'm going to be sick.' But she goes back next Sunday and the next until the day you go to school with a black rosette on your lapel, and the flag is flying half-mast for your Uncle Dick who was gassed. You are small, and you go into a room unexpectedly, at night, because something has disturbed you when you are visiting Grandmother and she, that fierce little old lady, is kneeling on the floor, her face turned up to the family portrait taken in 1914, and you know she is praying for Jack, the beautiful boy, and Stephen, the laughing roly-poly, her sons, who were 'missing' at Lone Pine, August 1915, although she never mentions it to a living soul. (Except the night World War II was declared and she suddenly says, 'Wouldn't it be funny if they found the boys wandering round – and they got their memories back!' And none of us look at her.) You are sent to take soup to a family down on their luck in the depression. You hate going: once you saw the husband's leg being 'aired' when you entered without their hearing your knock, and you tried to avoid him ever after, and sometimes took the soup home and lied to your mother, 'they were not home', rather than smell that smell again. And the hook instead of a hand, the 'Stumpy' in a wheel chair; one man even skating along on a little trolley, his hands taking the place of his absent legs; the man who shook and trembled and the other one who stuttered from 'shell shock' and regularly had to be 'put away'.

They were the flotsam and jetsam of war but no one told you. This is what the world is, was all your child's mind knew; we had no way of knowing that it was the world only for some of us.

There were the artifacts of war, trophies 'the boys' brought back to a new, isolated land which had not seen the things they had seen, and the other mementoes that were never shown. You waited till your parents were out and pried, in terror of what you would find of that sombre land of muffled drums and strange, uncaring revelry. You found a postcard, addressed to Grandmother at Calrossie, Yarram-Yarram, Victoria, Australia, saying 'I'll be in touch with you soon, Jack' and the date is July 1915, one month before Lone Pine. There were postcards from your father, to *his* mother asking her to write – always they wanted letters from home, these men. And there was a piece of jagged, heavy metal, three inches long – was this what was in cousin Jackie Pearce? You remember a conversation overheard – 'You could hear him roaring. He'd scream like a horse, hanging on to his stomach'. You moved so you couldn't hear, but then moved back to hear more. 'They'd got a big piece out but the fragments had gone everywhere. He is lucky to be alive, old Jackie is!' There is a bent bullet, three inches long, twisted from some impact; a neat swagger stick of Uncle Dick's, hand carved, with both ends decorated with bullet casings. You know 'every man who went to Egypt had one to beat off the beggars and Eggs-a-cook men', but you don't touch it; you remember mother retching. There is a leather pouch and you get your smaller-than-mother's hand in a pocket and winkle out a letter, a love letter to father. You try to put a face and dress on the writer from 12 000 miles and twenty years ago. She has written, 'Dearest the day is over, ended the dream divine; you must go back to your life, I must go back to mine'.

You put all the mementoes back, uncomprehending, but the thread of 'Roses are Blooming in Picardy' runs through the waking hours of all your young days and when you learn the piano, you play every Sunday night for visitors to sing: 'Pack Up Your Troubles'; 'It's a Long Way'; 'Australia Will Be There'; 'One Two Three! Australian Boys Are We!'

Then, one day, carelessly, your guard down, you tell a girl at school about the postcards, the jagged metal, the bent bullet. 'They must be funny, your parents,' she says. 'Why?' 'All that rubbish from that war!' Her father wasn't there, nor her uncle, and you envy her. Suddenly embarrassed, you realise you've never seen her at the railway station seeing-off 'stumpies' or blind men tap-tap-tapping with their sticks or Lew who stuttered and wept. 'Oh, they just keep them for a joke!' And you hate, hard, the things that embarrass you. Even on Anzac Day, when you wear the medals on your left breast as do all the other kids of returned men. When you are in your teens, those kids whose fathers hadn't gone tease you, 'Think you're smart don't you! We know why your father went to the war! Well he came a gutzer didn't he!' Your father had been invalided out when he was aged 21 and for a long time he was too sick to work and wouldn't go for a pension, but you didn't know that others knew. That night you ask truculently, with fear, 'Why did you go to the war?' And he doesn't know. He, who has an answer for everything, says, 'Oh, well, a man feels he's got to go you know'. There was no conscription. 'No, but, a man feels it's his duty.' This had sufficed before, but now it seemed as vapid as my tormentor had said it was. 'The uncles – Jack, Stephen, Dick and Jackie Pearce, Mick Byrne – you didn't all go for duty!' I tried to sneer and he, that quiet man, looked up at me, 'Well, what do *you* think we went for? The good of our health?' Four dead out of that group, Jackie Pearce twice wounded and Dad invalided out before he had long been a grown man; but still the question remained. *Why did they go?* You ask the kids next day, not cap in hand, but taking up a fighting stance, 'Why do you think my father went to the war?' They say in unison, 'So he could have a good time!' You are too stupid with youth to wonder what sort of time a man could have patrolling the North Sea, out of sight of land, for four unbroken years of his youth. Even if you had thought of that you still would not have known what sent him and all the others. You were too close, the nearness blinded, deafened, stupefied you with its immensity.

Your mother is not so quiet, not so monosyllabic as your father and yet, on this one subject she is inarticulate and resorts to cold, aching rage (that breaks your heart while you taunt her) when she senses your doubts.

'Pack up your troubles!' she hears you criticise. 'That song is evil in content and intent.' She is taken aback a little by that, and for one sentence humours the growing child. 'And what do you think the intent is?' 'It was to drug men into forgetting what the trenches were really like, what killing men was like, to make them fatalistic about death and to believe that nothing can be done to alter anything in life.'

Pack up your troubles in your old kit-bag
And smile! smile! smile!
While you've a lucifer to light your fag
Smile boys that's the style!
What's the use of worrying?
It never was worth while –
So! Pack up your troubles in your old kit-bag,
And smile! smile! smile!

'That song made it easier for them to go back to the trenches each time didn't it?' I thrust at my mother. She was quiet, looking at me, and then she said a terrible thing, softly. 'Yes,' she said. And I was too young, raw, obtuse to know the truth of the necessity of which she spoke.

Of course there were things I never doubted. Horror for instance, the one vignette above others that all children can conjure up at the chance hearing of the sketchiest remark. That the Germans butchered babies was brought home to me nightly in my dreams. '*There was this picture with a Hun with no less than 6 Belgian babies skewered on his bayonet!*' Walls were thin and ears long.

'And what they do to the women no man can repeat even to another man.' (To a child brought up in mid-Victorian prudery even a wild imagination couldn't fill the gaps there.) But there were the posters. There was a harsh red and green painting of Norman Lindsay's with the Hun with his face of Beelzebub slavering over a globe with the blood from his fingers running over Europe and trickling down towards Australia; another of his with Huns (the word was as common and unthinkingly used as was Dago for Italians) already in Australia – you knew it was Australia because the outback Aussie 'cocky' had his back to a galvanised iron tank as the bayonets pressed towards him and his wife cowered back from hands clutching and eyes leering at her. There was Belgium, the Madonna-like figure trampled and beaten but still refusing to acquiesce.

For a child of the nineteen-thirties, when a map of the world with the dominions of the British Empire painted over in red was on the wall of every school throughout the land, the call to defend that Empire was still strangely immediate; while reading Macaulay – 'How can man die better/than facing fearful odds/for the ashes of his father/ And the temples of his Gods' – we were transfixed: we could believe in the rush to avenge 'Little Belgium'. We learnt, 'Never the Lotus closes/Never the wild fowl wake/ But a soul goes out on the east wind/That died for England's sake', and thought we knew what sent our fathers to the war. The fingerpost of our youth was that lexicon of names, that rosary that began with Gallipoli, Sari Bair, Lone Pine, Beersheba, Amman, and went on to Fromelles, Amiens, Mouquet Farm, Pozières, Passchendaele, Villers-Breton-neux; as though slipping the beads between our fingers, the names were as familiar to us as they once were unfamiliar to our parents in their schooldays. We felt the pitch of an excitement that nothing else engendered; we felt the delicate sting of the champagne bubbles of adventure the like of which these men knew; no other group of men we encountered had the freemasonry of comradeship that these had; and we knew that war gave to man the chance to defy his mightiest enemy – death – and the trace of the combat was etched on him for all time. 'My mate used to say', wrote a soldier, 'that there are two days you need not try to escape death: the day you are not going to die for nothing will harm you on that day; the other time is the day you are to die for nothing will prevent your death that day. When we were called out to "Hop-over" my mate would say "Come on! Let's see which day it is!"'

For twenty years, until the next 'world' war engulfed us, we lived with that first 'great' war shrouding us, as tangible and real as the event of the day. The fabric of our lives, of the country itself, was knitted by the event. As Noel Coward had Jane say in *Cavalcade*, 'Let's drink to our sons who made part of the pattern, and to our hearts that died with them'.

Later, as adults, many of us rebelled against war and, in our anger, linked the men who had gone to war with war itself. Many found it impossible – some still do – to grant to the survivors of that greatest tragedy the world has known the memories that made those years peerless, inimitable, irreplaceable. For those five years they were away from Australia were both the best and the worst of times men had known. They had been brought up in an age of belief, allied to an epoch of incredulity but now it was 'the season of light, it was the winter of despair'. No men since (and perhaps before) have lived through such an age.

We who had grown up admiring them as fathers were still in doubt: why had they gone to a war for which no man has been able to give any logical reason for its being? Why did they stay? (And this author had the uncanny experience of being asked recently by her own daughter after reading of some of their travail: 'But why didn't they desert?') And why, seeing they lost most battles except the last, were they so quietly proud that the depth of their pride made it impossible for them to articulate it?

To answer my own perplexities I began to read voraciously, to search through the countryside for diaries and letters of these men, then to tape-record the reminiscences of others so as to leave a record of matters not recorded elsewhere. Finally, I travelled to Jordan, Egypt, Gallipoli, France; I walked over the battlefields, up and down the cliff-face of Anzac Cove, up those narrow stony valleys where the bullets had whistled; I waded shoulder-deep into the Aegean Sea to try to recapture the moment of the Landing (and, note, we always use the majorscule). Then up and down the flower-scented, silent cities of the dead who overcrowded sixty miles of the banks of the River Somme in France and Belgium. To this day, sixty years later, the inhabitants drink *eau minérale* (mineral water) because they believed when they returned to their valley in 1918 that so many 'missing' bodies, 110000 men of the allies, lay unrecovered in that narrow strip that the water seeping through to the river must be polluted.

At the end of such an Odyssey one is no nearer the whole truth. But one is unshakeably certain that tattooed on the folk-memory of these men was an urgent drive as old as pre-history, the blood-sacrifice of a nation. In the almost epicless land that is Australia the diaries of these men become our Homeric *Iliad*. Their patriotism might not be the beliefs we hold today but *they were the dominating sentiments of their times.*

To a man, the belief had been drilled in them by tradition, legend, lore, verse, story and song that nationhood is forged in battle, that glory consummates the rag-tag and bob-tail of humanity into a nation.

> It's only an old piece of bunting
> It's only an old coloured rag
> But many have died for its honour
> And shed their life's blood for the flag.

They quoted such Brittanic themes but beneath the words was the knowledge that it was not *their* flag they sang of. Their nation was only thirteen years old and no blood had been shed for it; a document had been signed, a parliament prorogued, but there had been no selfless act of valour to crown its coming of age. This they would do.

Within eight months of the outbreak of war the deed had been done. By 29 April 1915 the newspapers of the world had emblazoned the baptism of a new nation, not least those of Britain, whose press was deep in admiration of these men who, up till now, had been thought of as Colonials. 'Before the war who had ever heard of Anzac?' wrote General Sir Ian Hamilton. 'Hereafter who will ever forget it?'

By the time the Gallipoli Peninsula was evacuated, it had become hallowed ground, the forging place of a nation. The blood sacrifice had been enacted albeit by the most unchivalric wild colonial boys the 'mother country' had ever despaired of.

It was Australia's Shrine, her Westminster, the cradle of her traditions; and the tomb of her princes; as an élite free-masonry the survivors were given the deference due to a fraternity comparable to the 300 who stood the ground at

Thermopylae; men who were not at Anzac saluted the survivors – and envied them their immortality.

The 'White Gurkhas' they were called on Gallipoli, and the Australians at home passed the story on. 'The supreme exploit of the British infantry in the whole of its history,' the Melbourne *Argus* recorded on 22 December 1915, while in London a British officer wrote of the Australian soldier, 'The bravest thing God ever made'.

'I tell you', Henry Lawson had written in a clarion call, 'The Star of the South shall rise in the lurid clouds of War'. So it had, in that first wild magnificent gesture, but ahead were four years during which they must maintain that which they had begun. 'A hero', wrote R. W. Emerson, 'is no braver than an ordinary man but he is braver five minutes longer'. They had fallen for one of the most ancient and dangerous of human illusions – the belief in the possibility of a short, decisive war.

2
Moulding the Lads

'Captain Walter Gamble's 1 200 cadets demonstrated rifle drill and firing outside [the Exhibition Building], and bayonet exercises, cutlass and flag drill inside the building'.

It was 7 September 1900 and many of Captain Gamble's cadets were twelve years of age. By 1914 they would be aged 26. And so they got them ready.

In 1906 Gamble, now 'Major', a Victorian State School inspector, was appointed State Commandant of the Cadet Corps. By 1907 the cadets were assumed to be part of the Commonwealth Military Forces and by the Defence Act of 1903–11 all Australian boys were required to serve: all medically fit boys between the ages of twelve and fourteen were junior cadets; the senior cadets were older boys still at school or those who had left between fourteen and eighteen years of age.

Further, in accordance with the regulations of the Commonwealth Defence Department, the training of junior cadets was carried on under Defence Department instructors. Saluting the Flag, Military Drill and Cadet Corps loomed large on the educational programme.

Victorian State School Inspector Gamble had advocated this for many years. As far back as his annual inspector's report for 1885–6 he stated that the military inspection of school boys should be transferred to the Defence Department 'which has a large number of drill inspectors to render assistance in *moulding the lads who will form our national army'*. (Author's italics.)

Military Drill had been insisted on from the 1860s, the Colonel Commandant of Volunteers (Permanent Army) presenting certificates to trainee teachers who passed the examination as Military Drill tutors. At the passing-out ceremony a Brigade Sergeant-Major from the Defence Department snapped the lines to attention, 'The Queen was played, three cheers for the flag was given', and speeches were made: '. . . military drill is becoming more general in the schools and is found to be an important aid to discipline. We attach great importance to this subject and shall see if anything can be done to extend it without injury to subjects which are, *perhaps* more important'.

In 1875 S.S. Inspector John Ilkington, commenting on the recent issue of a *Manual of Drill for School Use* by the local military authorities, said, 'The personal duty of every male citizen to render himself competent to bear arms in national defence is year by year becoming more apparent'.

In 1884 the movement to establish Cadet Corps in Victoria was begun and by August 1885 thirty-eight state schools had established corps. 'The members of the corps will have opportunities before leaving school of becoming versed in the use of the rifle and infantry field exercises and such of them as may hereafter join the militia or volunteer forces will have comparatively little to learn in order to attain efficiency.'

By 1889 Inspectors from Victoria Barracks reported: 'The discipline is generally good and will undoubtedly improve as the teachers realise that they are, for the time, officers and those under their command soldiers of the future.'

In 1890, 16 053 boys trained in Victorian schools alone. Lieutenant-Colonel Snee reported, 'While it is not the duty of the State to foster a war-like spirit for simply fighting's sake, the Commonwealth demands that every man (and our boys, the men in future years) shall *prepare* and be in readiness to defend his hearth and home'. That year the supervision of S.S. Military Drill was transferred to the Defence Department so as to have that branch of study examined by military officers.

The Boer War stirred the patriotic fervour and devotion to Empire as did almost any royal occasion. Two thousand cadets had marched through the streets of Melbourne in 1896 in the celebrations to mark the Jubilee, but it was the formation of the new Commonwealth that set patriotism running an all time banker: and the flood would not recede until the blood sacrifice had been paid. 'With the help of bugles and drums', Lieutenant-Colonel Henry reported in 1900, 'the marching is regulated and smartened'. All through the first decade of the twentieth century the sparks that kindle fiery war were fuelled, the bugles were shrilling. In Germany, all over Europe, even in America who was said to be pacific, boys were being schooled in martial arts, ostensibly 'without injury to subjects which are, *perhaps* more important'.

Theodore Roosevelt, in a speech to the soldiers at Camp Upton, USA, in 1917 said, 'The man who has not raised himself to be a soldier, and the woman who has not raised her boy to be a soldier for the right, neither one of them is entitled to citizenship in the Republic'.

Drum to drum rat-a-tat-tatted, trumpet spoke to trumpet, thunder to thunder. Throughout the few years that were left they all drilled the impressionable young, children that by now had fathers who had drilled in the same temper.

As well as training for the brain-spattering, wind-pipe slitting art of war, they sought to educate those not already persuaded by mounting eye-catching displays of children. The *Sydney Daily Telegraph* of 27 January 1901 was ecstatic about the drill display by 10 000 Sydney school pupils to mark Commonwealth Day.

Imperialism and patriotism being the dominant themes immediately prior to and following Federation, the schools acquired two ceremonial occasions that were honoured by millions of Australian school children: the Monday morning observance and Empire Day. In 1900 a Victorian committee including representatives of the Ministry of Defence set about arranging for every state school to be supplied with a Union Jack and, as well, devised the ceremony to be observed when Saluting the Flag (capital letters were always used for such expressions). Apart from every Monday and Empire Day there were plenty of other days to be celebrated: King's Birthday, Queen's Birthday, Commonwealth Day, Coronation Day and Ascension Day. An 'appropriate uniform ceremony for hoisting and saluting of the flag as an expression of patriotic sentiment' was devised. 'Every boy will be eager no doubt to obtain the post of Flag officer in his school'. In a memo headed 'The Grand Old Flag' they continued, 'Nothing can be more appropriate or tend more to stimulate patriotic feelings and impress the idea of the unity of the British Empire on the minds of old and young than to hoist the Union Jack over all our schools'.

As though a fever, an emergency, was upon them the nation urged on the young, as though believing without question that man is a military animal, glorying in gunpowder, loving parades.

In a supplement to the *Education Gazette and Teachers' Aid* of 29 October 1901 the Minister for Education stated that 'While recognising in full the good work that has been done by teachers in the past in fostering in those under their care devotion to the Sovereign, and love of their country' he considered the time opportune for systematising effort to maintain and increase if possible the patriotic sentiment in this state. To this end, on national occasions he ordered that 'lessons inculcating patriotism be given, songs of a national character be sung, and the ceremony of saluting the flag be performed'. A suggested programme was given:

Oral lesson: Life of King Edward VII
Patriotic song
Oral lesson: The Union Jack
Saluting the Flag
Patriotic song
Oral lesson: The British Empire
Patriotic verses by the children
The National Anthem

Every Monday morning the children were to be formed up in a hollow square facing the flagpole and at a given signal the boys should salute, and the girls stand to attention. Then all, placing the right hand on left breast, should say the following words simultaneously: 'I love God and my country, I honour the flag, I will serve the King and cheerfully obey my parents, teachers and the laws.' Immediately after, three cheers for the King should be given, the boys uncovering their heads.

The school was to be decorated with 'greenery, bunting, pictures of the King and Queen and of the late Queen (draped in black) and mottoes such as *One People One Destiny* and the *Crimson Thread of Kinship* framed in red, white and blue. Several children may be chosen to hoist the flag, say, 6 girls dressed in red, white and blue and six boys in sailor costume'.

The same publication of 20 May 1904 carried this message to teachers: 'The school flag, if used judiciously . . . will foster sentiments of loyalty to the Commonwealth and the Empire and periodically refresh the memories of the pupils regarding important historical events and keep them in touch with what is transpiring at the present time.' Issue followed issue with headings of 'The National Flag' and 'Flags for State Schools', this latter notifying teachers that the Education Department had for sale flags in two sizes: '12' × 6' for 26/- and 6' × 3' for 6/6'. The composition of the Union Jack was described at length, the width and placing of the various crosses emphasised over and over.

It was not until they were all swept away in 'the greatest tragedy the world has known' that there was any relaxation in the 'preparation' of youth.

As the reality of war was brought home to the public the idea of Junior Cadets in primary schools became repugnant. From 1916 onwards the minister's reports make no mention of Military Drill or Cadet Corps. In August 1917, as the never-ending casualty lists mounted higher, compulsory cadet training was suspended.

3
The First Man, the First Shilling

On Anzac Day 1937, our little bush school in the Koo-Wee-Rup swamplands combined with other equally small one-teacher schools for the annual Anzac Day ceremony. Six words ricocheted around my eleven-year-old head when I first heard them and if a drum had begun to beat outside the Mechanics Institute I would have marched to wherever it called without looking back. The terrible dichotomy of our childhood, our intimate knowledge that war is the ultimate evil, and against it the thrilling call of a bugle, was washing over me and the bugle won. The guest speaker was telling of his walking from the swamplands to 'jump the rattler' to Melbourne to enlist.

'I couldn't help myself,' he said. 'Mum was a widow and she needed me to help her run the farm because the other kids were too small. But I read what Andrew Fisher said and I went.' Fisher's message to England was that Australia would stand behind her to 'the last man, the last shilling'. The Garibaldian rallying cry of it! And twenty-three years later those words could still move a small Australian girl as they had moved a young man in 1914.

So the first of the men came in, and the first of the money began to be spent.

While the 'men from twelve years of age' were drilling in the new lands, old Europe was drilling as it had for centuries and, with centuries of old scores to settle, was sparring, one nation with another, treading the traditional steps of the dance that leads to war. Most, if not all, of these squabbles had origins lost in antiquity and though the *Dominion* newspaper published such news the man on the street knew of them but little.

What really set tongues wagging apart from the hurly-burly of football and the threat of a double dissolution bringing on an election was the news that the British Association for the Advancement of Science would shortly be holding conferences in Australian capital cities and this really *was* something to talk about in a land where, to date, nothing much had happened.

When they read of an obscure arch-duke being shot in an obscure country they were not much interested until the newspapers began to report in a manner suggesting war. It seems incredible over sixty years later, but they were suddenly interested, overjoyed. Some writers at the time pointed out that it was the nearest any nation could get to being unanimous on any subject. 'It is our baptism of fire!' jubilantly cried the *Sydney Morning Herald*.

'We'll gather round the banner of our country,' sang the crowds that gathered in Martin Place, carolling the popular song of the day.

> On land or sea, wherever you be,
> Keep your eye on Germany!
> For England Home and Beauty
> Have no cause to fear!
> Should auld acquaintance be forgot?
> No! No! No! No! No! Australia will be there!
> Australia will be there!*

As the thrumming of the drums drew nearer many men had already offered themselves. My Uncle Jack had left the farm in Gippsland and gone to join the militia. Uncle Dick, my father's giant of a brother, had left his Neerim timber lease where he was splitting sleepers for the railway and 'gone down for the army'. Uncle Stephen also was 'in the military'. My father, the youngest brother of eight timber-

---

* 'Australia Will Be There' – W. W. Francis. August 1914 (Allans Music Australia Ltd).

getters in the hills behind Neerim and Tanjil Bren had, in 1913, joined the crew of the first flagship of the Australian Navy, HMAS *Australia*, and was at sea on manoeuvres. Down in the far north-west of Tasmania young Rupert Clare Garsia, lieutenant in the Royal Navy, was on leave with his family in the isolated potato growing area back of Irishtown. On 29 July 1914 he rode a horse into Smithton and read the local paper, the *Advocate*. That night he wrote off to Lieutenant Darling of HMAS *Australia* asking if Australian ships were likely to be tied to Australian waters in case of war as he'd just read of 'the trouble between Austria and Serbia'. Next day he was to ride to Woolnorth on the far tip of the island, but when he got to a settlement with a telephone he put a call in to the *Advocate* for news: 'They say the Mediterranean fleet is coaling and provisioning at Malta to go full speed for London,' he wrote in his diary. He handed his horse to a friend: 'I tell Blackett I can't come with him and am catching coach next morning. Walked home carrying as a swag 5 loaves of bread and all sorts of heavy things besides. Margie's tea very welcome to perspiring individual. Spent rest of afternoon feeding pigs, catching "Con" ready for morning and cutting up firewood. At dinner (I'd packed) Eric very *piano* but I insisted on opening a bottle of '34 port which was a great success. Up at 4.30 a.m., drove "Con" in jinker to catch the coach . . . caught the 9.30 p.m. *Oonah* which sailed for Melbourne . . . me on't.'

It was Sunday 2 August before he reached Melbourne and there the Navy office told him HMAS *Australia* would be getting away to sea as fast as she could be coaled in Sydney. He tried to catch the train – but it might miss the ship. He tried to hire a motor vehicle – but that would cost £75 to take him to Sydney and even that might break down. He was in a '*terrible stew*'. Eventually he wired the Commanding Officer of HMAS *Australia*. 'Emergency Lieutenant, 4 years seniority, left HMS *NZ* last January ready for service.' He decided on the train and while waiting he wrote, 'Great cag about war, everywhere. Two navvies cutting a new line here; I overheard one say during smoko: I tell you we *must* go into this'. He gets to Sydney and talks his way onto the flagship which sails immediately. '*Wed. 5 Aug. 9.30 p.m.*: Ship sails. Crew must be tired poor beggars. Have been going hard since Saturday coaling, making ready for sea etc. Left for German held Pacific Islands.

'*6 Aug*: Yesterday we received news at 1.30 p.m. *War Declared*. Created no surprises, (on board) so much so I forgot to enter it in my diary.'

The following day he heard that a seaman who should have slept at his sea-going station down at 4 Gun Supply had decided to sleep in the mess instead. He sent for the man and told him he was liable to be shot in wartime for an offence of this nature. 'There is no doubt it has not been realised yet by a lot of men that we are at war – I don't think it has sunk right in with any of us. After Divisions we cleared for action.'

The wattle was out along the bush roads in the southern states, the wildflowers were beginning to blaze in WA, and in NSW waratahs were blooming like crown fires through the forests when word came that war had 'broken out'. The first intimation had been at 3 p.m. on 30 July in a cablegram, in cipher, to the Governor-General, Sir Ronald Munro-Ferguson. It read:

'See preface defence scheme. Adopt precautionary stage. Names of powers will be communicated later if necessary.' (The first sentence of this message was the pre-arranged signal that war was probable.)

At 5 p.m. the Australian fleet, then on manoeuvres off the Queensland coast, was distributed according to plan. The flagship, the battle-cruiser *Australia*, came full steam south to Sydney to refuel in all haste: so large and valuable a ship could not afford to be caught in the vulnerable position of having insufficient coal on in a harbour where she could not manoeuvre. From that day the country was on the alert.

Another cable arrived on 4 August: 'Be on your guard

against possibility of attack in advance of any formal declaration of war. Understand clearly that this is not war telegram.'

The Australian Government had already cabled the offer to 'place the vessels of the Australian Navy under the control of the Admiralty. The Government is further prepared to despatch *further* expeditionary force of 20 000 men . . . to be at complete disposal of home government. Cost of despatch and maintenance will be borne by this Government'. Although each Dominion would automatically be at war if Britain went to war, none of them was obliged to send one soldier or sailor, or move a ship or merchandise in any effort against the common enemy. Mother England was very much the Victorian matriarch and provided protection for her brood, even when adulthood had changed them from colonies to dominions.

The Governor-General was able to cable London on the morning of 5 August (4 August in London): . . . There is indescribable enthusiasm and entire unanimity throughout Australia in support of all that tends to provide for the security of the empire in war.'

In a few hours the final message of the series arrived: 'War has broken out with Germany.'

The Rt Hon. Andrew Fisher, then leader of the Labor Opposition, announced 'we shall pledge our last man and our last shilling to see this war brought to a successful issue'. He had used these words as early as 3 August in an electoral campaign (the Rt Hon. Joseph Cook was Prime Minister at the outbreak of war) and later in September, when he became Prime Minister.

Ronald Smith, the famous Tasmanian bushwalker, son of 'Philosopher' Smith (the discoverer of the 'mountain of tin' at Waratah) and an intimate of Gustave Weindorfer of Cradle Mountain, was at Queenscliff (Vic.) in the militia. The day war was declared he wrote home to his wife in Tasmania's sparsely settled north-west: 'Isn't this war awful. One does not know what it will end in but it is better to have it now than a few years later when Germany is stronger. What a way they are going on running over any country they like . . . I had to go into town today . . . and the excitement is tremendous. I have never seen so many anxious, worried faces . . . Everyone had a paper and they came out every hour nearly. Special war editions. There was great excitement in the city when the fort guns were heard at the Heads. A German boat was trying to sneak out and they told her to stop and she didn't so they let off a few guns over her head . . . she very quickly stopped then.'

Shortly after noon on that first day, when dawn had not yet risen over Europe, what is believed to be the first shot of the war was fired within earshot of the citizens of Melbourne. It was the Fire Commander at Fort Nepean (Lieutenant C. Morris) firing a first shot across the bows of a German merchant ship with the promise that the next one would not be in front of her but in her. The *Pfalz*, no doubt having received a warning cable from her owners, had left Victoria Dock at 7.45 a.m. and steamed away down the bay before war was proclaimed. Her captain was ready to make a run for the open sea even after the first shot but pilot Robinson of the Port Phillip Pilot Service grappled with him on the bridge and persuaded him to steam back to Portsea where the ship was seized.

By 8 August the Queenslander, Major Cyril Brudenall White, had organised the scheme to create a special force and on the tenth of the month recruiting was opened and arrangements were made for the force to sail in six weeks time. General W. T. Bridges, who was to die with a bullet through his head on Gallipoli, called the new army the Australian Imperial Force, the AIF. By 17 August they were ready to march recruits into grandstands on racetracks, showgrounds, anywhere they could shelter men, and to shape them into battalions.

At Enoggera (Qld), the third Infantry Brigade charged with bayonets through the light scrub in glorious sunshine. My Uncle Jack Adams, who had enlisted in the militia in Queensland the previous year, wrote: 'It's very exciting but we get hot charging around in the sunshine.' Stephen was in training in NSW. (Exactly a year later, at Lone Pine, the beautiful youth and the roly-poly boy charged again in brilliant sunshine and disappeared from the face of the earth and their mother, who could never believe they had died.)

The weather was good at Blackboy Hill (WA) as it was almost everywhere except Broadmeadows (Vic.) and the rifle ranges in Tasmania. Fooling with his new mates of the 3rd Field Ambulance at Blackboy Hill, Private John Simpson (real name Kirkpatrick) posed for a photograph with a skeleton they'd used for demonstration purposes and wrote to his mother, 'I've got an appetite like a horse'. The tough stoker off a coastal trader was only twenty-one years of age and growing big. He too would be dead this time next year.

Out of 'The Meadows' (Broadmeadows) the Victorians Carl and Ernek Janssen were writing home regularly, as they did until they were killed on Gallipoli Peninsula.

In Queensland, 1 400 men had poured into the Town Hall by 11 August and tents began to sprout like mushrooms in Bell's Paddock, Enoggera: as pretty a place as any army camp was placed. Here were trained the men who made up the 9th Infantry Battalion. On 22 August a contingent of 123 men from Northern Queensland climbed on board the old SS *Bombala* at Townsville and headed south to the capital, picking up ten more men at Mackay and reaching Brisbane on the twenty-fifth. Of these men, seventy-seven joined the 9th Battalion and the rest went to the Light Horse. Country districts were recruiting with vigour and sending their men down to the capital city: for some it was a journey of over one thousand miles, something few, if any, Europeans would be doing.

On 3 September, only one month after war had been declared, 1 849 men were in camp at Enoggera. For the first week or two at any of these camps scattered around Australia little training for battle was given; they were too pre-occupied with pitching tents, building cook-houses, carting and unloading stores and preparing camp sites.

Leave was given sparingly but on Sunday afternoons the

camp was thrown open to visitors, and relatives and friends flocked in with picnic baskets and hampers, the men with visitors sharing both visitors and hampers with those who had none.

Men were marching in from the city office blocks, the farms, the sheep runs, deserting from ships as soon as they berthed; men came from the outposts of empire as recognised in this land. Bill Harney, later to become Australia's best known 'bush' writer, rode out from the Gulf country where he had lived at Borroloola to catch a boat to Darwin and sail around the coast to join up in a capital city. 'Struth!' he told me years later when I camped with him near Ayers Rock, 'I was dead scared when I went to join up – scared it would be all over before I got there!'

Out at Meekatharra in Western Australia Barry (B. F.) Murphy had just driven his team of beautiful tall camels 150 miles in from the Never-Never country where the small copper mines were providing him with so much ore to cart that he and his 14-camel team were kept occupied all year round. Barney and his three brothers were amongst the most famous of the camel teamsters of the Wiluna–Meekatharra area. He was brought up at Nannine and, like the rest of his Irish family, had gone off with a camel team while still in short pants. Then he heard about the war, immediately sold his famous tall team and went down to Blackboy Camp.

Along the flat stretch of the greatest engineering endeavour of the day South Australians were dropping their 'banjoes', the shovels of the navvy, and riding on the empty materials trucks along the construction line back to Port Augusta, en route for Adelaide to enlist. Only forty years before their state had been largely unexplored. In 1913 the railway had been begun, one thousand miles of track across a waterless wasteland, and every available navvy was needed. Yet, on the outbreak of war, the men flocked to the city to join up, encouraged, goaded, by their own hand-written news-sheet *The Desert Echo*. Week after week this double page, sweat-stained news-sheet published the latest list of volunteers and a report of the farewells and gifts made as they left the world's most arid work camps.

> Many Trans-Australia Line boys
> Are off to fight the foe

began what they themselves called their 'doggerel debut'.

> They told us they were willing
> Their lives to sacrifice
> In order that their country
> Victorious may rejoice.

> And as they lay there thinking
> Of you they left behind
> They know you're fit and able
> And for trench-work just the kind.

> They call to you to join them
> Tom, Dick and Paddy too
> What makes you linger longer
> There's such a need for you!

The young men who walked, shyly, diffidently, in under the shabby freestone archway at Victoria Barracks, Paddington, had that great common fear, that of being turned down. Miss the great adventure? Not likely! Young Private Brew, No. 714, had joined up in Melbourne the day enlistment opened only to be successfully reclaimed by his parents as a minor. Next day he 'cleared' from home, 'grew older' on the way to Sydney and was accepted into the 2nd Battalion; his parents next heard from him after the Landing. He was lucky, as men viewed it then. In the overwhelming scenes of loyalty and enthusiasm that each day witnessed at Victoria Barracks, there were men who wept because they were unacceptable through age or physical disability. Many had travelled hundreds of miles to join up, had left good jobs, had been fêted as heroes before they left their country towns and they would die rather than go back as rejects.

Captain J. W. B. Bean, medical officer at the Barracks on

17 August, wrote: 'Some I have to refuse and they plead with me and almost break down. In fact, some do go away poor chaps, gulping down their feelings and with tears of disappointment in their eyes. We do the best we can for the rejects – write them a certificate to say they have been rejected, and why, and pay their railway fare home. This helps them to get taken on again at their work, but it does seem so awfully hard. Poor beggars. Such awful mouths the Australians have, many of them. You couldn't fail them for teeth too rigidly, or you'd never have made up your battalion.' Of the first fifty men examined four only had passed the medical requirements. Later it was arranged that those otherwise physically fit should be passed after their teeth were treated.

So off to 'The Chamber of Horrors', the dental pavilion at the Agricultural Showgrounds, they went and lined up awaiting their turn. Some returned in the afternoon with swollen faces having had a dozen and more roots dug out.

The Army requirements were for men of 5 feet 6 inches or over, a 34-inch chest expansion, and aged between 19 and 38 years, but so many men offered that the authorities could be openly selective. When the recruiting tables were set up on 11 August for the first time, a pushing, jostling mass of some thousands turned up. Enlisting officers passed as medically fit over 3 000 of them on that one day. Over 10 000 men had enlisted in Sydney by 20 August.

That month saw such activity in Sydney that it was likened to 'a disturbed ant colony' with its streams of men coming in from all corners of the state to volunteer, and many hurrying off after acceptance to make final arrangements to leave home and business before entering camp. So many crowded the entrances, corridors, verandahs and yards of the recruiting centre that they were moved to queue in double lines in catherine wheel formation to prevent the jostling and urgency to 'be in first before it's all over'. They lined up in their thousands, stripped, were examined by doctors while hundreds of clerks wrote particulars 'as if their lives depended on the number of forms they could fill in a given time'. Sergeant-Majors took charge of more men than they had ever dreamt of handling and taught them to form fours in a rough way before marching them off to one of the racecourses, Randwick, Kensington or Rose Bay, or on to the showgrounds.

'How I remember that first night in camp lying on the cement floor of the Randwick grandstand, trousers folded round boots for a pillow, one blanket and many a shiver, while a terrific southerly buster drove the rain in clouds of spray over all who were not fortunate enough to be at the back,' wrote Private H. W. Cavell of the 2nd Battalion.

New South Wales organised and fitted out the Naval and Military Expeditionary Force to German-held islands in the Pacific, they recruited their First Division and Light Horse regiments as well as other special units, and still the recruits rolled in, all worried lest it would be over before they got there. So many presented themselves that the doctors were unusually selective and for the duration of the war, the 13th Battalion was called 'The Battalion of Big Men'. The Ordnance Stores Staff used to ransack the back shelves for 'out sizes' for the Battalion. When someone found 'A bag of elevens' he was told, 'Send them to Rosehill', where the 13th were camped. A bundle of OS tunics? 'Put them in that 13th heap!' They selected their largest men for guard duty and could turn out guards patrols who averaged 'well over 6 foot in height and 14 stone in weight'.

Among the original NCOs few had any training. A sergeant of the 13th one day said to his men on parade, 'I'm supposed to give you chaps an hours fixing and unfixing. Does anyone know about it?' One newly formed company was asked, 'Is there anyone here who would like to be a sergeant?'

Some interesting, tough men came in on that earliest batch. Men such as Rex Hall, who at the age of nine had ridden with his Uncle Tom on a journey through southern New South Wales to drove sheep from Moulamein. Riding was no effort for the young farm boy. From the age of three he had ridden 'Sovvy', a cunning white pony who knew when enough was enough. By the time Rex was six and ready for school Sovvy was not only foxy, but plaguey, and four young Halls to carry to school was too much. With Rex occupying fourth position on his back he turned straight in to the local creek, sliding on his forefeet down the muddy bank and catapulting all the young riders over his head. Rex was a bush boy who had gone yabbying, fished for bream and black fish, and once, when he was very little, 'brought up the rearguard when my older brothers allowed me to hold the tail as they proudly carried up to the house a cod fish weighing thirty-nine pounds that we'd caught in Barr Creek'.

The tiny bush school of Koroop in Victoria's Northern district is still there, with its Roll of Honour recording the names of five young Halls: Ray, Glen, Rex, Jack and Roy.

When he was nineteen war was declared. Rex Hall rode in immediately and by 18 August he was at Broadmeadows in the 1st Light Horse Field Ambulance. 'I was given two stripes and felt I had the Field Marshal's baton in the bag!' Rex believes, along with many others, that the Shepparton-made water furphy was the origin of 'furphy', slang for rumour. 'The little iron water cart trundled through the lines at "the Meadows" and brought with it rumours of our departure.'

The rations were never enough for young men who spent a long day in the fresh air and the food wasn't what they had known at home. At meal times, armed with tin plates and issue knives and forks the men sat at long wooden tables in groups of forty. Two men's orderlies who probably had been farmers, bankers or teachers a week before did their best as waiters but it was rarely good enough for these hungry impatient men. At Randwick, one volatile man, fearing lest the supply of potatoes should run out, mounted the table, walked its whole length and personally speared his own helping, and a mess orderly walked along the table dropping a chop on each man's plate.

Colour patches were authorised for the first time, those small badges of cloth stitched beneath the shoulder line of a coat. The upper colour showed the battalion, the lower colour, the brigade. These emblems, Australia's nearest equivalent to heraldic devices, quickly became badges of honour and esteem, a pride in a battalion as deep and sincere as any of the traditional regiments of the 'motherland'.

If all was bustle for the front-line recruits, there were others who were equally busy. Uniforms had to be made; harness and wagons, the food for the ships and the army had to be arranged as well as medical stores, the refitting of freighters and passenger liners. All were to be ready to sail by 21 September. Within five weeks of their having marched in to camp the men were sent off to march through the streets of their capital cities. From Hobart to Perth, Brisbane to Adelaide, Melbourne and Sydney, the big-boned, early-enlisted troops swung down the streets in their uniforms cut loose to allow more freedom than the to-that-date traditional, tight-fitting, shiny-buttoned and braided, elegant walking-out outfit. The excitement was at fever pitch.

All over Australia, it seemed, the people wanted to see 'the Boys' march through their capital cities. In NSW the whole 1st Brigade marched through the city of Sydney 'to continuous and enthusiastic acclamation'. Later, when the casualty lists came out day after day, the people found it harder to come to cheer but now they cheered the marching men who were 'going off to their baptism of fire'.

Many good horsemen had dismounted and joined the infantry for fear that the war would be over if they were too choosey – even though they did feel that being a 'foot-slogger' was only one rung up from being a 'bum-brusher' (officer's servant). Conversely, when the Light Horse began to recruit, many men who had never been on a horse rushed to join – the real horsemen declared that these men were 'just too tired' to join the infantry. Many men brought their own horses with them. These were purchased by the Remount Officer and issued back to their previous owners. A large number of those horses supplied by the Government were unbroken and some of the best and quickest breaking was done on these among the trees of Enoggera. When the

'Second' rode through Brisbane prior to leaving to join the first convoy, the horses were still very raw and many of the riders had a lively time keeping them in any sort of order.

The 9th Infantry Battalion left their Enoggera camp on 24 September to join the convoy on board the Orient liner *Omrah*. There had been no publicity about the departure but before the ship sailed nearly two hundred people came to farewell the battalion that would have one of the longest and toughest of campaigns and would endure till the end.

It was a remarkable achievement, the outfitting of 20 000 men with accoutrements for war and equipment for their horses, wagons and domestic matters (such as pay allotments of money to dependents etc.) and the outfitting of the transports with mess-tables and hammocks. The lower decks looked like barrack rooms. But it was done as ordered by 21 September. (The Australian staff had been ready to ship away the mounts for the Light Horse on 21 August.) On this day transports began to glide out of their home state ports to rendezvous with the convoy in the lonely sound at Albany, Western Australia. Shipping masters were perturbed. The great German raiders *Scharnhorst* and *Gneisenau*, part of Admiral von Spee's Pacific Flotilla, were rampaging across the Pacific and this convoy, some of them small ships, many of them slow, armed with ludicrously meagre small-arms with a full complement of Australia's finest young men on board, would be a fine prize for the Germans. But all around the long coastline they began to creep down towards the rendezvous.

The Australian Government was anxious, Labor Prime Minister Andrew Fisher was 'extremely restive', the New Zealand Government refused to permit her men to sail until an adequate naval escort was provided, and then the British Government sent the strongest note: they deemed it imprudent to venture so large a convoy into lanes infested by some of the enemy's most daring ships to sail in any century. Relieved of the responsibility the Australian Government ordered all troop ships into the nearest port while the Royal Australian Navy swept the Pacific clean.

4
Goodbye to AE 1

When he was aged 82, I recorded my father's reminiscences on tape, hoping to learn about the life below decks on the first flagship of the Australian Navy. It was my mother, like a Greek chorus in the background, that nudged the information out of him. A direct transcript reads like this:

Me: Where were you living when you joined the Navy?

Dad: Neerim South. (Mum: Out the back of the bush, miles from anywhere.)

Me: Where did you go to enlist?

Dad: Melbourne. (Mum: You walked the fourteen miles into Warragul didn't you?)

Dad: Yes, to get the train to Melbourne.

Me: Had you been to Melbourne before?

Dad: Well, I don't know about that . . . (Mum: When would *you* have been to Melbourne? Timber cutters! They never leave the forests and the hills!)

Dad: No, I hadn't been to Melbourne [and before Mum could come in again] and I wasn't missing much either.

In 1970, six years before I made this tape, we had gone to a 'Back to Neerim South', out there beyond the now close-settled farms, out to where the great forests had grown, and there in the open by a fire made of tree trunks the old settlers were gathered. After a while a very old man came to my 76-year-old father and said, 'You're one of the Smith boys?' Dad said yes (there had been eight of them). Then the old man said, 'I know who you are! You're the young one who went away to the navy and sailed *right around the world*!'

It was fifty-eight years since the young axeman had left
that place in 1912 and yet the memory of the great journey
he had been swept away on had so engrossed the tiny
settlement that even in 1970 his exploits were remembered
and wondered at. Being in the navy would have been a
matter for remark in all events, because only 3 200 men
were on active service with this, the world's newest navy.

The Royal Australian Navy was created during the years
1911 to 1913 and when war broke out a Naval Board was
functioning, a Naval College had been opened at Jervis Bay
(NSW), a training ship (*Tingira*) had been acquired, the
building yard at Cockatoo Island had been taken over by
the Commonwealth and work had started on naval bases
at Western Port (Vic.) and Fremantle (WA). Planned as a
basic squadron, when war broke out the service consisted
of:

Battle-cruiser *Australia*   19 200 tons   44 000 h.p.
   (arrived in Sydney from
   Clydeside, October 1913)
Light cruisers:
  Melbourne
  Sydney   5 400 tons   22 000 h.p.
  Brisbane
  (under construction)
Destroyers:
  Parramatta
  Yarra   700 tons   12 000 h.p.
  Warrego
Submarines:
  AE 1   800 tons   1 750 h.p.
  AE 2

Besides these ships the Commonwealth owned or controlled
the light cruiser *Encounter*, the small cruiser *Pioneer*, the
gunboats *Protector* and *Gayundah*; and the torpedo-boats
Childers and *Countess of Hopetoun* (remnants from the old
colonial flotillas).

Coaling to clear harbour before war was declared, the flagship HMAS *Australia* was ordered to escort a force to seize the German island territory in the Pacific, German New Guinea, the Bismarcks and Samoa. Two infantry battalions, known as the Australian Navy and Military Expeditionary Force, had been hastily recruited in Sydney and sailed for Rabaul (New Britain) the instant the ships completed coaling.

This expeditionary force was swiftly mobilised and despatched. Driver B. A. Cripps, a Queenslander, headed his diary '1st Aust. Expeditionary Force in the Pacific Ocean on HMTS *Kanowna*'.

'*4 August 1914*: Troops mobilised at Townsville 4 Aug. 1914. Members of rifle clubs and those who volunteered came in at all times. *7 August*: Received orders to leave by the SS *Kanowna* for Thursday Island. *8 August*: Busy all morning loading troop ship with stores. Had a few minutes talk with Jan [his girl-friend]. Ship left wharf about 12 o'clock midst the most enthusiastic farewell that Townsville had ever seen. [There were alarums caused by the German raiders *Scharnhorst* and *Gneisenau* being on the rampage in the Pacific.] *14 August*: The troops were issued with ball cartridges last night ready for an attack which was expected from the Germans. *15 August*: About 11 o'clock tonight the Captain came and told us that 4 volunteers were wanted to join an expeditionary force to go on the Pacific Ocean. Company Serg. Major Collum, Drivers Johnstone, Graham and Cripps volunteered at 2 minutes to 12 o'clock. We signed an oath of allegiance, as we were to be under the Imperial authorities. We then went and had a light supper and toasted good wishes to the Force. *16 August*: We left the harbour about 10 o'clock tonight with all lights out as it was rumoured the *Scharnhorst* was about. Our destination is unknown. The boys have started a paper on board called the *Latrine Leader* and the *W.C. Chronicle*.'

Within a week Lieutenant Garsia was sent back to Australia in charge of a prize crew on board the *Zambesi*, a little vessel belonging to the German Pacific Administration that had been captured on 12 August. Far from being pleased at his new command Garsia fretted furiously. By now it was known that the German raiders *Scharnhorst* and *Gneisenau* were in the Pacific and he was afraid he'd be left out of the chase. 'It's not likely but quite possible that [the flotilla] might be called away suddenly to chase Scharnhorst and Co and one would miss everything,' he wrote. There was an irony in this: within three months, with no thought of action, Garsia would be able to write of taking part in the most dramatic action – the first battle – of the Australian Navy, and this on the other side of the watery southern world. He badgers his way onto another little ship going out to rejoin the squadron.

'*11 Sept*: We will get into Rabaul tomorrow and then we'll coal-coal-coal; 1000 tons in sweltering heat – my oath. *12 Sept*: Coaling Ship.

'We arrived at Rabaul at 11 a.m. to find Flagship lying at Herbertshöe and to hear accounts of fighting on the previous day. It is bad news too to hear that Elwell and Dr Pockley have been killed . . . To begin with 25 men were landed from the *Berrima* to march 4 miles inland to capture the Wireless Station. And what is more they did it after fighting all the way and with the 4 miles turning out to be 9 miles. Within 100 yds of the landing Elwell was killed and Dr Pockley while attending to a wounded German was shot from a tree probably by an ignorant nigger. Later *200* men were landed to reinforce.'

So the first Australian casualties fell. A greater, more tragic blow came in a few days time. Rupert Garsia had by now got a berth on HMAS *Sydney* and on 16 September wrote: 'Left Rabaul for Sydney. *AE 1* is missing since yesterday. But we are only really anxious today. It is the worst submarine disaster that has yet occurred anywhere in the world. 35 lives lost. The officers are Besant, Scarlett and Moore. I knew C. L. Moore very well at Whale Island.'

AE 1 was indeed lost. 'We looked out across the water', my father told me as a child, 'hung well out as we passed islands in case she was anchored with radio and engine both gone, but we knew we'd never see her again. They had all been devoured, swallowed up by the sea. These were very crude little vessels these early submarines.'

In that 'ditty box' of memorabilia I found as a child I came on a poem the seamen had written.

The fate of the AE 1 - - -

She faced no battle flames, she heard no German gun,
The ship without a name: the luckless A.E. 1.
Yet were her sailors lives no less for Empire lost
And Mothers, sweethearts, wives will bear the bitter cost.
Australia's war-ships swept the broad Pacific Main
But she from out the deep will never rise again,
And we shall not forget all the years that run
The fate that she has met. Good-bye to A.E. 1.

Pent in their iron cell they sank beneath the waves
Untouched by shot or shell they drifted to their graves
Until their painful breath at last began to fail
Upon their way to death; let pity draw the veil.
They could not strike one blow, but out of sound and sight
Of comrade or of foe they passed to endless night
Deep down on ocean's floor, far from the wind and sun
They rest forever more. Good-bye to A.E. 1.

A harder fate was theirs than men who fight and die
But still, Australia cares and will not pass them by,
When Honours lists are read their names will surely be
Amongst the gallant dead who fought to keep us free.

Their winding sheet is steel, their sepulchre is wide
The sea birds scream and wheel where silently they died
Their's is a monument to history just begun
When down to death they went.

Good-bye to A.E. 1.

'A.B. Albert Smith RAN copied these words, 19 Sept, 1914 on board the flag ship *Australia* in Rabaul Harbour.'
Lieutenant Garsia is quickly snapped from thoughts of

the *AE 1* by a message received on 17 September while they were searching for the lost submarine. 'When *Australia* and *Sydney* were south of Rossel Id we recd news of the *Scharnhorst* and *Gneisenau* being sighted off Samoa and then off Fiji. So we turned about and made straight back to Rabaul arriving there Sat. Sept 19th.'

It was these two ships of Vice-Admiral Count von Spee's East Asia squadron that were to hold up for many weeks the despatch of the troops now gathering in Australia. Up and down and across the Pacific they raided, using their island territories as coaling stations. In mid-September the German Governor in the Pacific agreed that all resistance in the islands of German New Guinea should cease. (Australian troops remained in occupation of these – and the other territories in the Pacific that once were German – until after the war, when the League of Nations gave Australia a mandate over them.) The loss of these would not embarrass the two raiders as far as coaling went, as they had colliers well positioned with very little dependence on the German colonies, but the presence of the powerfully armed *Australia* in the Pacific certainly did. One of the most modern battle cruisers afloat, she was capable of 25 knots, had eight 12-inch guns, fourteen 4-inch guns, a 4-inch anti-aircraft gun, a 3-inch and four three-pounder guns; 5 machine guns, and two 18-inch torpedo tubes.

Lieutenant Garsia kept a very good diary. '*Sept 19th*: Sat. night filled up with coal finishing 3 a.m. *Sept 21st*: 11.30 a.m. Weighed and proceeded en route to Angaur in the Pelew Islands to destroy the 2nd Rate Wireless Station there, and we are going via a German Rendezvous we have got wind of – but a bit late by 2 days I think.

'The *Scharnhorst* and *Gneisenau* are believed to be coming over to the New Guinea Coast, but a generally pessimistic view prevails that we are never going to see them. *They* have never actively advertised their where-abouts by means of Wireless, while the *Flag* and other ships have used theirs with an energy that must have knocked the heads off the German Wireless Operators. "Stoker Jones' allotment" has become a byword.'

All around the eastern states of Australia ship-loads of men were still prevented from sailing because of the menace of these two daring raiders. The New Zealand Expeditionary Force was similarly held up. When the last of the German radio stations in the Pacific was put out of action Garsia recorded the next message from the Admiralty.

'HMAS *Australia* is to go and follow up the *Scharnhorst* and *Gneisenau* who have now bombarded Papeete, Tahiti. It is a bit of a problem for the Admiral for if von Spee had good colliers there is nothing to stop him doubling back onto the Australian Coast. We presume he is going round the Horn and up onto the Argentine Trade Route, but this is not certain. One has no conception of the big distances involved in the Pacific with the coal problem continually acting as a drag on all movements. If one is going to steam to find the enemy at a place 6 000 miles away, one must coal some 2 days before there is any chance of falling in with him, otherwise one could not fight the action, which generally means a convenient anchorage must be found at the right distance, for coaling in mid-ocean is no easy matter . . .'

So HMAS *Australia* steamed off in the wake of the *Scharnhorst* and *Gneisenau*. 'They were like phantom names we heard whispered in the night,' my father said. 'We knew we would never see those ships this side of Davy Jones's locker.' And neither they did. As Garsia had predicted, the two raiders rounded Cape Horn. HMAS *Australia*, with little but intuition to direct her, tried first to bluff her way through the Panama Canal but, being neutral, Panama turned her back. She steamed at her 25 knots down the coast of Chile, passed through the roughly charted Straits of Magellan south of the Horn and was hard on the heels of the enemy she had hounded since war began when a signal came that British warships ahead had intercepted the two ships as they came up from the Horn and sunk both.

5
The Great Adventure

Now, with the Pacific free of the raiders, transports began to creep down and around the coastline of the continent to the rendezvous at Albany and HMAS *Sydney* steamed to join them as escort. In Sydney for dry docking, Lieutenant Garsia laconically mentions the fact, while the newspapers were crying in headlines: OFF ON THE GREAT ADVENTURE.

'*Oct 23*: Left dock in our right mind. Coaling. It transpires we are to escort the Australian and N.Z. Expeditionary Force from (hush) Albany to Aden. *Oct 31*: Arrived Albany. Found here the Australian and New Zealand Convoy. And the *Minotaur* and *Melbourne*. The transports are a fine lot of ships between 30 and 40 in number. Coaled ship . . . We are all furious at the news of the resignation of Prince Louis. The *Globe* ought to be smashed out of existence and the editor publicly flogged. [This was in reference to the hounding of the Admiral of the Fleet, Lord Louis Battenburg, who was of German descent. He was the father of Lord Louis Mountbatten.]'

They left home in October 1914 to the sounds of 'Sons of Australia', 'Dedicated to the Australian Expeditionary Force', it was as naïve and unsophisticated as the men themselves.

We're from the land of gum-trees, where the sun is
    mighty hot,
Where the 'possum and the kangaroo reside;
From the far-back country and from many a lonely spot,

Where you have to know your way without a guide.
From the land of tea and damper, from the forest and
    the plain,
We have come to help our kindred in the war;
Because their blood, and ours, too, is of the same old
    strain –
It's British, and we don't ask any more . . .

Chorus: For Britain! good old Britain!
            Where our fathers first drew breath,
            We'll fight like true Australians,
            Facing danger, wounds or death.
            With Britain's other gallant sons
            We're going hand in hand;
            Our War-cry 'Good old Britain' boys,
            Our own dear motherland.

The newspapers might claim that the men were 'off on the great adventure' but the diaries of the young soldiers rarely give evidence of their having any such emotions – for the most part it was the saddest moment of their young lives.

Signaller R. J. Kenny of the 4th Battalion, was moved, as were most men, by the women on the wharf. 'When we left Sydney nobody knew we were going. We were trammed from camp to Circular Quay, where lighters were waiting to take us to *Euripides*. How it leaked out that we were going I don't know but soon people came flocking from everywhere. The police cordon could hardly keep back the women bent on giving father or brother a parting kiss. We were reminded before leaving camp that breaking ranks or any breach of discipline would be severely dealt with; and every man stood like a statue. But I shall not forget the tear-dimmed eyes of the women and girls that I saw on the morning I left Sydney.'

'I did miss you coming in,' Ronald Smith wrote of parting from Kitty, his wife in Tasmania. 'It is a struggle to keep from crying. I was terribly afraid I'd start before getting in to Kindred and then I'd be unable to stop.'

Meanwhile, the women, too, wrote of their emotions at parting. Annie Riddell saw her cousin Walter Hackett of the 13th Light Horse ride off to war from Melbourne. '. . . On Thursday afternoon I met Ella at the tram terminus and we went by the horse tram to Coburg and started from there to walk the five miles to the camp . . . Walter as well as the whole of the regiment had to go on parade . . . All the time Walter kept squinting round to see if we were still there . . . the minute it was over, he came bounding over to us . . . we walked over to the road together and said Good bye – and started once more to walk back to Coburg . . . Walter was in the highest spirits and a whole new uniform – more green in it than the others and no end of straps and things about it . . .

'Next morning a friend of Miss Courtney's rang up from Coburg and said the troops were just passing . . . ran up to the top of Albion Street – but it was only the A squadron – so we came home and finished breakfast – then I rang up head quarters at the camp and asked if Private W. Hackett were still in camp – and if I had been Lady Ferguson I could not have had better treatment – so he asked if I would mind waiting a minute! While he went to find out – he came back to the 'phone and told me his squadron was just leaving the camp at that moment – so we calculated how long they would take to get down [and we] all went up to the Rd. and saw them come along – they did look splendid – with their waving black ostrich plumes [*sic*] – As Walter got near I handed him your letter. He gaily waved his hand and we waved and cheered him. Then I came home changed my dress and started off again to town to meet Ella at 11 a.m. As we neared the Hay Market I saw the squadron disappearing round the corner to the back streets – so when I met Ella we started off for the Queen's bridge thinking to see them there – sure enough we only waited a few minutes and on they came – we handed Walter his bible – though his horse swerved very much at our approach.

'Then we went by Port Melb tram and passed them again

(they only walk). We lined up near the pier – and right in front of us there were Archie Hackett and his wife and Mabel – they were delighted to see us, and had been waiting there since 10.30 – by then it was 11.30 – of course I introduced and we went along the Rd to point out Walter at a more convenient place – Archie buzzed right up to him, caught his hand and shook it – and a minute after – the squadron came to a stand still so I managed an introduction.

'Then the men rode along to the beach and stood in a single line all along the shore and at a given signal – they rode right into the sea – it was a sight for a cinematograph – then they came out and the men dismounted – they then led their horses toward the pier, so we lined up and kissed Walter – Mabel dashed forward and flung her arm round him. Good bye! Walter dear! she said. . . . We were so glad of those few minutes – we waited till 2.30 in the hope of getting on the pier – but found it impossible . . .'

Carl and Ernek thoughtfully prepared their family for the weary months ahead, Ernek writing to his father: 'I am sorry you were not home the other day but would like to see you all before we go . . . We are sailing Tuesday by the *Orvieto* (A2) is her number. She goes from Port Melbourne. My number is 395 [this number he pencils heavy and black].'

Though they may not have thought of it as adventure, the Queenslanders of the 2nd Light Horse were jubilant. Waiting at their temporary 'shake-down' on Melbourne Show grounds they were visited by Prime Minister 'Andy' Fisher, who eventually yielded to their constant requests for permission to wear the emu plume on the left side of their turned-up hats. Of all things calculated to undo the disappointment and boredom that the broken journey had brought on them it was this bestowal of emu feathers (known to most of them as 'kangaroo feathers'). They were worn with a pride of soil and homeland as deep as that of any heraldic device dating back to the crusaders and worn still by the sick old nations.

The 'Battalion of Big Men', the 13th, set off to war by
train, going down to Melbourne via the golden wheatfields
of the Eastern Riverina where the whistling of the train
engines brought farmers and families and townspeople out
to wave and cry 'Good luck!' They roared on through the
vineyards of the Murray to where the ladies of Albury had
food awaiting them and the townspeople gave them a
rousing farewell. They arrived at Broadmeadows to mud
and more mud. So tenacious was this mud claimed to be
that the New South Welshmen swore that in Egypt and
Gallipoli there were still 'Broadmeadows' mud marks on
our clothes'.

But as if to prepare them for the Homeric lands and
battles that were awaiting them, many of the ships carried
the names of men and landmarks of the heroes of ancient
literature and of the *Iliad*. Into that great, lonely, safe King
George Sound at Albany, transport after transport carrying
men, horses and guns crept. There were the *Ulysses*,
Euripides, *Medic*, *Ascanius*, *Hororata*, *Benalla*, *Afric*,
Orvieto, and the tiny *Southern* able to make only 11 knots.
To escort them was HMS *Minotaur*, from the British China
Station, HMAS *Sydney* and HMAS *Melbourne* from
Australia and the *Ibuki* from Japan who had recently
entered the war.

Most of the men had been no more than six weeks in
camp – and much of that had been spent in getting uniforms
together, learning to drill, and arranging their papers. On
board ship men who would be signallers for infantry
regiments were drawn from the ranks and trained in
semaphore and message carying. All ranks were given
instruction in semaphore signalling and all officers 'should
be able to send and read semaphore by end of voyage'.

Officers must learn many things: war diaries, for instance
(taken only to mean the official diary kept in each battalion,
as private diaries were officially forbidden). 'The guiding
principles to be followed in regard to the matter to be
entered in war diaries are that war diaries ought to serve as
a record of important facts not recorded elsewhere, and as
an index of important orders, instructions, or messages

received or despatched.' Luckily for us, many ordinary soldiers kept a tiny, albeit illicit, diary.

The men had come on board with much of their personal kit such as 'soap, piece of, in wallets; Boots, ankle, brown. Laces (spare), for boots, ankle, pairs; socks, worsted, pairs – one pair on person, one pair in pocket of greatcoat and one pair in kitbag at base'. The final instruction regarding kit was: 'Soldiers when discharged will receive a suit of plain clothes and a cap free or sum of 20 shillings in lieu', a fair indication of its value.

During the voyage they were to be paid 1s 0d per day for 50 days. The pay of a private, apart from on board ship, was to be 5s 0d per day plus 1s 0d deferred pay. A corporal, 9s 0d, Lieutenant-Colonel, £1 17s 6d, and Colonel or Brigadier £2 5s 0d. The allotment to dependants must be 'Not less than 2/5 of pay to wife or de facto and no less than 3/5 if children'. Illegitimate children were to be allotted one-fifth, and pre-maternity orders would be in the order of one-fifth. Colonels of regiments were obliged to ensure that soldiers retain at least 1s 0d per day for their own use while abroad.

On board the *Benalla* were nurses. Most were enlisted with the Australian Army Nursing Service, others, afraid as were many soldiers that the war would be over before they could get in, had volunteered for the Queen Alexandra Imperial Military Nursing Service Reserve (QAIMNSR) and were on their way to hospitals run by the English army.

Pretty Effie Hargreaves sailed off this way in March 1915 under the following terms of engagement:

'Free Passage: from and return to Australia either by 2nd class mail steamer or by military transport.
Pay: Sister £50 p.a.; staff nurses £40 p.a. with allowance of 15/- or 21/- weekly according to place of service.
Free Uniform.'

The terms of engagement for Australian Army Nursing Service (AANS) after 1 July 1915 were:

Pay: Matron 12/6 per day
       Nursing Sister 9/6 per day
       Staff Nurse 7/- per day.

They were granted an outfit allowance of £10 10s 0d with which they might 'purchase or make the whole or any portion of such articles'. They were later granted £16 per annum for maintenance or renewal of uniform.

The most exquisitely detailed diaries this author has collected are those of a nurse with the Australian Army Nursing Service, Sister Alice Kitchen. Reading this woman's diaries as she hovered on the edge of battles, reached out to recover maimed and sick men, it is impossible to remain unmoved. Alice Kitchen was forty years old when the convoy left Australia in 1914. That she survived the following five years is a tribute to her stamina and dedication.

With no preamble she began her diary in a clear hand, in ink, in a leather-covered book:

'*19 October 1914, Troopship "Benalla"*, *A.24*: Came on board 12 noon, leaving all the family on the pier. Moved out 2 p.m. after luncheon. Learned we were going straight out to Albany, without any escort or cruisers. Those parts are evidently considered safe. They say there are scouts out "somewhere". An anxious time is expected after leaving Albany in spite of the convoy.'

In this brisk fashion Sister Kitchen began to write as she joined that first convoy taking the first AIF to war. Ahead were Gallipoli, Ypres, Pozières, the Somme – a score of battlefields – and five years of what has been called 'the greatest tragedy mankind has known'.

While the *Ibuki* and four other naval ships shepherded the New Zealand transports across the Tasman Sea to the rendezvous, the men of the Australian states once again set off to converge on the lonely waters of King George Sound. Here, in the wide, deep harbour near the little town of Albany, the greatest flotilla to leave Australia began to assemble. There would be twenty-eight transports from Australia and ten from New Zealand meeting in one of the finest anchorages in the world; sheltered from the winds by encircling flower-scented hills.

But apart from relatives and friends of the men, few Australians gave little thought to those who had gone. Indeed, the newspapers had not even published reports of the seizing of the German-held islands in the Pacific. There was far more exciting news from the countries where most Australians believed the action would occur: for all that they cheered the announcement of war, and waved and blew kisses to their troops marching off, they still had no realisation that Australia was *in it*. Europe was where wars happened and tragedies befell the participants. Now the retreat from Mons, the rallying on the Marne, the horror of Belgium and a town new to Australians, Ypres, took all their mind. Their own laughing lads merely seemed to bob and float on the eddies of that maelstrom of Europe.

Alice Kitchen continued her daily diary unperturbed by anything except tobacco. '*Oct 23*: . . . 9 pats. We have been travelling close to the *Wiltshire* all day and drawing near to Albany. An entertainment took place tonight but we missed it, being too busy to go. We were in time for some singing. We did not stay long on account of the smoke which is one of my greatest trials [and about which she complained for the five years of the war!]. *Oct 24*: Albany this morning early – a good many troopships already in . . . able to post letters and send telegrams to relieve their anxiety at home. I wish we could send a wireless daily but that cannot be . . . nice to see our own land once more. Sorry to hear the *Emden* has been busy again.'

On 30 October she mentions that 'The men went for a route march and some gave trouble by not returning and the pickets were sent out after them; all were found but one – and the rest were had up next day and dismissed and sent off the boat to return to their homes'. The nurses occupied themselves with shopping, knitting, learning French and writing letters, until on 1 November, All Saints' Day, 'At 8 a.m. we began to move out in single file to the sea; it was a fine sight to see the long line of ships, going out one by one and forming into 3 long lines, the Cruisers leading . . . We travel about 800 yds behind each other, and a mile between the 3 rows. It seems a little difficult to get the correct speed and they occasionally have to drop out of line if they get too close, but seem to have all sorts of arrangements made for contingencies . . . It is an anxious time for all those in charge. We hear the Capt. never leaves the bridge at night. If attacked by enemy cruisers we are to go 3 miles out of our course till the cruisers do their work. A cruiser leads the way then the *Orvieto* then 3 lines of ships 3 abreast, a cruiser on each side, and one far away in the rear. They say there are scouts as well beyond these . . . If the *Emden* comes in amongst us in the dark what a commotion there would be. Most of them would be horribly mixed up in collision. We all realise our danger but are in God's hands. At night all portholes are covered when the light is on and as few as possible used, partly to minimise the difficulty of steering by the boat behind each one . . . Our Jap Cruiser is like a pillar of cloud opposite my porthole . . . I often rise in the night and look to see if it is still there and feel safer when I see its huge cloud. It draws in much nearer to us in the dark night hours.' (It was just such a 'pillar of smoke' that the *Emden* relied on to lead it to its victims.)

Then, amongst entries about measles, sore throats and the heat, comes that of 9 November: 'It was announced that a German Cruiser, name unknown, had been beached to save itself from sinking. We hope it is the *Emden*.'

The *Emden* certainly had been busy. She had been at Tsingtau on foreign station when the captain, von Muller, received the wireless message that Germany had ordered the mobilisation of the whole army and the fleet. By the time war was declared (2 August for Germany and Russia) *Emden* had, by her captain's own decision, headed out into the open sea as a lone wolf raider. On 4 August, the day when Britain entered the war, she took her first prize, the Russian *Rjasan*, a near-new speedy passenger ship, such a valuable ship that she was promptly made over to the

German navy to be used as a sea-going warship. Within the next three months *Emden*'s epic adventure rivalled that of any of the daring voyages recorded by Hakluyt. It was more in the tradition of the swashbuckling Englishmen Drake and Hawkins than of modern sea warfare, but unlike these men there was a chivalry about the German von Muller. By 1 November *The Times* had recorded, 'The German light-cruiser *Emden* has, up to date, sunk 15 English ships, a total of 93,000 tons and captured and set free again five'. And this was only the English. The German newspaper *Der Volkerkreig* reported on 4 November, 'The Iron Cross 1st and 2nd class is awarded to the Captain of the *Emden*, and the Iron Cross, 2nd class to all officers and subordinate officers and to 50 petty officers and men of the ship's company'.

Striking the Colombo–Calcutta trade-route on 9 October she picked up the Greek steamer *Pontoporos* soon after dark, the next day *Kabinga*, and *Killin* two nights later, *Diplomat* at noon on the thirteenth and late on the fourteenth the *Trabboch* and *Clan Mathieson*. Six ships in four days and this by a ship without support of any kind, dependent on the coal carried by her prizes to refuel, surrounded by enemy or neutral ports which refused her permission to lay up for repairs, or ordinary sea-going maintenance.

The shipping lane was used by neutrals as well as enemy shipping and every time he was sighted by a neutral ship Captain von Muller, knowing his whereabouts would be reported, had to abandon the area, wait for dark, and head off somewhere else. On the twenty-fifth he had been driven off one lane – so he headed for another. That day he took the *King Lud*, on 26 October the *Tymeric* and *Gryfevale*. The following day he captured the *Buresk*, a British collier full of coal, the *Ribera* at noon and the *Foyle* six hours later, before he was sighted by a Dutch (neutral) ship and forced to disappear into other ocean areas.

Earlier. on 14 October, he sank the *Clan Grant*, *Ponrabbel* and *Ben Mohr* all on the one day; on the eighteenth between the hours of 7.15 p.m. and midnight she took *Troilus*,

St Egbert and *Exford* and at 9 a.m., the next morning, the *Chilkana*.

On some of these ships von Muller put crews to work them as colliers for the raider, others he sent off to ports with captured crews – and mostly with carefully planned stories to decoy other ships into the new seas to which he intended to disappear. On 30 October he captured his last prize, the British steamer *Newburn*. It was toward this daring and brilliant enemy that the Australian convoy was heading.

6
What Price Me Now?

While the convoy was awakening to another day at 6.30 a.m. on 9 November the *Melbourne*, at the head of the three long lines of transports, picked up a wireless message from the cable station at Direction Island in the Cocos–Keeling Group. It was imperfect, flung out as the station itself was besieged: 'Enemy warship off island.'

The convoy was less than sixty miles from Cocos Island. With her stokers 'working like demons' the *Sydney* reached top speed of 27 knots when sent off to the attack and reached the *Emden* two and a half hours later, at 9 a.m. By 9.45 a.m. the battle had begun. The *Emden* had ten guns of only 4.1-inch calibre and it was her policy to fight at comparatively short range. The *Sydney* had 6-inch guns and could use her tactical advantage, staying either outside the range of the smaller guns or at a distance where the extreme range would make good shooting difficult. The battle lasted one hour and forty minutes and Lieutenant Garsia recorded every second of it, this time in a letter he despatched from HMAS *Sydney* in Colombo to his father. Within a few days it was to flash around the world.

'I was in my bath when Bell-Salter came in with news that the enemy was within 40 miles of us. I of course took it for a "leg haul" but he soon convinced me and the noise made by the propellors going at rapidly increasing speed, soon left us in a state of great elation. . . . at 8.30 a.m. I went on the bridge as officer of Forenoon Watch. We were going about 24 knots by now. As soon as the men had had their breakfast some few steps began to be taken to get the ship thoroughly ready for action, but it was not till after I had been relieved by the Navigating Officer to go to Divisions and Prayers at 9 a.m. (the ordinary daily routine), that after these ceremonies were over "Prepare for Action" was piped. It could be misleading to say we went into action unready. But we were undoubtedly not ready in every detail and these details were being attended to right up to the time the "Action" bugle sounded. . . . We opened fire from our Port Guns to begin with. I was standing just behind No. 1 Port and the Gunlayer, (Atkins 1st Cl. Petty Officer) said "Shall I load, Sir?" I was surprised, but deadly keen there should be no "flap". So said "No, don't load till you get the order." . . . At 9.15 a.m. the tops of the cocoanut trees of Keeling Islands were sighted. At 9.20 we sighted the *Emden*, or rather the tops of her funnels, 12 or 15 miles away. At 9.40 a.m. she opened fire at a very big range and shortly after that we started in on her. . . . I being officer of foremost group of guns. . . . Right near the beginning though I knew nothing about it, a shot hit the range finder, without exploding, within a few feet of the Captain, Rahilly, Johnstone and three men. They were all on the little, exposed, Upper Bridge known as "Monkey's Island". The poor Range Finder operator, Hoy, Able Seaman was done for, but a youngster called Miller who was at his elbow was not touched. Later I heard a crash and looking aft saw that a shell had hit near Gun . . . A_3 (No 2 Starb). But owing to the Screen being in the way I did not know it had knocked out practically the whole of that gun's crew. And not seeing any flame or smoke rising (we cope with the smallest fire *immediately*), went on with my job. This required continual attention. The men are splendid at *loading* drill, but practice *supply* of ammunition is almost impossible in peace time. To have a big supply stacked on the Upper Deck is far too dangerous when proceeding in Action, and what with getting an even distribution of projectiles and cartridges between the two guns, getting the safety caps off, with fiddly pins and things to take out, attending to misfires, cheering up the one or two who seemed to be "pulling dry", you can imagine I had little time to be thinking much about the *Emden*. I noticed once or twice when going forward the Starb side to the Fxle Gun, that we seemed to be in the thick of it. There was a lot of "Wheee-oo" "Whee-oo" – "Wheee-oo" and the "But-But-But" of the shell striking the water beyond us. Many seemed only thirty yds beyond and as the range was pretty big, this is quite possible, since the angle of descent would be pretty steep. Coming aft, I heard a shot graze the tops of the shield of No. 1 Starb. . . . All the time we were going 25 and sometimes as much as 26 knots. We had the speed on the *Emden* and fought as suited ourselves. We next changed round to Starb Guns and I then found Sharpe the Gunlayer of No. 1 Starb had been knocked out close to the Conning Tower, so I brought Atkins over to fire No. 1 Starb. I was quite deaf by now as in the hurry there had been no thought of getting cotton wool. This is a point I won't overlook next time. Coming aft the Port Side from the Fxle gun, I was met by a lot of men cheering and waving their caps. I said "What's happened?" "She's gone Sir, she's gone". I ran to the ship's side and no sign of the ship could I see. If one could have seen a dark cloud of smoke, it would have been different. But I could see no sign of anything. So I called out "All hands turn out the lifeboats, there will be men in the water". They were just starting to do this when someone called out "She's still firing Sir" and of course everyone ran back to the guns . . . a cloud of yellow or very light coloured smoke had obscured her from view, so that looking in her direction one's impression was she had utterly and totally disappeared. Later we . . . engaged her on the other broadside. By now her three funnels and her foremast had been shot away and she was on fire aft. We turned again and after giving her a salvo or two with the Starb guns, saw her run ashore on North Keeling Island. So at 11.20 a.m. we ceased firing, the action having lasted 1 hour 40 min. While chasing a collier (which had been in attendance on *Emden*) we had time to see our hits and losses. Able Seaman Hoy and Ordinary Seaman Bell were gone poor beggars, and

Petty officer Lynch and Able Seaman Sharp died one that afternoon and the other next day. Of the 8 or 9 wounded only two are permanently affected, or so we greatly hope. Hampden who has "bites" out of both calves will be all right in 6 weeks.

'Our hits were not very serious. We were "hulled" in about 3 places . . . When we boarded the collier, we found they had opened the sea cocks and the ship was sinking fast so we took everyone off her and returned to the *Emden* . . . now occurred something that could not be avoided but which has taken all the gilt off the gingerbread. It was the only subject on which the Captain was really rude to the Captain of the *Emden*, when we were taking him up to Colombo, and they were very good friends before and after the subject was mentioned. We got back to find the *Emden*'s colours still flying. It's true she was ashore, but as we had no means of knowing whether they had not means, if we left them there of going over to the Cable Station (15 miles away) and capturing it and we did not dare approach too close . . . The Captain got a lot closer than any of us thought wise and we could see two guns pointing at us to say nothing of the risk that they might have a torpedo ready for us. Then we signalled "Do you Surrender?" They waved a *red* flag back saying "We have no signal books". Now the point is, with their colours up, they were *absolutely entitled* to lure us as close as we were fools enough to come and then let us have it. After trying to get an answer out of them for about half an hour (and even with colours up if they had waved a *white* flag it would have helped matters) we opened fire again and gave them three salvoes. I believed it finished 15 or 20 men out right. Then at last they sent a man aloft to cut down the colours and waved a big white flag from forward. It was getting dark and we did not know for certain that the Cruiser *Konigsberg* might not be near, so we could do no rescue work that night and had to steam away. A cry in the darkness and we were stopped and lifeboats lowered to pick up a nearly exhausted German sailor, the 4th rescued from the water that day.

'*10th Nov*: Early in the morning we made for the cable station to find that the party landed by the Germans to destroy the station had seized a schooner and departed. The poor devils aren't likely to go far with a leaking ship and the leathers removed from all the pumps. Although they had broken up all the instruments the Cable people had a duplicate set buried . . . [The "poor devils", after a journey that took in 3 ships, camel riding, and miles on foot arrived safely in Germany within a few weeks.] At 11.10 a.m. we arrived off the *Emden* again. I was sent over to her in one of the cutters. Luckily her stern was sticking out beyond where the surf broke, so that with a rope from the stern of the ship one could ride close under one quarter, with the boat's bow to seaward. The rollers were very big and the surging to and fro and so on made getting on board fairly difficult. However the Germans standing aft gave me a hand up and I was received by the Captain of the *Emden*. I told him from our Captain that if he would give his parole the Captain was prepared to take all his crew on board the *Sydney* and take them straight up to Colombo. He stuck a little over the word "parole" but readily agreed when I explained the exact scope of it. And now came the dreadful job of getting the badly wounded into the boats. There were 15 of these. Luckily we have a very good pattern of light stretcher into which men can be strapped. We got away 3 . . . in each boat. The Germans were all suffering badly from thirst, so we hauled the boats' water casks up on deck . . . When I got a chance with all the boats away I went to have a look round the ship. I have no intention of describing what I saw. With the exception of the forecastle which is hardly touched, from Fore Bridge to Stern Post, she is nothing but a shambles. And the whole thing was most shocking. The German Doctor asking me to signal for some Morphia sent me aft and I never came forward again. By 5 p.m. we had all on board the *Sydney* from the *Emden* with the exception of some 30 men who had swum ashore to the island. These had missed their way to where they were told to go and when we arrived off the only landing place (N. Keeling is uninhabited and no harbour) they were none of them there.'

Lieutenant Garsia took the whaler and some crew to the island to bring off some wounded men whom they heard were ashore. They had difficulty landing in the surf and were forced to stay overnight. Next morning they collected four wounded men from the beach opposite the *Emden* and transferred them to HMAS *Sydney* which then steamed for Colombo. 'It quite shook [the German lieutenants Schal and Vitthoef] when they found out the Captain had asked that there should be no cheering on entering Colombo . . . At Colombo we dropped all our wounded. . . . It was very interesting talking to some of the German officers afterwards. "You fired on the White flag." I at once took the matter up and went into what had happened straight away, and the torpedo Lieutenant [Vitthoef] and an Engineer both said emphatically "No that is not so, you did not fire on the white flag". But we did not leave it at that, one of us went to the Captain and he got from Capt. von Muller an assurance that we had done nothing of the kind and that he intended to assemble his officers and tell them so. The day von Muller was leaving the ship at Colombo, he came up to me on the Quarter Deck and thanked me in connection with the rescue of the wounded, shook hands and saluted.'

When HMAS *Sydney* berthed in Colombo young Lieutenant Garsia sent his letter off to his father who, seeing it as great propaganda for the fledgling Australian Navy, sent it to *The Times*. From there it spread quickly. In 1953, when sending the original of the letter to C. E. W. Bean, the official war historian, Rupert Garsia (now Captain) explained the consequences:

'The most interesting point about the letter was I think the immense interest in the Action shown in England at the time.

'The letter was perfectly timed to meet this interest. It left Colombo the day we arrived there, while Captain Glossop was still drafting his despatch. It went straight from my father in Somerset to *The Times*. It was translated into many languages and used as propaganda. It took up the whole of the single sheet official gazette at Gibraltar the day of our arrival there for Action Repairs, having arrived there from England the day before. When we arrived at Bermuda and Halifax and other places all the Press people in those places knew about it and got on my track.

'From my own point of view at the time it was a good thing I had no idea my father would send the letter on. But he said, everyone was asking about the Action, when my letter turned up and without hesitation he sent it straight to *The Times.* So my wrath was unavailing and soon evaporated, when it had proved so useful.'

Australian *Punch* had as its cover a cartoon that expressed what all Australia felt on hearing the news. The sailor boy, with HMAS *Sydney* on his tally band is hoying out 'Hip Hip Hooray! Alone I did it! What price me now!'

'What did people at home think about the *Sydney* sinking the *Emden*?' John Simpson Kirkpatrick wrote home to his mother in England. 'The *Sydney* belonged to the Australian Navy!' He is very proud. 'The old colonel shouted beer for all hands on board and we all drank the health of the *Sydney* pretty deeply I am afraid.'

Sister Alice Kitchen wrote in her diary: '*Emden* was within 20 miles of us so providence must have protected us. It was evidently hoping to attack us in the rear. We hear it is beached and everybody is so pleased. One sub. said to me he hoped they wouldn't say much about it in the *Herald*, and added, "It's my mother I am thinking about, she'll be so anxious".'

In his report Captain Glossop stated that 'a terrible sight' had met them on the *Emden.* 'Corpses and fragments of human remains lay about shrivelled by the blazing fires under the deck and the hardly less blazing tropical sun. The wounded had been without food and water for twenty four hours, their wounds were corrupted and gangrenous, with maggots a quarter inch in length crawling in them.'

The later sights on board HMAS *Sydney* were scarcely less dreadful. Captain Glossop wrote that the cruiser had become '. . . nothing but a hospital of the most painful description'. The *Sydney* had been a crowded ship when she sailed but now, with almost two hundred of the *Emden*'s crew on board, the wounded and dying were in every hammock and lay thick on the deck. The planking, gymnasium mats and the men's own bedding that they had handed over was bloodied and stained with human excrement. The two surgeons available worked around the clock. 'At midnight [November 11th]', wrote Surgeon L. Darby of the *Sydney*, 'we went to bed after a spell of 40 hours without any sleep'. Next morning the medical team started again and 'by night we had finished off all the operations and the bigger work but had been unable to get up to the theatre all the cases which required attention'. Not until they left Colombo were the men of the *Sydney* able to clean away the foetid evidence, throw overboard the stained mats and bedding and scour the decks. The final casualty figures reported by Captain von Muller to the German Admiralty were 134 officers and men dead, 65 wounded, leaving 117 unwounded officers and men from the *Emden*.

Ships were now fitted with the newly invented radio, and there was truly a babel of messages over the waters. Though it was a radio message from the Cocos Islands – 'unidentified ship entered harbour' – that brought about her end, *Emden* on no occasion gave her own position away by careless use of the morse or radio in her wild rampage across the sea lanes. At times, as they were in the process of despatching one ship to the bottom, another smoke cloud on the horizon would herald the approach of more booty. Their routine on approaching a vessel was to signal, 'Stop your engines, don't use wireless, what ship?' Sometimes they were steaming along with a 'convoy of 7 captured ships, unable to spare time to sink them or unwilling to risk the sound of gunfire', Franz Joseph, Prince of Hohenzollern and Gunnery Officer of the *Emden*, wrote of their swashbuckling Indian Ocean extravaganza: '. . . thanks to us, not a single ship [was] to be seen. We had made the Indian Ocean as unsafe as possible . . . English ships dare not navigate the Indian Ocean.'

The *Emden* had harried industriously but her need to be coaled regularly meant that she must rendezvous with her tender – the captured English collier *Buresk* – and lie alongside for hours, vulnerable. She could have caused untold harm to the approaching convoy in spite of the escort. 'We should have got in among the transports from astern', some of her officers later claimed, 'and then we should have done all possible damage with our guns and torpedoes. We should have sunk at least 6 and possibly 12 before your escort came up and stopped us.'

But alerted by that message from the Cocos Islands where, ironically, *Emden* had gone to put the cable station out of action, the *Sydney* left the convoy and, with its vastly superior weaponry and range, despatched the raider. Sir Henry Newbolt, 'Admiralty Laureate' as he was dubbed, in ecstasy penned a poem to commemorate the feat and in it attributes to the gunners of the world's newest navy a most extraordinary feat!

> Their hearts were hot
> And as they shot
> They sang like kangaroos.

When news of the sinking of the *Emden* was received at Lloyds in London they tolled the Lutine bell for the ship that had cost the underwriters of British commerce five million dollars Australian.

Back on the convoy the news of the first victory, not only of the new navy but of Australia itself, was received with jubilation. Carl Janssen wrote to his parents: 'Colombo was full of ships . . . all our fleet and the rest mostly big grey warships. It was here we saw the *Sydney* for the first time since she left us to fight the *Emden* . . . how proud we all felt that an Australian ship got the very ship that so many English and Japanese had been looking for. Our ship took . . . some of the prisoners. 43 men, 3 Petty Officers, the Captain and 3 other officers one of whom is a Prince. I am

on guard today. Guard means much more than it did. Each
man on guard carries a loaded rifle and instead of 9 posts
we have 15. It takes me just about 30 minutes to post
sentries from one end of the ship to the other. The Germans
are a fine looking lot and pleasant. The officers are in
cabins and the men have a space in the stern barred off . . .'

Ernek told his sister Beatrice that the *Emden*'s capture
'was the only great excitement of the long journey . . . It is
very warm, all we are wearing at the present is a singlet
and trousers, no boots or socks, we all look like a lot of
orphans with our blue trousers rolled up to our knees.
Some of them go about in bathing costumes'.

Jack 'Simpson', whom they called 'Murphy', mistaking
his Durham accent for Irish, was in evidence on the *Medic*.
'Where's me possum,' was his constant cry, as he searched
the ship for the baby possum he'd brought on board with
him. When he tracked it down he put it down the front of
his shirt or in his hammock.

Carl Janssen wrote about their route marches. 'This
morning after church service we went for a 2½ mile walk,
which is only 10 times around the first-class deck and
thoroughly enjoyed it. It feels good to march to a band
again.'

'And don't forget', Ernek wrote to his sister, 'they will let
us receive letters and I don't care how many you write me.'

Sister Kitchen was working up to twelve hours a day
every day, but she carefully wrote up her diary each night.
'*Nov. 11th*: Our Jap guardian still at its post and never
shows a speck of light unless it is signalling . . . Band plays
very well under Corp. Treherne from Ballarat. Dinner is
improving in its conduct, when the band performs at Dinner
it plays the N. Anthem, just as the toast of the King is
called and is quite an institution. I did not think I should
like the red capes so much, but love looking at them round
the table. One of us sits at each corner of the table. Another
death on the *Euripides* . . . Typhoid innoculation today, 2
companies done. Dr J. advised me to have it also. *Nov. 12th*:
Great preparations made for baptisms crossing the line. A

large canvas bath erected into which all and sundry were tipped. Looking down at the seething mass of warm and moist humanity the fun was fast and furious dozens being in at once and buckets of water being thrown everywhere even on to the hospital deck. I kept well in the background. . . . We had 8 casualties, cut head, broken ankle, and faint, or (feint). . . . It served to let off some of their superfluous steam. *Nov. 17th:* Very tired of the intense heat which seems to burn through one's body and makes you shake, while moisture streams from every pore. We left Colombo about 7.30 p.m. moving out in a different way, some of the boats having left before 3rd Division of 10 ships, going on alone. These waters are evidently considered safe now the *Emden* is out of the way. After we leave Gibralter they will begin to feel anxious once more. We hear very little war news nowadays and no signalling from ship to ship being allowed, we might as well be 1 000 miles from anywhere as 80 yds from the next ship and know nothing of what occurs there. We were all disappointed at getting no news at Colombo from home . . . disgusted at hearing that all the letters we wrote at Albany were carried on to Colombo before being posted. We all picture the anxiety of those at home, not knowing our whereabouts and how we are. *Nov. 25th*: Feel frayed at the edges. Had a day off, first whole day since leaving Albany. At Aden this morning, a barren and dry looking place with fierce blazing sun . . . Saw a few Arabs in a boat, but no shore leave for anyone. . . . Heard England had declared war with Turkey and was bombarding some port in the Red Sea. It will make all those responsible very worried about mines etc . . . All sleeping out tonight are to take life belts with them. *Nov. 27th*: All lights were darkened very much last night and it is surprising how little the long lines of dark ships show on the sea . . . when the moon is clear . . . We heard today that the troops are to be landed at Cairo. No one knows exactly why, so we may see Pharoah's land . . . On the whole every one seems pleased that they are to go to Egypt. We do not yet know what our fate is to be, or where we are to go . . . 3 or 4 lads were court martialled for refusing innoculation with antityphoid serum. *Dec. 1st*: Reached Suez this morning, and anchored outside the Canal. It is a wonderful sight to see the ships of our convoy gathering in one after the other . . . We are to move off into the Canal tonight.'

They leave for Alexandria, and learn that, after disembarking, they are to go first to Cairo and then to Mena House Hospital. 'Everyone quite demoralised at the prospect of getting off the boat.'

The nurses were taken to Mena House, a fine large house with Australian gum trees about it right at the foot of the pyramids which was to become a familiar hospital to the Australians. Sister Kitchen's diary continued to record everything, including the fact that their luggage was unavailable, being hopelessly mixed up with the kit bags and baggage of about 600 men.

'*Dec. 10*: Had a busy day; all muddle and confusion. Samsing lost her bundle of rugs and was very worried till Henderson got the native police and found them in a hut. I was off [and went] for a walk round the foot of the Great Pyramid and look[ed] at the lovely sunset colours, pestered by Arab guides . . . dozens of soldiers climbing the Pyramids, and having the time of their lives riding camels and donkeys. Went along the road to see where the camp lay behind Mena House and along an avenue of trees which met overhead, on the road to Cairo, but found it dreary wandering about alone . . . After dinner Coulter and Bennet called to see their "adopted" Sisters and promised us an "8" to wear to show we belonged to their Battalion, the 8th. The food here is very nice, but strange in taste, queer vegetables and queer unsalted butter which we rather fancy is goats' or buffalo. The fruit is nice, especially the fresh dates . . . All the waiters are natives with long white gowns, red sash, fez and slippers. Col. Ryan came to see us, and it seemed very nice indeed to see a familiar face in a land of strangers.

'We are getting in crowds of patients daily and filling up. This place is to be organised for 400 beds and is costing the Commonwealth something like £75 per day at present.

'*Dec. 12*: Tonight we have 40 patients between Samsing and myself and one orderly, mostly influenza and sore throats. This afternoon I met in the hall several of our own *Benalla* patients who had been having a rough time at Alexandria or where-ever they went to and they rejoiced greatly at meeting us. This afternoon I went for a walk round the Pyramid and down to the Sphinx . . . was surrounded by soldiers, arabs, camels and donkey rides . . . I saw one [soldier] climbing and another cutting his name on one of the stones of the Pyramid. I never thought to be here and see it all. I came back at 5 and helped in the wards a bit. Everything was so rushed and muddled and so many meals to get around. It was late before we got to dinner.'

She was beginning what was to be her lot until 1919. The nurses were working twelve hours on, twelve off, with one day a week free – if they could be spared. Some went on record as working up to thirty days without a break.

'*Dec. 16*: Sister Samsing sick tonight with what appears to be influenza. Went to see the 8th Batt. and saw their wonderful patchwork linings in the Mess Tent and their little streets and stone decorations round the tents.

'*Dec. 24*: Samsing still sick. Xmas Eve in a strange land and no news from home for all these weeks. We hear there is a large mail at Alexandria for the troops which may arrive tomorrow . . . After duty went for a long rough walk in the moonlight with J.E.W. round by the bank overlooking the native village and then to the Sphinx . . . talked of home and friends and wondered what they were doing and if they were thinking of us . . . Being Xmas Eve, we allowed ourselves a little latitude and stayed out till 11 p.m.

'*Dec. 25*: Xmas Day in Egypt. First thing, our chambermaid knocked at my door with a parcel for me from Sr. Samsing which was a lovely grey silk Kimona . . . We spent the morning decorating the ward with flowers and greenery. Col. Bolton came to wish us the usual compliments and our *own* 8th Band came up to play selections. Mr Finlay and many others came up to see us too and in the afternoon I got my first letter from home, written 2 months which had been to England and back here. . . . the one event calculated to make me feel a bit happier to know that at last we may expect . . . letters regularly. The one question all our soldier friends ask when we meet is, "have *you* had any letters?" I think I will always be glad we came to Egypt. The sunsets are lovely, soft and tender tones, nothing crude, pink, violet, and heliotrope and beautiful blues, softly blended into a beautiful indescribable whole: all softly reflected over the dry and yellow sands of the desert. The sunrises are just the same lovely sight with the base of the pyramid shrouded in a pale blue mist out of which the peaks rise in their great splendour.'

At the end of January they left Mena House and 'after seeing our luggage off went up to the Sphinx to have our photos taken to send home. On camels too. The weirdest sensation when a camel kneels and rises; feels a bit like an earthquake'. The next day, they settled in at Heliopolis 'Palace', which had had a chequered career, being at one time planned as a casino. They met a few old friends and farewelled some of the nurses who were returning home on the *Kyarra* with the sick. The 7th and 8th Battalions were sent to Ismalia and Alice Kitchen is anxious for their safety, although, in fact, the men did not see action on this particular occasion. But by 21 February she is remarking: 'Hear that the Australians are to move out of Egypt on the 17th of March. The air is full of rumours.'

7

Painting Egypt Red

And so these latter-day crusaders came to the ancient land of Egypt. Their naïveté astonishes us. 'Last night saw the c-c-dance,' a young soldier writes of the Can-Can.

'From the summit of these pyramids', Napoleon had declared to his army in Egypt 115 years before, 'forty centuries look down on you'. And two thousand years before Napoleon, the Roman Legions had camped here. Now the encampment was of the men from the newest nation on earth and they were awed by, and themselves awed, the land of the Pharoahs.

John Simpson's forte was to saunter in to a tea-shop with his possum tucked down the front of his shirt and delight the waitresses with the furry animal. (It later disappeared from Mena Camp and was not heard of again.) Lieutenant Ernie Harris, 3rd Machine Gun Company, 12th Battalion, wrote to his mother from Cairo on 29 March 1915: 'Nothing to do. Rotting in camp. They say patience is a virtue. Then a soldier must be full of virtue. You need never be afraid of me going to the dogs after going through this campaign because the things I see at times instead of attracting me simply fill me with disgust.'

Corporal E. R. Robson, 4th Battalion, wrote: 'One night there were 50 New South Welshmen of the 4th Btn waiting for the last tram from Cairo to their camp at Mena but when they saw it coming realised it was packed. Quickly they threw a few piastres to a boy and commandeered his donkey, put their most inebriated member on its back and started running round shouting, "The Sultan's Coming!"

Everybody got off the tram to see the Sultan and we leaped on board taking the donkey with us. The donkey was put off at the next stop.'

Ernek Janssen wrote: 'My dear Mother, Father, Naja [sister] and Bosco [his dog], we are camped below the pyramids with the sky for a covering. They have not got enough tents for us all but there are some more coming shortly. It was very pretty coming through by train from Alexandria.

'We have just received your letters and snap-shots which you wrote on the 22nd Oct. 1914. They must have gone to England then had to be sent back here. I was disappointed that they were not of a later date, but they were better than not getting any at all. There were three tram loads of mails come out to this camp, yesterday. All of the transport is carried out here by the Electric Trams . . . they run right into the camp.'

Carl Janssen wrote off from Mena Camp to one of his artist friends: 'We landed at Alexandria 3 weeks ago and I had the good fortune to be chosen with a Sergeant to remain in Alexandria with the Captain and 12 men to form a guard for a rest camp for sick horses. . . . Our camp was in one of the lowest native suburbs . . . We never went out singly and always with side-arms. I expected a wealth of colour but some dirt predominated. There is a fine square or series of squares in the city proper and from there the native streets stretch in all directions. The Sergeant and myself penetrated to some most interesting parts apart from the beaten track. Queer Arab cafes, bakers' shops, confectioners, metal workers and all sorts of places around. There are special shops where those Tarboosh caps are blocked into shape while the customers wait. . . . Alexandria is famed as having one of the biggest brothel quarters of any city and I can believe it. The first thing a cabbie says to a soldier is "Sister Street"? There are about 6 streets containing nothing but prostitutes of all nationalities. These women are inspected once a week and all produce their certificates before doing business. Some of the girls are very fine and some are worse than awful. I saw one or two French girls with beautiful figures but these were in the better class houses. Business is done quite openly and the prostitute and the old woman in charge tout at the doors. There are very few comparatively speaking native women prostitutes. Some of the unmarried women who wear a white veil are beautiful up to about 18 years of age. The married women wear a heavy black veil with a metal arrangement over the nose. . . .'

Carl's letter to his parents was not quite so frank: 'This camp is practically at the foot of the Pyramids and on the edge of the Sahara desert. It is sand and more sand and we drill in sand up to our ankes and march in sand and eat sand but it is decidedly cleaner than Broadmeadows' dust. It is very cold here at nights and the dew is equal to a heavy rain. 2 others and myself have dug a hole and covered it with rubber sheets till we get a tent. We have no rest day here. Even Sundays we go for a long march after church. I guess we will get fit after a few weeks. I was terribly glad to get the prints of mother. We got a special tram to Mena and reached the Pyramids just at sunset. I will always remember that first view of the Pyramids. They stood out as masses of purple against a gorgeous sky.'

It was a strange four months. Rumours of embarkation for a battle-front were rife from the time they left the first convoy; there were rumours in the newspapers back home regarding their behaviour; they lived through exotic and remarkable environmental changes for young men from a land 12 000 miles away and a country 4 000 years younger than the one in which they now found themselves.

The writer who best summed up those months in Egypt prior to leaving for the Dardanelles was Carl Janssen, in his reply to a student friend.

'This mail was rather an exciting one as the day before we had received word of our departure in a very short time and also because it is the first we have heard of Mr Bean's letter re behaviour. (Our departure this time is "dinkum" and no mere rumour. Some of us believe we go to Marseilles and then Amiens which will be our base.) To explain a few things. First of all the only reliable man writing for Australian papers, from what we can read in copies received, is Capt. Bean. No acct of his which I have seen has been incorrect in any detail but one very slight one and that immaterial. . . . Also there have been numerous letters published, evidently by fond parents, from members of the Force and I guess a few young men are blushing unknown to us when they hear the remarks made in camp. There is a special notice board in one of the Company lines kept specially for these sublime examples of the art of writing fairy tales. One real beauty published in the *Herald* under the title of "Fall In" has, I see, found its way into the *Times History of the War*. Also from paper accounts our stay in Egypt has been one long picnic. In the main the statements are correct because we did receive chocolate and we did get Plum Pudding for Xmas but till 3 weeks ago no leave but night leave was ever granted. I saw a statement that we got 1 whole day in five. This is the routine we had without any exaggeration: For the first 3 weeks reveille 6.15 a.m., breakfast 7, Fall in 8. March out about 3 miles in ankle deep sand with one bread roll per man and 1 tin sardines to 4 men for lunch (no variation in diet for lunch and breakfast, bread and jam, one slice per man) return to camp at 4 p.m. Training consisted of skirmishing for about 2 miles across the desert. Then Reveille was changed to 5.30 a.m. and return to camp at 4.30 some mornings leaving camp at 7.30 a.m. and returning at midnight. The upshot was that on Sunday 3 weeks ago there were 800 men in hospital with disease brought on by overwork and a protest was lodged by the Doctors. The record morning for our Company was 43 men parading sick out of 200 and the Doctor exempting 30 from duty. 10 cases were marked exhaustion. Everybody, including officers, was glum and irritable. Those men not on duty turned in to bed at 6 o'clock very often too tired to eat their evening meal. At Broadmeadows (the Australian training camp) in the evenings there was singing and tale telling and letter writing in the tents, but here things became absolutely dead. While on guard at the entrance to camp I collected one night 252 passes between 7–8 p.m. which were available to 11 p.m.: "Too tired to stay in town." And even Sundays were not free. Reveille same time, Church Parade 9 to 10 a.m. then a route march over the desert for about 5 miles, return to camp at 1.30. Dinner and then clean up lines for inspection. Inspection meant standing on parade from 3 o'clock to 4 and then dismissal. Then the heads took a "tumble" and great is the changes. We have 1 full day holiday per week and Sunday excepting Church Parade is free. General leave excepting to defaulters is granted both days. Everybody is light hearted and fit. Our work has been cut out in a sensible manner and is done cheerfully and well. You would not recognise us for the same soldiers who left Melbourne. There is a confidence in the bearing of all which I have not seen in any but soldiers with training and it makes me realise how unfitted we were to go to a war such as the present one with our Broadmeadows training. Now for another dark patch. There are 400 cases of Venereal Diseases. We were warned on ship of the terrible forms of Venereal disease in this country, but of course there were the usual scoffers. But honestly I believe the proportion of victims would not have been so great had we been worked sensibly and granted day leave. Night leave left the men with weaker natures and nothing to do but visit hotels and Brothels. . . . Now that day leave has been granted the men spend their money on trips to the hundreds of interesting places round Cairo and crime has decreased tremendously. Our Guard tent has been empty for 3 days. This is unprecedented even in Broadmeadows. Now for Mr Bean, there is nothing to quibble about in his statement. There is a "leaven of wasters" but they have been mostly culled out. A large proportion of those wasters are not Australians, but Emmigrants from England. There are some very bad Australians I admit but their badness is of a different type. The Australians' chief weakness has been drink and violence but the Englishman is a dirty sneak and in some cases a deserter from the Imperial service. When I say dirty I mean slovenly and filthy. . . . I am afraid this letter must go round as I cannot possibly spare time for more. Active service cards have arrived at one company office and in future all we may do is to cross out unwanted phrases such as "I am not dead yet", etc. . . . One thing I nearly forgot. What kind of crowd is this second force? They talk a lot and seem in some instances to be rather proud of their exploits in Melbourne and Colombo. I guess it is the small leaven again and I guess the sand is going to make a difference though their training is not as severe as ours was.'

The final paragraph is repeated in a hundred letters and diaries: those first voyagers saw themselves as an élite.

Carl Janssen wrote frankly on venereal disease probably because he had had a more sophisticated life style than most letter writers at the war and he was, after all, writing to an equally sophisticated friend and not to his mother. However, it would have been difficult, if not impossible, to tell the truth to the majority of Australians, for the firm belief was that our soldiers were noble and going to be heroes: such men did not do that sort of thing. They were to be proved right on the first two points, but because the realisation of these demands that the subject be a normal man, they must be wrong about the third. The double standards of the Victorian Age still blinded them to truth, and against the men's wishes they had put haloes on them.

Of course, venereal disease was not unknown in Australia; many men were suffering from it when they joined. The official history of the Australian Army Medical Service says that 'all who were found to be suffering from venereal diseases were discharged from the AIF (September 1914). Though health in general was good a small cloud on the horizon showed itself in the comparative prevalence of measles, influenza and venereal diseases'. Some men were taken off the first convoy, some were detected en route. In Egypt, by 28 December 1915, the numbers were such that because of insufficient hospital space they were returned to field units who were not equipped to deal with 'unfits'. Colonel A. G. Butler, D.S.O., V.D., B.A., M.B., Cl.B. (Camb.), the author of the medical history of the war, wrote, 'Venereal diseases introduced the medical service to its most difficult problem in the war'. 'Influenza was the greatest cause of illness in these early days. Next in point of numbers was the whole group of respiratory infections and of greater importance from the military and national point of view was the outbreak of the venereal contagion which during the four months [preceding Gallipoli] incapacitated over 2000 men and sent three per cent of the force constantly sick.'

This 'wilfully contracted disease' bore a terrible stigma for some men; for others it was a joke, a comment on their virility, almost another feather in their larrikin headdress. But the primitive measures taken against it were grim. The orders issued to the 'military guard' of the barbed wire compound in which venereal cases were camped on the Egyptian desert at Mena were: 'All patients will wear a white band on the right arm. The hospital is in quarantine and the O.C. guard will take all measures to ensure its isolation. He will post four sentries, a flying picket will move amongst the tents and a picket on the southern side of the hospital near the latrines. He will be responsible that the sentries do not speak to the patients, that no patient is allowed to leave the hospital lines or receive food or other articles from outside; that no visitors are allowed into the lines, that any unauthorised person entering or leaving is placed in the guard room.'

This fierce discipline was held to be necessary, but that the medical profession were not to blame and indeed had a sympathetic concern for these men is shown as early as this in the war from a memorandum by Major B. T. Zwar, AAMC:

'The following are the result of careful personal enquiries from the first 300 patients under my charge in No. 2 ASH Jan. 1915. The vast majority were youths, some still in their teens, others in the early twenties – 85.3 per cent had been infected for the first time. The greater number of these assured me they had been ignorant of the risk they ran. I have reason to believe most of them. In those early days of the AIF education of officers – medical, clerical and combatant – and men in regard to sex hygiene, the risk of illicit intercourse, and the effects of venereal infection, was not effectively undertaken. There was a harmful – and erroneous – belief among officers and men that venereal disease is easily cured, and that continence is harmful to health and that it is unmanly.

'This punitive method of treatment regarded the contraction of VD as a crime to be punished. The man must lose his pay and the hospital must be a penitentiary to impose a dread of the consequences of sexual misconduct. The man must have his disgrace kept well before him: it must be well branded in his pay book. The natural consequence – concealment of disease – was bound to follow but was to be heavily punished if detected. The patient was made to feel like a criminal and the deterrent motive appealed to was fear, fear of losing his pay, fear of being found out by his family, of losing the respect of other men, fear of the grisly sights and circumstances of a VD hospital. Complete loss of self respect tending to reckless living often resulted.'

One month after Carl Janssen wrote his letter, the men broke out in a way not totally unexpected. Mention of 2 April 1915 brings a sly grin to the face of many an old soldier, but if he was there he doesn't talk about it.

8
The Battle of the Wazzir

'No,' said the old man I was interviewing, 'I won't put anything about that on tape . . . but I will say this: the night we fired the Wazzir was the best fun any of us had till the war ended four years later.'

Many men have given me details of the famous 'Battle of the Wazzir' but none wanted their name mentioned. After all, it *was* the most famous fight in a brothel any Australian had known.

On Good Friday, 2 April 1915, when the troops were about to leave Egypt for Gallipoli, some of them determined to exact retribution for certain injuries they believed themselves or their mates to have incurred at brothels in the street known to them as the 'Wazzir' – the Haret el Wasser near Shepheards Hotel in Cairo. They sacked the houses – some eight storeys high – threw the bedding and girls' dresses down onto the street below and set fire to both the houses and the gear on the street. The 'red-caps', British Military Police, were called and when they failed to quell the riot the Egyptian Fire Brigade was sent in, but the men made short work of their hoses: 'By the time we were done', confided one of my grey-haired informants, smiling away at the memory while his eighty-year-old wife made scones out in the kitchen, 'by the time we were done there was scarcely a piece of hose longer than twelve inches left – well, a few feet long anyway. We hacked them with our big pocket knives.'

Later, in June, men of the 2nd Australian Division

repeated the scene in the 'Second Battle of the Wazzir'. 'These two affairs', says the *Official History of Australia in the War of 1914–18*, 'made a good deal of noise at the time. They were not heroic, but they also differed very little from what at Oxford and Cambridge and in Australian universities is known as a 'rag'. (Which may lead many of us to believe that if 'rags' in those days were anything like the 'Battle of the Wazzir', then today's university students are ruefully lacking in imagination when plotting their annual forays.)

C. J. Dennis, when he heard of the battle, promptly wrote some verses covering it for inclusion in his new book *The Moods of Ginger Mick*. In the poem, he said it happened because the AIF were doing 'their little bit to scrub Pharoah's dirty kingdom clean and to shift 'is ancient 'eap of sin and shame'. That's not what the survivors told me. They say the raid took place for three reasons: a rise in price, bad drink, and an 'isolation compound full of our mates with V.D.' Tens of thousands of reinforcements landed in late February and early March and, the demand being greater than the supply, the girls put the price up. Several men have told me similar stories. Others spoke of the alcohol sold in the Haret el Wasser: 'It was expensive and it was reckoned that the Gippo's pissed in it to give it colour – if you'll pardon the expression.' All remembered the sights in the compound where the treatment for V.D. was primitive (as it was everywhere at the time). The social effects for a soldier were gross – his pay was stopped and his pay-book branded with his shame – and the misery of their mates incensed those lucky enough to have escaped or avoided the same fate.

Dennis intended to include the poem in the longer work telling of Ginger Mick at the war, but when the censor intervened he stopped publication and issued only a few copies in 'unrevised proof' form, dated 12 July 1916. The story of course purports to be told by The Sentimental Bloke on the authority of Ginger Mick 'who was there'.

Now Ginger Mick 'e writes me a long, ixited note,
An' 'e writes it in a whisper so to speak;
For I guess the censor's shadder was across 'im as 'e wrote,
An' 'e 'ad to bottle things that mustn't leak
So I ain't got orl the strength uv it; but sich as Ginger sends
I rejooce to decent English fer me friends.

As Dennis says, he didn't get 'all the strength' of it, but
then the official Proceeding of the Court of Inquiry at Mena
Camp on 3 April 1915 didn't get much either. With terms
of reference enabling them to 'elicit all information possible
regarding the disturbance in Cairo last night' they examined
witnesses, possibly none 'friendly'. From the Captain down
to the Driver the men gave evidence on oath that attested to
eyesight and powers of observation lamentable in any
military man, or to an *esprit de corps* that any army would
be proud of. The Secret and Confidential file reads as
follows:
'First evidence: –
'Thomas James Entwistle, Captain, Commanding 3rd
Reinforcements, 8th Light Horse Regiment, on oath saith:
– I was in Cairo on the afternoon of 2nd April and left the
Continental Hotel about 6 p.m. From outside appearances
the town was normal. I was with Captain Daly, 6th
Battalion Infantry, and Lieut. Robinson. A Sergeant came
and reported to Capt. Daly that a serious riot was taking
place down in the native quarter. He himself had foot-
marks on his neck and said he had lost his bayonet in the
scrimmage. We at once went to the native quarters guided
by the Sergeant and got close enough to see soldiers tossing
articles of bedding and furniture from all windows of the
building which was six stories high. As far as I could see
the men were New Zealand Privates. They were setting fire
to the furniture in the middle of the street. I did not
recognise any of the men.
'President: – 'Was there any Australians in the crowd?'
'Witness: – 'Yes; New Zealanders predominated.'

'Witness continuing saith: – 'We returned to Shepheards hotel and a British General asked us if we could do anything in quelling the disturbance and we told him we had already been down there and would do anything to help. We fell in as many men as we could find to act as picquets. I had about 95 men. Lieut. Malcolm of the 9th Light Horse took over my Picquet and I was provided with a horse and tried to move the men on in company with Mr Chanter of the 9th Light Horse. I heard firing but did not see any. I could give no idea as to what started the trouble. The Maoris were about one in ten. Men in uniform were shoving the women out of the houses. They were native women.'

Captain Entwistle recognised no man 'as far as I could see the men were New Zealand Privates'. And that must have been right – because every other man on oath said the same thing.

The enquiry must have been the delight – or the despair – of Colonel F. G. Hughes, V.D., the Court President and his two assistants. One wonders if they would have secured any witnesses at all if it hadn't been for:

'Alick O'Gilvie, 5th Battery Field Artillery saith: I was on duty in the streets where the disturbance took place from 8.30 a.m. to 4.30 a.m. next morning. I took 14 identity discs from men who were looting grog and handed them over to Lieut. McFarlane.'

'Yeh don't hear much about it,' Ginger Mick tells 'The Sentimental Bloke'. 'But', he says, 'The Battle uv Wazzir took the bun.'

The poem is a strange mixture of insight, naïveté and the favourite games of the day, chauvinism and ostrich-itis.

When they wandered from the newest and the cleanest
        land on earth,
An' the filth uv ages met 'em, it wus 'ard . . .
They wus children, playing wiv an asp, an' never fearin' it,
An' they took it very sore when they wus bit.

And 'bit' they were. With the primitive and none too effective treatment applying at the time the army had little option but to bundle many of those wounded in horizontal combat back to Australia and ignominious discharge. The official history of the Australian Army Medical Service recorded that, 'With the possible exception of mumps, venereal infections were the most difficult to prevent, the most troublesome to treat and the most productive of absence from duty . . . During the year that ended February 1916, 5 924 Australians were treated at the isolation hospital for venereal infection with an average stay in hospital of 35 days. Of these 1 344 were returned to Australia. A system of "personal prophylaxis for the careless or uncontrollable" was later developed with little success'.

The moral stigma back home may have demanded such righteous chauvinism as was expressed by the Sentimental Bloke, but the official report doesn't quite bear out the indignation – well, not the 'righteous' kind anyway. 'Of the means taken to abate the violence of attraction towards sources of infection such as moral suasion, counter-attractions, fear and stoppage of pay – the only one fully effective was distance from the sphere of influence.' Leave was cancelled from the Canal to Cairo and the training depot was removed to a distance which even the 'careless and uncontrollable' would find it difficult to cross. There were at that time 2 000 cases under treatment and the Divisional medical superintendent had informed the corps commander that drastic steps must be taken to deal with the situation. Because of this, the number had dropped to 914 by April but equally, because of this isolation, the fighting fit men awaiting embarkation were really fighting mad.

They had known for weeks they were moving. 'New rifles,' wrote one. 'We must be going in soon.' The Janssen brothers began to write daily letters to their parents, sister – and dog Bosco. They would write few more. These letters were received in May 1915 when both the boys were already dead – Carl was killed at the Landing, and Ernek on 8 May. To his sister Beatrice Carl wrote: 'I believe we are leaving on Tuesday. We all thought that we would have been gone before as it is over a week since the 9th, 10th, 11th Battalions left, and my word they are keeping it quiet where they have gone. Nobody seems to know. I dare say that you will know where we are before you receive this . . . we have been doing some more night manoeuvres lately . . . and my word it was a cold night out, we did not have our blankets either, ours went astray somewhere. The whole of the Division was out, it was a big sham-fight and they even had mounted men (imaginary), falling out and being treated by the Ambulance Corps. The wounded men were lucky as they were taken back to camp and were able to have a good sleep in the tent.'

Ernek wrote to his parents on Easter Sunday: 'We are in the station yard waiting to get into the train, we have just walked in from Mena and are pretty tired. We left camp at 6.20. . . . I hope we have seen the last of it. I am writing this on the off chance of getting it posted, for I suppose it will be a long time before we can write again. Carl and I are together and both well, and I hope we come out of it alright. You will hear plenty about us in the papers. We will be travelling all night and get to Alexandria some time in the morning and I suppose we will go straight on the boats. It will be only a short trip this time. We will miss the mail unless they keep it back at Alexandria and give it to us. We will soon be moving. Goodbye, with heaps of love. From your ever loving son Ernek.'

9
The Arena

They sailed in to Mudros, the harbour of Lemnos Island. On the island's peaks Agamemnon, King of Mycenae, had lit a chain of fires to signal to Clytaemnestra, his queen, that he had taken nearby Troy. Here, to the one place consecrated by poets to the conflicts of heroes, to the forces and passions personified by the Olympian gods and goddesses, half Europe, half Asia, came the new men, bred beneath a cross of stars that Herodotus had not known of when he portrayed the localised war at Thermopylae as global conflict. It is the most famous arena of the world, the birth-place of the *Iliad*. Men had tried their mettle here before Australia was dreamt of.

Many men knew something of the history of the area and wrote of the dynastic field they were to contest. Through their diaries one hears the footfalls of approaching tragedy, the shuffling of the unknown gods behind the scenes. They would forge a new name there and would share spiritual possession with Achilles and Agamemnon, Paris and Hector. As General Sir Ian Hamilton wrote, 'Before the war who had ever heard of Anzac: hereafter who will ever forget it?'

They learnt, a few days after arriving, that they were to 'land on Gallipoli and give the Turks hell'. Many warriors must have smiled wryly down from Olympus when they heard this. The Dardanelles, the Hellespont of the ancients, is a narrow forty-mile strait linking the north-east corner of the Aegean to the Sea of Marmora, and from Homeric times it has been celebrated as a theatre of war. Near the entrance on the Asiatic shore stand the remains of Troy. Across the

77

strait, just above the Narrows, Xerxes built his bridge of boats to carry his armies into Europe for the invasion of Greece in the fifth Century B.C.

On 18 March 1915 an attempt was made to force the passage of the Dardanelles by naval power alone – a feat which had been accomplished a century before by the *Royal George.* It was unsuccessful. Winston Churchill, First Lord of the Admiralty, suggested the strategy of a naval attack, hoping to open a sea communication with Russia. Early in 1915 Russia had made representations to Britain to stage an attack elsewhere, thereby relieving their forces battling against the Turks in the Caucasus. During February and March British and French warships bombarded the forts in the Narrows at the entrance to the Dardanelles, but could go no further. It was then decided to send a military expedition under General Sir Ian Hamilton.

Because there was little water on Lemnos the men were kept on board their ships until the day came when the battle would begin. Private A. J. Gourlay of the 24th Battalion wrote home that 'the SS *Knight Templar* is so rat infested that the men are afraid to swing their hammocks for fear that rats would gnaw the ropes and send them crashing to the deck so instead, they spread their hammocks direct on the deck'.

And all the while the ships came into the harbour until the waters were speckled with a vast armada.

'Murphy' Simpson (John Simpson Kirkpatrick) was there. 'You will hear about the Australians as soon as we make a start,' he had written to his mother. He rowed the men ashore for fresh vegetables, and promptly set off to barter for wine for his mates. 'He was good at that sort of thing,' Private Jim McPhee of the 3rd Field Ambulance recalls.

Day by day they practised scaling rope ladders over the ships' sides, while back in Egypt those left behind wondered where they had all gone.

Sister Kitchen had been abroad on that fateful Good Friday: 'Samsing and I went to Cairo about 4.30 and had some tea at Shepheards. Saw soldiers on donkeys with brass and bead necklaces. Cairo stiff with khaki today. All the soldiers are now branded well by having stripes on their hats and sleeves. 'Ours' red and white, others green and white, red and blue, blue and white. [They were the first 'colour patches', a device by which men can recognise comrades-in-arms. The red and white patch immediately became known as 'blood and bandages'.] Great rumours of our men going away next week so I am striving to finish the promised gloves for J.

'Great excitement down a little street just beyond Shepheards – fire carts and military police rushing everywhere, motor cars and gharries flying, natives rushing pell mell everywhere and we heard shots fired. When all seemed quiet, later on we walked down the street and suddenly there was a great rush of people, so we got under the protection of 2 M.P.s. Heard after that the Australian and U.K. soldiers had burned down some undesirable places, defied the "red caps" who fired at them, killing one man and injuring several and cleared the street with fixed bayonets. It may be the usual yarn. [It was no yarn, but the 'Battle of the Wazzir'.]

'*April 3rd*: Capt. Lind . . . told us they had got their orders to go tomorrow . . . Most of the girls feeling blue, so many relations and friends among them. Feel glad I have no brothers to be grieving over. *April 4th*: Samsing and I went to Mena in a motor ambulance to see if we could say Goodbye to the "8th". Got there just in time to see the first half of the battalion marching away with Col. Gartside: and the band playing them off. All the tents gone and the place cleared up and looking deserted. Saw lots of the lads we knew. The Brigadier told them that in a month's time most of them would probably be dead!! A nice cheerful soul he must be. God grant he may be much mistaken. Saw Col. Bolton in the Mess tent, and had a cup of black tea; which we were glad of as the dust and sand is just awful, like fine flour thickening the atmosphere, no wonder so many are sick. Col. B. looks very well and so do many of the men. We walked up to the tram. On the way in we passed the "8th" marching . . . Samsing and I had a dinner at Saults and then went to the station just in time to see the 8th come in and spoke to some we had missed at Camp . . . came away before they entrained. God in his mercy protect them all. Came back, everyone feeling depressed and blue. Realise that on an expedition of this kind, love affairs must be a heart-breaking business and feel that Europe must be full of heartbroken women, who have lost sons, husbands and brothers and others dear to them.

'*April 10th*: Samsing and I went to Cairo which seems deserted. We had tea at Shepheard's . . . Tommies and N.C.O.'s allowed on the terrace now. We missed all the familiar friends who used to gather there on Saturday afternoons and the soldiers' band. It seems longer than a week since they all left and Easter Sunday was not characterised by any feeling of joy at the thought of all the possible grim work ahead of all our men. Tonight more marched away . . . we heard them passing, with bands playing and people cheering. About 40 000 men will by this time have left here.'

On 11 April more troops departed. There were rumours of 'disasters and Australian casualties at the Dardanelles' which sensible Sister Kitchen disregarded. While the transports gathered in Mudros Harbour, Alice Kitchen and Sister Samsing shopped for hats, nightdresses and corsets during their hours off. Quite unaware – as indeed were the people in Australia and all except the men themselves – that the most momentous day in the country's history was about to dawn, they went on with their work 'moving patients and beds, making room for the wounded who may sooner or later arrive from the Dardanelles'.

On Board SS *Galeka* at Lemnos a husband was writing. Major J. W. Hamilton, 6th Battalion was sending a last letter to his wife before the day dawned.

' . . . We are on the eve of landing on the Peninsula . . . I am going to leave this letter with Mr Williams the 3rd Officer who has promised to post it at the first port. Dearie, this may be my last to you. But cheer up and if I fall

tomorrow morning, well, I will be one of the many brave
fellows who have died trying to do their duty for God and
Country. We are about to undertake a task which is
extremely bad. We are to land in the face of the enemy.
They have any amount of artillery in hidden spots and we
have to face that in the boats. If they get a shrapnel in them
and sink then of course we have no chance to swim with all
our equipment but then we do have the knowledge that the
fleet are behind us and will pepper the Turks if they can
only see their guns. Well dear, I hope that by the time you
are reading this that I am still in the land of the living and
may have got into communication by cable or otherwise
after we get ashore. Anyhow Dearest there is one consolation
that we are the Reserve Battalion of our Brigade and will be
the last of the 4 to get ashore. But then another aspect to
look at is we will have alarmed the Turks with our first
shore party and as it will be early morning by the time we
are getting off from the ships we may cop all their artillery
fire whilst we are in our boats. Anyhow dearest, I hope that
this is not my last letter to you by long chalks. We are all
bustle. Each man has 200 rounds, 3 days iron rations,
1 quart water, a waterproof sheet and his greatcoat. So we
all have to live for 3 days without any more supplies. I
cannot conscientiously tell you any more about myself as I
know all about what is going on but you will have it all in
the papers long before this reaches you, it is useless my
telling you. Anyhow love, believe me that if I fall I will do so
happy in the thought that I have done my duty to you and
my country. . . . I have your testament in my hand and as I
gaze at our little daughter Boyne, holding the candle and
looking at me with her darling little face I think that I have
been a brute to leave you all for this life with all its danger
but, I don't know, I can't explain, the only thing I can say is
that if I didn't come I wouldn't be worthy of my name.
Dearest, this is rather a gruesome letter but pray consider
the feelings of your dear old hubby on the eve of going in to
action. "I have never been in such a position before," I
fancy I said the same thing the day I made my wedding

vows but how different the conditions. I am not the hardened soldier until I get my baptism of fire. We are about 5 hours steaming from our landing place. It is now 6.40 p.m. Interruption by Mr Williams who has promised to post this at the first port this ship comes to after this scrap. It is now 7.5 p.m. We have just had our last dinner aboard this craft and at daybreak we get into our tow and land. I wonder what it will be like. I must say goodbye to you my darling wife. I trust that the Almighty in His mercy will guard my life and bring us together when we will live a holy and happy life till He us two do part in twain. Goodbye love and God bless you and my darling little Boyne. Your loving and true hubby, Jack.'

10
All Those Empty Pages

The worst of working with the diaries is all those empty pages. You turn back one page from the one you find empty and re-read: '*27 April, 1915*: All around me have been killed or wounded. I escaped so far'. And there is no more. He was aged 28.

In an almost epic-less land, the 'Gallipoli diaries' are precious. With such a diary in our hand we experience the true headiness of an historian, that of the wisdom of hindsight. With this hindsight our mind can slip back to that date, which to the diarist is as yet of no significance, but it is tattooed on our folk memory. There, on 25 April 1915, we stand waiting, watching our writer on his fatal, irreverent progression to this dividing mark in time, and as he comes towards us it is not possible to be wholly objective. We know too much.

There is the tiny diary of 'Alfred M. Love; Corporal; No. 1375; Weight 12st 10lb; Height 5ft 9½ins; size of hat 6⅞; Hosiary 8; Gloves – (Private); Collar 16″, Shirt 15½; Shoes 9. Will made out in favour of my wife'. On 22 December 1914 he left Broadmeadows Camp for the troop-ship that would take him overseas. 'Had lead pencil thrown up from some young lady on leaving. Very rowdy on board tonight. Feeling well.'

'*Wed 23rd*: Weighed anchor 5 a.m. Submarine *AE 2* in tow bound for duty in North Sea England. *Thurs 24th*: On duty as ships orderly. Submarine broke away, picked her up again. Concert on board tonight. Xmas eve. *Friday 25th*: Xmas day. Church parade at 9.30. Xmas greetings exchanged from crew of submarine and boat. Had good dinner. Thinking of home and wife and child. *Sat 26th*: Still feeling very well. Having good trip across the Bight. Have bayonet fighting every day from today. Vaccinated today. . . .

'*Thurs 31st*: Left Albany today at 8.30 a.m. 17 ships, a very nice sight to see all of them steaming out together. Learning French 1st person. Concert on board tonight very nice. Seeing old year out and new one in. Thinking of my dear ones at home. May God bless them. *1 January 1915*: Holiday on board. Burial at sea this morning at 11 a.m. All boats stopped for 5 minutes and flew flag at half-mast.'

Knowing the fields these men were heading for, one is struck with the irony of time standing still for five minutes and a flag being flown at half-mast for one man. Was the man on board who later wrote in France, 'We ran out yesterday to the attack across the bodies of the dead we hadn't been able to bury and today we retreated back across those same bodies but now there were more of them'? Or the soldier who wrote, 'It is hotter today. The smell of the dead is almost unbearable'.

They cast off the submarine casually and headed for Colombo.

On shore in Egypt, like the other soldier diarists, he became a tourist, seeing Heliopolis, Cairo, Alexandria, scaling the pyramids, touring the museums and sights. 'Went out to the pyramids, inside the pyramids, on top of the big one; visited the sphinx and tombs. Finished up night in Cairo.'

All the time they were being intensively trained – on the rifle range, in mock attacks, trench digging, pack drill and route marching. '*Wed 3 March*: Went 28 mile today. Very tired. Thinking of home and Glenora and Essie. Wish I was home with them tonight.'

As well as training, they were playing up. 'On duty tonight rousing the drunks out of Cairo. . . . On guard duty today. 35 prisoners in boob. Pretty busy tonight with drunks and absent-without-leave men.'

He isn't above a bit of A.W.L. himself as an earlier entry shows. '*Wed 3 Feb*: I went into Cairo tonight on French leave.' And the following day: 'Went in to Cairo again today. Got home alright without getting caught.' Next night in Cairo, 'Saw the C-C-Dance [Can-Can].'

Sometimes he gives way to a little pride, as when there was 'a march past the Brigadier of our Brigade. He said he was very proud of us all'. And at the rifle butts, 'I done very well today at shooting at both targets'. But the most common entry concerns his wife and child. '*Thursday 4 March*: 8 years married today – Glenora and Essie's birthday today. Many happy returns of the day to them. May God bless them. On guard tonight. Very tired. Glenora . . . God bless her and keep her true to me until I can return to her.'

By 13 March the air was thrumming with anticipation: 'Inspection of kit today ready for going at any time. Saw George and said good-by to him. He expected to sail tomorrow afternoon. *Wed 17 March*: Feet and rifle inspection. The officers sold a dead man's kit today by auction and the sum of £27 was raised to send home to his people. *Sat 20 March*: Packing all wagons today, beds and bags. Tents ready to strike and to march out of camp.'

The following day the troops were lined up and inspected by 'the High Commissioner & Sultan. Between 20 and 30 000 troops. It was a fine sight to see'. In margin, 'Got letter from wife'.

Then Alfred Love became ill and for a week suffered a temperature of 103° and fever. At the hospital, 'one of the largest palaces in the world', that had been taken over by the army medical corps, he was cared for and well fed: 'I will miss the chicken and pudding when I go.' And he had left by the following week, in time to embark. Perhaps now we could walk day by day with him, for there is only a little time to go.

'*Wednesday 7 April 1915*: We are told we are going to the Dardanelles to fight the Turks and will have to land under fire so we will have all our equipment ready to throw off if the small boats we are to land in get hit. It looks like a hot time for us. [The next page of the diary is missing.] *16 April*: The harbour has plenty of shelter for all kinds of boats. There are over 12 battle-ships, the old *Queen Elizabeth* and *Lion* and French and Russian and a lot of destroyers. It is only 3 hours sail to the Dardanelles where they are bombarding.'

The following day he trains: 'not much room on boat though. Thinking of home. *19 Ap*: Still in harbour. There are still a lot of transport boats to come on here. We were issued with 200 rounds of ball cartridges today and practised disembarking and embarking. *20 Ap*: A lot of Tommies arrived today, also French and Aust. troopships. Feeling very well.'

On the next day he records: '120 days away from home now. *Friday 23 Ap*: The warships are . . . getting steam up. 6 p.m.: Some transports (7) + 4 battleships have gone out tonight. *Saturday 24 Ap*: A lot more troops left today. The battle starts tomorrow morning in earnest at daybreak. [He then writes in the margin] Thinking a lot of home and wife and child. *Sunday 25 Ap*: We can hear the big guns firing this morning. 9.50 we are now moving ourselves. Reached the scene of action 5 p.m. and landed and dig ourselves in under fire.

'*Monday 26 Ap*: Daylight now, the Turks are driven back a mile or two. Very heavy losses yesterday for the Australians. About 400 come on our boat last night. We are now ready in trenches to give them hell. We move right up to the firing line in the morning. The allies are having it pretty rough but we will win. *Tuesday 27 April*: Arrived at firing line at 10 o'clock this morning. Having a very bad time of it so far. Machine guns played hell on our men for a start, they are getting hit and killed all around me but I escaped so far.'

And there is no more. You turn the pages quickly: perhaps he's only wounded, he'll write when he gets to hospital. But you are on to the back cover before you see his hand again: 'In the event of my death I wish this book to be sent to my Dear Wife to let her know that my last thoughts were of her and Essie my darling daughter' – and here is her address. Quickly, turn back to his final entry and, yes, there it is in the margin, scrawled in the pencil that a girl threw to him as the troopship left Melbourne. 'Thinking a lot of wife and child.'

The *Queen Elizabeth*, flagship of the expedition, had led them out of Mudros with cheers flooding the harbour. Sailors, soldiers from Britain, Ireland, New Zealand, France and India cheered everyone else, crews to soldiers, soldiers to sailors. Once out of the harbour and close to lovely Imbros Isle the order came from the Commander on the bridge, 'You fellows can smoke and talk quietly but all lights out when I give the orders'. Old sailors moved among the men handing round hot cocoa – the night was chilly – sailors shuffled back and forth buying gifts from their canteen for the men close packed on deck. Then, 'Lights out. We're going in now'. The boats were alongside at 1.30 a.m. 'Man the boats men.' And they were on their way.

Taken as close as possible to the point of landing by three old battleships and transports, they then climbed over the side on rope ladders into rowing boats or destroyers. The rowing boats were in twelve strings, three to each string (or 'tow') with a small steamboat towing them.

No other men, not even Caesar's army of invasion in Britain, have had to land in an enemy's country with such a difficult prospect before them. They were to land on a foodless cliff, five hundred miles from a store. They had to take with them all things – munitions, guns, entrenching tools, sandbags, provisions, clothing, medical stores, hospital equipment, mules, horses, fodder, even water to drink, for the land produced not even that. These military supplies had to be arranged in boats and lighters in such a way that they might be thrust ashore with many thousands of men in all haste but without confusion.

At the reaping and the shearing,
At the sawmill and the mine,
In the stockyard and the clearing,
At the pressing of the vine.
By the camp fire of the drover,
By the fence with slip-rail drawn,
Men will tell the story over, Of the landing at the dawn!

There, at the western entrance to the Dardanelles, where Saul of Tarsus had heard the voice from Europe call 'Help us!', the Landing was made, and what has been called 'the most dramatic day of the whole world war' began.

Sergeant G. E. James of the 7th Battalion had entered in his notebook directions as they were given him.

'*24 April*: Water bottles to be carried on top of pack. Hot breakfast for all troops. Disembark at 4 a.m. Sunday morning. Clothes to be worn suitable for cool period. Magazine to be loaded with one charger, cut-off closed. See to closing of cartridge pouches. Rifle to be slipped over one shoulder. Men once in boats to sit down and place rifles between their knees. Four ladders available and to be kept in use (no waiting about).

'On destroyer men must remain steady. Strict silence. Never leave wounded behind for they might be mutilated.'

Then, in case of need he listed helpful Turkish words:

'Halt: *Doo-er*
It is an Englishman: *Bir Ingliz*
Hands up: *El yokar-dah*
Throw down your rifle: *Selagh brack.*'

Norman Harvey recorded the landing of Queensland's 9th Battalion: 'As soon as the men were in their tows, the battleships, which had been stopped since 1 a.m., began to move in slowly through a sea as smooth as glass. The tows advanced with them, each drawn by its picket-boat. About 3 o'clock the moon vanished. Half an hour later, the battleships having arrived as close to the shore as they could without running the risk of being seen, an officer on the bridge of the "Queen" called out in a clear loud voice, "Go ahead and land". Thereupon the tows quickened their speed, and as they left, the sailors lining the sides of the "Queen" gave a "silent cheer" by waving their caps and uttering a subdued whisper, which was barely audible to those in the boats.

'The naval officer in charge of the most southerly tow, one of those containing 9th Battalion men, was to give the direction to the others keeping in line with him at intervals of about 150 yards. It was now very dark on account of a thick mist, and the men in the boats could hardly distinguish the tows on either side of them. Not a word was spoken above a whisper, and barely heard was the splash of the boats as the little waves lapped their sides. The suspense in the crowded boats was very trying. "I was shaking all over with nervousness and excitement," wrote one man.

'On reaching shallow water the steamboats cast off their tows, leaving the troops to row the remainder of the way to the shore. Shortly afterwards at 4.29 a.m., there appeared on the top of a dimly-seen hill to the south a bright yellow light, which lasted for about half a minute. A single rifle-shot rang out from the shore, followed a second or two later by several shots. Then a heavier fire began.

'At the sound of the firing the feeling of suspense ended. Some began singing in the boats. A voice was heard through a megaphone "Make your landing, lads, where you can, and hold on." The boats almost immediately began to run aground, and the men climbed over their sides and waded ashore as best they could. This was no easy matter, as the weighty equipment and arms impeded their movements, and underneath the water the bottom was slippery, rounded shingle, not very easy to walk on with military boots. Some of the men found themselves in water half-way up their chests, but scrambling to the shore, they ran across a narrow stretch of beach until brought up by a sandy bank about ten feet high. Here they lay on the ground, took off their packs and laid them down, and fixed bayonets. Some had vainly attempted to fix their bayonets while in the water. Orders had been given that no shots were to be fired until daylight.

'Tradition has it that it was a 9th Battalion boat that was the first to ground, and a number of its men had already reached the bank at the far side of the beach when the first shot was heard.

'To Lieutenant Duncan Chapman belongs the honour of having been the first Australian to set foot on Anzac.

'It had been forcibly impressed on all that on landing they must advance at all costs, so as to clear the way for the main body. Consequently they began to climb the steep hill in front of them. Besides being very steep, the hillside was covered with scrub. A machine gun was firing from the top of the hill, but some of the men climbed up to it, quickly drove the Turks away from their gun, and captured a small stretch of trench from which it had been firing.

'As they climbed the men cheered, swore and joked; one of them afterwards said: "The swearing that went on, as well as the jokes, was marvellous." When they encountered any of the Turks they chased the enemy with shouts of "imshee yalla", "eggs-a-cook" and other expressions which they had picked up in Egypt.'

Direction had been lost in the strong current and the troops waded ashore a mile or more north of the beachhead shown on the operational maps, on the area of which General Birdwood had said, 'The country there is so difficult and broken that it is impossible to attempt a landing there while it is dark'. The landing ground therefore had not been studied and every movement had to be improvised through the thick thorny scrub and the precipitous ridges. In the darkness the strings of rowing boats converged so that battalions became mixed up on the small beach and only the roughest reassembly was possible.

The tows kept coming, and by now the Turks defending their homeland were alerted and 'some boats drifted off full of dead with no-one in control', Birdwood wrote. The living set off into the unknown. The impetuous Australians,' the leader said. That first day the holes were scratched at the furthest point the men were to reach. Later these perimeters became known as Pope's Hill, Steele's, Courtney's and Quinn's and each was held with daily casualties until the evacuation.

When the men landed they met little opposition in comparison with what they later faced.

The Turk's defence plan had been prepared by the German general, Liman von Sanders, who had at his disposal six infantry divisions. This astute man concentrated his main force in rear areas and stationed only out-posts on or above the beaches. By calling in reinforcements under the command of Mustapha Kemal he could thus direct his forces against the main invasion wherever it happened.

The type of terrain they could expect to meet had been described to the men. The reality was entirely different but they moved on up the gullies and slopes in pursuit of the Turks. All day the fighting was bitter. Enemy reinforcements were pouring in according to plan. Fire from the Turks, who they could not see, and whose defences were well prepared and camouflaged, and the need to hold on hour after hour to their exposed positions with Turkish artillery raining shrapnel over them, caused heavy casualties. At this stage the Australian artillery had not gone into action.

At the end of the first day 16 000 men had been put ashore, 2 000 had been killed. And instead of driving a mile and a half inland with a front of four miles, our troops were clinging to a bare foothold on the Second Ridge, little more than half a mile inland on a front of one mile. Both sides had fought each other to exhaustion, and the Turks, though ordered to advance, could not carry out the order.

That 'baptism of fire', as the men called it, was to set the pattern for the next eight months: the Turkish army would always look down from the heights onto the attackers below. (It was said that when the War Graves Commission went to Gallipoli after the war ended they were able to identify bodies as being Australian (or British) troops by a bullet hole in the skull.)

This day saw 'The Linseed Lancers' come into their own

most honourable place in history. 'The Body Snatchers', as
the troops had jokingly called them in training camps, now
arrived to the sudden cry of 'Stretcher bearers!' The 3rd
Field Ambulance landed with the first wave. Three of their
men were killed and 14 wounded at the Landing in the
early dawn light and the remainder were on their knees
attending to the wounded on the beach. As the infantry
pushed up the cliff side they followed along the ridges,
establishing collection posts as they went. In camp there
had been distinction between 'fighting men' and others, but
from the time the first boat grounded on the beach it was
recognised that the toughest men on the peninsula were
those carrying the wounded down the gullies in the blistering
heat of the day and the dark, stumbling abyss of night.
'After the Landing', Stretcher bearer Jim McPhee said,
'there was no distinction at all.' The bullets spat around
them as they spat around the fighting men. 'We didn't carry
arms, just water bottles and a big field dressing for shrapnel
wounds, you couldn't manage any more by the time you got
a weight on a stretcher. . . . I remember we carried a little
bundle of kindling wood on our backs that first day. The
sailors had broken up cases and bundled the pieces for us
so we could boil a billy. My brother Vic was with me. He
was killed later in France.' (The brothers were bank clerks
from Victoria.)

In the flurry of battle Ernek Janssen scrawled a few
words in a diary.

'*Sunday 25 April*: Arrived at our first landing place.
Started a fearful battle. Went ashore early in the morning
under fearful shrapnel fire. Started fighting as soon as we
landed. We went waist deep in the water getting ashore.
Carl was hit with a piece of shrapnel getting out of the
boat.'

He makes no more mention of Carl. Perhaps he did not
know that his brother had died on the beach with shrapnel
in his throat. Ernek himself is to make only two more
entries in his rough diary, the last one being at the entrance
to the Dardanelles.

From the transport *Devanha* the irrepressible Jack 'Murphy' Simpson transferred to the torpedo boat *Ribble*. On deck they could talk – 'but quietly chaps' – and smoke. They were given hot cocoa. The midnight air was bitterly cold. They huddled into their greatcoats. Then, 'Lights out men. Stop talking. We're going in now', the commander of the *Ribble* said quietly, leaning out over the deck of waiting men.

The medical parties went ashore with the fighting men and, as they landed, were hit as were the fighters. Their work at first was right there on the beach with the men as they fell. Later they followed the fighters up the gulches, searching for the wounded, bringing them back to the beach. Simpson found a little donkey and began his business in Shrapnel Gully, named because of the ceaseless death-rattle of shrapnel on that highway to the front line. All men, at all paces, came down here: the stretcher bearers, strangely delicate, placing their feet carefully amongst the debris and stones; signal men running, dodging the strafe and bullets; the walking wounded leaning on their mates; and through all this strode 'Murphy' with a wounded man straddling the back of the little donkey. It was an incredible thing to do: not the getting of a donkey, which in itself was a sensible, practical method of transporting wounded men, particularly those with leg wounds, down that rough terrain – the incredible thing was that he not only exposed himself to the snipers who held a twenty-four-hour watch on this thorough-fare, but that his route must be clearly seen and his times of passing certain points noted. 'My worries,' he is said to have laughed when this was constantly pointed out to him. The laughing larrikin had traded his possum and cattle dog and Lilly, his terrier back home in Durham, for a donkey the like of which he hadn't led since he was a boy and worked during school holidays for a man who sold 'donkey rides' along the sands. For sixpence a day, from 7.30 a.m. to nine at night (when he rode them two miles home) he had grown to know donkeys. Now he led a beast up the gully, carried water up for the wounded (for he had, on the day of the Landing, found men parched up there on this waterless peninsula) then, 'Here mate', came the call. Leaving the donkey under cover of the cliff he dived out, lifted the man and got him back to the animal and began the descent through the storm of bullets that kept him in constant employment.

In Cairo, Sister Kitchen heard of their exploits when the first of the wounded arrived on 29 April, 'our first real war heroes from Turkey. They were mostly minor injuries from bullet wounds about arms or shoulders. We had 50 tonight. All seem ravenous for food, and full of excitement and all eager to hear the news. We hear rumours of their doing very well'.

The British had landed at Cape Helles on 25 April and fared no better than the men at Anzac Cove. Now, supplemented with men from the Anzac area, they launched a large offensive. For this, Ernek had gone south with his battalion. 'On the afternoon of 9 May the Australian Brigade advanced over open ground towards the Turkish positions. In the face of heavy and increasing machine-gun fire their swift advance was the spectacle of the battlefield,' states the official Australian War Museum bulletin. 'With men constantly falling, however, the lines became so thin and the front so weak they could push no further. In one short hour the Brigade lost 1,000 men.' Ernek Janssen was listed – still is listed – 'missing'.

Robert 'Mac' Calder of the 14th Battalion heard the wounded calling. 'For two nights and a day the wounded were calling, "Have you forgotten me, cobbers?" and "Water". In the nights the chaps left the trenches to give them water. We dug down about four feet in our trench and found water and only for that would have been without water. Before I'd got to the trench I'd given half the water in my bottle to an AMC man who wanted it for the wounded.

'Three days after we'd made the run we got orders to leave the trench. There was only one thing for it and that was – make a bolt for it. So in twos and threes we left the trench to make a bolt for the 400 yards back into cover. I believe I lived 5 years in that run. I got out of the trench and ran for my life, I could see the bullets cutting up the ground at my feet as I ran . . . I'll remember that run if I live to be a hundred. A few days later we were joined by the battalion and 300 did not answer the roll call.'

To collect the diaries and letters of these men is to get together the only major writings of the working-class man this country has. For many obvious reasons working-class men have not left written records. As they said themselves, it took a war to make them 'put pen to paper', and perhaps it was only this war because World War II produced nothing like the amount of diaries and letters of World War I. The artlessness of almost all the soldier diarists makes for a clarity that in turn transports us sixty years and twelve thousand miles into the heart and heat of the matter.

Signaller R. J. Kenny of the 4th Battalion had landed and raced inland but with his company was ordered back to the beach to work around to the right to reinforce the Third Brigade. 'At one place our dead and dying were packed close together. This stretch of beach couldn't have been twenty yards wide. We passed between them and the waters edge. We sang out to the boys that we would give the Turks an extra crack for them. Those that could, waved their hands back in acknowledgement. They were nearly all young chaps and it hurt to see them flattened out on the first day . . .

'Men saw and heard most terrible things. After the advance of 26 April when we were then driven back we set to and dug in deeper. The Turks attacked in great numbers but couldn't move us. Immediately in front of us was a gully running roughly parallel to our trenches. All night a wounded Australian somewhere down there was singing out, "Water! Water! For God's sake cobbers bring me water!" His cries were heart rending. "Don't let a man stay here!" I asked to be let out to try to bring him in or at least give him a drink but was refused because it was dark and both sides were shooting at anyone in front of our trenches as being night, friend could not be distinguished from foe. Towards morning the cries ceased and I hoped the Turks took him and attended to him. They were very good to our wounded and I'm sure if they found him alive he has been fixed up.'

Each had his own way of facing the death that he expected. A young man writing from Egypt on 5 May 1915 to his minister of religion back in Brisbane, wrote that while he was sitting in the packed recreation tent writing letters home a Padre entered and told the men to go on writing but that he would say a few words. 'The Padre is saying there is nothing necessarily terrible in death, that the word in the New Testament means "a place of safe keeping" and in other words that "who lives for England sleeps with God". His last text was "There are none dead but live unto God". It is an extraordinary scene – hundreds writing what might be their last letter home and the chaplain speaking . . . he is making us realise more fully that we shall not be forgotten in prayer by our comrades if we do fall. We shall all be members of one glorious body marching forward, the Captain of which is Christ. The rooms of his mansion are being filled, that is all.'

Ernie Mack, wounded at Gallipoli, wrote to his sister Nell while on his way to Hospital in England. 'By jove, who would have thought a year ago that I would have seen so much of the world. Even if I never get back to Australia I will be quite satisfied in a way as this has been a good experience to finish up on.'

Even when 'resting' from the trenches they were not safe. as Corporal F. J. Ponting related in a letter: 'While having a rest out of the trenches, I, with Pte E. T. Chalker of the 4th Battn like myself, went down to the beach to have a swim and replenish our water bottles. After swimming, we sat on one of the barges to get dressed. I had puttees and Chalker had slacks so he was dressed before me and while waiting walked away and rolled me a cigarette. I went over to get the cigarette when Whiz! Bang! a shell from Beachy Bill burst on the place I'd been sitting ten seconds before.'

Many men recorded brief anecdotes such as this one by Private E. R. Jeffree, a stretcher bearer (1st Field Ambulance). 'One day a barrel of wine floated ashore, in June this was, and although it was in the direct line of Turkish Artillery fire boys were crowded round it filling tins. The Turks thought, with so many fellows around they would make a bag so fired away like mad but all the boys did was hide behind the barrel and some just ducked without leaving their positions for fear they would get no wine. Another time I saw a chap bathing on Brighton Beach and a Turkish Sniper got him in his sights. Every time the Turk fired the lad would duck; and, when he emerged, he would wave his hand in signaller's fashion to indicate a miss. This was repeated several times; but the Turk didn't get him.'

Others recalled poignant moments such as when Corporal Robson D.C.M., 4th Battalion, saw 'a young fellow get shot in Shrapnel Gully while putting a cross over his brother's grave'. Another time he offered to help 'a young fellow crawling down to the beach with his hand and half his leg off but he said there were plenty more needed help more than he did and, "Anyway", he said, "I don't think I'll last more than an hour".' Robson was awarded the D.C.M. 'For carrying water and ammunition under heavy fire, taking charge of 50 men, and shooting 13 Turks with a rifle'.

There were no non-combatants on Gallipoli: every man was in the line of fire. Corporal F. E. Quintal of the 6th Light Horse wrote of a cook whose wrath was monumental when the Turks hit his cooking fire and destroyed the breakfast he'd prepared. 'The cook – a typical Australian bushman – had gone down twice to the beach before daylight and carried up 16 gallons of water for the men's tea. The track leading to the Water Supply Depot was steep, narrow and tortuous; it really required unusual strength to bring up 8 gallons at a time. He got his fire going, no easy task with the scarcity of fuel, and set to work to get breakfast ready.

'Hanging over the shallow cooking trench were three

kerosene tins exclusively for tea, another tin for stew, and numerous quart pots which he allowed men to place there for their own private use – a great concession this, as it meant that each man with a private pot had to crouch over the fire and with a stick keep his can on the perpendicular, getting very much in cook's way. Just when the lot of us were longingly casting furtive looks in the direction of the temporary "kitchen" shells began to fall thick and fast and like rabbits we sought our burrows. But Cooky, true to his breed, stuck to his post and paid not the slightest heed to the shells that were falling all round him – until one landed fairly in the middle of his fire, and with a terrific explosion, sent pots, tins, pans and cans to the four corners of the earth, but luckily left Cookie standing in the midst of it all. He stood there quite unscathed with tall gaunt frame and a hard face with two weeks growth of raven black beard on it. His hairy chest was bare, he wore "shorts" that didn't even approach his knees, his feet were protected by huge ammunition boots – and no socks. He cut a figure.

'Then he started with a yell of rage. He faced about in the direction from which the shell came, and with his knobby, hairy arms uplifted, poured out his wrath upon the Kaiser's head in such language as I never heard before – and I've heard some. Having grown hoarse with invoking curses on one and all our foes, he suddenly wheeled round and, without saying another word, even in acknowledgement of the many words of sympathy extended him, gathered up two kerosene tins, and grimly started back to the beach with all the work to be done again.'

The wounded were got off the beach under cover of darkness and taken to Egypt where Sister Alice Kitchen was feeling her forty-plus years. '*May 1st*: Another strenuous day, some worked till late at night, others till nearly 11 p.m. (having gone on duty at 6 a.m.) Batches of wounded came in, many bullet wounds, every room crammed and such a puddle of disorder. Ray Bennett came in with a flesh wound in thigh, and told us that Capt. Hodgson, Sargeant, and Stanley Close had all been killed and R. Barrett killed or missing. Barry badly wounded, Col. Bolton a wrist injury and grazed scalp but returned to the front from Alexandria. No doubt many of the men have gone too. We heard a rumour that Col. Coulter had been shot in the head, but it may be only rumour, many of the wounds are slight, some marvellous escapes and some horrible injuries. 25 or so died on the boats coming over, such dreadful news for so many of them at home to hear. It all makes one realise the awfulness of war. H. Elsie J. is said to have got a bullet through the shoulder strap but no injury. One dreads to hear who next has gone. Worked till nearly 11 p.m. Another train expected in at midnight. I suppose it makes a good record to say that so many patients have been through this place but it will end in a good many breakdowns on the staff. The war will wear [them] out . . .

'*May 3rd:* Another horrible day. Everyone working all sorts of hours and scarcely time to think of meals for one's self. So many men have arm and hand injuries . . . One poor lad had to have his leg amputated, gangrene from injury to main artery, I fancy . . . Most of them think the casualties were heavier than anticipated but it is very difficult to really know. Many think 6 000 about the number, but one man told me 8 000 would be nearer the mark. There will be grief and sorrow in many a home and I am afraid few of the 1st A.I.F. will return except as cripples. It is all too dreadful and every day we hear of someone we knew being killed or wounded.

'Everyone has felt the awful strain of the last week . . . if we had been nursing strange troops we may have felt it less, but among our own people the horrors of war are brought home to one more intensely. Almost everyone on the staff has some relation or friend at the front and so you are constantly dreading to hear the latest news . . . God preserve them all, but that seems an impossibility unless the war ends suddenly. It is a bit amusing to hear that their war cry was Imshee Allah!, and I suppose anyone who has been in Egypt will always say Imshee Allah! as next to "Backsheesh" that seems the most frequently used phrase.

'*May 6th*: . . . The Light Horse are being dismounted leaving their horses here and going as infantry, leaving Egypt on Sunday. There is evidently no use for their horses at present. . . .

'*May 10th*: Over to Luna Park . . . hundreds of beds and only very few helpers . . . Met a bandsman from the 8th. Heard another friend had been killed . . . Every night a train comes in with wounded and sick from the transports and we hear of them bringing 700 and 800 over with only 2 or 3 Drs. and a few orderlies. The medical service seems to have broken down completely.

'*May 11th*: The morning star rises just outside one of our ward windows and it and the morning light over the dry desert sand are lovely in the dawn and make up for the depression that is the usual accompaniment of night duty. I love this old Egypt so much and shall be sorry to leave it and always hope I may come back to it again. The Jacaranda trees are in bloom everywhere and look a delightful sight with their beautiful heliotrope flowers. I have never seen so many or such fine ones anywhere. I asked one man who came in from the front where he had come from and he said he thought it was from "Hell". It seemed like that to him. I am afraid our losses have been heavy and the lives lost too many for the positions gained. It seems such reckless waste of useful human life.

'*May 21st*: Sr. Samsing came back last night and also brought word that Col. Gartside had been killed. Gen. Bridges died of wounds and Lt. Mathieson. He was such a nice kind little man. It is all too tragic. One by one our soldier friends drop out of the ranks . . . Sister Heath's fiancé also killed a few days ago.

'*May 22nd*: Still 3 cases of tetanus, one not doing well and the other two are having lumbar puncture . . . Sticky, little flies a pest . . . Yet another very hot day and another glorious night, the moon flooding the desert with its silvery beams. I wonder on what scenes of horror and death at Gallipoli this same moon looks down upon, how many broken lives and hearts all over this sad old world.'

On 19 May the Light Horsemen who had volunteered to come from Egypt without their horses were beginning to land when there occurred the strongest Turkish effort of the campaign to drive the Anzacs back into the sea. From 2.30 a.m. for seven and a half hours the Turks hurled themselves repeatedly against the whole Anzac front, especially at the centre, but at 11 a.m. when the attack finally flickered out, the Anzac trenches were still intact, and some 3 000 enemy dead strewed the ground. 'On May 20, some of the enemy wounded from the big attack still lay between the lines. Each of us, them and us, watched them die. Everyone wanted to help, none of us knew how to,' Sergeant A. S. 'Good-time' Charlie Nicholas wrote. 'Several attempts were made by both sides, always ending in misunderstanding and resumption of firing. At one stage the Australians hoisted a Red Cross flag and instantly two bullets brought it down. Scarcely had it fallen when a Turk ran from the enemy lines direct to the Australian line. He gasped out an apology, and explained that many of the Turkish troops did not know the meaning of the Red Cross. A written message was sent to the enemy suggesting that if an armistice was desired it must be formally arranged through an envoy sent along the beach from Gaba Tepe. This envoy duly appeared beneath a white flag and was blind-folded and was taken past Hell Spit, through the water on a stretcher carried by some Australians who were swimming, and deposited at General Birdwood's head-quarters. A "Suspension of Arms" from 7.30 a.m. to 4.30 p.m. and size of burial parties was agreed to. On 24 May at 7.30 a.m. all firing ceased at Anzac but not at Cape Helles 13 miles away.'

He was among the burial parties: 'Incredible! Nine hours silence! The machine guns stopped, the sound of bullets died away, the roar of bursting shells and the blast of grenades ended. Then we unarmed men walked out to meet our enemy and bury our dead. It was the dead that forced the armistice. Some of them had lain there since the Landing. Thousands had been killed since the big night attack when they tried to throw us into the sea. The Turks' bodies lay in heaps all along the narrow No Man's Land even up to the parapets of the trenches. The weather was hot, and the bodies rotted rapidly. They bred a plague of flies. A nauseating stench. Our army doctors feared a plague.

'My own experience, with that of others, was the strange effect of the silence. I found a sort of "hurting" of the ears, obviously caused by the sudden cessation of heavy, continuous firing that, from the time of the Landing, had never ceased for a moment. It was an amazing sensation – nearly as great as the sudden realisation that for a few hours a man was *safe*!

'The burial parties consisted of 200 men from each side, the Australians wearing Red Cross armlets, the enemy Red Crescents. A line was pegged down the centre of No Man's Land, the Turks burying bodies on their side, while the Australians and New Zealanders did likewise.

'It was impossible to identify all bodies, as many Anzacs were lying on the Turkish side of the demarcation line, and it is considered that those who were buried this way were listed by a later Court of Inquiry as "Missing, believed killed".

'In some parts of the line men mingled freely with Johnny Turk. . . . For these few hours in No Man's Land there was not the slightest sign of personal hostility.

'While the written conditions of the truce were observed, both sides took advantage of improving loopholes or trenches while "the heads" seized the opportunity to thoroughly survey the ground held by the enemy. At Quinn's Post both sides buried dead in unoccupied trenches, filling in trenches that would have been handy for the opposing side in any attack.

'Anzac burial parties greeted the enemy with odds and ends of Arabic phrases, and with Australianese that must have been incomprehensible to them. "Backsheesh – Saida – Eggs-a-cook" – even "Play you again next Saturday".

'They exchanged cigarettes and souvenirs. The men

returned to their trenches at 4 p.m., bringing in a few badly wounded men. The uncanny silence continued. The Turks disappeared behind their parapets.

'The temporary armistice had been honorably kept. With the front line again fully manned, the whole of Anzac "stood to" as time ran out. Slowly cruising along the Gallipoli coastline, with their guns trained shorewards, steamed the destroyers and cruisers, while further out a squadron of battleships lay motionless.

'The minutes ticked away. Still the silence.

'Then, far to the right, came the whipcrack of a Turkish sniper's rifle.

'A tremendous fusillade of rifle-fire broke out, both sides blazing away at each other's parapets, as if to say, "The Armistice is over – now it is WAR!"'

The 'Special Instructions for Action during Suspension of Arms' of 24 May 1915 included the following clause: 'A bearer party of 200 strong will inter the dead and remove the wounded to their respective lines except in front of sections where corpses are not very numerous. Six picks and six shovels for interring much decomposed corpses are to be held ready at 8 a.m. in each section of the defence. Dead and wounded are to be cleared from the vicinity of our trenches first, gradually working towards the dividing line.'

After the dead and wounded had been removed the men must collect the rifles and equipment found in the area, load it into their stretchers and deposit it on the demarkation line. The bolts of the rifles were to be removed and the rifles returned to their respective owners. 'Arms or equipment of dead or wounded officers will be returned to their own side without restriction.'

Private B. Jackson of the 2nd Battalion wrote about that 'big' armistice of 24 May, 'I came to a spot where the dead were lying two and three deep, and I saw an Australian and a Turk who had run each other through with their bayonets. Both apparently had fallen dead at the same instant as their bayonets had not been withdrawn. In their death struggle, their arms must have encircled each other, and they were lying exactly in this position when I saw them. They had been in that sad embrace for at least a week'.

'Murphy' Simpson was still making his daily runs down Shrapnel Valley, mostly bringing down men with leg wounds; fatalistic, cheerful – no man spoke or wrote about 'Murphy' but they mentioned his laughter – he had been reported missing from his unit on the second day. He had set off independently with his donkey that he called 'Duffy' or any other name that came to his tongue. 'Imshi Abdul' he shouted his vocabulary of Egyptian, or 'Come on *Queen Elizabeth*', referring to the great ship offshore. He camped with an Indian ambulance unit, sleeping little and be-grudging time to eat. Up and back, up and back. 'Here mate!' One man a trip.

For three weeks he toiled up with water and back with men, all day every day. 'Has the bloke with the donk stopped one yet?' was the common question when men came down from outer posts. 'My troubles,' said Simpson when warned of the impossibility of his escaping forever.

No man was immune. On 15 May General Bridges was killed at Simpson's own unit, the 3rd Field Ambulance Brigade in Shrapnel Gully. On the night of 18–19 May the Turks came across in masses, waves and waves of men. The wounded were thick, in the bushes, on the rocks, on the parapets, on trenches, everywhere. There was plenty of work for 'Murphy' Simpson and Duffy.

War

Out in the dust he lies;
   Flies in his mouth,
Ants in his eyes . . .

I stood at the door
   Where he went out;
Full-grown man,
   Ruddy and stout;

I heard the march
  Of the trampling feet,
Slow and steady
  Come down the street;

The beat of the drum
  Was clods on the heart,
For all that the regiment
  Looked so smart!

I heard the crackle
  Of hasty cheers
Run like the breaking
  Of unshed tears,

And just for a moment,
  As he went by,
I had sight of his face,
  And the flash of his eye.

He died a hero's death,
  They said,
When they came to tell me
  My boy was dead;

But out in the street
  A dead dog lies;
Flies in his mouth,
  Ants in his eyes.

Mary Gilmore
(later Dame Mary)

As the attack slackened Simpson was hit; the big hearty laugh ceased, the man was dead with a bullet through his heart. The Indian Field Ambulance men with whom he usually camped squatted and threw dust over their heads and wailed their dirge for the man. He was buried that night, and only after his death did they realise he belonged to none of the medical corps in the area but, separated from his own unit, had initiated a one-man rescue outfit. One of the most likeable men on Gallipoli, this 'starveling of fate forgot himself into immortality'.

Trooper A. S. Bartlett of Western Australia's 10th Light Horse had said as the Infantry marched off to Gallipoli, 'I hate to hear their sympathy with us light horsemen for having been left behind here in Egypt!' He knew that in the rivalry of battalion and corps pride there was more derision than sympathy. But the 10th didn't have long to wait. Within two days of the Landing it was recognised that the 'wastage' (as deaths were called) at Anzac was going to be huge. Reinforcements must be brought up immediately to fill the gaps left in the ranks by men that were now crowding the few spaces where graves could be dug. The Western Australians watched the hospital trains unload bodies at Heliopolis and when Colonel Brazier, their commanding officer, asked them if they were willing to volunteer for dismounted service he was able to report to the Brigadier, General Hughes, 'They have volunteered to a man'.

They left behind their bandoliers, leggings, and spurs and put on the cloth puttees, web equipment and pack of the infantryman, but not without regret. 'I hate leaving my leggings and spurs off,' said Trooper Bartlett. Twenty-five per cent of the men were detailed off to stay behind to care for the horses – they would be needed later for the long campaign in the desert, a long drawn-out thing that did not end until 1919. But few of the men who went off in the *Lutzow* to Gallipoli on 16 May were alive to ride their horses in those magnificent charges across the Jordan River.

It is claimed that while the bayonet sharpening went on as they neared Gallipoli the old hymn 'Oh God, our help in ages past' was being accompanied 'by the hiss of revolving grindstones'.

They were insanely excited. Lieutenant-Colonel Olden claims that when the first shrapnel began bursting round the deck of the *Lutzow* as they reached Gallipoli waters, 'realising they were under fire for the first time [time] promptly climbed the masts and rigging to get a better view of it'. They went ashore in the, by now, time-honoured Gallipoli way: over the side onto destroyers that took them close inshore, from there in tows of barges and small boats. This was 21 May, near the end of the brave attempt by the Turks to 'drive us into the sea'. When the 10th got on shore and dug in at Plugge's Plateau they saw 7 000 enemy dead stretched out in front of the Australian trenches. Their introduction to war was swift. On the twenty-fourth they assisted in bringing in the wounded and burying the dead during the 'armistice' and the following day, 25 May, watched with every Australian on Gallipoli the sinking offshore of HMS *Triumph* in clear daylight. No man writing of the shock of seeing this 'huge battleship disappear' refers to it in terms other than melancholy and dread. They were prisoners on this two-mile by one-mile strip of land, crowded dug-out to dug-out, the hole they had dug to live in often caving in under the footfalls of troops crossing above on the way to repel attacks. And now, 'in broad daylight. I couldn't sleep properly this night. To see that big ship so easily wiped off the sea'.

11
The White Ships

Meanwhile Sister Kitchen and Sister Samsing wandered through the streets of Cairo, admiring the 'magnolia blooms and a sort of tuberose . . . tentwork, fly switches, and silver shawls . . . while the crippled and badly clothed Australian soldiers increase daily . . . Their woollen khaki are most unsuitable for this climate'. Regularly she wrote up her diary until, on 8 June, she misses making an entry for the first time since leaving Melbourne. We learn the reason on the ninth, when she records that 'On Monday (7th) night about 11 p.m. Samsing came and told me we were detailed for transport duty to Dardanelles and I had to be relieved and get ready by 7 a.m. tomorrow. The sorting and packing and tidying of my room took me till morning.

'We got the 9.30 to Alex . . . We were met by Miss Oram (Lady Superintendent of Nurses) with a motor ambulance and she went with us to the Quay and arranged about a boat to take us to the *Gascon*. Pointed out a ship which had last night brought in 1 500 wounded, and she said she had robbed the hospitals of 36 sisters for transport work. Got a cabin to ourselves. Everyone is kind and nice and glad to see us as the work is heavy. The C.O. seems especially to be liked. We hear we are going to ANZAC Cove and perhaps to Gaba Tepe and do hope we shall see what is left of the dear boys of the 8th . . .

'*June 15th*: Woke up to find ourselves at Gaba Tepe opposite the 'Anzac' Beach and the hill where so many of our casualties took place. It looks an awful-looking spot to land men to fight in modern warfare. An aeroplane did some scouting over the vicinity all the morning and had several shots fired at it, and the *Monitor* fired at least 20 shots during the morning, great heavy booms echoing round the hills and over the sea dealing out destruction, or trying to. The aeroplane circled overhead like some huge bird. On the hills opposite we heard rifle cracks off and on all day. We had no visitors, though the *Cecelia* is lying close to us and the heacy not far off. The *Pincher* and 2 or 3 other destroyers patrolled round all day like watchdogs and a trawler or a mine-sweeper brought over an odd patient or so till we had 3 in. At night the rifle shots got more frequent and the hill looks well lit up but we are told that they are not visible on the shore. We see a vessel using its searchlight, and as the moon, which is a new one 2 days old, sank, the *Cecelia* went away and we are to carry on her work.

'*June 17th*: About 3 times in 24 hrs the mine-sweeper brings over patients, the last batch generally about 11 p.m. Got in one poor boy from the 8th with his hand blown off (Scott). Very warm down below. At 9 p.m. the portholes are closed for fear of submarines. The watertight doors can be closed quickly and then it would take us longer to sink. Though we continually hear guns and shells being fired on the beach and from the torpedo boats, we all seem to pursue our ordinary work, scarce giving a thought to the possibility of being torpedoed or shelled. "In the Great Hand of God we stand."

'*June 18th*: Last night we got in another man with his R. hand off with a hand grenade. Things they make themselves out of jam tins . . . They occasionally go off too soon and then there is tragedy, or in throwing it, hit the back of the trench. Col. McPhee came over today and we were so pleased to see him once more. He looks thinner and older. He gave us all the news of the 8th or what is left of them. Gave me a little picture of Lemnos of his own taking. Got in a spinal injury – such sad cases they are and so hopeless and tragic. . . . how good and patient and uncomplaining they are with all their terrible injuries.

June 20th: Several large shells were fired at the store ship near us today, so we were promptly moved away a bit. Got 2 bad abdominals; one died. The work gets heavier daily and the flies a pest and the atmosphere very oppressive down below and there is so little time to take the air on deck.

'*June 30th*: Got off all the sick [in Alexandria] by noon though we had about 12 stretcher cases and it was a business to try and get the men fit to travel again in their torn and bloodstained clothing. . . . we were free after lunch and Samsing and I went off to Alexandria to shop and look round.

'*July 4th*: . . . We got to Gaba Tepe early – about 11 a.m. Another hospital ship, the *Neuralia*, standing by and still taking on patients. Tonight it looks pretty with its dado of green lights and brilliant red cross which sends a red reflection over the sea like a great red sword.

'*July 8th*: Spent the day struggling with a bad abdominal – in vain. After 9, Samsing and I sat on the deck and watched the last of the sunset . . . *July 10th*: Another poor abd. died tonight: had no op. he was too bad. . . . if they are operated on, they die and they mostly die if nothing is done. *July 11th*: A busy day: on till 10 p.m. A poor dying abdominal begged us not to leave him, as he felt he was going. The Staff is not adequate for the heavy demands on it especially the night when the wounded always come in, in 2 or 3 batches. When I think of all the "technique", and the fuss and bother over a clean abd. op. I wonder the more. These poor ones have often to do with such scanty nursing when there is a rush and 2 or 3 are urgently ill or even dying, you feel torn . . . to have to leave them at all.

'Tonight at 7 p.m. a cruiser came up and did some business with heavy guns and made a great commotion, 2 or 3 destroyers did scouting for submarines. The shells fired in return whistled and shrieked as they passed over or beside us and made huge splashes as they fell, often near the destroyers. Our anchor always gets hauled up and we get a wriggle on, on these occasions.

'*July 14th*: Samsing and I were up till 1 a.m. A large batch of stretchers came in about 9.30 – about 30 of them and we had to put them on the hatchway. We stayed with a dying man making the 3rd that day and one more in the night. Tonight we were up till 10 p.m. working trying to straighten things out a little. We left for Lemnos before midday: the *Cecelia* relieving us.

'*July 15th*: We arrived at Lemnos safely, took on 9 more cases on the hatch or "atch" as the boys call it: making 40 in all. We heard during the course of the morning we are to go to Malta and rejoice . . .

'*July 18th*: Arrived at Malta early in a.m. and got up in good time to get the patients all fixed up and off but it was a long tedious business: dressings to do, patients to feed and dress and kits to be got out and tied up; stitches etc. all to be lined up ready for removal. Felt fearfully tired and fagged after the long trip and heavy, but got dressed and was ready to go ashore in a little boat at 3.30 p.m. It all looked very charming with its old high walls and streets. We went to the Blue Sisters, where we spent a pleasant hour or so. They showed us over the hospital, gave us tea and supplied me with Altar bread for Fr. McAuliffe.

'*July 22nd*: Arrived at Mudros Harbor and found an hours' notice to sail. Did all our ironing with a box iron. In the afternoon we went with Mr Williams in the boat to the *Argylshire* to see if any Australian Sisters were on board. Found about 40 E. Reserves and Canadians whose varied collars and costumes were a marvel and enough to upset Miss Oram completely. We did not stay long and had to tack to get back while the *Gascon* tooted wildly and flew the *recall* flag and the Capt. hung anxiously over the side, having received orders to proceed to Cape Helles which we reached about 9 p.m. It does not look so familiar as Gaba Tepe.

'*July 23rd*: A wild windy day. A French hospital ship and the *Grantully Castle* were both here, the latter leaving this morning; and we are to take up the work. This evening several patients came on and Night Duty began. *July 24th*:

. . . In the silence and dusk, broken only by the lapping of the sea against the ship, the torpedo destroyers came up and down and round us like dark silent shapes, making no sound, showing no sign of light, like great dark crocodiles. A search light plays in the distance and an occasional rocket and we hear sometimes rifle and shell fire . . . Here the last lot of patients come in about 7 p.m. so they generally get settled down about 9 p.m. or thereabouts unless an odd one or 2 a little later, but the bringing in of large batches of wounded at night is not so customary as it is at "Anzac". I watched French Destroyers creeping round and round us all night, dark silent shapes: and wonder why they don't keep out of the shining moontrack on the sea! A perfect dawn and a golden red sunrise that compensates for night up.'

The next three nights were comparatively quiet, and early on the morning of the thirtieth they departed for Mudros Bay. On 2 August the *Gascon* 'Arrived at Alex. at 4 a.m. and stood outside till 10 a.m. or so. It was late when we got off the patients. The heat during the night was frightful and after an hour or so downstairs I was so soaked that I had to redress. Everything on the ship moist and sticky.

'*August 3rd*: No letters from home for nearly 3 months now. Went to bed for a sleep last night in the dark and felt better for it. Went ashore in the morning and did some shopping, laid in a stock of Mothersill and Worcestershire sauce.* Got back to lunch with the aid of 2 native policemen and an interpreter of some sort . . .

'*August 6th*: Had a quiet restful day getting to Mudros Bay this evening 6 p.m. After dinner we saw 6 or 8 hospital ships going out till only the *Gloucester Castle* and ourselves were left. Also cruisers and transports etc. and it looks as if all preparations for a big attack were being made. We may go tomorrow or next day.'

---

* Remedy for sea sickness.

12
The Lonesome Pine

In faint lead pencil young Private T. Oliver of the 7th Battalion wrote home on the eve of the most terrible battle.

'*Doctors Ridge, Near Lonesome Pine, 3 August 1915*: My loving Mother, father, brothers and sisters and friends . . . Don't have any fear for me, I am ready for whatever comes and quite prepared to die for my king and country and the dear ones left behind . . . The shells are lobbing about us . . . we have got our marching orders now so I will close with fondest love to you all, it may be good-bye but God be with you all until we meet again.'

They didn't talk much about it. It is in their letters that the chilling realisation is expressed, and not often even there. Their demeanour exposed them. They became quieter, they made preparations, they exchanged letters to be posted home if they 'went west'. They subtly changed from talking of getting home, to talk of making 'another blow for the allies'.

They were thinner now, illness had eaten into seventy per cent of them, but they stopped going on sick parade; those already in hospital tried to desert back to their units.

'Feints' were begun along the narrow strip of land at 3.50 p.m. on 6 August, and the bombardment that had been going on for three days was increased. The men who would attack Lone Pine had been busy since early morning sewing white calico patches on the backs of their tunics and as armbands (they would be fighting as darkness fell), collecting their ammunition and 'iron' rations, and filling their water bottles. Each man could be seen carefully cleaning his rifle; many set to work once more sharpening their bayonets. They began to file up into the trenches facing the Turkish-held Lone Pine by 4.30 p.m. At 5.30 p.m. they were on the fire-step, some running down at the last moment to get near a mate so as to go over the top with someone they knew. Then the order for the hop-over was given and the first line leapt out with the setting sun at their backs, and ran. The Turks took a few seconds to fire and by then the first of the Australians were running along the edge of what the surveys had shown to be the Turkish trenches. The men back in the Australian trenches watched them, bewildered. They had bunched up, and as others joined them they spread out 'like a line of spectators along a street kerb'. By now the Turkish machine guns and rifles had their range and they began to fall. What the Australians found was that the Turkish trenches here were roofed in with thick pine logs covered with earth and entry was nearly impossible – while the enemy were free to fire out at them from safety. When they realised this, some men began to claw at the heavy timbers and slowly drag them aside while others ran on over the logs to the open communication trenches beyond and from there charged back to the forward trenches beneath the canopy of logs. Above them the parapet was lined with men lying still. After a time, the observers back in the Australian lines realised that all these men were dead. It was some time before the fate of the men beneath the log roofing was known.

Into the warren of dark tunnels the men leapt, followed by wave on wave of reinforcements until the trenches were choked with dead and wounded men. No bombs were used. The fighting was too close for this. Rifles, but mostly bayonets and, at times, hands did the killing. By 6 p.m. Lone Pine had been taken, the 'casualties' removed, reinforcements brought in and 'a few jars of rum' broached. The Australian commanders, unlike officers of other troops, found that rather than issue rum immediately before a battle it was more efficacious when the men were tired and 'battleworn'.

During the 'wild rush' across the open ground to Lone Pine, several men had run over the log covering and on past the trenches and come on a sight no Australians had seen before: behind the Turkish trenches of Lone Pine was a depression in which battalion after battalion was sheltered as reinforcements. But these few Australians did not get back to their own lines to give warning – their bodies remained on the open ground where they had been shot until the burial parties moved on to the peninsula in 1920.

The Turkish reserves were rushed to Lone Pine and bombing began as they attempted to re-take the trenches. This bomb-fight continued from 6 to 9 August. In the official history C. E. W. Bean wrote: 'The bomb-fight went on almost continuously, flaring up four times into many hours of desperate fighting when successive Turkish reinforcements were thrown in. Even at Quinns Post, there had never been such bomb-fighting. Noting that the Turkish bombs had long fuses the Australians constantly caught them and threw them back before they burst. The Turks then learnt to shorten the fuses and many boys' hands were blown off, and others were blinded or killed. Hundreds of times bombs falling into the trenches were smothered with sandbags; but others burst, killing and wounding the groups behind the barricades, and the stream of wounded was continuous.

'At intervals when Turks were clearly massing behind the barriers the Australians would clear them, exposing themselves above the parapet in the process, and with rifles or a machine-gun sweeping down the enemy. The Turks dynamited a barricade, but the Australians rushed, and re-established it. The Turks set fire to the logs of the head cover. The Australians twice extinguished it. The Turks twice penetrated far into the trenches they had lost; the Australians turned them and chased them back. Jam-tin bombs, though pouring from the factory on the beach, were still in far from sufficient supply. On both sides the dead clogged many of the trenches till the garrison gave them such burial as it could underfoot or in the parapet – or dragged them clear. On the enemy's side, the Turkish dead, with a few big Australians at their head, were laid out in a horrifying procession beside the pathway leading up through the Cup along which Turkish reinforcements had to climb; on the Australian side the wounded and the heap of salvaged rifles, crowded the corresponding depression of Brown's Dip.'

From the hospital ship *Gascon*, Sister Kitchen recorded those August days:

'*August 8th*: Sunday morn – calm and peaceful, no startling news except from a transport that the troops had made a successful new landing. About 4 p.m. we got orders to go to Gaba Tepe and off we went arriving about 9 p.m. 5 other hos. ships anchored here and one went out, also the *Liberty*, as we came in.

'*August 9th*: Was awakened at 1 a.m. . . . a large number of wounded were arriving in spite of the fact that about 6 other hospital ships were in the vicinity. Got up and worked till 4 a.m. . . . About dinner time tonight we went over to Imbros Island. Many ships are here and we are to put off all our cases on to transports to go on either to Mudros Bay or elsewhere. They say there are 10,000 beds at Lemnos. Kent Hughes came on board and is "fed up" with the way things are being done already.

'*August 10th*: Had a busy day getting all our cases dressed and ready to be transhipped. Most went on to the *Ionate* and the balance to the *Canada* and we then returned to Anzac for another load. We are acting as a clearing hospital at present having put through about 650 patients in 2 days. At Lemnos – 3600 went through a clearing hos. there (in a 600 bed hos.) in a day or so. Bullets fell on our deck and one wounded the dispensary Indian tonight, although the anchor was got up and we moved. Then a large lighterful of wounded came alongside about 200 patients on it. Never saw such a lot at once before, about 20 stretchers . . . The stretcher bearers have lost heavily, also many others of all units. The hill 971 has been taken and lost several times by the accounts of the men and the casualties have been frightful . . . One middie off the Sweeper who brought off the wounded told me how tired he was, no sleep for 5 days except snatches, working all night, and being sniped at also – cold from want of suitable clothing, no gear, sent off in a hurry. Today when getting off our men we gave out all the brilliant coloured pyjmas and shirts . . . They are all so dirty and ragged, their uniforms or what remains of it, stiff with dried blood, boots and socks caked with sand and all grateful for a wash. I had 10 Gurkas and 3 Sikhs. Some presented me with their badges . . . a dreadful war . . . more like wholesale murder.

'*August 11th*: Started off at 7 a.m. and worked till 11 p.m. We got a full ship and were back at Imbros in exactly 24 hrs since leaving it. We had often 3 boatloads of stretcher cases alongside at once and 2 or 3 more coming up and as fast as they moved off another 2 or 3 boatloads, so we soon got full. The men today are more badly injured . . . many compound fractures of arms, 6 C.F. femurs and all other sorts thrown in. All seem thankful to get away from it, and appreciate the comfort of a wash, and dressings done. The men all say the casualties were awful and they were simply mown down, often by our own artillery. Snipers seem particularly bad also and account for a good many. We expect to put this load off tomorrow on to transports and go back for another load tomorrow night. As there are still hundreds on the beach it seems the best thing we can do them . . . one can't forget what they must feel like lying about with little food and no dressings done for 4 and 5 days as some of them are – especially when in inaccessible places. No hospital arrangements except dressing stations and those not safe from fire and shells and bullets. We do not appear to have so many deaths . . . Before leaving Egypt and Malta last time we heard the authorities were preparing for 22,000 casualties so are not surprised that there are thousands already.

'*August 12th*: This morning we set off for Mudros Bay and got here early in forenoon . . . Opinions seem varied as to the numbers of wounded which have been taken off from

Gallipoli but "Chief" thinks 15,000 near the mark as he knows the ships running and the numbers they are likely to carry. They say Alexandria and Malta are crowded full and the *Aquitania* here in the Bay with over 3000 on board. Lemnos is supposed to be able to take 11,000 but we doubt it. All seem agreed that to winter at Gallipoli was out of the question, to retreat impossible unless they wish to admit themselves beaten, and it is said to be so rough that no stores could be landed or wounded taken off. Still the cost has been heavy and the N.Z. suffered greatly, also Imperials. Today the ward got well in hand though 2 C. Fractures of arm died from gangrene, only boys though one was 20 and married. It is so very rapid and horrid. . . . The wounded we received this time are on the whole much less serious and fatal than those we used to receive when we were lying near Anzac for 10 and 11 days. No doubt the worst here have died on shore . . . All the patients tell us that there are hundreds and hundreds lying everywhere, many in the broiling sun not even able to get a drink and many have come on board with dressings not done for 4 and 5 days and some even wept for food, they were so done up with hunger, pain, and shock. It makes us anxious to get on and get back for more. So many septic wounds, so many limbs likely to be lost. . . .

'*August 13th*: Two unlucky days in one! After waiting here over 30 hrs for orders we got them! Malta. . . . I shall get no letters for weeks. Heard tonight about the *King Edward* with 3000 troops sunk by a torpedo. . . . We suppose they will scarcely send the *Aquitania* or any other transport with wounded now. It will be too chancy. [The 'Black Ships' such as the *Aquitania* were transports, not hospital ships, 'White Ships', and as such, even though they carried wounded were not guaranteed immunity from enemy attack.] We had a busy day [in] Ward I . . . I have abandoned collar and cape for the time being as I cannot cope with too much ironing and a collar only lasts 10 minutes in the heat of Mudros Bay, just now. Stooping on the hatchway, anything but pleasant . . . I hope no torpedo attacks us and trust in God.

'*August 16th*: Got to Malta early about 9 a.m. . . . but the patients did not all get off till after 7 p.m. It always takes longer to unload here, and there was a dearth of stretchers. We leave tonight 7.30 p.m. again for Mudros.'

One of the wounded men she had taken from Lone Pine was the Private Tom Oliver whose farewell letter was quoted at the beginning of this chapter. Later, in September, he wrote home from Egypt. 'Well, since I went to the Dardanelles my mates and I have had some experiences. I had one sad one the first parade when they told me the little lad was killed [his brother]. I had some very narrow squeaks but I wasn't touched until 10 August when I was wounded and sent to No. 1 AGH Heliopolis. Was very bad for days. They operated on me 20 August and my temp. was 105.6, respiration 124 and then they put a thick needle in my side on the 24th and pumped out 2½ pints of fluid from my lungs.'

He spent the next month in and out of the operating theatre having 'fluid pumped out'. He would recover for four or five days, then again collapse. Eventually he wrote, 'I don't think I would be much good for the trenches again. It would have been grand if the both of us were coming home. I wish they could get the Turks on the run and finish this cruel war'.

Where possible the wounded were being collected, but the dead were left to rot where they fell. Because the ground was so exposed it was impossible even to record the details on the identification tags of the corpses. It was a dolorous disaster that caused the name of Lone Pine to be whispered for decades in many families, including my own, as if speaking of the tomb of the living dead, of mystery and horror and the dark engulfing of young noisy boys. It was better not to dwell on it. That my mother's brothers, grandmother's sons, were 'missing' in that land of the lonesome pine was a thing none of us could forget. The song from which the place received its name was still popular in the 'twenties and 'thirties and invariably someone would turn the radio down when they heard 'On the Trail of the Lonesome Pine' begin. We felt a pinch of some nerve that was inexplicable, unbearable. Perhaps the worst of it was that this loss of life was not even a 'battle': it was designated a 'demonstration', or a 'feint', to draw off Turkish opposition from a British landing being made at Suvla Bay.

The three British divisions that were to land at Suvla Bay, the flat salt lake country to the north of Anzac, were called 'Kitchener's Army' but there was one Australian group with it. Private R. G. 'Tommy' Thompson came ashore with the 'Dry Land Sailors', part of a unique group, the Naval Bridging Train. 'We were formed from all states. We were to build piers and construct bridges. Mostly using pontoons. . . . We set off for the Dardanelles on 16 June 1915 and apart from a few days at Lemnos we went straight to the August landing. While the Anzacs were continuing their "demonstration" as it was called, we went in to Suvla Bay with the British divisions as they landed. We had to scramble off our ship in darkness, over the side into the pontoons we were to take ashore. About 16 of us in each pontoon. We each were given an oar and told to row for the shore "over there". The pontoons were blunt ended and hopeless to manoeuvre and we lost contact. When daylight came there we were stretched miles up and down the coast. It took about three days to get us rounded up and drag the pontoons along. But all the while the Tommy troops were being landed and sent inland. Time and time again men doubled back and asked us where the front line was. They had no idea where to go. They'd head off into the scrub, thick bush it was; Officers and men alike asked us "which way to the lines?". They were all green, inexperienced. The officers, dressed up, were picked off right away by snipers and often the sergeant led the men into action. There was no water except what was in their little water bottles. And it was terrible hot. A man would come down with thirty bottles over his shoulder trying to get water from somewhere to take back up to the lines.

'We couldn't see anything of what was happening to the Australians. We heard terrible reports.'

As letters, including Private Tom Oliver's, show, the troops had 'got wind' of the great attempt that was to be launched. That they were to be sacrificed only as a 'demonstration' seemed not to affect them unduly. What did affect them was the fact that after all they had gone through they now faced the prospect of never again returning home. No man had any illusions at all. Instead of the cheering crowds massed to greet them on return, and thoughts of the gaiety and welcome now came a vision of battle after battle until death claimed them or hideous wounds took them away.

'Captain Stout said to me before we went over at Lone Pine, "We'll make a name for ourselves tonight Mac,"' Lance-Corporal Alex McQueen wrote. 'Well, I was outed in the early part of the night, but he made a name for himself alright. He was a Lieutenant when going in to the charge, made a captain next day, gained the V.C. the next, and the following day eternity.'

They wrote about friendships that men in civilian life would never understand. Private Angelo Humphreys, aged 19, leaving Sydney on the *Karoola* on 16 June 1915, wrote in the third person to conceal the identity of the teetotal lad he was. 'One of the men didn't drink strong liquor or spirits and he was called "molly-coddle", "girlie" and half a dozen such names until Private McClure put a stop to it. "Leave the kid alone. If he doesn't drink what's that to do with us?" In Egypt McClure took this lad under his care and stopped the other lads from leading him astray; he was kindness itself . . . On 6 August in the Lone Pine attack I lasted until about 6.30 p.m. when I was wounded. I looked around to see if I knew anybody alongside me and noticed that my chum and friend McClure was also wounded. I had started to bandage him when I felt dizzy – I suppose on account of loss of blood and he said, "Lay down, sonny, and when you feel better you can bandage me up". I lay down and he said, "We are fairly safe here", and a shot came past me and killed him instantly.

Decorations were issued – 7 V.Cs for Lone Pine itself, but as Private W. Percival, a New South Welshman, said of the disastrous attack on Hill 971 on 7 August 1915, 'Of the whole of those good comrades who were with me I can honestly say that these lads performed deeds of heroism and utter fearless bravery sufficient to warrant the issue all round of V.C.s, but nobody of high enough military rank saw them. We, their mates, saw it all. On the following day we buried some of our dead under whatever shelter the unoccupied ranges near us afforded. We crept on, scrambling and slipping on rugged slopes and across huge crevices in whose depths were often reposed the unheeded bodies of the dead, enemy and friend mixed, the result of that bloody struggle up steep hill-sides exposed to the spray of machine bullets and shrapnel.'

Trooper J. W. Garratt of the 1st Light Horse wrote of bomb-thrower R. M. Carr from that same day, across on 'Dead Man's Land'. 'We knew we hadn't a ghost of a chance but we charged. A Turkish machine gun right in front of our group gave us a lot of trouble. Several bombers tried to get it but they were pinged off the instant they got over our parapet. Carr then crawled up to within five yards of the gun, stood up, threw two bombs at it, put it out of action, saving scores of lives. He got no mention at all.'

Private W. S. Percival of the 15th Battalion told of 7 August, after the futile but desperate attack on Hill 971. 'One man was caught through the side of the head, severing his right ear, but not killing him. He lay . . . in a dangerous position – right in line of a point from which some snipers were potting our lads as they passed across a bit of a rise . . A man crawled out of our shallow trench and wormed his way along the ground to a position within a couple of yards of this man. Ping! Zipp! Zipp! Bullets hit the ground in little spurts of dust all round the rescuer's body. "Bob down!" yelled one of our boys, he was the would-be-rescuer's brother. But the rescuer worked his way snake-wise until he got to the wounded man. Clumsily turning the man over, he shouted, "How's she going, mate?" There was no answer. He yelled, "Strike me pink the poor bugger's just about outed", and began to drag him towards a bluff of rock and bush-studded earth nearer them but away from us. He got a bullet through his ankle but managed it at last, and we all cheered him. He looked over and grinned. He bound the wounded man's head up but didn't bother about his own wound. [Percival here had to move on, leaving the two rescued men isolated.]

'Down at the Base Hospital at Lemnos Island I heard the sequel. He managed to attract the attention of some stretcher bearers and the wounded man was stealthily carried away at night. The bearers promised to come back for the rescuer as soon as they could but it was no use. The Turks machine-gunned the whole of that range on which he lay and he stopped one of the bullets and the man he rescued survived for two days after that.'

Young Private L. G. Carrick of the 18th Battalion wrote in a sort of doggerel but nevertheless telling style, 'Thoughts of Home'.

We are waiting tonight for the Turks to advance.
We are still short of men, but they won't stand a chance.
To break through our lines – their advance we'll retard.
If they want to win through, then they'll have to fight hard.
    Tis the dawn of the day and they haven't come yet;
    But they're sure to come at us before long I bet –
    'They're coming! They're coming!' I heard the boys shout.
    In less than a minute they'll all be knocked out.
But that isn't as easy as some folks suppose,
and to make a Turk fight you don't tread on his toes;
Now they're into our trench and the bayonets clash,
Bullets whizzing, bombs explode, and the rifles all flash.
    The wounded are moaning, the dead are so still;
    But the men who are standing fight only to kill;
    The noise it is awful, the Shrapnel shells scream,
    Our bayonets are reddened and no longer gleam.
The victory is won and we just need a rest;
The wounded are taken, their wounds have been dressed,
To bury the dead – well, it makes our hearts sore
So now, I think Mother, I've really seen war.

The 'Fair Dinkums', the young, green reinforcements, were crowded into the many blood-baths of battles of those few days. Many died before coming to grips with the enemy of that empire they had come so far to fight for. One of the battles or 'feints' to draw Turkish troops away from the main objective at Suvla Bay was at 'German Officers', a point near which Australian tunnellers had dug a network of underground trenches. To enable the troops to make a surprise exit from these subterranean alleyways 'lids' of turf had been removed from twenty-one of the black tunnels from underground. From these caverns the raw boys were to scramble out into the spatter of bullets and ribbons of machine gun fire. The attack failed; those who got out through the 'plug-holes' were hit by bullets as they ran and killed as they lay exposed. Others, wounded as they climbed out, congested the tunnels and blocked the outlets.

At The Nek the 3rd Light Horse Brigade was to storm the Turkish trenches. The hill crest along which they must charge was so narrow and the precipices either side so steep that the number of men in each line of attack was limited to 150. 'On a given signal, silently, and without rifle-fire, with bomb and bayonet only' the 8th and 10th Light Horse regiments were ordered to 'engage the enemy'. They were warned that the numbers to be engaged were 'not light' and that machine guns in five positions 'commanded the approach to the Nek and fighting might disclose others'.

This was the first pitched battle these men had fought (they had had only eleven weeks of trench warfare). They must cross a narrow causeway under fire from three sides – and the five groups of machine guns were 200 yards behind the Turkish trenches, which were eight feet deep.

They believed they 'would take the hitherto impassable trenches and move through green and open country. The prospect filled them with a longing akin to home-sickness'.

Whatever chance such a plan had of success was ended at 4.23 a.m., seven minutes before the 'hop-over', when the artillery ceased fire. The Australians in the trench had orders to commence their attack at 4.30 a.m. when the artillery fire was to cease but now – it has not been satisfactorily explained to this day but is thought to have been inaccurate synchronising of watches – the bombardment stopped, and the Turks rushed to their parapets and took up positions ready for the attack they knew must come. One line sat on the parapet of the trench and the other stood behind it. They nestled their rifles into their shoulders, took aim, and waited. Their machine guns swivelled across the field they would sweep when the attack came.

The two lines of trenches were only twenty yards apart at some places across the bullet-riddled stumps of thorny bushes.

Perplexed, the Australians waited for the artillery, 'the softening-up', perhaps to give a final burst, but none came. There was silence for seven minutes until, at 4.30 a.m., the order was given: 'Go!'

From their observation point the Australians could see the Light Horse run across the sky-line, 'go limp and lay down'. Some had fallen back into the trenches as they attempted the 'hop-over'. The rest lay dead five or six yards from the parapet. All the officers – ten men – were killed, but Private D. McGarvie and two others got as far as the parapet of the Turkish trenches and threw bombs over until they had none left, called back to their comrades for more only to receive the reply that there were none – and over their heads they could see the bayonets of the Turkish troops behind the parapet. Lieutenant E. G. Wilson reached the Turkish parapet at a distance from the other three. He sat there with his back to the wall beckoning to his countrymen to come and join him until he was killed by bomb lobbed over the Turkish parapet. The other three men, now out of bombs, crawled off towards shelter. Two nights later McGarvie, wounded through the ankle, reached the safety of his own lines. The other two men were not found. That first group of 150 men were annihilated in half a minute.

The next 150 men to follow realised that they must be destroyed but mounted the step to climb from the trench. Two minutes after the first line had gone the second line leapt out into the fire. Later, when the battle was done, it was found that the second got a little farther than the first: their bodies were a few yards further on. They had passed over the bodies of the men who two minutes before had left their trench, running and shouting. Captain Hore of Hobart ran swiftly through the hail and was leading when he 'looked around and found he was the only man running'. The rest lay dead behind him. Hore threw himself to the ground and none passed him.

About this time a flag was seen – a small yellow and red flag on the enemy's trench. It will never be known who planted it there but it is surmised that some man of the first wave must have got into the trench and raised the small flag as a signal.

Those first two waves were Victorians, of the 8th Light Horse. Now followed the 10th Light Horse from Western Australia. Only the historian C. E. W. Bean could adequately describe what then happened.

'The West Australians filed into the trenches which the Victorians had just left. In addition to the fire which had previously swept the parapet, two Turkish 75 mm field guns were now bursting their shrapnel low over No Man's Land as fast as they could be loaded and fired. The saps were crowded with dead and wounded Australians who had been shot back straight from the parapet and were now being carried or helped to the rear. Among the West Australians who occasionally halted to let them pass, every man assumed that death was certain, and each in the secret places of his mind debated how he would go to it. Mate having said good-bye to mate the third line took up its position on the fire-step.

'It was then about 4.45. The third line, formed by the 10th, went forward to meet death instantly, as the 8th had done, men running as straight and swiftly as they could at the Turkish rifles. With that regiment went the flower of the youth of Western Australia, sons of the old pioneering families, youngsters, in some cases two and three from the same home, who had flocked to Perth at the outbreak of war.

'Sergeant W. L. Sanderson who went over with the fourth wave of men had found himself out alone as had Captain Hore. Running, he tripped over a spiky rhododen-dron bush and lay on the ground. His commanding officer crawled by him and shouted "Retire the fourth line first" and only then did Sanderson look around and see there was no one near him except the dead. Making his way back to the Australian lines, passing dying and dead he found that about 50 yards of the line had not a man in it except the dead and wounded: no one was manning it. It was 6 p.m. and the sacrifice was over. Of the 8th Light Horse half those who started out had been killed and nearly half the remainder wounded: out of a total of 300, 12 officers and 142 men had been killed and 4 officers and 76 men wounded.

'Each of the actions being inter-dependant one on the other for success, the day of 7th August drained first one, then the other, regiment. The 1st Light Horse Regiment of New South Welshmen made an exceedingly brave dash on Baby 700 with few of their officers remaining unwounded. Of the original 200, 154 were casualties, every officer but one being hit.'

Battalion after battalion suffered, almost every group on the Peninsula was thrown up into the maelstrom during those August days, but The Nek remained the ultimate in slaughter. 'During the long hours of that day [said C. E. W. Bean] the summit of The Nek could be seen crowded with the bodies of the Light Horse men. At first here and there a man raised his arm to the sky, or tried to drink from his water-bottle. But as the sun of that burning day climbed higher, such movement ceased. Over the whole summit the figures lay still in the quivering heat.'

For sixty years my own family has nurtured a small piece of folklore about that day. Mick Byrne, my cousin, was killed at that time and my Aunt Anastasia, when hearing of his death, cried out a seemingly irrelevant remark, 'He must have taken his jacket off!' The legend is that Mick was born with a caul over his head – the skin some babies do not slough naturally and which is removed by the midwife. This caul has been revered throughout history as a safeguard against sudden death. In Dickens's time, for instance, a caul fetched a high price on the waterfront, sea-captains depending on possession of one to save them from an untimely end. 'When Mick went to war,' my aunt told me, 'I stitched his caul in the left breast pocket of his jacket.'

In August 1975 when I was on The Nek it was humid and heavily hot, I removed my jacket and suddenly remembered the photographs I'd seen of the troops waiting for the hop-over on 7 August 1915 – they were all without jackets under the hot sun.

When I visited the Peninsula in 1975 the famous Turkish guide, Mr Dilman, was describing to me the various moves of 7 August 1915. He was standing behind me. I was sitting on the edge of a ridge overlooking The Nek. The old man, who was there when the Australians landed, began to describe the last moments of the Light Horse attack across The Nek. 'The sun was here', he pointed to the horizon, 'when the first wave did come over'. I was looking across at that narrow causeway that opened out onto hundreds of rifles, machine guns and artillery and bayonets 'bristling row on row on row'. 'Then, we see, they all lie down. Right away over come another wave, they go a little further and they lay down. The sun has not begun to move, it is all so quick. Another line of men jump out and run, and they fall down and then we see another begin to come over and a Turkish officer cry out . . .' In his telling, Mr Dilman lapsed into Turkish. I grabbed his ankle. 'Speak English!' I called, 'Tell me!' and he said, 'He say, Stop it!'

They had succeeded in drawing off the Turkish troops from Suvla Bay, but at what a cost for so undeserving a cause! For a reason that has never been clearly understood 'Kitchener's Army' did not advance. They landed to only token opposition, turned inland, and stopped. 'Tommy' Thompson of the R.A.N. Bridging Teams commented that they were so ill-informed they could not find 'the front'. The official history accuses General Sir Ian Hamilton of being unduly secretive but the main denunciation must be of the senility of the commanding officer of the newly landed force who kept the troops immobile, paralysed. 'It was good to see the British land,' Private Klu wrote. 'Only a little shrapnel.' Yet no advantage was taken of this lack of fire, of the flat ground or of the absence of the enemy who was being occupied by the Anzacs. Of the three Mack brothers (all from the 8th Light Horse) who served at Gallipoli, two wrote home letters critical of the campaign. The long, frank and obviously uncensored letter from Lieutenant Ernie Mack to his sister Nell has pertinent comments on the campaign including the Australians' comments on the fighting ability of the English. It was written after he was wounded, on his way to hospital in England.*

'Aug. 6th . . . was expected to be the beginning of the end. On that evening the New Zealanders' Maoris and 500 Gurkahs . . . drove the Turks back while our 4th Brigade, that is the 13–16 battalions moved further out to the left and came in on the Turks diagonally and drove them further back . . . While this movement was being carried out an English Division was secretly landed at Suvla Bay, a small bay about a mile and a half from our left and the idea was that it was to move on over the plain country with the exception of a couple of hills that were known to be only guarded by 100 Turks and swing right around on our left to Anafarta township and then spread out and connect with our flank.

'The A.I.F. and N.Z. did heroic work that night and when morning came they looked for the English who were

* He returned later to Egypt and was killed in the battle of Magdhaba.

supposed to be on their left front . . . the English had landed alright but instead of pushing straight on (they were all landed by 9.30 p.m.) the G.O.C. of the Division had kept the men all night on the beach and did not make a move out till just on five. . . . The enemy scouts had discovered the landing . . . and had immediately brought up . . . troops from Maidos and had strongly fortified the hills on the plain with trenches (and the Turks are wonderful in regard to trench digging) and there they held the English back while the A.I.F. were two miles ahead with their left flank completely at the mercy of the Turks . . .

'Some English regiments that were sent over to reinforce the A.I.F. had no more idea of fighting than kids a year old. Mind you these were not the regular British Tommy but part of Kitchener's army and a bigger collection of dead and dying men you never saw, they have not the pluck of a louse and all their officers think of doing is to ape the regular officer when on parade, but when in action the first thing he does is to lose his head and tell his men to retire.

'It is an absolute fact that the A.I.F. and N.Z's out on the left, though they had been fighting continuously from the 6th, point blank refused to let the English relieve them in the firing line as on two other occasions where they did the Englishmen raced them down to the bottom of the hill as they considered the fire was too hot to hold the trenches. Of course the Australians had to turn round and drive the Turks out of the trenches again . . . losing a lot of men in doing so . . . On the 21st Aug. another move from the left was started. The idea being to work right round from the left across the Peninsular to Maidos. The A.I.F. advanced, took and held all they were told but the English only advanced and in three or four places were driven back again that night. . . .

'It is taken as a recognised fact by everybody of the A.I.F. that there is absolutely nothing left for anyone but to get killed or wounded, though being wounded does not save them for as soon as they recover they are sent back again.

'The A.I.F. are being used as nothing else than gun fodder . . .

'You know you always hear people say that they would like to be in a bayonet charge, but the bayonet charges of previous wars are absolutely child's play to present methods and the person who says he likes them is fit for the asylum. I was talking to a N.Z. Major last night and he has been through four [bayonet charges] each one successful, but during the last one he had a big lump of his skull removed and he says that after the first one he always had a queer feeling when he got out of the trench to another, none of them liked it, it was only duty that made them go.'

Stan was writing to Eva from Egypt, as incensed as was his brother Ernie. 'In my letter last week to Mother I think I said we thought we were going to make a move. Well the lot of Australians did so and from what I can hear so far they have been cut up terribly. . . . I have got nearly all my information from Cliff Pinnock of A troop who is in Luna Hosp. . . . He cannot understand how any of them are still alive . . . They knew they had to charge in the morn, so had all their packs ready to bring back if wounded and each man prepared himself. They had a chain and half to go to reach the Turk trenches and got the order at 4.30 just as day was breaking. A number got killed before they got clear of our trenches and fell back again, others rushed on some running about half way, lying down then rushing on again. In the first charge only two reached the Turks, Roger Palmer and Cameron and the last seen of them was their jumping into the trench.* We'll never see them again . . . Two more lots of men including the 10th Reg. of our 3rd Brigade tried to get across but got mowed down . . . Then Major Todd of the 10th [was] told to tell the men to retire back to our trenches. Those of them not dead came back only then when they got the order. They knew the risk before going out as it was the maddest idea to attempt it and there was not a single shirker. The thing which saved those who lived was a small rise just against the Turks and some of them lay down here but all the time bombs were thrown by Turks at top of the rise and rolled down amongst

---

* Could these be the two who planted the red and yellow flags?

them. . . . Cliff says he never in his life heard such a noise –
machine guns, artillery, bombs, rifles, cheering and battleships down in the bay firing broadside after broadside. He
does not know how he felt, like all the others I have spoken
to. They just had the idea sticking in their minds that they
had to get to the trench in front of them. . . . The worst part
of it was the waiting for the word before they charged – it
got on their nerves. I've seen a lot of our wounded . . . Some
cases I don't like going near are those who have lost their
nerve but they'll get all right soon the nurses say. . . . I was
speaking today to a few of the 15th Batt. (Queenslanders
who have a pretty good reputation) who are wounded in
Luna. They were sent round on our left towards Salt Lake
with the Ghurkas in marching order – sections of four.
Then they turned straight inland. When they got inland
they came on to the Turks. That was the end of the
Ghurkas' rifles. We may have gathered them up since for
them but the Ghurkas still have their knives and from what
the 15th tell me, made good use of them too . . .

'It used to be first rate after we landed with the battleships
down at the sea to look after us. Whenever the Turks
brought up a fresh gun to annoy us one of the ships would
promptly quieten it with a few 12 in. lyddite shells . . . By
jove, they do hit hard . . . You hear the guns go off down in
the sea, then a hurrying rush overhead, next a metallic sort
of roar quite different from any other shell. I soon found out
to keep my mouth wide open and block up ears when shells
land close. The Turks used to give some very disagreeable
shells when I was over there – 11.4 in[ch] ones high
explosive – not many pellets in them fortunately mostly
explosive stuff. They were a great nuisance as they knocked
our trenches and dug-outs about so. They make a most
frightful noise when they hit the ground and explode and
the fumes smell too. You can hear and see them coming
from a good way off and a lot of men saved their lives by
running out of their way but you want to be careful as you
may run into them as their line, though straight is hard to
judge. Getting into a dug-out is no good as you'd get buried.

These shells have deafened as well as blinded a lot of men I hear . . . A few thousand Australians sick and limbs off etc. left for Australia today. I saw them leave but have no inclination myself to return till we are finished with over here.

'It's a little more than a month now since I left Anzac but I'm feeling very fit . . . so will soon rejoin the boys and the quicker the better. . . .'

Lance-Corporal George Garland, a young New South Welshman of the 18th Battalion, wrote of 22 August 1915 that after a 'wild mad charge on the enemy trenches with fixed bayonets – order had been given that rifles were not to be loaded, the job having to be done by bayonets alone – a tornado of fire came from flank and front and the battalion as a fighting force almost ceased to exist, 800 men going down in less than half an hour. A bullet in the head had sent me unconscious and when I came to the things that impressed me were the terrific din, the heat and thirst, and the flies burrowing into my mouth and nose. Then I heard a voice telling me to turn over onto my stomach. Try as I might I could not do it, yet this voice continually suggested that I should "turn over and crawl to me". Eventually it roused my will power and I reached him. It was only a few yards through the undergrowth but my face was scratched and bleeding through rubbing against the earth and brambles. And how the bullets did zipp and whiz and twang as they ricocheted off the ground.

'The Turks had evidently seen me moving amongst the bushes and just to make sure would every now and again let go a few into the scrub. But though he was wounded in the leg this man never left me. As soon as the fire slackened he gave me water and bandaged my head, and immediately started to get me to a place of safety. I had not the power to help myself nor the will to try. I just held on to his boot with both hands and he scrambled along the ground pulling me with him. Every now and then he would have to stop and give me water and let me rest because I was seized by a fit of retching brought on by shock. I must have been a great burden to him apart from his wounded leg but he never left me till he handed me over to the stretcher bearers. I afterwards heard that his name is Pte Tuckwell of the same company as mine but I cannot call him to mind nor have I seen him since.'

Throughout the month the battles continued, with Hill 60 being among the most fearful.

The 18th battalion had gone into battle on 21 August with 1 004 men; at roll call on 29 August 386 men answered their names.

13
Fight I Must

Must you go, need you go?
Is it wrong to say no?
Answered he, with a sigh
Fight I must. It's do or die.

Back home in Australia they were turning out patriotic
songs as fast as hand-knitted arm stump socks and flannel
cholera belts. The writer of the above lines coyly retreated
behind the pen-name of 'Juliet' – but put her photograph on
the sheet music of 'A Soldier's Song'. There were 'Sons of
Australia'; 'He's a Young Australian Soldier'; 'Roll Up!';
Tasmania's own 'Our Boys in Egypt' and a score of other
recruiting and patriotic songs. Customers in music
emporiums were urged to 'try this over on your piano' – an
arrangement entitled 'Heroes of Anzac'.

Hark the cannons' tragic roar
Thundering in Aegean sea
Watch and ward for men of Anzac
Landing at Gallipoli

The fallen heroes now are sleeping
Numbered with immortal brave
Though they fought with matchless courage
All they won was but a grave.

Much of the local product was doggerel set to tumpty-
tump music, but some of the imports were fine and musically
pleasing like the haunting

God send you back to me
Over the mighty sea
Dearest I want you near.
God dwells above you
Knows how I love you
He will bring you back to me.

Every war needs its songs, as much for the folk back home to identify with the endeavour as for the men 'at the front'. The men now left at Anzac after the month of August didn't know there were songs written about their efforts and heard none of them, yet few soldiers have more needed the relief of songs to take their minds off reality. Behind the lines the infantry were singing of the boredom of jam, parodying 'A wee Doch and Doris':

Plum and apple, Apple and plum, Plum and Apple
There is always some
The A.S.C. get strawberry jam and lashings of rum
But we poor blokes in trenches, we get – apple and plum.

But of all the songs they sang none was more loved than this:

There's a long long trail a-winding
Into the land of my dreams
Where the nightingales are singing
And a white moon beams
There's a long long night of waiting
Until my dreams all come true
Till the day when I'll be going
Down that long long trail, with you.

Like Lieutenant G. W. Harris, a Western Australian from the 12th Battalion, they wrote home, 'I wish this blessed old war would end. I think there would be great jubilation among our crowd. The continuous shelling here is apt to get on one's nerves, nothing but the sound of continuous firing of big guns and small arms. Goodbye dear Mum, keep your pecker up. I'll be back to you one of these days and tell Tim he ought to be here as it's exciting at times'.

In a PS. he added, 'Fancy poor old Charley Barnes shot dead two hours after landing and poor Harry Roe has lost his arm'. He too had watched the *Triumph* sink off Anzac. 'It was heart rending. A sight I don't ever want to see again. . . . There's always someone getting hit or killed. It's getting on our nerves horribly.'

Harris had been evacuated twice already, both times with shrapnel in the back. He'd been sent from hospital back to Gallipoli on 7 August only to leave again on 9 August with more shell fragments embedded in him. 'I wish to Heaven the whole thing was over,' he wrote at that time. Then, 'the game's up to mud'. And he ends, 'God bless you dearest Mum and keep you safe always'.

Back again on Gallipoli on 29 September, he again writes to his mother: 'At present I'm suffering from an attack of homesickness to the fullest degree. I think this place would make anyone the same. Wouldn't it be great if I could get home for Christmas. I wouldn't swap places with Lord Kitchener if that came to pass. I dreamt the other night I was out with you all and then I was awakened by a shell bursting near our dug-out.'

He criticises a friend at home who does not enlist. 'If he could see the *young boys* here, I'm certain some of them are not more than 16 and see how they behave themselves under fire, as plucky as the oldest veteran. It makes me feel like crying to see some of the poor kids – they're not more – and the way they stick to it although in some instances it means their life. . . . I don't think you people understand the monotony of it all and how nerve-wracking it is.'

The remarkable thing about the aftermath of the August battles was that the men gave no thought to withdrawal. They stayed, faced the Turks, and slogged it out like two evenly matched boxers in a ring. Weak before the battles of that terrible month they now grew weaker still. Colonel Sir J. Purves-Stewart, examining the non-sick men on Gallipoli in September, men still in the trenches, noted that the contrast between the old and the new troops was striking, and found that 'The newly arrived men were of splendid physique, in the pink of condition, active and alert. The older troops were emaciated in 77% of cases, and nearly all of them showed well-marked pallor of the face; 64% of these men were suffering from indolent ulcers of the skin, chiefly hands and shins; 78% had occasional diarrhoeal attacks, but not enough to put them on the sick list. Most striking of all was the rapidity and feebleness of the heart's action: 74% of the old troops suffered from shortness of breath. The spirit and morale of these soldiers new or old, was excellent. Not one man hinted at the slightest inclination to be relieved from trench duty'. These figures are not of *sick* men but those on active duty. It was suggested that they be given a brief spell on Lemnos Island, 'The ordinary rest camp with the usual games and other amusements is unsuitable. Most of these men are too tired to play football or cricket etc'. A few days on Lemnos enabled them to get an unbroken sleep at nights and freedom from bullets and shrapnel by day but it was only a bandage over a gaping wound. Conditions on the peninsula meant that the relief from unbearable tension afforded to 'weaker vessels' by wine, women and AWL was not available. Nor was there respite from intolerable strain by leave, except for the rare three day 'leave' to Lemnos or Imbros, and neither of the islands could be regarded as 'resorts'. Physically, the men were in a quite terrible condition but with the highly intense and individualistic school of conduct they had built up they ignored, even joked about it.

'We called Apricot jam "Deakins Diarrhoea", stretcher bearer Jim McPhee of the 3rd Division Field Ambulance told me. 'We got plenty of both. Funny, you didn't get despondent. Oh, occasionally you'd wonder where it was all going to end but always someone came up with something. We had some silly sayings. "An Anzac button" was a nail in place of a trouser button. Things like that. The one thing you did get sick of was the flies. They were so thick in the warm weather they'd be floating on the top of the boiling tin of tea, scalded, sealing the top in a mass. But when you look back – shaving with a blade razor in the open with bullets whizzing by. Phew! I don't know how we did that. You know, there were aimed and stray bullets, it was the stray ones that worried us.

'Carrying a stretcher a man saw everything. You knew who the real men were. There was Commander Cater, an Englishman, Beach Master at Anzac, he directed traffic. He had a commanding voice and a megaphone. He'd been on the beach since the beginning. In August, when he fell on Watsons Pier from shrapnel, men ran to him from everywhere. Two of us ran down with a stretcher and carried him to the hospital behind the beach but he died. We felt bad. He'd been such a fearless man.

'Were we stretcher bearers ever afraid? All the time. At one time on Gallipoli so many bearers were killed that carrying during the day was banned.

'There was a similarity about the men we carried on Gallipoli. Every man there was determined to pull his weight. Carrying a man down to the beach he'd crack hardy and imitate the "Chooms", the English. "Gie us a fag, choom," he'd say. Lots of them did this. Then the next thing always was, "Fancy collecting one after all this time". A man who'd only been there a week would marvel at that, because it seemed a lifetime had been spent dodging bullets and running from shrapnel. Then, "I gave them hell before they got me". We'd light a fag up for a man and he'd look at his wound and say, "Fancy collecting one now".

'When we were in the Sari Bair stunt in August we got a patient down to a dressing station and . . . a chap waiting for a limb to be sawn off . . . became so whimsical in the Australian vernacular that his pal, not long off the table, complained, "If he doesn't stow it I'll burst me stitches laughing at the coot". We had a hardened old bearer who'd seen service in India. "Game by God!" he said. "These Wugga Wugga blighters are the gamest a man ever did see." I wrote that down. Bearers brought in men during that stunt with wounds gangrenous and crawling. One man was charred black from a close shell burst.

'And of course there were some "strangely exciting

experiences", like the night march on 6 August across the plain of Suvla with the Ghurka Infantry behind us. "One hundred disasters (piastres) we can beat Chunder if it comes to a run!" We were marching silent, stray bullets falling amongst us, the stretcher bearers picking up the wounded and heading back but otherwise steadily on we went. Instead of the homely fires of the dug-outs along the tiers of the cliffs of Anzac we were marching across a spectral plain with bayonets glistening like a sea of spear grass all around us. Then wildly from close ahead came whoops and cheers and thankfully firing, to warm our blood with excitement. Lead spurted all around, bearers and dressing station staff fell . . . Throughout the night the watercourse we'd brought the stretchers to filled with wounded, who lay there exposed to the cold and bullets and all next day to the hot August sun.

'Now came September – we still got wounded of course – but the dysentery cases were terrible. Men just almost collapsed before they'd give in to leave the trenches.'

Individual acts of cool courage were as evident as the mass rush in attack with war whoops, cheering and 'chiakking'. Sergeant Hugh Gooch, a grazier from Cooke's Plains (SA) was one example of a man acting coolly, knowing intimately how little chance he had of surviving his act. On the twenty-eighth, when most of the battles around the perimeter had settled down to a lower key, he was with fifty-three men of the 9th Light Horse trapped in a communication trench only a few yards from the Turks – as both discovered after dark and immediately began throwing bombs at one another. It was necessary to take information back to the command post as to exactly where the Australians were and what the enemy's position was. Gooch did this once successfully but was killed as he ran across the open ground a second time with a message. This man had had a narrow escape earlier in the month when a large shell burst near him. 'It was a big shock to his nerves,' a friend recalled. 'It left him off colour for a while and like all of us he was run down with work and the food.'* When the battalion got back to Egypt in January 1916 a friend wrote to his parents: 'There are not many left now of the original 9th who have not had sickness or wounds. A mere remnant, but on all sides I hear Hugh spoken of with respect and regret at his death. From one who was fighting at his side on the last day of his life I learnt that the 9th attacked under a heavy fire and but few who left the trenches returned.

'Hugh was shot a few yards from the trench and lay for some hours before he could be brought back. His body was brought in and buried I believe behind Hill 60. The 9th Regiment has been reformed.'

Sister Kitchen's favourites, the 8th Battalion, were decimated, The 'diary' officially ordered to be kept by each battalion bluntly records details:

'31 August: strength of battalion 22 Officers, 683 other ranks. (Number of original battn. left, exclusive of all reinforcements now here, 7 Off. 300 O.R's. Out of this 300 O.R's, 10 have been promoted by commission.) Still away wounded, 8 Off. 376 O.R's = 384. Still away sick, 17 Off. 324 O.R's = 341. Still away missing, 22 O.R's. Grand total killed, wounded, missing and sick: 37 Off. 860 O.R's = 897. Total casualties since coming into trench on 19 July 1915–31 Aug 1915: 7 Off. 485 O.R's = 492'.

The men of the 8th were ill when they went into the trenches for the 'August stunt'. The diary entry for 18 August read, '419 men diarrhoea, 118 with "Barcoo rot" (sores, scabs, skin eruptions, vomiting, nausea, digestive problems). Battalion not physically fit'.

Before the battle of Lone Pine the battalion strength had been 22 officers, 894 other ranks, a total of 916. The number of men who had left Broadmeadows with the battalion in October 1914 was reduced to 12 officers, 472 other ranks, or, 484 men. Of these, 6 officers and 297 other

---

* Hugh Gooch had served in the Boer War in 1900.

ranks were away wounded and 16 officers, 145 other ranks were sick. 'Grand total of casualties since landing, 22 Off. 538 O.R's = 560.' The frontage the battalion protected extended from Courtney's Post on the left to Scott's on the right – over 1 yard per man.

Private Roy Rankin, 21st Battalion, went to Gallipoli with reinforcements, from there to other battlefields and, like many who escaped death on the Peninsula, did not survive France. The collection of his letters commences on 29 April 1915 as he was about to leave Melbourne – four days after the Australians had landed at Gallipoli – and four months later he wrote from Egypt just before they departed for the front, where he hoped 'to be in the fun when the Turks are driven back to Constantinople'.

'We struck tents yesterday, and got our bayonets sharpened. The Australians have made a name for themselves, and the Turks will not face their bayonets; though they will come at the British and French. That is what wounded Australians tell us, though it may be mostly "blow".'

His ship, the *Southland*, was torpedoed out from Alexandria and his next letter tells of his rescue.

'There was a crash and the ship seemed to stop dead. . . . we had been torpedoed. . . . I reached the deck . . . fell in opposite our boat which was left swinging from one davit and was overturned in being lowered. The crews of 2 or 3 boats let the same thing happen. I was one of the first to strike the water and took a neat header with the rest on top of me. It was impossible to reach a boat being hindered by boots, belt, clothes and waves and was drifting away with dozens of others clinging to bits of wreckage until I saw a rope and grabbed it and hauled myself along to an over-crowded, sinking boat. Our concern was to keep our little boat from sinking.

'Presently a streak of smoke was seen on the horizon, and very quickly a ship came into view; she was a hospital ship, and six others soon came after her, and began picking up the scattered boats. Three of them were destroyers, and it was a grand sight to see them streaking, yet sneaking through the water at their top speed. We were taken on a cruiser where the sailors fed us, dried our clothes, and gave us cigarettes. That night we were brought into port and put on board a troopship.'

A week later he is writing from 'my little dug-out in the west' (Gallipoli). 'As we have been under artillery, rifle and machine gun fire we can realise as no one else can what the first Australians did, and put up with . . . It is just before and after sunset that the artillery is in action and shells can be heard whizzing from one hilltop to another. It is a pretty sight to see an aeroplane flying (always at a great height) across a blue sky, when suddenly a puff of white smoke, just like a tuft of cotton wool appears near her and a report is heard a few seconds later. Sometimes a dozen shrapnel shells will be fired at an aeroplane, the puff of smoke making her go off course, but none of them ever hit. Sometimes the aeroplane drops a bomb which explodes with a powerful explosion, but it is very hard for her to hit her mark. . . . Could you send an old book or novel, or any old thing except papers and war news? The *Sydney Mail* is very welcome, but a book in which there is no war news would be even more acceptable . . .'

From the firing line on 12 October he describes front line warfare, including one of the features which illustrates an Australian attitude to the Turks. 'The Turks are great sports and in places where the trenches are only a few yards apart exchange cigarettes for tobacco with the Australians, by throwing them (the cigarettes) across the intervening space. And if the stuff falls short they do not shoot at one another as they reach up for it. At other times they are continually throwing bombs at one another's trenches. There is plenty to talk about in this sort of warfare but it is difficult to put anything in letters without its being censored.

'At night time there is generally no artillery fire at all and machine guns, bombs and rifles do all the talking. It is a pretty sight to see rockets and flares go up when one side fears the other may be going to attack. They are of different colors and light up the whole place as bright as day. The brightest is a white light which would put an arc lamp in the shade. After the rocket is fired the flare is kept in the air by means of a little parachute which slowly descends and drifts away on the breeze carrying the flare with it.

'We get news here in the form of telegrams, copies of which are posted up in the trenches. According to a telegram received yesterday the Germans are beginning to have a very bad time of it, we are all looking forward to a quick ending of the war. I have just received a couple of boshter pairs of socks from Aunt Alice. They are just what I wanted as the issued socks need washing and it is impossible to get water for that. [He later wrote his mother remarking that her advice to him in case of *cold feet* to put on two pairs of socks was 'what the boys over here say about young men who won't enlist'.]

Food interests him constantly. When on water picket, guarding tanks behind the firing line for a week, he is delighted. 'We draw our rations raw and cook them ourselves so we can have roast meat instead of boiled and make ourselves dough cakes, etc. This climate gives one a powerful appetite, and as long as we are well fed we are happy. We have been ten weeks in the trenches now, and naturally are tired of the food supplied us and long for better tucker.

'It would amuse you to see us cooking for ourselves whenever we get the materials. All we need are flour and fat and onions and we can cook anything from pancakes to grisoles. The grisoles are the best and are made by mixing bully-beef with minced onion and mixed with flour or bread crumbs, and then fried. Fat is the hardest thing to get as there is such a demand for it. We get plenty of jam to put on our pancakes and dough cakes, but bread is not too plentiful.

'If all else fails we can always make porridge out of ground up biscuits, and fried biscuits are very good, though they require a lot of soaking first. So that you can see the only thing we have to occupy our minds is the question of tucker.

'I have only seen one Turk since I've been here (except prisoners) but was not quick enough to get a shot at him. It is very seldom Abdullah shows himself and all we have to shoot at are periscopes. Needless to say we do not show ourselves, either.

'A chap is like a rabbit here, always digging himself holes called dug-outs to sleep in, and it is not hard to make oneself very comfortable in the coldest weather. A hole dug in the side of a trench makes a very snug nest if one has plenty of blankets and a water-proof sheet over the mouth to keep out the rain and the cold. But that is not the only reason we are like rabbits. We sometimes have to work down tunnels and saps, and my work for the last few days has been carrying sandbags out of them. Need to be a mule or mountaineer carrying stores up these hills.'

Ronald Smith of Tasmania, who wrote about the excitement in Melbourne when war was declared, was one of the older men to enlist, being thirty-four when he sailed off to war. He had belonged to the militia for many years and had been active in his local rifle club. By July 1915 Smith was a Captain in the 26th Battalion and writing pages of instructions from Egypt to his wife Kitty on how to manage the farm and business in his absence.

Captain Smith was soon to see Shrapnel Gully, and in October he wrote from Gallipoli: 'So Jim Kelly is going after all. A defective right eye ought not to block a man because plenty here fire from the left shoulder using the left eye. I am quite well and eating with a good appetite but sickness is prevalent here, mainly diarrhoea . . . I wish Roland Leas were with me. No one cares for exploring here but myself. I wish you would tell him. I expect the seeds are coming up nicely now. I'd like to see them.'

The chance meetings miles from home happened all the time, even on Gallipoli. '15 September, Mr Ron Smith, Dear Sir, just a note hoping to find you quite well. No doubt you will be surprised to hear from me. I am from Forth and will try to get around shortly. Yours sincerely, Dale Elliott, A.Co. 12th Battn.'

Life went on. The letters chronicle it all. Smith's 'own

darling Kittiwake' gives birth to a son. 'You poor dear darling. How I wish I'd been with you. What will you call him? The bullets are coming over thick and fast now. It is 6 a.m. and dark and I am writing this with the light of a candle. The Billardia I suppose is quite big by now. I hope it flowers, but I suppose what grew this year will flower next.'

Then on 10 December Kitty receives a telegram: 'Regret reported Captain Ronald Edgar Smith disembarked Malta from Hospital ship Karaparo December fourth wounded will promptly advise if anything further received. Base Records.' It is quickly followed by another: 'Bullet shoulder. Not Serious. Walking About. Ronald Smith Naval Hospital Malta.'

The wound took a long time to heal, and he was troubled with recurring weakness and collapse as well. He was so weak on 20 February 1916 that when he saw his wife's handwriting on an envelope he was so overcome he had to go to his room and lie down. On 26 March he was invalided home. (By 1917 he was on his way back again, this time to France.)

Sergeant Harry Kahn (WA) was another 'Fair Dinkum'. Like most men who went to the peninsula he was observant of the little things, 'We started off with flannel cholera belts with sundry tapes to fasten them round your waist. They were all made to fit portly gentlemen and I was fine. None of us would wear them. They ended up as strips of cloth to clean our rifles. I don't know how it was supposed to prevent cholera. But many medical things were essentially Victorian in outlook and intent, i.e. when we arrived in Egypt we were under the command of the British and it was forbidden under Imperial regulations to shave the upper lip. Perhaps it lent an appearance of ferociousness or maturity on our childish faces but anyway that was soon forgotten and we were allowed to shave. I didn't grow a moustache because at that age I couldn't grow sufficient whiskers to cover my lip. "The Australian Eleven" it was called on us young fellows – 11 hairs growing on our upper lip.

'The improvisation was a wonderful thing at Gallipoli. Ingenious. When the long, drawn-out hates went on after August they made draught boards by scratching the squares on an old bit of trench timbering with a nail.* They made stew ladles from damaged water bottles, a grater from an empty milk tin with holes punched in by nail. This was for grating hard army biscuits up for porridge.'

During this period the New Zealand artist Sapper Moore Jones went up in a balloon to do a series of water colors. From his eyrie he could see the lines of trenches; he saw the 'bivvies' on the safer slopes which men called home, where they could have their own little cooking fires, sleep almost in safety and dream of anything but the throbbing crackling machine gun that spoke of death by day and night from the vantage point of the higher ground. He saw the tracks that had been cut around the slopes and the snake-like lines where men toiled upwards with water and rations, and food for the guns. He saw the stretchers coming down the tracks with their burden of pain and broken youth and maybe, in sheltered hollows, he saw groups of men shrouding a comrade in his blanket and laying him in a shallow grave. Hung in mid-air he saw all and he painted it 'with his heart's blood' as a friend wrote of his series done of the Peninsula. His balloon was anchored to a warship out with the fleet on the Aegean enabling him to view the land and the men, and these are the things he painted. Incidentally, this was the artist who painted 'Simpson'. 'I don't think much of it as a painting,' he later said. His balloon was a break in the monotony for the diggers. They stared at it by day, as by night they gazed with fascination at the hospital ships lit up with green and white lights and with a large red cross.

Sergeant E. R. 'Bill' Richards of Bendigo (Vic.), whose family were miners, joined the Engineers and in his letters home he tells of the new kind of warfare that followed the August hand-to-hand fighting. 'At present we are in the trenches having a lively time – underground warfare – we

* There is one of these boards in the War Museum, Canberra.

generally see a mine or two go up with Turks etc. We have been very careful for they have only caught one of our trenches as yet. We generally counter-mine and catch their drives or saps as they are called. You would not have thought I would have turned out a miner.' As an after-thought he writes, 'Coming to look back over the ridges and hills I cannot understand ever being allowed to take this position. I have managed to escape so far. I expect I am very lucky as the odds are about ten to one against'.

As Bill Richards said, the fighting was now mainly confined to mine tunnels. The Turks were mining and so were the Australians. On one occasion the Australians cut across a Turkish tunnel and watched the legs of Turks passing the entrance.

John Buchan at this time was writing that 'men returned to the habits of their first parents. The Australians and New Zealanders especially showed a noble disregard of apparel. In mid-summer, heat burned to a dull brick red. Coats, shirts, boots and puttees disappeared in succession, then trousers shrank to shorts, as they toiled . . . till the hour of relief came and they could wash in the shrapnel-dotted Aegean'.

The Egyptian newspapers reported the state of dress of the Australians in the heat of a Turkish summer. 'Not since the pre-historic stone ages has such a naked army been seen in civilised warfare as the Australian army corps fighting on the Gallipoli Peninsula. They display an utter abhorrence for superfluous clothing. They are famous throughout Europe for their hard-fighting, hard swearing and nakedness, even to a sense of indecency.'

This provoked Signaller Tom Skeyhill to write 'The Naked Army':

We ain't no picture postcards,
Nor studies in black and white;
We don't doll up in evening clothes,
When we go out to fight.

We've forgotten all our manners,
And our talk is full of slang,
For you ain't got time for grammar
When you 'ear the rifles bang.

The 'eat an' the vermin 'ad drove us nearly balmy,
So we peeled off all our clobber, and we're called 'The
 Naked Army'.

In London they were singing a song to the tune of 'Pretty
Red Wing':

Now the moon shines tonight on Charlie Chaplin
His boots are cracklin' for the want of blacknin',
And his khaki trousers they need mendin',
Before we send 'im to the Dardanelles.

Men – boys sometimes – were still writing to Australia
to relatives of men killed, wounded or missing. Sergeant
Jim McDonald, whom Carl Janssen had been so happy to
have in his company at Broadmeadows only one year
before, was writing to Carl and Ernek's sister Beatrice.
 'Poor Carl of course fell but a few yards away from me. I
don't know whether he was hit in the boat or not but I
clearly remember the shell that did the damage. Two of our
sergeants and Lieut. Adams and a few privates of our
company are with me and they say that there is no doubt
but that poor Ernek was killed at Cape Helles. You can
understand that it is very difficult for me to write thus to
you. How he met his death I don't know. In Carl's case, the
same shrapnel shell which caused his and others' deaths
burst just as the platoon which I belonged to moved off.
Had we remained one minute longer a good many of us
would have fared the same. Poor old Carl was shot through
the lower part of the neck and was propped up against a
rock at the foot of the cliff . . . we had to move off and I
never saw him again.'
 Ernek had taken part in that dash down at Cape Helles
of which the official history records: '. . . heads down, as if

into fierce rain, some men holding shovels before their faces like umbrellas in a rain storm. The firing was by then intense, spurts of dust rising from the plain like drops splashing in a thundershower. Their swift advance was the spectacle of the battle-field. Men fell constantly until the lines were so thin that the front was too weak to push further . . . the Brigade [2nd] already reduced at Anzac to 2 900 men lost in one short hour another 1 000'.

Carl had been seen to die and to be buried but Ernek was 'missing'. His parents wrote to every agency possible begging for news but none came.

Reg Mills, who had left his job as Manager of Swifts Creek Butter Factory in Gippsland (Vic.), wrote 'It will be a great blessing when the war is finished. It is only when one is here that he can realise to the full extent what war really is. . . . It is hard to get rest for the lice and fleas. I'd heard of them before but never realised what it meant. They are something awful here in this trench. They get into the woollen underwear. I don't know what I look like, something like one of those wild pigs. I broke one of my front teeth off eating a bit of bacon with a bone in it. I manage to get a look at my face and whiskers in the mirror of the periscope rifles in the trenches'.

Later, on 22 November, he wrote from hospital in Egypt that he had been hit by shrapnel on 29 October. 'I got so awfully sick through being bad for a fortnight before with diarrhoea. I got septic cellulitis and it was very painful, the leg terribly swollen up because the stuff would not come away. I straightened my leg for the first time today and hope to be able to get up in a week now. There are 50 in this ward, mostly serious wounds and I can tell you some of them are frightful. I am very satisfied with mine when I see some of the other fellows. I have the piece of shell that hit me. It is ¼ lb. weight.

[Later, after nine weeks in bed,] 'It gets very tiresome lying in bed so long. I feel now that I will not be able to go through a second spasm of what I have just gone through, of course if I have to go to the front again I will willingly go but I am not one of those heroes *dying to go back to the front again.* "*Once bitten twice shy*" with me, and I am certain anyone who has once been to Gallipoli if he speaks with his heart he doesn't want a second go. I have not received any of the parcels you have sent me as they would go to Gallipoli and only letters are sent on from there. As long as some of the poor fellows in the trenches get them I am quite satisfied as I know their circumstances and do not begrudge them anything.'

Lieutenant C. R. Morley, a storekeeper from Tweed Heads (NSW) was with the 5th Light Horse when they dismounted.

'*13 May 1915*: Last letter from here as we're off to the Dardanelles tomorrow. We are to go as infantry as they wouldn't take us with our horses. Pretty rotten isn't it to carry a pack after all this time. We have handed in our spurs and saddles. Everyone is having great fun here trying on putties and wondering what their legs look like. I look a real dag. Big feet and thin legs. Some wounded infantry said to a nurse when they heard we were going over as infantry, "*Now* they won't have spurs and leggings".

'*29 May 1915*: Gallipoli. This is a funny place. It must be the only place in the world where you can't spend money. I will always take my hat off to the infantry who took this place. I reckon it was one of the most brilliant feats in history.

'*14 November 1915*: Tigne Military Hospital Malta. I was brought off in hospital ship on a stretcher. My word I was sorry to leave. One hates the life but . . . This is a Tommy place. Military everywhere. It gets on a fellow's nerves. Everywhere notices stuck up and you can't do this and you can't do that.' Lieutenant Morley survived until 8 October 1917 when he was killed during a mounted Light Horse charge near Gaza.

The hospital ships still lay in the Aegean taking on cases, but these were now medical rather than wounds. Sister Kitchen was still on the *Gascon* shuttling back and forth from Anzac to base hospitals.

On 25 August they took about 200 medical patients to Mudros and the following day she complains, '. . . moved up to the inner harbour in the morning, up against the *Camdor Castle* which has been a troopship and is to take our patients on to England or elsewhere. Eleven sisters have been sent on board and all the beds are on the floor. No stores or dressings. In the afternoon our walking cases went on to the shore and after dinner the rest were sent on board the *Camdor Castle*. A nice officer has promised to send us over from Cape Helles some cartridge [sic] cases to make hot water jugs, gongs, etc. Rain today: a very rare event since we landed in Egypt.

'*August 27th*: . . . Left in the afternoon for Imbros to do "Fleet Sweeper" work and bring away some of the lighter medical cases. Got there outside the boom about 9 p.m. *August 28th*: Took on a good many during the night. During the day the anchor . . . let go and taken up 6 times while we took on cases from various barges and beaches . . . in all 940 cases, thick everywhere on the floors and hatches till there isn't a speck of room anywhere. Fortunately they are nearly all minor . . . some bad dysentery cases among them. "Gallipoli Gallop" some wag called it. We left Imbros this morning and got to Mudros Bay about 11 a.m. . . . Every place seems to be full. *August 30th*: The usual rushing day with meals and drinks. Early this morning we came up to the inner harbour and lined up against a transport which had been a German prize, and it took on 230 of our patients. We also sent off the Indians and 10 Turkish sick prisoners. It all relieved the strain on the ship's resources and food; of which we have only 6 days supply left. We were at last able to clean up the ward a bit and get the kits from under the beds. (Left Lemnos about 11.45 for Alexandria.) *September 1st*: (Wattle Day at home!) Got to Alexandria at 4 p.m. . . . letters from home . . . Fearfully hot tonight. We are to take back to Mudros 8 Sisters for the *Stonus* as they are afraid the boat may be torpedoed: and need the sisters when they get there. *September 4th*: Went ashore at Ports and Lights and drove to see 8th, and then after hearing some of the news, Samsing and I went to Groppi's for tea and found boat was to sail at 5 p.m. so got an arabeyah and picked up the Matron and tore back . . . all the wards have been sulphured to make them a bit sweeter . . . *September 9th*: Started taking on early and kept it up all day. Mostly medical cases. (p.m. 2.30) Capt. Jackson and (now) "Major" Ebeling arrived on the scene and we were very pleased to see them. After waiting so long for a visit, we had given up all hope. E. looks pale and thinner after 8 weeks in the trenches. . . . We spent all our spare moments talking to them, as Samsing says – "We can see the patients any time!" They had dinner on the boat and left about 9 p.m. It was a great pleasure to see them after so many months.'

Roland Mills, sick and weak from exposure, poor food and exhaustion, was rested for a few days on Lemnos. 'You mention in your letter about the long lists of cases of illness published in the *Herald*. Is it any wonder the boys being crook after 5 months of fighting and being fed mostly on those hard biscuits and bacon. They have not been treated at all fairly. They ought to have been relieved months before they were. During the Suvla Bay landing one of the tommies told me that in France the troops were treated far better than the poor old Australians. He had been in the trenches there and said they had only 4 days in and 4 days out. While they were out of the trenches they were not under shell fire and were able to go to places of amusement but on Gallipoli one is never out of range of the Turkish artillery. Of course no-one expected theatres or anything like that but there is no doubt that had they been relieved sooner there would not have been so much sickness. Now that we have had a bit of a spell everyone is looking fit and well again.'

On arriving back at Gallipoli the following week he swiftly wrote again to his brother. 'We are now back again on the Peninsula and my word it is colder than when we left. I think we are in for a pretty rough time. The weather is now enough to freeze you, so what will it be like at Xmas? We have copped onto a bonzer dug-out, just the pong. As soon as you get this letter I would like you to send me something to get rid of the lice. They are getting unbearable. When I was here before I used to get about with only a pair of shorts on and boots and socks and used to have a swim every day and they had little chance to trouble me. I suppose you think I am not clean having lice on me but everyone is the same, officers and all.

'Arnie Shaw was telling me the other day that 16 fellows enlisted with him and now there are only 3 of them left. The others have either been killed or wounded. . . . I think the people in Australia realise the seriousness of this war and are urging on recruiting and not in vain, 1 000 a day in one city (Melbourne) is not bad going.' (Roland, of the 1st Division signal company, was nineteen, not to be confused with 'Reg' Mills, another Victorian.)

By December he was explaining to his mother, 'Perhaps you don't quite understand what to send. What I want is a few tins of "Keatings Powder" or something in that line. . . . No doubt you got a bit of a surprise to hear I was lousy but it's a fact. You ought to see us having a louse as we call it. Going through our underclothes looking for them. . . . The first time I saw a chap having a louse I couldn't get over it. He looked such a character with his head down to it going through all the folds and corners of his shirt. I often think it wouldn't be a bad idea for George to send a drawing to the Bully with a joke about a soldier at the front lousing himself. . . .

'Here behind the trenches we ought to be safe but we get most of the bombs that "Joe Bourke" slings over. They are mostly what we call Broomstick Bombs. Great big beggars with long sticks attached just like a broom. They are evidently fired out of a trench mortar and the stick is used to make them fall in a particular way. A chap in our section was hit on the legs and had his face cut about by one of these bombs falling outside his dug-out the other night. We don't expect to see him for some time. I'm quite content to let half a dozen bombs burst outside my dug-out. It's a bonzer. We've tunnelled in about six feet under the ground from our old dug-out with the waterproof sheet for covering so you see we have a two-roomed dug-out now, one for sleeping, the other as a reception room or dining room. Of course the main idea of tunnelling in was to make sure of keeping dry if we got a heavy downpour of rain and the waterproofs fail us.

'Sis says in her last letter Cliffie Middleton is disappointed that they won't allow him back at the front. Don't take too much notice of this talk. Once a chap gets away from this place he's not too anxious to get back again. . . . There is a lot of talk going about that Andy Fisher is endeavouring to get the 1st Division back to Australia for a spell after we spend the winter here. I don't think it would be too much to expect . . . The Tommies in France have a few days in the trenches, then a few days out of range of the guns. Our boys here say there is more danger out of the trenches here and I am of the same opinion.'

Alan Campbell, 2nd Light Horse, wrote after revisiting Gallipoli in 1963, 'Peculiar feelings arose when I got to pondering the many human skulls and larger bones lying around exposed to the elements. I cannot describe these feelings'.

Enlistment was accelerated fantastically by news of the Landing at Gallipoli. From August to December 1914 there had been 52 561 enlistments. The peak at July 1915 was never again reached, or indeed challenged during the years that followed. In 1915 the figures were as follows:

January	10 225
February	8 370
March	8 913
April	6 250
May	10 526
June	12 505
July	36 575
August	25 714
September	16 571
October	9 914
November	11 230
December	9 119

Keith Murdoch (later Sir Keith, the press 'tycoon') visited Gallipoli as an Australian press correspondent during this time. Although his reporting on Gallipoli did not have the impact of the American, Ashmead-Bartlett, his trenchant criticism of the British command on the peninsula was a part of the pressure that caused the British Government to recall Hamilton and replace him with General Sir Charles Monro. On his arrival Monro was quickly aware that 'Apart from the Australian and New Zealand Corps' no other troops on the peninsula were equal to a sustained effort and he recommended withdrawal.

14
The Face of
a Hero

There had to be a hero. The people demand one. Wholesale slaughter, wholesale bravery are too immense for the puny human imagination to grasp; they overwhelm and depress the collective mind. So there was a hero. But this one was different, this was a man as redolent as a gum tree, as Australian as a kangaroo, a real colonial spirit. He had scarcely begun his task when he was killed, and with the slower communications of the time he was dead before Australia knew he was alive. But they were sure that they knew what a hero looked like.

Boozers and brawlers and ships' deserters and blokes who hump their blueys don't get statues, don't get painted; neither do cane cutters, miners or those toughest, roughest of all men, the ships' firemen, shovelling coal with a bullocky's tongue following the 'banjo' into the furnace down in the tomb below decks where the temperature could and did go to 135 degrees Fahrenheit. And who has seen a statue to a larrikin?

No larrikin could fit the traditional mould that has been cast for heroes since time immemorial, that mould of a man of noble countenance, erect, far-seeing, serene, quiet spoken, gazing into a distance beyond the sight of other men and brave beyond the courage of mortal man.

The aesthetically beautiful statue of the Man with the Donkey at Melbourne's Shrine of Remembrance, and the famous painting of John Simpson Kirkpatrick are of that man, the traditional hero of the public mind. That 'Simpson' was all the things we believed made up a 'dinky-di digger' was ignored, and school children since before Anzac was evacuated were taught to revere him as 'a hero' in the fictional mould.

That, perhaps, is one of the great tragedies of that war of tragedies, for 'Jack Simpson' was a *real* man, and when he died real men wept in the sight of others. He had flouted the rules and 'never heard' of the regulations. In camp before he left Australia, in Egypt, and at last on Gallipoli, he was a man to have beside you when the whips were cracking. In the back streets of Cairo when there was a stoush on and the call went out 'Aussie Here!' he answered and was as nippy with his knuckles as the next man.

He was an Englishman with all the qualities of the legendary Australian, and a pride in the country few could exceed. 'You will find out where I am when the Australians make a start,' he wrote to his mother when he left Egypt. (And she had written back, not knowing he was already dead, 'You said I'd know when the Australians made a start . . . well, the Australians have done gloriously, they have made England ring with their bravery.')

He had left his home at South Shields County Durham on 14 October 1909, three months after his seventeenth birthday. 'Now mother,' he wrote, telling her of his work at sea as third fireman and steward to the engineers, 'I do hope you are keeping your pecker up and not worrying about me for there is no call. I eat enough for two horses at meals but I am always "ungry". I am getting an appetite like a horse but there is plenty of grub.' His mother, a widow, had his favourite sister, Annie, at home with her. 'You'll catch it orlright from me if you don't do your school-work,' he told Annie. He was heading for 'Sidney' he thought, but as the ship was 'a proper wreck and the fore-castle has been flooded all the time and everything floating about and in the bunkers are very nearly up to our knees in water and nearly everybody is about full up with her already. Everybody will be clearing out at Sidney as she is a rotten packet altogether'.

From London in December 1909 he wrote that he hoped

to be home for Christmas: 'Mind mother I like poultry now. At first the engineers wolfed it all but mind they didn't after that I watched them. For I had my wack shoved in the cupboard before I told them dinner was ready.'

By April 1910 he was on the way back to Australia on SS *Yeddo*. 'I hope we are going to Newcastle for if we are I am going to go to the pits [the coal mines].' He jumped ship on 13 May and carried his swag to Northern Queensland, eventually reaching the mines. '. . . Am sending you a postal order for a quid. I start work at the pit on Monday night but I have to work for 3 weeks before I am paid so it will be three weeks before I can send you any more money . . .' Always he wrote of sending money home. 'Only sent 15/- as only had 7 shifts this fortnight and after paying two quid board and paying for my fags I am about cleaned out. I will send you 7/6 for the New Year licence for Lilly [his Yorkshire terrier he'd left with his mother]. I have such a nice dog out here, a cattle dog, such a pretty dog he is and the licence here is only 2/6 per year.'

He always called a spade a spade. His mother tells him she has given two lodgers their marching orders. Of 'Antonio' being told to 'git', he writes, 'I wish I had been home. I would have made that Russian Jew bugger dance a hornpipe on his ars'.

Then he is off again as Second Stevedore on coasters shuttling back and forth from Fremantle to Adelaide, Melbourne, Sydney and Rockhampton 'in the stokehole'.

Time and again, almost every letter, he adds, 'I'm sending you a couple of quid'.

He enjoyed a good punch-up. At sea on the SS *Koringal* on Christmas Day 1912 they dined 'on goose and plum pudding [then] we drank each others health quite a number of times until each man thought he was Jack Johnston, champion of the world, when my mate suggested going over and having a fight with the sailors. . . . things went pretty lively for the next half hour. You couldn't see anything for blood and snots flying about until the mates and engineers came along and threatened to log all hands forward. We all had trophies of the fray. Someone bunged one of my eyes right up and by the look of my beak I think someone must have jumped on it by mistake when I was on the floor but as they say, all's well that ends well.'

On arrival in 'Sidney' he wrote to his mother, who was worried about his humping his bluey, 'Now mother, keep your heart up. . . . what are you making such a song and dance about those so-called hardships. There are no hardships about it at all. It is just about the best life that a fellow could wish for "carrying his swag", or "humping his bluey" as the colonials call it, going all over the country with your belongings strapped on your back, that is your blankets and a change of underclothing "if you have got any" and a billy can. Now mother you would think we would be like the tramps in the old country but what a mistake. The best of respectable men with a house of his own when he gets out of work just packs his swag and off he goes to where he heres the work is on'.

But, 'I wish I were at canny old Shields for Christmas. This place is so quiet I can feel my whiskers turning grey.'

He was stoking in temperatures that melted the weight off him. 'It is 135° in the stokehold and it is heavy enough to fire without towing this great big hulk we have in tow from Melbourne to Fremantle. . . . [Later] I've got very white and thin now I'm a greaser. Don't eat like a horse as I did when firing. I look more like a corps than anything else and if the exchecker will hold out I will leave and go up the bush for a while as I am sick of the sea.' By 1913, 'dead broke and looking properly consumptive', he hopes he will soon feel strong enough to start firing again 'for a man don't want to be feeling weak firing on this coast now that summer is coming'.

He joined up as soon as war broke out, jumping ship at Fremantle and enlisting in Perth because he wanted to get back to England and was sure that the first convoy was going there. Later, the army medical historian, Colonel A. G. Butler, was to write: 'A stretcher bearer of quiet disposition enlisted as "Simpson".' Of such statements are legends made.

'*13 September 1914*: Blackboy Camp W.A. We are expecting to get orders to leave at any minute for the old country. I left you 4/- a day out of my pay. We only have 5/- a day and 1/- deferred pay. So you take 2/- a day for yourself and put 2/- per day in the bank for me when I come home from the war. I will be having a good holiday. *14 October 1914*: AAMC. I am in the Australian Medical Core. My address when I get to England will be:

Pte Jack Simpson 202
C Section, 3 Field Ambulance
A.A. Med. Core,
1st Aust. Contingent, England.

I think we are going to Aldershot.' (For reasons of his own he was now known as Simpson, not Kirkpatrick.)

On Christmas Day 1914, he wrote from Egypt: 'I would not have joined this Contingent if I had known they were not going to England. I would have taken the first ship home and had a holiday at home and then joined the army at home and went to the front instead of being stuck in this Godforsaken place.' In a letter dated 3 January 1915 he says, 'I see in this mornings paper that Australia is going to send 100 000 more men. I am not surprised for men were simply going mad out there to go to the war. There was many a man envied us 1st Contingent for being so lucky as to get off to the war.'

When a man was killed or died at war, his personal effects were sent back to base and from there to his next-of-kin. Among Jack's effects were the letters that arrived after his death, including two from Annie. Jack had written to his mother two days before the Landing, and her reply to this letter was starkly marked on the envelope for return to sender with the one word, '*Killed*'.

'You said in your letter that I would find out where you were when the Australians made a start. Well my son, the Australians have done gloriously – they have made England ring with their bravery. Mr Asquith said in The House of Commons that the Australians had fought like heroes and that they had surpassed themselves in the annals of British warfare with their bravery. The Red Cross, he said that they worked like heroes to save and rescue the wounded.

'Jack my son, my heart is fairly bursting with sorrow and with pride to think that you are amongst such a lot of brave men – but mind they have paid dearly for their bravery. I saw the Australian list of casualties this morning and I am sorry to say that it's very heavy. I see that the 3rd Field Ambulance has got some wounded but thank God that your number was not there. . . .

'My dear son I wrote to you last week – you said that you hadn't had a letter from me for a month, but Jack my dear lad I didn't know where to write to you for you wrote and told me that you were leaving Egypt and you were coming either to France or England. I didn't know where to write to but I wrote you last week on speck and I addressed it to The Dardanelles, so that I hope you have got my letter. . . .'

On 3 September his mother wrote him for the last time. She had had no word from Gallipoli. 'Now my dearest lad I wonder if this war will keep me from seeing you again. I hope not. Now my dear son I will have to stop for I am broken hearted. I cannot settle. I am worried to death and I can't help it. Goodnight and God bless you. XXXX and take care of yourself and write soon for I *feel crazy*.' Jack was the last of her sons, the other three having died in childhood. This letter crossed another addressed to Miss A. Kirkpatrick, dated 2 September 1915 from Captain Fay of the 3rd Field Ambulance and postmarked from Gallipoli. 'I was extremely sorry to hear that you had not had word from us about your brother. Colonel Sutton, then commanding the Ambulance wrote very shortly after the occurrence. [Enemy shipping was then most successful and lists were constantly being made of dates when any mail sent would have been lost at sea.] Your brother landed with us from the torpedo boat at daylight on 25 April so taking part in the historic landing. He did excellent work during the day. He discovered a donkey in a deserted hut, took possession and worked up and down the dangerous valley [Shrapnel Valley] carrying wounded men to the beach on the donkey. This plan was a very great success so he continued day by day from morning to night and became one of the best known men in the division. Everyone from the General down seems to have known him and his donkey which he christened Murphy. The valley at the time was very dangerous as it was exposed to snipers and also was continuously shelled. He scorned the danger and always kept going, whistling and singing, a universal favourite. So he worked for three weeks. On the night of 18 May as you will have read in the papers, the Turks made a heavy attack on our position. Early in the morning as usual your brother was at work, when a machine gun played on the track where he was passing. The days of his almost miraculous escapes were past, for he fell on the spot, shot through the heart. He truly died doing his duty. We buried him that night on a little hill near the sea-shore known as Queensland Point, Chaplain Green, reading the service. The work your brother did was so exceptionally good that his name was mentioned in the orders of the day. He gave his life in the performance of a gallant and cheerful service that has been excelled by none.'

Later again, there was a letter from a soldier whom Jack had brought down to the beach on the donkey. This man, Corporal A. C. Towers, was in hospital in England when he sent the letter and a poem he had written. 'Beneath the cliffs of Sari Bair, Lion Hearted "Anzac Murphy" lies, The bravest of them all.'

The Official War Historian, C. E. W. Bean, said: 'On the night of April 25th he annexed a donkey, and each day, and half of every night, he worked continuously between the head of Monash Valley and the beach, his donkey carrying a brassard round its forehead and a wounded man on its back. Simpson escaped death so many times that he was completely fatalistic; the deadly sniping down the valley and the most furious shrapnel fire never stopped him. The colonel of his ambulance, recognising the value of his work, allowed him to carry on as a completely separate unit. He camped with his donkey at the Indian mule camp, and had only to report once a day at the field ambulance. Presently he annexed a second donkey. On May 19th he went up the valley past the water-guard, where he generally had his breakfast, but it was not ready. "Never mind," he called. "Get me a good dinner when I come back."

'He never came back. With two patients he was coming down the creek-bed, when he was hit through the heart, both the wounded men being wounded again. He had carried many scores of men down the valley, and had saved many lives at the cost of his own.'

Colonel (later General Sir) John Monash, at that time Commanding Officer of the 4th Brigade, in a letter dated 20 May 1915 to H.Q. New Zealand and Australian Division, wrote: 'I desire to bring under special notice for favour of transmission to the proper authority, the case of Private Simpson, stated to belong to "C" Section, 3rd Field Ambulance. This man has been working in this valley since 26 April, in collecting the wounded, and carrying them to the dressings stations. He had a small donkey which he used to carry all cases unable to walk. . . .

'Simpson and his donkey were yesterday killed by shrapnel shell and inquiry then elicited that he belonged to none of the A.A.M.C. units with this brigade, but had become separated from his own unit, and had carried on his perilous work on his own initiative.'*

The story of Simpson is, to a large extent, the story of all stretcher bearers. Unsustained by the hot-blooded heroism exhibited by men in violent action, unable to retaliate, with only the often meagre protection afforded by a red cross flag, these men calmly exposed their lives to danger to save their comrades and so built up the tradition of selflessness and cool courage that is a feature of their service.

* No award was made to Simpson as *one single act* of valour was
  what the citations called for.

15
T.P. (The Padre)

This man was different from others of his kind. You sense it in his letters, his diary and the photographs that showed him weary, thinner, concerned for his flock. I never met him, but I did know his son Bill for twenty-four hours on our only meeting before he died in 1975. A Church of England minister like his father before him, Bill spoke of his father in a free, fierce, unyielding way that helped me know him, understand his sensitivity, toughness and sympathy for the men thrown into the pit of war. The cryptic notes in the diary I did not attempt to decipher – unadorned, they are witness to his ability to gain the confidence of the men: in this way he heard, saw and experienced much of their life on board ship, in Egypt, on Gallipoli and on Lemnos when it was all over. His observations are perhaps the most pertinent records of the way the men spoke, played, joked and died. Bill told me his father was a popular public speaker and the 'key-word' type of entry was probably meant to be material for future talks. Neither have I commented on his tender letters to his wife, themselves unique in that age when many men wrote to their wives as though to a chance acquaintance. But I did see photographs of her – a pretty, round, merry-faced girl with a strand of hair escaping and tumbling round her laughing eyes.

Padre T. P. Bennett went over with the 22nd Battalion in May 1915 on *Ulysses*. Unlike the first convoy, they had a rough trip.

'*11 May 1915*: one of the men who had been acting as

Good Samaritan to one of his seasick comrades told me, "I was holding his head on my shoulder and trying to make the beggar comfortable and what do you think he said to me? 'Oh damn it all. Let me head drop on the deck.'" Poor beggar. Such a lot feel very bad.'

He stayed with the 22nd throughout his year's service and on Gallipoli buried boys that he mentions in his diary as having played cards with or laughed at in the deck sports on board *Ulysses*. He brought a little portable organ along with him and used to have sing songs on the deck. They sang:

It's a long way to go to Melbourne,
It's a long way to go.
It's a long way to go to Melbourne,
To the Australian girl I know.
Goodbye Yarra Yarra and the girls we left behind,
It's a long long way to go to Melbourne,
Tho we don't come home till after Xmas you can bet we
    don't mind.

He was president of the Sports and Amusements committee, and wrote in the news-sheet called *The Odyssey* (as on the *Ulysses*!): 'Programme next Saturday: Spar and Bolster; sling the monkey; Potato and Sack Race; Blindfold Boxing and the First Stage of the Boxing Championships.'

On the same day as he organised all this he wrote to his wife: 'How strange that in a population of 2 500 people there should not be a single woman in this floating town known as Transport 38A. All the same, I wish I had my dear old girl with me'. And next day his diary entry reads: 'Buried Private David Madigan at sea. Must have come on board ill, determined to get to the war for after fleet sailed he very ill with measles and bronchitis. Convoy stopped. Engines silent. Widowed mother, Rose Madigan. A 19 year old from sheep station Corowa. . . . You hear some funny things. A fellow in the hospital wanting a soldier to move on, he was obstructing the light from the port-hole, "Ere! Get out of the way or I'll chuck a b—— measle at yer!"'

By the time the ship reached Aden on 1 June he had buried seven men at sea and trained himself to record their names as well as some small personal details with which to comfort the next-of-kin whose names and addresses he also noted. On Gallipoli, when the burials were daily and often in the dark, under fire, he continued this practice to help him write home those letters that took great time, thought and pain.

'In Red Sea. Getting round in singlet, pantaloonlets and shoes.' He never rested. 'Tug-o-war on deck. I played three games of cards with the men lounging around. Amongst those near-by I came on one from Illowa and another from Terang and had a good yarn with them. Met nine men from Warrnambool [his Victorian parish].' He visited the hospital every morning for an hour and a half after breakfast to chat with the men 'as well as visits of one or two hours duration to the troop decks with copies of the New Testament in one pocket and patent buttons and large safety pins in another, looking glasses in another and various other small sundries too numerous to mention. The troop decks are unbearably hot. I think I'd peg out if I had to stand up to all the discomforts of the soldiers. . . . Went right round ship seeing as far as possible working under tropical conditions. To Engine room, where firemen shovelling at rate of 5 tons per hour into fire in this heat . . . they are in a furnace'. Then, 'Get this note away to my darling girl. Wouldn't I love to be crooning it into her ear as she lay on my arm. She's a brick to give me the opportunity of this magnificent experience'.

Egypt startled him but at no time is he sanctimonious or hypocritical, whether making notes on the city, its denizens or the AIF. 'There was a rumpus last night down in the Wazur, the lowest native quarter, between our Australian soldiers and the natives, women again being the trouble as was the case with the first contingent and again because of the disciplinary measures by the authorities. The soldiers raised a riot in Heliopolis − a few wild spirits − with the result that both Heliopolis and Cairo are out of bounds so you will probably see in the Australian papers all sorts of articles about the wild behaviour of the Australian troops. Don't worry. Things are not so bad. NSW men were the leading spirits I understand. The long voyage was too much for them.' He notes what he saw and heard on the day of this second Battle of the Wazzir: 'Hot wind off the desert. 121° in the shade. 80 000 pound damage to Wazur.' Then, cryptically: 'Fire at Wazur. Capt. Abbot. Wazur. 4 Syrian girls. cigarette – suck-off-French-rubber and hair – balconies. Dr Drummond and Craig on balcony light behind call out to soldiers.' Another entry: '2 donkeys, 2 women, 3 men, 3 children, 1 room not 14 foot square. Dens Beds Soldier with garment on – women at supper. Drink. Scent. Slater, McKay locked in. Nudity everywhere. Saw sights with my very own eyes. I see why Cairo is looked on as one of the wickedest cities in the world, things today have not improved since the days of the Old Testament history when God's wrath fell upon Israel because she disregarded God's warnings against allegiances with Egypt. We were glad to get back to camp even though it is full of dust and lice.'

He makes no criticism of the men, even after overhearing the following: 'Breakfast 13 August 1915: "you fucking xt I've only just got the f . . . . . g thing off the other f . . . . . g table you b . . t . . d".' Later, on Gallipoli, he notes the story of the night sentry challenging passers-by in the dark:

> Who are you?
> Bucks . . . Pass Bucks.
> Who are you?
> Ghurkas . . . Pass Ghurkas
> Who are you?
> West Kent . . . Pass West Kent.
> Who are you?
> !!! . . . Pass Australian

Padre Bennett had more pressing tasks than to fuss over small things, things that were unimportant to him. Crowding the hospitals were 40 000 wounded and sick boys who were being moved perpetually from one hospital to another, and he must find all those whose mothers, desperate for news after receiving the stark telegram, had written to him. 'Walked miles over the desert to the infectious diseases hospital. Found 7 of my 22nd Btn boys there. They were indeed glad to see me. I feel I am getting to know my congregation better. . . . Sunday: Sermonized all the morning. Visited Heliopolis in the afternoon. . . . a patient who knew me called out. . . . He was wounded at Achi Baba. My word I've seen some sights and heard of some escapes in these hospital wards. I'm getting hardened to it a bit but the experiences will last as long as my memory lasts.

'At Heliopolis I met two lads from Hamilton, one with both eyes gone, one with four wounds in body. You can't imagine the size of this war until you see it with your own eyes. Over 4 000 in the one base hospital (and sending men out every day to convalescent homes).

'They don't give you time to feel sorry for them. You hear things – all the time – like, "Pass the commode" and, "Grand to feel a jerry under you. Like being at home again".'

But he *was* moved: 'Buried my first man in Egypt. With body of this young boy from Nhill we left for the cemetery . . . these military funerals always move me very much.'

And the men cheered him immediately after: 'The soldiers volunteer to write signs for the many small businesses which have sprung up. You see signs for:

Barbar and Shavar	Stickly cash payments
Eggs – good or bad	Boiled ice-cream
Little Bourke St. Cafe	Pijamas and jakets

Like all the others before and after him he was in two minds about Egypt: 'This hole of a place. Heat moist and frying.' Then, 'I'm getting accustomed to Egypt and yell out Imshi Yalla! Get out! Move on!'

By this time he and his battalion were moving on. By 2 September he was off to Gallipoli on board the *Southland*, half an hour behind the *Scotian* which was sunk by a submarine on 4 September. He arrives on Gallipoli carrying two days 'iron' rations, and goes over the ship's side into a barge. 'One man hit by bullet in our barge. First time under

fire. Ducked one's head. Two hours with packs on barge.
Then, biggest trial up to the present, went on up the road
till I had to give in. Slept in a shelter. Soldier moved me in.
Shrapnel holes in roof. Cheerful prospect.

'*5 Sept*: Moved up to Shrapnel Gully. First morning on
Peninsula. Went to trenches and understood what Australia
did: "The Impossible". Met some from the *Scotian*. They
had 1½ hours in the water, singing: "Here we are, Here we
are, Here we are again", and "Australia will be there".
6 Sept: Guns going all night. Quite long walk up valley.
Bullets flying. Shrapnel sending us all into our dug-outs
now and then. Battalion moved into trenches. Self had to
stay in Shrapnel Gully. [In a few days his work told him
why.] *7 Sept*: Visited all our battalion in the trenches. From
my dug-out I look across from Troas on the left to
Samothrace on extreme right. Sunset indescribable.'

He learns that his tasks are to censor letters, write to
relatives of dead or badly wounded men, reply to queries
about soldiers, bury the dead and record the graves. '*15
Sept*: First funeral on Peninsula. Buried 1106. Pte W. S.
Samways aged 20, Station Hand, Methodist, Single, also
1690 Pte A. T. Hotham aged 21, Commercial Bank,
Nagambie.'

The dead from the terrible battles of August were still
lying outside the trenches, as they would until the war's
end, and he found the flies very troublesome. 'Sunsets,
mules, water carriers, lonely crosses, makes one sad. Flies
very tame indeed.

There's a little wet home in the trench
where the rain drops continually drench,
There's a dead turk close by
with his toes to the sky,
who causes a terrible stench.
Underneath in place of a floor
there's some mud and a wet piece of straw,
and the Jack Johnstons tear
through the rain sodden air
in my little wet home in the trench.

There are snipers who keep on the go
So you keep your nappers down low
And the star shells at night
Make a deuce of a light
Which causes the language to flow.
Then bully and biscuits we'll chew
But with shells dropping there
There's no place to compare, with my little wet home in
    the trench.'

Two days running he narrowly escapes death, walking out of his dug-out minutes before shells kill the other inmates. Almost every day he goes right round the trenches. Every night he buries some boy. '*19 Sept*: Buried 9 p.m., 147 W. H. Walker, 22, C of E, Buried 151, A. J. Elliott, 23 . . .' In spare moments he does what everyone else on Gallipoli does: he hunts 'uninvited guests' in the seams of his clothes.

'*Sunday 26*: Two services then visit Quinns, Courtneys, sing-song with battalion cooks. [He goes back to his cryptic style occasionally: 'dead turk with hand out. Half packet cigarette butts'.] *1 Oct*: Turks hitting us with shells. Buried 2 in Shrapnel Gully, one, Pte Newhand, 21, C of E *Suicide*.'

Always on Sundays he celebrates Holy Communion, then censors hundreds of letters, 'late at night, 2 candle stumps'. '*13 Oct*: Buried 8 p.m. 124 Pte G. Brooks, aged 22, C of E, Mother 75 Hanover Street, W. Brunswick. *14 Oct*: Wrote Brooks' parents. [He received a reply from Mrs Brooks, 15 Jan 1916.] *17 Oct*: Sunday: Service, 9.30, Holy Communion 10.15, Funeral 11 Service 6 Service 8.'

And so he continues, burying, writing to next-of-kin, visiting his congregation in the forward trenches, giving up to five services on Sundays, always with prepared sermons, and all the time running confirmation classes.

'*29 Oct*: Shrapnel Gully bombardment. Letters, Sermons, round trenches, 2 p.m. confirmation class. D company Sap exploded, 30 carried out – worked hard with Dr Brandy, finished 7.30 p.m., buried 7 men all in their twenties including Lieut. Frederick Bowra of W.A. The saddest day

I've spent on the peninsula. Bowra a gentleman in every sense of the word, Churchman, communicant, chorister. The number of his men present in the Gully an eloquent testimony. Will Good's two brothers present heartbroken. A sad walk back. [Next day he is out again.] Men playing football. Turks bombarding. Our men cheer a miss and go on kicking football. Buried two men Shrapnel Gully. Shot in head by sniper.

'*23 Nov*: 3 p.m. buried 498, 19th Btn., Thomas Burke, 22, RC, N. of K. J. Burke, Yougall, County Cork, Ireland.'

Then, there appeared a strange phenomenon for Australian troops: snow. '*28 Nov*: Snowed all night. Went for services, impossible to hold them. 12–18 inches snow everywhere. Sad experience of self and Q.M. at the Orchard (alone with a body to bury). Ice had the sticking tendency of glue. 156 men down for boots to be replaced. Got a buster on ice, very slippery. Too dark in dug-out to read or write after 2 p.m. What is in store for us? My first Advent Sunday on which I have missed my communion. How I miss my Eucharist. Heard this: "You got any ammunition?" "one up the funnel and nine in the tin box underneath." Heaviest bombardment to date. Lone Pine knocked to pieces. Heavy casualties. Major Johnson, Green, Fogarty and about 60 men. At 6th Field Ambulance all day till shelled out. [For the third time a man in front of him was hit by shrapnel.] Man with 2 fingers off told me he "hit a bomb and it hurt my two fingers. This fag's great, padre". Lots of killed and wounded at 6th F.A. Buried 42 at Browns Dip. Buried 3 from Quinns Post including Michael Maher, R.C. and Alfred Hobbs.'

He suffers, as do the men, from colds, jaundice and diarrhoea, but still he goes around his flock, toiling up Shrapnel Gully, stopping only when ordered to do so with everyone else so that lack of movement will warn the Turks that a stretcher party is bringing a mortally wounded man down. Immediately the stretcher bearers move past traffic is resumed and the bullets and shrapnel fall again. He has got very thin and haggard, his clothes hang on him. He no longer wears an ecclesiastical collar but huddles, as do the men, in anything that suits that terrible land. His parish is wherever the boys of the 22nd Battalion are crouched and he visits them whether they're in the dug-outs behind the firing line as 'reserves' or in the firing line itself. Quinn's, Courtney's, Steele's, were all in his parish, the outposts nearest the enemy who in places were less than ten yards across No Man's Land and who raided and were raided incessantly. He seems never to have thought that he was not obliged to take the same risks as they did, live under the same conditions, exist on the same meagre food, get the same diseases, duck the same bullets and occasionally, as did they, silently cry in his diary, 'Dear God, what is to become of us?'

Some idea of the regard with which he was held by his congregation is reflected in this poem, published in 1915 in the local paper of the town of Warrnambool (Vic.), his parish back home.

'Sent from the front by Captain Craig of the 22nd Battalion and penned by Colonel Crouch, O.C. The lines refer to Chaplain Bennett who has been nicknamed The Padre (T.P.) and who is beloved by the whole regiment.'

The Padre
Who is the friend of all the corp
From Melbourne pier to Anzac shore
And tries to serve us more and more!
THE PADRE
Who, when in ship we were not well
Would come and liven our sick spell
And story, joke and yarn would tell?
THE PADRE
Who came on deck at close of day
To start the songs and organ play
And brighten up the soldiers way?
THE PADRE

And when old Egypt's land was seen
And wandering steps had hellwards been
Would try our lives and lips to clean?
                         THE PADRE
And if we strayed far from the road
Would point the path that should be trod
And guide our erring feet to God? –
                         THE PADRE
Who comes along the trench we fight
Gives us the means to Home to write
Then censors all that is not right! –
                         THE PADRE
And if at last we bite the clod
Who sees our bodies 'neath the sod
And asks us mercy from our God?
                         THE PADRE
And when in soldiers' grave we rest
Who writes to Folks at Home distrest
Tells them we did our very best?
                         THE PADRE
Oh Padre good, our help and stay
Our love for you grows day by day
We are but men, so for us pray
                         Dear Padre

Gallipoli
30.10.15   R.A.C.

On 16 December at 6 p.m. he left Gallipoli with two
other padres. The evacuation was under way. 'Lighter
much more comfortable than when landing 15 weeks ago.
Said goodbye to Dexter on Anzac Cove. Man on beach
bumped into cart. "I'll complain to the council about this!"
he said. *17 Dec*: Arrived Lemnos Harbour 8 a.m. Harbour
just crowded with shipping and motor and steam launches
everywhere. Busiest shipping scene I've ever witnessed.
Warships, transports, sailing boats. Got ashore. Long
march – met friends. Tea on ground with pocket knives,
pineapple and sardines. Strange, the freedom from fire.
God has been so good to me.'

He is sleeping in a one-man tent with three other men. Accommodation is over-taxed, as still the transports creep in with the beleaguered Anzacs. '*22 Dec*: Went to every tent in lines. Saw every man. Rain. Men are all suffering badly through lack of tent accommodation. Tents full of wet beings. *24 Dec*: Went round tents. Saw every man. Christmas billies being opened. Fun. Men could not get things back in billies. My billy contained: pipe, 2 tins tobacco, peanuts, 10 envelopes, pudding, curry powder, laces, chocolates (2) veal and tongue, pencil, digestive tablets, handkerchief. From Mrs a. E. Cook, Craigs Hotel, Ballarat, Victoria; a pudding from A. Rogers, Koroit, Vic.'*

Then, an entry reads, 'a great treat: Mudros. Wash all over. Slept in pyjamas'.

Early January saw him back in Alexandria, cabling his superiors to advise them that he is returning home as soon as permission is granted 'to resume charge of my parish'. A reply came immediately from General Headquarters: 'My dear Bennett, twelve months of the strain you have had is as much as any parish priest ought to undergo and I think you are quite right to return. With best wishes.'

While awaiting transport home the letters kept coming to him, touchingly brave, sane, but distraught letters from those searching for news of sons, brothers, husbands.

Mrs E. Brooks, whose son he buried in Shrapnel Gully, replied to his letter: 'I thought it was so kind of you to write and let us know how our dear boy was killed but it came as a great shock to us not knowing that he was at the front. I received 3 letters from him after I received news of his death. I prayed for him every night that God would spare him and bring him safe home again. There is none feel it like a mother. He was my youngest child. He had no fear in his brave young heart. I am so glad he was buried decent and that he never suffered any pain and also to know that he was so well liked by all his comrades.'

From the Shetland Isles of Scotland Mary J. Mouat

---

* This billy is now in the Historical Collection, La Trobe Library, Melbourne. It is not known if another has been preserved in Australia.

wrote: 'I was very glad to get your letter telling me about my dear son Daniel. Shourly it was a great kindness for you to wret to me about Daniel words could niver explain how graitfull I am to you. I am in grait trouble about him as I am niver had word from him sine before your letter was wretten. I alwise fear the worst. I have no one I can ask about him. And as I am had experience of your goodness already I must ask you pleas if you can tell me anything about him as I not able to wret what is the matter with him if you are not having no word from him I am wretten after to him but got no word from him. It was grief to know him sick but the want of word from him is still more affliction.'

Jane Hindhaugh of Yambuk, Victoria, wrote on black-edged paper enclosed in an envelope bordered in black: 'I am writing to ask if you can give me any information [and as you read the letter, you begin to wonder how many others she has written and sent off whenever she has heard of someone who might help in her quest] of my son No 1906 Pte J. W. J. Hindhaugh, 6th Inf. Bge. Our Vicar, Mr Jessop of Port Fairy, had written to find out from the Defence Department where my son died and after some time I received word that it was Malta but did not know what hospital or any other particulars. It would be a great comfort to us all if we knew he was cared for and buried decently. Probably some day some of the family will go and see where they are laid as I had another son killed in action on 7 August in the Anzac charge of the Light Horse and have a younger son in camp that will be leaving shortly. The boy who died at Malta left Melbourne 26 August and only stayed one week in Egypt and then went to the front on the 14 October. Last week we had letters from him written on the 7th and 13th. He was in the trenches and expected to go into the firing line the following Saturday. He was taken off Gallipoli to a hospital on Malta 28th and died on the 30th. It was a great shock to us as only the night before we had received his letters. I have written to the Anglican Chaplain of the Light Horse Brigade about my other son but so far have not received a reply. Of course I understand it must be very hard to get particulars of everyone when there are so many together. Their cousin, Major Hindhaugh, 4 LH wrote and said he would send me any definite news he could learn about Russell. I am afraid this note is perhaps not very well written or made clear what I want you to do for me but it is so hard for me to write. My thoughts are always about the boys and I wonder where they are laid to rest. I lost another son 3 years ago. He was at High school and contracted pneumonia and only lived 10 days so my trials have been many and hard.'

The Padre sought these letter writers out on his return. I asked his son, Bill, who made available the letters and diary, if this distressed his father overmuch. 'I only remember one thing,' Bill told me. 'He once said: "War is about mothers searching for their sons amid that vast carnage. They were persistent and terrible and tragic".'

16
What, Gone?
The Australians Gone!

What gone! The Australians gone! From Anzac gone?
The lurid crater where for eight long months
They lived with death, dined with disease,
Till one in every two fell ill and one
In every four was shot and one
In every eight lay dead.
Yes, gone! From Anzac gone!
And left behind eight thousand graves.

Sapper J. C. Hackney, 1915

They wrapped sandbags round their feet to muffle their
tread and, in groups of twenty, silently ('no talking lads, no
smoking') moved out of their trenches behind the guides
sent up night after night to fetch another group. Down past
the graves they were escorted, to the beach and the waiting
boats. The ceremony of the blood-sacrifice was over and
Gallipoli was being evacuated. Field Marshal Earl Kitchener
had visited Anzac on 13 November and decided so. He
could spare no men for reinforcements, and the troops
'camped like sandmartins in holes all round the semi-circle
of gravel cliffs overlooking North Beach' were besieged. It
was 8 December before the British Cabinet agreed and the
final secret order came to the peninsula.

Of the two Englishmen, Hamilton had advised the British
Government that withdrawal must cost 'not less than half
the total force', and his successor, Monro, reckoned on a
loss of 30 per cent. The Australian commanders took over
the organisation of the withdrawal of their troops and

determined to effect the operation with far less casualties. General Brudenell White, Chief-of-Staff at Anzac, devised a plan for conditioning the Turks to sudden silences when fire from the Anzac troops would cease. This went on for days until the Turks became puzzled and moved forward, when they were suddenly shot down. The Turkish commanders therefore assumed that the Australians were preparing their winter quarters (which they themselves were doing).

The troops were not told the reason for these cessations of fire. Such were the measures taken to ensure secrecy that even *The Anzac Book* which had been planned went ahead. This was to have been for troops on the peninsula as a Christmas treat. Literary competitions were now held and the men sent in hundreds of contributions. (The book was eventually published, but after the last Anzac had left Gallipoli.) When the news broke the troops were left in a state of shock. There were English, Irish, French, Indian, as well as supportive troops, but to none of these was the news so oppressive as it was to the Australians and New Zealanders 'to whom this first great test of their nations in war had meant so much'. C. E. W. Bean, as usual, better described this moment than any other writer. '. . . What hurt all, and hurt most deeply, was to leave behind to an enemy not only the heights and valleys that so much effort had won, but the bodies of their mates who had given their lives in that effort. From 12 December (when they first were told of the evacuation) onwards the cemeteries of Anzac were never without men, in twos or threes or singly, "tidying up" the grave of some dear, dead friend, and repairing or renewing the little wooden packing-case crosses and rough inscriptions.'

Their burial march was the big guns' roar. Their great-coat
Their winding sheet. Their head
Is to the firing line and the ocean
At their feet.
Tom Skeyhill, 8th Battalion 1915.

'I hope *they* won't hear us marching down the *deres*,' said one on the final day.

Men were taken off for several nights – boats did not approach Anzac until after dark. Over eleven nights 35 445 men were got safely away, 20 277 of them being taken off on the last two nights, 18 and 19 December.

The weather was perfect, the sea calm. The men made sure the Turks could see them at the points visible to the enemy. They played cricket on Shell Green, they fired no more or no less than they had on other recent days. Men in all sections of the line were employed fixing devices to make rifles fire after the trenches were empty.

The official diary of the 13th Battalion (NSW) briefly details the final days. (This Battalion had fallen in strength from 800 to 473 men during the August battles.)

'*17 Dec*: Birdwood inspected Sub. section at 1330. Personnel detailed to echelons vide operation order No. 13. Tested device for firing rifle automatically after a set period. Tests successful. *18 Dec*: First day of evacuation. Turk work party observed on sky-line. Everything normal. *19 Dec*: Second day evacuation. Everything normal. Enemy bombarded Hill 60 Apex and Canterbury Knob at 1215 with 8″ high explosive. Enemy still wire fixing. *Night of 19th and 20th*: Destroyed all ammunition and bomb reserves and all stores left on post. Placed damaged rifles so fixed so that the last man to leave trench has only to light a candle and the rifle would fire 5, 10 or 15 minutes later. During daylight parties sent to wander round the Deres [gullies] to show signs of traffic. Echelon A, 3 officers, 169 O.R's marched off under Lt Barton at 1715. Other parties at 1930, 2115, 0155, 0205, 0215. Private Butler of D Coy. tended Little Table Top lamp until 2400. Hotchkiss [gun] blown up by engineers at 0200. Battn. completed embarkation without a casualty.'

After midnight the eleven miles of the Anzac front was held by only 1 500 men moving from loophole to loophole firing and throwing bombs at the Turkish trenches a few yards away. Then these men, feet padded, began one after

another to creep away. At 2.40 a.m. the last men left Lone
Pine and at 2.55 p.m. the last defender crept quietly from
Quinn's Post where the greatest bomb fight of the campaign
had constantly been warred. The Turks kept up their
desultory night fire. The last boatload left the beach at
4 a.m.; the last of the Anzac staff waited ten minutes for
stragglers, and finding there were none, pushed off. With
them went the tradition of a standard of endurance that
had already been taken up by their countrymen back home.
To again quote Bean, 'Anzac stood, and still stands, for
reckless valour in a good cause, for enterprise, resource-
fulness, fidelity, comradeship and endurance that will never
own defeat'.

At 7.15 a.m. the Turks attacked – and found the trenches
empty, the invaders gone.

The Anzacs were different men now from the rowdy
boys who rampaged ashore in April when they were called
'the impetuous Australians'. They now had definite traditions, an identity, and they clung to it, clung to the battered
hat, the shabby, faded, ill-fitting tunic, the armour that set
them apart from all other men. But they were soberly,
deeply inconsolable over the evacuation.

Because of this feeling, a Special Order of the Day was
issued on 25 December by Major-General A. L. Bell, Chief
of the General Staff. Psychologically the men were stunned,
bewildered, and this message was devised as a means of
removing the feelings that ran deep in them of having
deserted their post. Part of the Special Order was as follows:

'No soldier relishes a withdrawal before the enemy. It is
hard to leave behind the graves of 9 000 comrades and to
relinquish positions so hardly won and so gallantly maintained as those we have left, but all ranks in the Dardanelles
army will realise they were all carrying out the orders of
H.M. Government so that in due course they could more
usefully be employed elsewhere for their King, their Country
and the Empire. There is only one consideration: what is
best for the common cause. In that spirit was the withdrawal carried out and in that spirit the Australians and

New Zealanders of the 9th Army Corps have proved and will continue to prove themselves second to none as soldiers of the empire.'

The communiqué may have been designed to assuage the sick and ailing troops but the following section was undoubtedly true.

'Officers, N.C.O's and men carried out without a hitch the most trying operation which soldiers can be called upon to undertake – a withdrawal in the face of an enemy in a manner representing the highest credit on the discipline and soldierly qualities of the troops. It is no exaggeration to call this achievement one without parallel. To disengage and withdraw from an enemy is the most difficult of all military operations and in this case the withdrawal was effected by surprise with the opposing forces at close grips and in many cases within a few yards of each other. Such an operation when succeeded by a re-embarkation from an open beach is one of which military history contains no precedent.'

Private Roy Rankin had left on 18 December and his experience was common to many. 'The Navy men treat us splendidly every time they get a chance because a lot of them saw our boys at the landing and, to use their own expression, they opened their eyes.

'As soon as we got on board some of the stokers asked half a dozen of us down into their quarter and supplied us with hot cocoa and salmon and *bread* and *butter*. Bread and butter was a luxury we had not been able to get and bread had not been brought on to the peninsula for weeks. . . . When we arrived at Mudros, the cruiser brought up alongside a battleship, the officers and crew of which were drawn up to welcome us, with band playing and sandwiches, cocoa and cigarettes ready for us. It was easy to see that they think a lot of the Australians, and take every opportunity of showing it. We had a good time on board and were then taken on shore and had to march about three miles to this camp and were allotted about one tent to eighteen men, as the number of tents was limited. That meant that we were

packed so tight that if one wanted to turn over everyone in
the tent had to turn over at the same time.'

The maverick Naval Bridging Train, among the last to be
taken off Suvla, was evacuated along with the rest to
Lemnos and there 'put on our own stunt'. Private Thompson
tells the story. 'Being Navy, although we were dressed in
khaki, we were a sort of odd-group-out. We hadn't been
paid for two months. We didn't have a bob between the lot
of us. The army had been paid but not us, and we wanted
to buy fruit from the islanders. So, one night, someone
came along and lifted up the flap of the tent and said,
"We're not going on parade tomorrow". To every tent he
went. To this day no one of us has told who that man was.
Anyway, they put a guard around us and took our rifles
from us and there we were. After a while they asked us if
we would go over to Egypt under open arrest so we said,
yes. They took us to Ismailia, to a little island and put a
guard on us. Then they paid us our back money and of
course that was awful. We couldn't go anywhere to spend it
and men gambled, two-up, with hundreds of pounds in the
centre. Some of us bribed guards to let us out to visit town.
Then Vice-Admiral Sir Rosslyn Wemyss of the Fleet came
to speak to us. "This action came very close to mutiny in
the face of the enemy," he said. Then, "But because of your
bravery at Gallipoli you may be freed". So we were freed.'

The diaries of battalions continued their laconic chronic-
ling of the 'campaign' to the very end – which in most cases
was, of all things, the childlike delight in a sort of Christmas
stocking in the form of 'Christmas Billies'. The 13th Battalion
records: '*20 Dec*: Went into Div. Camp at Mudros. *24 Dec*:
Battn. hold camp fire concert. *25 Dec*: Xmas day. Distribution of Xmas billies from Australia.'

The 8th (Sister Kitchen's 'own') Battalion recorded:
'*20 Dec*: Lemnos. Short of huts. Many men sleeping out.
Severe dust storm. *25 Dec*: Xmas Billies, 1 per man and
puddings 1 per 2 men given out.'

Christmas day was all excitement for the men. Sergeant
'Harry' Kahn, the Western Australian from the 28th

Battalion, could remember it all clearly in 1976, sixty-one years later. With a few other Western Australians he had a great Christmas Day. 'A few of us "borrowed" a boat but we couldn't find oars so we "borrowed" a couple of brooms and paddled out to one of the battleships in the harbour and they hauled us on board and each of us was "mothered" by a sailor. My guardian was a great big stoker, he weighed about 16 stone and was 6 feet high. I was less than half his weight after Gallipoli and he lent me a pair of pants and a singlet and got me a sailor's cap and you can imagine what I looked like in his gear but it was enough for me to line up and splice the mainbrace and the officer supervising the distribution of rum looked the other way – and we had plum pudding, everything. We had a good time. Then we went back on shore and got our billies . . . with the ironic label of a kangaroo with a digger's felt hat kicking the Turk off Gallipoli! The caption read, "This bit of the world belongs to us". They'd come from all over Australia. The contents pretty well indicated the type of person who donated them. A bookmaker or publican would put a flask of whisky and perhaps some money in the billy they packed; contents ranged from packets of flea powder to a pen. From children we got a fairly high proportion of lollies. Practically every digger I knew wrote to the donor, I know I wrote to two little girls on a Queensland station for some years afterwards; they were aged 6 and 8 when we first corresponded. The billies were like Christmas stockings to kids.'

Chaplain Bennett, the paragon among men, moved as usual around his 'parish'. 'The men were sitting around all over the place on the ground going through their billies, telling each other what they'd got. Some of them were trying to re-pack their booty but found they couldn't get all the contents back in the billies again.'

Roy Rankin wrote: 'A few days before New Year's Day we received our Christmas Mail. My word it was a wopper . . . we had received none for about five weeks. A column of men a couple of miles long (practically the whole camp)

marched into Mudros to bring it out rather than wait for it
to be carted out here.

'During our stay at Lemnos we got plenty of drill, the old
platoon and company drill, which we got rubbed into us in
Egypt, and which we hate thoroughly. It seemed strange
after the life in the trenches and we are very rusty on it.
There were fourteen of us detailed for guard over Divisional
Headquarters, and we had to be smart and neat in our
dress to say nothing of saluting all officers, a thing we
hadn't done since leaving Egypt! We got well fed there
however, and got as much bread as we wanted, which is a
thing that has not happened before or since.

'I am writing this on board a troopship bound, we believe,
for Alexandria, and as we left this morning we ought to
arrive there some time tomorrow night. But I must tell you
about the Christmas billies, etc. On Christmas Day we got
half a pudding each, but the next day the billies were given
out and we actually got one each. Every billy was different,
but most of them contained a pipe and tobacco, cigarettes,
chocolates, toffie, and tin of Christmas cake, as well as
useful articles like needles and thread and safety pins and
bootlaces, useful articles which a soldier cannot get, A
Godsend.'

17
The Tap Root

'If you are to go to that part of your country which is on the Galibolu Peninsula', Professor Ismet Giritli of Istanbul University told me, 'you must correctly approach it.' His plan was that I should travel in such a way that I would be attuned to the era, the area, and what he considered to be the wonder of it all. I was to stay at the small town of Cannakele, across the Dardanelles from the Anzac area. (The actual town of Galibolu is some eighty kilometres from Anzac Cove which is too precipitous, barren and geologically hostile to be cultivated or settled.)

'Cannakele is midway between two epics.' Ismet had a large map on the wall of his study. 'On the one side you have Troy, where Helen and Paris walked and Homer wrote of the Trojan wars. On the other side you have your Gallipoli, a new Iliad, an epic separated from the other by over two thousand years – but only by forty kilometres.'

So. I was to sail to the most famous arena of the old world where blood and nationhood were synonymous with youth and sacrifice. Early next morning, while the mist still shrouded old Byzantium which had first become Constantinople, and then, in our time, Istanbul, I sailed beneath the red flag of Turkey with its white crescent moon and star emblem. The little twice-weekly steamer that services the islands of these waters took me from the Black Sea through the Bosphorus with the breeze 'from Russia with love' which daily blows away the mists of Istanbul, and past that old city. ('. . . Win our way to Istanbul', said the English generals in 1915, 'and Russia, our ally, will have an unimpeded route to the sea.')

Now we were in the Sea of Marmora. Sitting on the deck I studied my Turkish phrase-book and dictionary. An old Turkish gentleman lying on the deck beside me – there were upwards of a hundred of us in the sun – had tried to talk with me but apart from yes, no, thank you, where is the ladies? and 'Ikki Bieri' (two beers please) I did not know the language. He took the phrase book and found two sentences. The English translation read, 'Where are you going? Why do you go?' To answer this was too diffuse, abstract, puzzling yet to me for an answer to be given. Where? A country of the mind perhaps, an acreage of the collective legend of a land? And why? I didn't know, except that I needed to see it and walk it and break my nails climbing its rocky cliffs as much as I'd needed to walk in Broome, Normanton, Halls Creek or Cocklebiddy and know their heat and dust and isolation. It was to me Australia, as much as any of those other legendary outposts.

The Turk was waiting so I went through my phrase book and with what was certainly execrable grammar I wrote one concrete reason for my visit: 'My mother is old (I couldn't find the word for elderly in my dictionary). She sends me from Australia with flowers for her brothers' graves.' In English I added, 'Lone Pine', and showed him the sprig of wattle mother had pressed in my field notebook. After puzzling through my grammar he softly said, 'Hah', and by gesture asked if he could show it to the others. I nodded, and off he went around the deck. The other passengers began to nod at me, some smiled, and I went to find the ladies' lavatory for a long time. When I came back the ship had tacked around to run for an island to put off some young Turkish sailors who even now were clambering up the highest vantage points of the ship to see their home island. No passengers remained on the side where I had been sitting but my notebook was there on the deck firmly anchored down with the largest apple I have ever seen. Had I been Herodotus I would have rushed after the old man to tell him I had lived for many years in Tasmania and never seen such an apple in my twenty-five years on that island.

Now as we sail down from the Sea of Marmora and into

the Dardanelles there is an epitaph of our own age picked out on the cliff-side. The English translation reads: 'Bow and listen. This earth is where an age sunk. This quiet mound is where the heart of a nation throbs.' Beside it the figure of a Turkish infantryman stands watch and ward over his homeland.

Down through the Dardanelles, the Hellespont of the Ancients, we travelled, a forty-mile strait that has been celebrated as a theatre of war since Homeric times. Near the entrance to the strait, on the Asiatic side, stands Troy. Just above the Narrows, Xerxes built his bridge of boats to carry his army into Europe for the invasion of Greece in the fifth century B.C. From here one looks across to Samothrace, to Mount Ida and the Plains of Troy, to Patrocles' burial place and the spot where Achilles damaged his heel and the land where Paris forsook the nymph Oenone; out into the Aegean Sea, past Lemnos and Imbros and on to Anzac Cove.

The graves lay untouched and many bodies were unburied until 1919 when the British War Graves Commission went in with the permission of the Turkish Government and collected all bodies believed to be British and buried them. Some graves in outlying areas, where men had been buried where they fell, were brought in and thirty-two cemeteries laid out. The Turkish Government granted land for cemeteries and memorials including 1 500 acres known as the Anzac Area.

The War Graves team which went to the peninsula had records of the burials in the battlefield burial grounds but were unable to locate the individual graves of some of the men known to have been buried in particular cemeteries; nor were they able to identify some of the graves they did locate.

Some of the cemeteries therefore contain tablets listing the names of the men known to be buried in that cemetery, as well as other tablets recording unidentified graves. Unlike the war cemeteries in France, the Gallipoli graves are not marked by upright stones but, because of isolation making repairs difficult, small tablets are set into a block low to the ground. The main wall of each cemetery has a simple cross carved in relief and the words from Ecclesiastes: *Their Names Shall Live Forevermore*. Because of the lack of water, flowers cannot easily be cultivated, but native shrubs have been planted around the graves and it is pleasant to smell the scent of native thyme drifting along the balmy August air as one's foot crushes the herbs growing on the pathways or an arm brushes bushes of rosemary. There is something not too heart-breaking about these graves. There are no fences, some just run right down onto the beach; the grass which has been planted is cut, but not shaven, the herbs telling of simple things perfume the air, and from where you stand by a man's name you can see the battlefield where he last lived. There is something reminiscent of Australian country graveyards about the cemeteries on Gallipoli.

Except for Lone Pine. It is away from the beach, but over-looking the most spectacular view on the peninsula, across to the dark Aegean Sea. There is something immediately different on this hill. No Australian graveyard is chilling in the way these impeccably kept rows of graves are; row on row on row on row of boys' names. All the boys you ever read about from those awful August days. 'He was running like a school boy, fast, with his head up, straight for the Turkish parapet when I last saw him,' they reported of a Western Australian Light Horseman.

I took the wattle my mother had pressed in my notebook and looked for her brothers' graves, the two boys whose names were made part of my own name but of whom I knew little. But of course there were no graves, Jack and Steve had been reported 'missing', so I began to search on the walls where the names of the missing were inscribed and there they were, J. Adams, S. Adams, carved into the golden stone. Realising that the inscription would scarcely show in a photograph because of the sandy colour of the stone, Mr Dilman, my guide, told me to sprinkle dust onto it, and brush it off with my hand, and the outer stone would be clean but the dust would remain in the inscribed names. 'Pick up a handful of dust and sprinkle it,' said the old man. So I stooped, gathered the dust and sprinkled it over the men who were dead long before I was born and as the dust left my hands I swear to God my tears followed it across – they didn't fall, they just spurted out. And I wasn't thinking of those two boys but of a girl who, 2 384 years ago, had stood only a few kilometres away from Lone Pine and sprinkled ritual dust over the unburied body of her brother lately dead on the battlefield. It seemed to me at that moment the saddest thing I had learnt in a lifetime, that men still killed men, and sometimes left them to rot and decay and be mauled by scavenging animals and birds. When Antigone refused to leave her brother Polyneices unsepulchred she, in her headstrong way, could have felt no more outraged than I did at the thought of the bodies of these two brothers of my mother 'receiving their obsequies from dogs and jackals; from some filthy scavenger of the air flapping to alight, then returning home. desecration reeking from its beak'; outraged at the bones of these my kinsmen being scattered down the precipices and valleys 12 000 miles from the green valleys and hills of their native Gippsland.

Later in the day we drove to the newly erected Turkish memorial and here I was asked to write in their visitors' book. 'Your Queen wrote in this book,' I was told, but I didn't care. I only wanted somewhere to record that 'these hills are the last that heard the laughter of two boys from "Calrossie", Yarram Yarram, Victoria, Australia', the family home to which Jack had addressed his last letter.

The Turks did not bury their dead. When the Anzacs and British left the peninsula the Turkish army was rushed to other battlegrounds as severe for them as Gallipoli had been. When the war ended they, as a defeated people, knew bad times. In the midst of this plateau of misfortune their inspiration of the days of 1915 – Mustapha Kemal, now known as Kemel Ataturk – led them into the creation of a new nation. This absorbed all their energies. The peninsula is so far from the settled areas of Turkey that till this day only a few families farm there and none on the barren wasteland of cliffs over which the Anzacs fought. So the Turkish soldiers' remains were left unburied, uncollected. One day when I was clambering down the cliff-side of Chunuk Bair with the War Graves' Superintendent to visit The Farm cemetery in the gulch, where no vehicle can penetrate, I clutched for support at a dry bush and dragged it out with my weight. As I grabbed for a foothold to save myself falling, clods of the cliff-face came away and, with the soil, bones fell on my face. Down in the valley where the tiny farm hut had once stood were skulls – I counted three and I was not looking for them but rather for an easy place to tread. There was a small patch of bones; they could have been several men, or maybe they were animals? There was certainly a thigh bone of a man.

On 'Baby 700', a small hill on the Sari Bair Ridge, the details of graves are evidence of the severity of the fighting in this rugged place: U.K. 1, Australia 32, N.Z. 10, unidentified 450. 'Baby 700' had been occupied on the day of the Landing but was lost again the same afternoon and although on 2 May and 7 August the Australians attempted to retake it, it never again fell to them.

The activity of the Commonwealth War Graves Commission and the building of monuments by the British went on for some years and must have somewhat bewildered the Turks. In 1965 the Turkish nation built a huge stone monument at Morto Bay to commemorate all the Turkish dead of the Campaign, said to number 66 000. (Mr Dilman and many Turkish scholars believe this number grossly underestimates the losses. Mr Dilman states: 'more like 100 000 is what is reckoned by the number of battalions pushed in here and the few who lived to fight again'.) There are no Turkish cemeteries on the peninsula. There is one small memorial stone to a Turkish sergeant near the British cemetery at The Nek, that is all.

Clambering along the cliff edge at the back of Quinn's Post I found excavations which Dilman recognised quickly as 'grave robbers' (his words). 'The odd shepherd who comes this way he thinks maybe these are valuables.'

One day here I waded out from Anzac Cove, near the Ari Burnu area, into the sea. I needed to know how it felt to be coming ashore. I waited till the water reached my shoulders then turned and headed for the beach. It wasn't easy. I found that the flat, shingle stones of that beach move underfoot and it is easy to slip as I did when Dilman called out, 'Put your hands up Smith! Your rifle. Out of the water.' When Smith's hands went up her balance was gone and over she went. Dilman reminded me, 'Your Australians carried great weights ashore, and kept their rifles dry.'

'At France it was different.'

Part Two:
After Gallipoli

18
Run For Your Life,
Dig!

After Gallipoli there was no known way that this band of brothers could be denied. There was no longer any need to use the phrase in quotation marks. The dramatis personae of what was now a closed shop demonstrated not so much in an overt way but in their very being that they were a tribe, a sept, a sodality. What affected one affected all. 'All you needed to do when you got into strife', said Tom Mahood, 'was to shout "Aussie Here!" and they'd come running. I've run to a point many times myself on leave when I heard the cry and we'd move in to rescue our mate we'd never seen before. It wasn't that we went in with fists but it's pretty unnerving to an adversary to see a whole tribe move in a phalanx upon him.'

A company of infantry with rifles and bayonets was ordered to surround a group of soldiers caught looting some small shops. The officers were running around calling, 'Don't let any men out of here'. Most men had gone but now and again a few came out with arms full of things, and rushed up to the lines. The guard would open out and let the man through . . . with a 'Run for your life Dig'; finally there wasn't a man inside and they were guarding the remaining shops.

The 'clan call' could work both ways, as Lieutenant Harold Wanliss found on his first night in Cairo. He went out with a military police officer. 'He has charge of one of the sections of the city and I went with him on his rounds. We caught a few Arabs running gaming schools but there was naught of excitement till we were in a Bedouin establishment which had been the means of the piquet capturing several deserters and was then being guarded against any reprisals by the deserters' friends. A fight took place outside and a peculiar cry was heard; immediately all these Arabs rushed out like a whirlwind and joined in the fray. It appeared that a sort of "clan call" had been given and they had answered it. But the cry of the opposition proved the stronger. "Aussie! Here!" A couple of soldiers waded in and the affair was soon over.'

Those were the 'rowdy affairs'. Where the blood tie showed most was in the quiet, everyday relationships. Men visited their mates in hospital with a tenacity that nothing moved. Some went from hospital to hospital searching for their wounded friends. 'It's funny to go into a ward,' Private Richard Smith wrote. 'A chap in a bed will yell out "Hey! Cobber!" and there's someone you haven't seen since the stretcher bearers took him off from Lone Pine or a fellow I gave a fag to as they carried him down Shrapnel Gully.'

Norman Mills tramped off to find his brother Reg. 'Went to the Palace Hospital but they said he was at Luna Park and they wouldn't let me in. It is a very hard hospital to get into as they have special days and hours for visiting. However this is possibly my last night in Egypt so I made frantic efforts to gain admittance and by seeing the Sergeant of the Guard I succeeded after a considerable time. Reg seems fairly well but the wound is not healing although he says he can hobble round a bit now.' Norman Mills had come from Omeo, up in 'The Man From Snowy River' country, and would not easily be denied.

The relaxation after their awful eight months took many forms. Although the reinforcements that were now flooding into Egypt from Australia had never been to Gallipoli they had a feverish hyperactivity, having arrived knowing by now what war was about. ('I had my photo taken time and again,' Richard Smith wrote. 'I was sure I'd never get out alive and I wanted back home to know what I looked like.') The 'heads' were constantly issuing circular memoranda complaining about 'horses being galloped through streets and lines' and such-like. On 10 January 1916 a confidential memo read: 'Gambling. The game known as Two-up is not to be played.' Ah well. Later, on 12 May from Headquarters, 5th Division, came this plea: 'I am anxious that the members of the division should drop the use of two words in particular which unfortunately are too commonly heard at the present time. Probably everyone knows that these words are F . . . and B . . . . . . They are both beastly, especially the first. In fact the use of that word really implies a low attitude of mind towards all our women relations and friends.'

It was not that the men had time on their hands that they indulged in these habits that so distressed their superiors – not that one is suggesting that the use of the words F . . . and B . . . . . . took up much time, but the fact was that the men were being given training the like of which they had never known before. Sergeant J. A. Stevens, official recorder for the 58th Battalion, wrote in his diary on 15 February 1916: 'At 9 a.m. we marched out of camp in full marching order each man carrying 220 rounds of ball ammunition – the lot weighing about 93 lbs. It was raining and that made it worse. We marched about 6 miles across the desert. I had the job of taking the names of those that fell out [he notes 32 men] during the march. I nearly had my own name on it several times but I stuck to it and got through. Our "dinner" today was doughy dry bread, sardines and water. It was the hardest days work I've done in my life, done to test the men, and it did, several of them falling down in fits.'

While the infantry was moving in to the line in France the artillery of the newly formed 4th and 5th divisions was completing its training in Egypt. It is claimed that 'the creation of that artillery was a task unparalleled in British experience, and is the classic example of the speed with which Australians could be trained'. Officers from non-artillery units were trained in some cases and they in turn instructed their men. The 3 000 officers and men of each of the two divisions had only five guns which they used in relays to train with, but were ready in April to move up to defend the Suez Canal from the Turks and thence to embark for France.

The official history of that march has recorded that a brigadier was removed from his post for the experience these men underwent in this march, and it was without doubt the harshest trial that any Australians had during training.

There was a shortage of trains to take the artillery men to Tel-el-Kabir – about forty miles – so it was decided that they would march across the desert over a period of three days with two fifteen-mile stages and a shorter stage on the final day. In the 14th Brigade, because the men broke ranks to drink from the 'Sweet-water Canal', their brigadier ordered them to march on without a break through the midday hours. Many observers have written of seeing the results of this march.

'At every step we sank to our ankles,' (the then) Private H. R. Williams wrote. 'The sand was very soft. The sun scorched our backs, the dust rose in fine white clouds, covering our faces like flour, choking our breathing and burning our lips and mouths. The craving for drink was damnable, but we knew the surest way to blow out like a broken-winded horse was to gulp water.

'Midday meal was bully beef and biscuits washed down with a drink from our water bottles. The sun fairly scorched us. We made shelters with our waterproof sheets over our rifles. After 14 miles we lay on our equipment and stretched our weary limbs. It was dark before our meal was ready, bully-beef, biscuits and strong tea. We fell asleep but the heavy dew had us awake and shivering before daylight. Breakfast was a small portion of particularly salt bacon, hard biscuits and jam with a little tea. At 7 a.m. we were told "your route is due east" and we were on the move again. During the hours of the march I had kept a pebble in my mouth; this had eased my thirst somewhat but now the roof of my mouth was becoming very tender. Now we began to march up hills of drift sand. At every step we sank to our calves and our packs became crushing burdens. The sun struck up from the white sand with the heat of a furnace. Men began to straggle and then to drop out. It was like walking on a treadmill. We reached the summit of the ridge in a very distressed condition. Our platoon sergeant fell unconscious under his pack. The general from his horse said the next camp was only an hour away. [It was three hours.] Thenceforward the march became a débâcle. Men fell unconscious on the sand and were left lying where they fell. Some became delerious and raved. Companies dwindled to mere handfuls. I went on with sagging knees, breath coming in gasps, froth on the lips. I was young, proud of my strength, had led for years an athletic life without smoking or drinking and was in a state of perfect physical fitness; still I found my strength ebbing fast. Our platoon officer collapsed in the sand. Shortly after, a corporal marching in front of me fell unconscious and some of us stumbled over his prone body. Captain Fanning was now the only officer left in our company and the company on the left was without an officer. A Company was not more than 20 strong [average 250]. At each halt we looked back. Away to the skyline we could see forms of men lying huddled in the sand, as though machine-gun fire had swept the columns. As we looked, some would rise and totter a few paces, to collapse again. The desert was strewn with clothing, equipment and miscellaneous articles. Queer thoughts surged through our brains as the sun beamed down on us. Perspiration was white on our tunics and our web-equipment had the white sweat stains seen on the harness of a toiling horse. At last Captain Fanning fell out – he'd covered a lot of ground coming backwards and forwards to keep us going – and there were 12 meh left of our company. Now we struck a patch of soft sand and we reeled like drunken men. Our packs seemed to have grown to the weight of mountains. We were foaming at the mouth like wild dogs, tongues swollen, breath gripping our throats with agonising pain, and legs buckling under us. Only 36 men of the battalion of about 900 got in. My mate Peter and

I got to the New Zealand cook-house and found a small quantity of dirty water. We joined about a dozen men in a mad scramble to drink this filth. We were parched with thirst, went on our hands and knees like famished beasts. One of the cooks saw us and pulled a dixie of tea off the fire for us but we vomited it up before it had time to do us any good. Word flew round the camp that there were hundreds of Australians still out in the desert and the Kiwis hurried out with water bottles, large stretcher parties, ambulance wagons, mounted men, camel parties, even an aeroplane flying low. All night long the New Zealanders worked bringing in men in all stages of exhaustion, some unconscious, others naked and in delerium, others with sunstroke. A few days later we had read to us a lengthy screed from Major Gen. McKay the divisional commander about our "disgraceful conduct". This made the men in the ranks the scape-goats for somebody's blunder. As punishment, for many mornings after, the battalion was marched round and round in a great circle under full packs for two hours, to teach us march discipline.'

These men later participated in some of the most terrible battles that took place in France, including that of Fromelles.

Beyond all the hard training, the shenanigans, the mateship, one thing obsessed each of these men who were waiting to go to France. Reg Mills tells of it: 'When the mail arrives there is a "hooray!" rush for it; it is impossible to hear the sergeant yelling out the names for the row that the lads make; they get that excited, and the looks of disappointment on some of their faces when their names have not been called out is pitiful.'

Chaplain Bennett had now left for home but among the chaplains in Egypt was an equally observant, kindly man, the Reverend Maitland Woods from Brisbane. In one letter from Egypt he writes, 'It is wonderful how well the Aussies get on with the Scottish Regiments – we have a small unit attached and they are really Anzacs *de facto* – there is a rugged sincerity about the Scotch character that seems to harmonize at once with the Anzac, and a tremendous amount of courage. Many of the Scotties are coming out to Australia, so they say, when the war is over'. He is optimistic – all the letter writers at some time are the same – 'I am beginning to think that the war will end comparatively soon – there will be some way out of this terrible impasse. In spite of all the Hun says, Germany has learned a bitter lesson. There *are higher powers*. The race is not always to the swift nor the battle to the strong as Solomon wrote in an embittered old age'. Like many men in this ancient land he read the Bible with renewed interest. 'Here on these very plains, David wrote "When I consider the works of thy hands" and over on the hills that were so very clear this morning, the B.V.M. sang the song of deliverance of all womankind, "For Behold, from henceforth, all Generations". And here on this plain where we are camped the lowing kine drew the Ark with the emblems from Gaza etc. back to Judaea.' His enthusiasm spread to his troops. 'The lectures on Egypt I give the men are really Bible classes only they don't know it, just what you and I have been giving our Sunday School children for years and years. It does amuse me when the Colonel of the Regiment says, "When are you going to give us another lecture, Padre?"'

Sister Kitchen had been back in Egypt some weeks. After a voyage with wounded from Gallipoli to London in November 1915, the *Gascon* had been ordered to Salonika, the Thessalonika of St Paul, as Alice, the meticulous chronicler, was quick to record. Then on 4 December came 'two lighters of patients to the *Gascon* and [we] took on about 74. Mostly men with badly frost-bitten toes after being out in the heavy snow of some days ago. They say some hundreds were affected by it in the same way. Wards were soon filled up and very quickly got settled down.

'5 *Dec*: After lunch we had to get a hustle on . . . about 280 patients coming down and nowhere ready to receive them, all the wards being full of cargo. Had to move quickly and were fixed up as far as the bedding went about 4.30 when the contingent arrived. Very many were frost-bitten toes and some fingers and the rest medical cases. The tale of their experiences is too pathetic. They were planted in a cold place without much winter preparation or equipment, broken boots, no mittens and insufficient shelter when the snow fell and then froze about 22 deg. below zero: not allowed to take off their boots to rub their feet and not relieved for hours. 6 froze to death and one was buried under 4 ft of snow when found. The patrols fared the worst, not being allowed to walk about: one man was given 28 days C.B. for taking off his boots. They say they came from Anzac in the same boots that were issued in July. Many of the feet are gangrenous and will be long and nasty. I got about 117, some put down below, 5 on the floor. Feet very tired when bedtime came and was very glad of help. Officers and orderlies sleeping on the decks, floors, and everywhere. Here there are about 300 frost-bite cases a day coming into the Canadian and Gen. Hosp. at the front.'

But there was to be some relief after the long heavy months spent nursing at sea. She was put ashore in Egypt and found herself back at 'the Palace' and in receipt of mail, '2 cases, 3 parcels, heaps of papers and about 75 to 80 letters. A message about several cases of things sent to me for the *Gascon* from people in Melbourne and I got many letters from strangers saying they had sent things'.

The entry for 14 December is indicative of her reflections. 'The outlook over the desert is charming and like old times again, but alas! how many are gone who were here last year.' The following day was spent quietly writing letters and by 16 December she was back having tea at Groppi's and chatting to Colonel Springthorpe. 'He looks aged, none the better for the summer in Egypt. Like many others, especially the older men, he has been harrowed by the horrors and hardships the men have had to endure.'

Then, on 22 December, came the news of the evacuation: 'Heard that Gallipoli had been abandoned; and that we had pulled out of it safely. No casualties – 45 000 men. . . . some one said: "Every inch of it is dyed with their blood and a grave for every yard". And I am sure the floor of the

Mediterranean is strewn with our dead. God grant them rest and everlasting peace. They have all done their best and if they failed it was not their fault. It is something to have conducted a good retirement.'

With Gallipoli 'Mafeesh' as the boys said, an air of marking time until the next 'stunt' swept over them.

'*December 25th (Xmas Day)*: Samsing gave me a little water colour of Cairo. . . . [we] were invited to dinner at Abassia at the Victorian Training Battalion and had an enjoyable evening. . . . good foods, puddings, wines, sweets, nuts, nothing desirable left out. They gave the usual toast "The King, The Sisters": and the C.O. replying said he would use the familiar phrase, "Our arms—our defence: their arms our recompense". Then the Silent Toast to the absent ones. We try not to linger on these moments.

'*December 28th*: Had dinner at the Continental with Col. Springthorpe, Major Hurley, Major Simmons and Sister Conyers. We had a little coffee cup as souvenir to be produced at the return dinner when "we all meet again at home". Cairo is stiff with soldiers of all sorts. Many seem too full of spirits. One grabbed me by the hand and shook it and said – "These are the women who look after us!"'

On the last day of the year from 9 p.m. till midnight the sisters organised a concert at Luna. It was 'successful on the whole. After supper the cornet duet took place on the balcony, "Life's dream is over" . . . and airs clad with memories of the *Benalla* and the original "8th"'.

January was quiet and uneventful. On the twenty-seventh she mentioned a 'big batch of patients who went to Australia. There is much joy at the call "Fall in for Australia", and no loitering about, everyone anxious lest he should miss the bus. There is always a shade of apprehension· lest he should be turned back at Suez etc. but it's a step nearer home'.

With the coming of February she notes that 'many Sisters have been off sick and others not too well'.

Like Alice herself they were suffering from the composite effects of twelve months of overwork, crippling conditions,

high drama and strange exotic new lands, and each had
seen and handled more tragedy than nurses in peacetime
would see in a full life's career. Sister Samsing was off
duty, ill, for days at a time, others for weeks; Alice now
showed signs of dangerous weariness and for weeks she
writes nothing but grizzling complaints. She was what she
herself would have termed 'upsplit'. 'Heliopolis full of
soldiers and smoke, and bread is scarce,' she writes. Bread
was often scarce in war zones and smoke, as she told us
when leaving Australia, was her pet hate. For a time she
even forgets to record the sunsets.

Her birthday comes and passes and she recalls that 'last
year Colonel Gartside and the others gave me a dinner'. But
that was last year. Now when she meets anyone from that
lost battalion, from a private to a colonel, she records as if
of a miracle, 'Saw a boy from the old 8th today'.

She goes to Pathe Pictures. *Charlie by the Sea* tickled her
fancy. In the sudden calm after the storm of the past year
she often writes of meeting an old acquaintance and 'talking
about old times'.

And then she is granted leave, and undertakes a voyage
of such charm that it sends her off into pages of rhapsodic
description; she goes up the Nile to Luxor and stops off at
all the temples and ruins she had ever read about.

The Colossus in the Ramesseum had her remembering
Shelley:

> I met a traveller from an antique land
> Who said, 'Two vast and trunkless legs of stone
> stand in the desert: Near them on the sand
> Half sunk a shattered visage lies.

She marvels, 'made of a single piece of granite 58 feet high,
length of ear 3½ feet, circumference of arm at elbow 17½
feet, length of index finger 3½ feet, area of the nail of
middle finger 25 sq. ins'.

There was something about the colossus, not just its
unbelievable dimensions lying there in the burning sand,
but something else. Having seen uncounted dead – she

later said she had no knowledge of the number of eyelids she closed, of the number of amputees she nursed – young men who died unwept, alone, unsung, the thing that to her was colossal in its unlikeliness was that any man could have built such a memorial to himself in the belief that generations to come would 'Look upon me, and wonder'.

That night, she came in from the silver moonlight and read Homer for contentment. 'I love Egypt,' she wrote as the sunset splashed across her page in a palette of subtle shades and the scent from the warm flowers and the yellow sands filtered through the senses.

All too soon she has to return to Cairo and the rumours 'that all Australians will be out of Egypt by June'.

The rumours become fact and on 27 February she went 'to the bank . . . after 3 p.m. and nearly died with the heat and the heavy serge dress and standing about . . . everybody else was closing their accounts also. Thank God we are getting out of it for the summer. Met Major Coulter of the 8th for a few minutes. Most of his men are gone. Felt quite exhausted . . . *March 29th*: Left the Heliopolis palace in cars. . . . A General with a row of ribbons was there to see us off on the train. He asked if we had plenty of room and were comfortable so we knew he was Imperial. No Australian official ever does that, especially if he is a M.O. We arrived at the *Salta* on the Quay at Alexandria about 1.30 p.m. and were formed into a ragged line on the pier and told off to wards which are to do duty for cabins. At any rate we travel in comparative safety. We were almost dead with heat, fatigue and want of tea and felt revived about 4 p.m. when we got some and had shore leave till 9.30 p.m. and tore off up the city to have a last look at the shops. I bought a little key of life for luck. Spent our first morning in Egypt here and our last. . . .'

The 1st Anzac corps began to sail from Egypt to France in March 1916. By this time the Germans had extended their line for almost 500 miles from the Swiss border to the North Sea. Since the First Battle of Ypres in November 1914 there had been a deadlock on the whole 'front'. The

greater part of the Allies' western front – 370 miles of it –
was held by the French. At the end of April 1916, 40 000
Australian troops were with the British Expeditionary
Force. Nearly all of these were combatant troops: their
ordinance, munitions and food were all British, Australia
paying so much per man for this supply. By July the
number of Australians in France had risen to 90 000;
another 90 000 were training in England and 25 000 were
in the Middle East.

The AIF doubled in size. Recruiting had been good
following the losses during August 1915 when, despite the
reports of 'victories', most Australians realised that things
were going badly for their men. To take up the raw recruits
and quickly get them in fighting shape, the old battalions
split into two and each expanded again to battalion strength
by taking in recruits who, coming into the veteran units,
quickly assimilated training and discipline – as well as
imbibing the tradition that each of these original battalions
was already cloaked with.

'The main object of the military is to get all the men fit for
the big push. The war will surely not last beyond the
summer,' wrote Sergeant George Scott in January 1916.

By the end of summer the terrible truth was known to
both sides: it was to be a long and hideous time before one
side or the other collapsed.

'Men, we are leaving for France and hell,' Captain
Fanning told A company, 56th Battalion. 'Make no mistake
as to what that means – death, privation, wounds and
suffering. Many of us will leave our bones in France.'
(Fanning himself was dead within a year.)

In March 1916 Roly Mills crossed to France from Egypt.
'We went by ship, five days to Toulon, then to Marseilles,
three days by train to the north of France. Then we marched
ten miles towards the firing line, spent the night in a barn;
next day we marched another five miles to the trenches. It
is a treat after Anzac.'

Two weeks later he was still delighted with the wide,
open fields, the green grass, trees, and the sight of civilians,

houses and some semblance of normality. 'My word this place is a treat to Gallipoli. . . . I can't help saying it again. . . . We only go in the trenches for a week at a time and then come out and rest. During the rests we are able to get a hot bath and clean change of underclothes besides getting all our clothes disinfected against vermin.

'I met Paddy Haig here. I was walking across a paddock and walked over to a chap who was on fatigue work to ask him for a match to light my cigarette and who should it be but Paddy. You can imagine the look of surprise we both had when he turned round.

'All the people as we passed on the march up through France had a wave for us. Some gave parcels of eatables to the lads.'

That part of the front held by the British extended from Belgium in the north of Ypres down to the river Somme south of Albert near Amiens. It was up and down this eighty-mile stretch that the Australians fought, and the names of the towns along that route became part of the folk-history of their own country – for as long as that generation lasted.

They arrived in spring time and marched past groups of smiling, sometimes cheering Frenchmen. There were flowers and fields; a man could see for miles. Their spirits were buoyant, they were happy. This place was so different from the ravine-rent cliffs of Gallipoli. They behaved impeccably, partly through enthusiasm at seeing so much beauty, partly out of chagrin and disdain at the assurance of British General Sir Archibald Murray in Egypt that the discipline of the Australians troops was such as to make him alter the plans for having them placed first on the list for France – to fourth. 'The most backward in training and discipline,' he believed. Feelings ran so hot that some senior officers suggested Murray's letter of accusation should be sent to the Australian Government to give it the 'opportunity to decide whether troops so valueless should not be withdrawn from France altogether'.

But now the men were in France. For a few weeks they

were kept quietly behind the lines with lectures on prevention
of frostbite, art of billeting, of disinfection in military baths.
They received for the first time tin helmets and gas masks;
some were sent to training schools in mortar, bombing and
sniping. By 7 April they were entering the line, marching
up through the long communication trenches that wound
through the countryside of green hedgerows and fields of
corn, farms and villages. In the villages were shops, and
people, even children. Farther back were army baths where
clothes were disinfected against lice and a man could bathe
regularly. They knew it would be a different war, sensed
that the tension would be less than at Gallipoli and the
sniping less keen, but they saw too that there was here no
shelter at all from even medium high-explosive shells: the
communication trenches were not dug down in the ground
because any excavation would immediately fill with water
in this low land; instead, breastworks built of sand bags
above ground gave them shelter of a sort.

19
The 'Fair Dinkums'

Louder the sound from out the gully comes:
The marching feet; the sullen roll of drums.
C. J. Dennis

They were marching all right. By June 1915, when 10 000 Australian casualties had been announced, the cost of nationhood had begun to be felt. It would worsen; the casualty lists would sicken; and fidgetty, nervous groups would hang around the notice boards in the cities to see the casualty lists pinned up as they were received, and murmur in anger as they searched for names they knew, but that first gallant deed was never regretted. For the whole of the war there was the enlistment of the waves of young men as they turned eighteen. Private Ivor T. Birtwistle, a junior reporter on the Melbourne *Age*, was one of these men and he fell into the habit of complaining as swiftly as the older men. Leaving Broadmeadows Camp on 6 May 1915, he began his diary:

'Extensive and chaotic preparations for our departure from Broadmeadows. Issue of equipment and general kit distinguished by lack of method and individual eccentricity, for instance, QM store left the issue of boots to the last minute when boots handed out irrespective of size, and I got 8.5, which I was told I could "change on board".'

It was said of the men who rushed to join up when war was declared that they were 'Dinkum Aussies'. The men who joined later, after hearing of the fearful death toll, were

208

called 'Fair Dinkums': men who enlisted even though they
knew the odds were against them.

Leaving Mitcham Camp (SA) Young Roy Bice (AAMC)
who later was awarded the military medal for bravery
under fire and died in the mud of Flanders, touches the
heart of the matter, writing in his beautiful hand in ink, an
achievement few soldiers rose to in those pre-biro days
when they could not easily carry liquid but must mix water
to their powdered ink.

'All is hustle and bustle this morning preparing for our
departure to a destination unknown. The waggons are
going this morning, the men tomorrow. I being a waggon
orderly go with the transports . . . Reached the outer
Harbour at 4.30 in the afternoon and found mother, Eva,
and the kiddies there waiting for me. Can tell you I was
pleased to see them. Had tea in the station kiosk and I was
wondering when we should meet again . . . But when their
train left, leaving me alone on the platform I confess tears
would come to the surface. Made beds in the ambulance
waggon and tried to sleep but it was useless.

'Troops arrived at 11 a.m. – the crowd a couple of hours
earlier. Barricades were placed each end of the wharf but
when the men came along there was a push and over went
the obstacles – girls rushed in and picked out their particular
friends – one girl clung round her boy's neck and wouldn't
let go for quite a while – Gee I'm glad nothing like that
happened to me – that's the worst of being in love.

'At last all the men were marched on board the old
Geelong – which was our transport . . . Streamers of
coloured paper were thrown up to the boys from friends on
shore . . . it was a great sight.

'At last the third whistle blows – and the cables are
released – the vessel slowly moves away from the wharf –
the paper streamers break – leaving [a] portion in the
hands of the people on shore, the remainder with the lad
who is going away to fight for them. Guess you would find
those pieces of paper in many a home today – as the boys

carefully rolled theirs up and placed them in their pocket books.

'The band is playing – everybody is cheering or singing – someone tries to shout a message to the shore but is useless – Everybody is happy.

'I kept my eyes on those heads and waved till I couldn't distinguish them from the others.'

'Leaving Australia behind is the most trying circumstances of all,' wrote Private John Millard of the 1st Battalion when he left in 1915. 'The scenes on the wharves where mothers, wives and sweethearts are weeping and not expecting to see many of their loved ones again are most trying.'

Once they were too far from the shore to distinguish the faces left behind, the men sought their quarters. Roy Bice found that the beds were 'hammocks – hung on hooks in the rafters overhead. When all the chaps were in the hammocks, they were touching, so you can imagine how closely we were packed in.

'Hadn't been in bed long before I felt the rolling of the boat. "Here's a go" thought I and it was – fortunately our quarters were on the well deck – so was not long reaching the side – one consolation I was not the only one – that night was a nightmare – first time I had been seasick . . . *June 3*: About sixteen hundred on board and I believe we are to pick up only a couple or three hundred more at Freemantle. Do not know where they are going to be packed – poor beggars – "Cheer up Society" sent on a good many cases of apples for the troops but have not seen any up to date. I notice the officers have fruit every day.'

They arrived at Fremantle on 5 June to see a 'crowd on wharf . . . All disappointed as we are anchored in midstream . . . There is great talk of a route march tomorrow. Men are very dis-satisfied at not being allowed to go ashore. When darkness fell many slid down ropes onto boats and reached the wharf that way. Hell of a row. Took the officers all their time to quieten the mob. Some of the heads were absolutely bluffed – in the end the men put their rifles away of course they had no ammunition but things were ugly for a time . . . 8 p.m., Had our usual sing song at the stern of the boat.

About four piccolos to accompany us. Sing ourselves hoarse.

'*June 7th*: Drew into the wharf this morning – took on the W.A. troops and then pulled out in midstream again . . . Boats loaded with people came out to us all afternoon . . . After ten the men applied for leave and were refused – so an attempt to lower the boats was made but was not successful. A few of our own lads managed to get off. Some had their people there – don't blame them . . . Route march is "Hoff". Going to bed early. Hundred or so on shore got there by boat or swimming with their clothes on.

'*June 8th*: The food is very much inferior to what we got in camp. You should see some of the stews – great pieces of fat floating around in dirty water – spuds boiled in jackets which have not previously been washed "Oh! It's a great life!" Bread is scarce – not enough by a long way – Orderly officer comes around at each meal time for complaints if any. He never leaves without a dozen complaints. It's the soldiers' priviledge to grumble – Left Fremantle without warning at 11 a.m. – though we were to stay there for a few days longer. Expect "the heads" took a "jerry" and sailed to stop further trouble – Only a hundred or so left behind – some of our lads among them – Behaviour on board much different to last night.'

Each state, as though they were still separate colonies and had to ask separately 'What Price me Now?', kept recruits coming. The small states, and those with great and (to the people of the cities) mysterious hinterlands, proudly recruited and sent away men as though they had them to spare.

News of the Landing sent another wave of volunteers into camps from Hobart across to Perth, Cairns down to Port Lincoln.

"Embarked from Brisbane 2 p.m. 28.6.15,' wrote Private W. E. K. Grubb, a Tasmanian from the fishing village of Stanley. He had enlisted in 1915 only six weeks earlier on 11 May. It was obvious that the enthusiasm of civilians had in no way cooled.

All around the entrance to the camp a crowd of Queenslanders had assembled to bid farewell to the 'Disorderly Tasmanians' and to wish them God speed. 'We moved off at 2.20 p.m. to the tune of "It's a long way etc" and the thermometer standing at about 103 degrees. There are about 2000 of us on board packed like sardines.'

By 1 September he was writing from Egypt while awaiting transport to the Dardanelles: 'Now the time is drawing close I feel calm and fit and just a little bit eager to get out and into the line of fire and avenge some of the wrongs committed on defenceless women. I shall hate to take life but I feel justified in wreaking vengeance on these allies of the *unspeakable* though "cultured" hun. I see thousands of wounded in the hospitals here and hundreds coming in daily as well as disfigured and broken down heroes.'

When he entered '13 Oct. 1915' in his diary, he was himself a part of the 'broken-down' army on Gallipoli. '. . . Fever and dysentery. I have seen men here big and strong and healthy one day and in a weeks time . . . walking skeletons. This is no exaggeration . . . Today I have been ill but working all the same. In Military circles it is a crime to be sick and not report but today I care nothing for pain or anything bodily for I have received two letters from my darling . . . *10 Nov*: Of all the ragtime armies in the world ours is in the front rank. Many men have undoubtedly lost their lives through inefficiency of officers and the jumbling of orders . . .' Later in the day he adds:

'Pack up and "prepare to go on tromp". Packs weighing something over 100 pounds. Head for Happy Gully. Bullets flying round and dirt coming over us, the closest call I've had yet. I went down fully expecting to be hit through the head and the next I felt dirt flying and kicking up around me and a feeling of relief. We got quickly to our feet and heard another [shell] coming and ran for shelter to a water tank behind which a crowd of men were sheltering. We reached this in time to escape being run down by the mule teams and Indians who were clearing out in all directions. From the firing line I can see Turkish trenches 30 yards away and between their lines and ours the bodies of some of our chaps can be seen lying in the positions as they fell. These poor chaps have been reported "missing" and will have to remain until the end as it is impossible to get them and in the heat of the day the Turks stir the bodies up with bullets to try to create disease from the stench. The flies are something fearful out here. No doubt this will some day be a fashionable watering place for tourists who will come to see the place on which their dead heroic friends and relations fought: "They shall know them by their bones along the way". I will try to sleep and dream I am back in Tasmania on the banks of the South Esk eating bananas 'neath the shade of its glorious willows as I did one summer not long ago.'

Two days later on 12 November he collapsed with enteric fever and was carried to the 13th Casualty Clearing Station, where he wrote that 'bullets are flying and shrapnel is screaming among the wounded and ill'. He was carried to hospital in Cairo and then sent back to Tasmania in 1916. (The doctors who had earlier turned away men with dental cavities were by now far less selective and many men who had been invalided home re-enlisted and were passed medically fit. Here he joined a militia group, was commissioned Lieutenant later in the year and by 10 February 1917 was on the way to France with the Seventh reinforcements of the 40th Battalion.)

Sapper Harry Dadswell enlisted in September 1915, a small, but wiry lad. 'A boy from the bush, eh?' the army doctor said. 'Did the Ararat [country] doctor sound your chest? Good! Go and put your clothes on, you'll do.' Later, like many of the men who returned, he liked to recall those early days of enlistment as though they were their boyhood – or perhaps because it was the end of it.

'I never forgot our first instruction in bayonet fighting. It brought home to us we weren't playing. After showing us how to hold and handle a rifle with a bayonet on the instructor said, "Go in with the point and if that is turned aside bring the butt to his face and kick hard to his middle". He looked at us and stopped. Then he lowered his rifle and said, "Take that shocked look off your faces men and get this into your heads once and for all. This is war and the only thing that counts is, you win and live. There are no rules, no umpires, and if you die think of what will happen to your folk at home. What will happen to your Mothers and sisters if the enemy beats us. If you die it doesn't matter how, there is no one to protest, no one to say it wasn't fair, so see the enemy dies, not you."'

Norman Young joined up the day he turned eighteen in 1917. The *Bendigo Advertiser* reported: 'Having attained his 18th birthday on Saturday, Mr N. M. Young, son of Mr J. N. Young, a member of the *Advertiser* composing staff, enlisted for active service, and in the evening a number of friends assembled at his place of residence in Honeysuckle Street to congratulate him upon the step he had taken and wish him "many happy returns of the day" . . . A very pleasant evening terminated with the singing of the National Anthem and "God Bless our Splendid Men".

> God bless our splendid men,
> Send them safe home again,
> God save our men.
>
> Keep them victorious,
> Patient and chivalrous,
> They are so dear to us,
> God save our men.

The following week the same newspaper reported the 'Dismissal Service' at St Paul's Church:

'Several hundred members of St Paul's church and Sunday school gathered . . . on the occasion of a "dismissal service", conducted by the Rev. G. H. Cranswick, for Messrs. W. Birch, K. Birch, Norman Young, H. B. Field and W. Buchanan, members . . . who have recently been accepted for active service and are leaving this week to enter camp . . .

'"We want to say to you," said Mr Cranswick, "we like the idea of saying 'good-bye' in this our dear old church, for we want you to remember that from this day on, God helping us, there will never go by a day until God in His mercy brings you back but that you will not be prayed for in the church. Every night at 5.30 o'clock, and every Sunday morning or evening your names will be put up before Almighty God, for His protecting arms to be around you. . . ."'

But Young and his friend H. B. Field were not quite eighteen and a half years old and permission to embark with the 25th Reinforcements was withheld. That they were not easily dissuaded is shown by the following letter to the Prime Minister, William Morris Hughes.

'Both of us are only two months short of the required age. We think it hard that we should be kept from sailing with our mates with whom we have trained since we entered camp. It has also come under our notice that a certain member of the Reinforcements also under the age of 18½ has been allowed to embark through obtaining the influence of a military official. Our parents have given their consent . . . we cannot understand why one can go and another be kept back. Both of us held commissions in the 17th Senior cadets and have been in camp three months. Apart from this we enlisted to do our bit along with the other lads . . . Also we shall reach the age of 18½ by the time we arrive in England.'

In reply they received a memo informing them that the Prime Minister 'is taking this matter up, and will advise'. They lobbied everyone they thought could help. Their persistence was unending. Permission to sail with their battalion was given, but in England permission for their transfer to the trenches in France was withheld. The correspondence started yet again, and once more they won out.

John King also joined in 1917 when he turned eighteen. Speaking sixty years later his recollections were clear – and honest. 'By the time I joined the army the war had been going for several years, it was well known it was no picnic but still at that time the propaganda that they used to put in the papers that we was winning this and winning that . . . always made us to believe we was going to finish the war next week. Even when I went away from Australia they told me I probably wouldn't get there before the war was finished but that didn't come to pass . . . they made everybody believe that it was not exactly a holiday but an experience that everyone ought to have. When I went there was people getting killed and we knew it wasn't any picnic.

'I think if I'd been working I would have waited a bit longer. My school friends were there and I joined the 37th Battalion, as I enlisted from Brunswick and I had to go in reinforcements for battalions of Brunswick men. Each municipality had a quota to try and fill and Brunswick Council would be notified that I had enlisted but you know, eighteen is too young, the strain is a bit too great. Anyway, when you went into camp you were told you'd be 7th Reinforcements to the 37th Battalion. In units raised in this way there was a fair chance you'd run into men you'd known in civilian life.

'Why did I enlist? Well, I was out of work. I was in the building industry and as all building supplies were brought from overseas and the shipping during the war was all directed to military purposes and the industry came to a standstill. You know, you've got to eat. You had the choice of being out of work or you joined the army, so I joined the army because . . . you know . . .'

They trained for three months at Seymour. 'Funny training! "Left turn! Right turn! How do we spend the money we earn", sort of thing.'

He sailed on the *Ballarat*. An extract from the famous diary of this ship reads for 26 April: 'Torpedoed by cripes.' The ship was sixty miles from Southampton.

'Like a lot of other people, I was repacking my kit-bag. I was marking with an indelible pencil my number and name on my underclothing, uniform etc. and lots of us were at this. And we were supposed to be on deck at 2 p.m. for a memorial service for the Anzacs who lost their lives at the

Landing in 1915. And all of a sudden this whoom! come and the boat shivered from end to end and not a soul spoke and all of a sudden I heard someone say, "The bastards have got us!"

'Fortunately for us the torpedo had struck on the stern of the ship. The submarine guard who were to watch out for torpedoes – you could see them travelling under the water – they had sighted the submarine earlier and saw the torpedo leave the sub, and they telephoned the bridge and the Captain began to slew the ship around and it only hit the stern and knocked the propellor off and we had a gun mounted on the stern and it put that out of action. There was wheat in the stern, and that swelled up when the water came in and they realised the boat wouldn't sink right away. I'll always give credit to the Royal Navy. They brought one of their destroyers right alongside and put planks over and there wasn't enough lifeboats to take all of us so was glad because I couldn't swim and you could imagine the number of men who got from one boat to another in a few minutes. But I got off in a lifeboat and it was like you read about – women and children first because there were two nurses in it and I was only a boy! All the life boats were hooked up one behind the other and before night fell there was the best sight I've ever seen in my life as all the ships came to our rescue. They'd sent out an SOS and all sorts of ships came from all directions and there were cruisers, destroyers, trawlers, passenger ships everything. At this time we were in the shipping channel nearly in sight of the English coast. Within fifteen minutes of abandoning ship we saw them begin to come over the horizon from every direction, smoke belching as they put on speed. The first though to come on the scene were the French aeroplanes who were over us in five minutes or so and that saved us from being fired on again and the planes were dropping depth charges to the Sub made itself scarce.

'We have a reunion for the survivors of the *Ballarat* every Anzac day and years later we received a letter from the German Commander of the submarine that sank the *Ballarat* and he put in the letter that he was only doing his duty as we were and that he was always pleased that there was no loss of life. He said that he was now the only man alive that was on that sub. when it sank the *Ballarat* because after he completed the cruise he was transferred to another command, leaving the crew on the submarine. The sub. then went back to sea and was lost with all hands.

'I was picked up by HMS *Hardy*, a destroyer, and put ashore at Southampton and we were told that the Germans had sunk 110 ships that week. For all that they had hot food waiting for us and some straw to kick around on the floor to sleep on.

'When I arrived at Larkhill I found that the English Army had decreed that no one was to go in to the trenches until they were nineteen. So we were kept for guard duty, they called us the "war babies". This caused me to be court-martialled. It wasn't for anything bad . . . I was on guard one day, our own men, and some of these fellows were particular bad characters and this day one . . . thought he'd put on a stunt . . . I was given a prisoner to take to the doctor's surgery. The Corporal sent me off alone with him, I knew nothing about the man but I learnt later he'd escaped four times before, he'd been up for court-martials but they didn't tell me. He nipped out the surgery window but I didn't know . . . eventually I found out and reported it . . . I always believed it was the fault of the administration who should have told me he was a desperate character. And we should have had an officer in charge of us war babies guard. They put me in a detention camp for six weeks where I had to sit on my backside and read books and when they marched me down to be court-martialled they had a guard of six men, a sergeant and a lieutenant in charge on me – and here I'd been sent off alone with that desperate bloke. It was all show. Now in the court-martial I'm not supposed to say a word, supposed to leave it to the Counsel allotted me but he was on their side and made no point of my being sent off alone with a dangerous character when it should have been several men in charge of an officer. Well, the sergeant and the lieutenant had been out having a few beers but now they say the lieutenant gave orders to the Sergeant, the Sergeant to the Corporal and the Corporal ordered me etc. etc. I could see how it was going but there was nothing I could do. I waited another five weeks in the detention camp. They had to find me guilty – otherwise they would have had to go the higher-ups and that would never do. So they marched me out on the parade ground, still under this guard. The men are formed up in a square and they read your sentence out, what you're charged with – I was charged with not paying proper attention to what I was doing and letting a prisoner escape . . . the least they could sentence me was seven days . . . So all in all I spent two or three months in the detention camp but I got my pay back, all except the seven days, so it was all an experience.

'Anyway it probably saved my life because by the time I got to France the Battle of Messines was finished and lots of our reinforcements were killed.'

Young Will Dodds set off on 22 December 1916 with a parcel of cake from his granny. Willy, aged eighteen, had known ever so slightly Glennie, of the same age. He wrote to her in a tentative fashion at first, and then became bolder and signed off as, 'Your own adoring Will'. Until 11 July 1917, as the battle of Passchendaele began.

'Dearest Glennie,

You must excuse this photo but I hope you will hold it dear to you as it is the last photo before crossing into real action. We fall-in to go over at 1.15 a.m. tomorrow morning. Accept my very best love and kisses once more today as this is the second note. Au revoir. Very best love from your own loving soldier, Will. [He then drew a circle and placed a large 'x' in it.] Strictly private. I have kissed this spot dear. [Until this time he had never called himself her soldier, and had been bantering, light-hearted.] Stop worrying about my meeting girls. They are all far away from us here anyway!'

Twice, Guy Martin ('Marty') Berry had attempted to

enlist but been 'knocked back' owing to a weakness left from typhoid fever contracted as a child. To avoid being handed a white feather in the street he wore on his lapel the big shiny badge issued to the medically unfit. After the heavy casualties of 1916 he volunteered again, was accepted, and sailed immediately.

He had his hair cut short to his scalp 'all except a little tuft or curl in front which the divisional signallers affect'. Like most of the letter writers he was anxious to cause his home folks as little heart-ache as possible. 'I shall write regularly but any number of unexpected things happen to prevent mail getting through. Should a man be wounded, notification would reach his people long before his letters stopped. Anyway, the Divvy Sigs seem to be a lucky crowd.'

The passing of the old year and welcoming the new was the last 'Marty' would see, and he enjoyed it as if he knew it would be his last. 'New Year's Day 1917: Given over entirely to the sports . . . Nearly everybody has entered for something just for the fun of it. Have you ever seen "cock-fighting"? Well, one chap is horse and the other rider. The rider is carried about on the horse's back. He tries to drag the opposing rider from his steed. The first pair that fall are the losers. Sometimes with an evenly matched lot the two riders take their arms from round the necks of their respective horses and fight with both hands. The scrap then generally resolves itself into a tug of war with each rider hanging on to the other and each horse pulling at the ankles of his rider. One of the riders must come off. . . .

'We have just been paid one pound and some have already started "Banker". Some of them will have lost it all in a few minutes. There was a poker school full swing and the port hole was open and a whacking big wave came and swamped them – now they're all changing their clothes!'

These last few months were full of interest for him. Durban was a delight. 'The Durban Corporation allows soldiers and sailors to travel free on the electric trams which run through the town and suburbs so we fly about everywhere – finishing up with a bathe in the surf. It was A1. Ever since leaving Melbourne we had promised ourselves a good dinner when we should land so us four sappers walked in to a hotel as though we were colonels and gourmandised to our hearts content.'

All too soon, it seems, his hour came. He was killed at Passchendaele (the third Battle of Ypres) on 4 October 1917. His brother Geoffrey was killed at Villers-Bretonneux.

Durban was one of the few stop-overs for reinforcements *en route* 'for the front'. Here they received a great welcome. The young 'Driver' Cripps who, on 4 August 1914, had volunteered to sail with the 'First Australian Expeditionary Force in the Pacific Ocean' is now Lieutenant B. A. Cripps of the 41st Battalion and leaving Brisbane. '*16 May 1916*: Left Enoggera station 8 a.m. en route for Sydney . . . All along the line the people gave us a real good time . . . The men decorated the carriages with ferns and it looked real well.

'*31 May*: At sea on Submarine Guard. All good shots. The Guard is known as the "Tin Openers". *18 June:* The "Yellow Jack" is flying on our fore-mast. In quarantine in Durban. Boer policemen and our guard preventing men from getting ashore. About 100 men broke leave today and a couple received their first taste of the bayonet when they broke through the guard. We leave the docks and anchor in the Bay. The people have been very good to us, gave us a lot of fruit and sweets. The ship stinks of sulphur from being fumigated.'

Ships were now shuttling back and forth across the world's oceans taking fit men out and passing ships returning to Australia with the wounded and sick. On the *Clan Macgillivray*, bound for the front in October 1916, the ship's newsheet (*The Macgillivray Magster*) wrote after leaving Durban, 'Many thanks Durban. Your doors were thrown open to us and we found a welcome in your homes; your trams were ours to make use of, the portals of your zoo were open wide. You showered us with kindness in a hundred ways and for it all you have our grateful thanks. As the Sentimental Bloke says, "I dips me lid".'

One 'Fair Dinkum' was in the unique position of being a

woman writing brave letters to her sweetheart who was safely at home. Matron Gertrude F. Moberly (later RRC) sent scores of very personal letters to her beloved 'Peter' from some of the world's most outlandish hospitals. 'Maybe', she says on her first night away in July 1915, 'the little fishes will be my companions. I hope not, they are cold. I like warm companions.'

'Here we are all on board the Troop Ship *Orsova*, and thrilled to the "marrow bone" at the "future all unknown", determined in our fluttering hearts to make good . . . Poor old boy! Do not worry too much; it is no fault of yours that that appendix had to be removed just when typhoid fever was doing its damnedest to make a certainty of your having "your toes turning up to the daisies". Oh, Pete, I . . . must confess to a prayer of thanksgiving to the "Bon Dieu" for making the M.O. definitely decide that you were unfit for active service. Of course, had you been fit and not offered, then I should have been equally upset, for you would not have been the man I believe in and love. We left the wharf at 10.30 a.m. and I sadly missed your dear old face among the crowd seeing us off. Thank you for those lovely roses . . . I kissed them all for you, and was aching to see you again. Our parting was so short . . . I shall write often, and you must do likewise.'

Gertrude was a Mosman woman, and, as time passed, an outspoken critic of the war. 'When I return I am going to go into politics on whichever side favours anti war. Those are the men I will vote and canvass for.' Another time she writes, 'What have we personally against the Germans? It is simply awful that millions have to suffer to satisfy the greed of a few in high positions'. But all this was later. Her first letters are a strange amalgam of many emotions.

'The *Orsova* arrived in Melbourne about noon. We have all been most excited watching troops being brought on board, also Sisters from Victoria, South Australia and Tasmania, and as we watched along came the HS *Kyarra* with all her poor wounded boys. Oh, what cheering they received. But, Peter, I could not stop the tears falling (my own two darling brothers killed), and Will, the only brother left, in camp at Enoggera, Queensland. All these 1400 boys, too; how many of them would return, or perhaps return, and in ten or fifteen years be forgotten? All this hectic talk of our "brave boys" . . . is sincerely said now, and every word meant, I grant – but a promise made now is not genuinely thought to be (and is, I feel sure) a bond, to be kept for all time. But, Peter, darling, why the Bible knows the unreliability of man – even princes. . . . Mark my words, "the day will come, and a retribution, when all this money so lavishly borrowed by those at the head of affairs all over the world will fall on the unborn men and women to come, a depression which will cause misery and starvation to many" for any thinking man or woman who studies the history of finance and economics knows the aftermath of war – heavy taxation, which, darling, you and I, as well as the millions, will have to bear.'

20
The Station Hands

From out at Hughes Park sheep station (SA) the station hands moved in to enlist. One who survived the war, Eddie (E. C.) Johnson, wrote memoirs of those days for his children. 'Four boys from Hughes Park – Joe Hamp, Arthur Hamp, Billy Elliott and myself – enlisted on February 14th, 1916. After being passed by the Army at Keswick, we arrived at the Jubilee Oval, Frome Road. We slept between seats, on the floor of a grandstand, owned at that time by the Show Society. While there, we were innoculated and vaccinated. . . . After a week, an officer asked each of us what our occupation was in civilian life. Joe Hamp explained to him that the four of us had come from Hughes Park sheep station, so we were told to step forward two paces, and with others were sent to Mitcham Light Horse Camp, where we commenced our drill.

'On observing a squad marching out of the camp with signal flags, I became very interested and told Joe that that kind of work appealed to me . . . My application was accepted, and, on arriving at the Signal quarters, I found that a signalling school course occupied a month, and the present school had one week to go. While waiting for the next school, I was placed with two efficient signallers, who gave me great encouragement in learning semaphore and morse code with flags, and also morse code with a buzzer. This helped me considerably for my turn in the next school. It must have been a lucky break for me, for on completion of my school exam, I managed to top the school, and was made a temporary Corporal with three others, for a following

school. . . . The signalling work became very interesting.
We would do Helio work by having four signal stations,
and messages would be sent out to these stations, on top of
the Pier Hotel at Glenelg, on top of the *Advertiser* building,
also to Windy Point, and back to the Signal School at
Mitcham. On other occasions a squad would be in the Hills
and would signal by morse code flags to a squad in the
signal school. Signalling would also be carried out at night
with lamps. . . . Eight of us had been informed we would be
sent off to England shortly as reinforcements with the
Divisional Signalling Engineers, and we were granted a
short leave . . . The following day when I left for Mitcham,
mother walked over the hill with me to Watervale. It was
hard saying farewell to her . . . At last the eventful day
arrived . . . Our eight Signallers paraded on the "gravel
patch", with others for inspection at 9 a.m. at the Mitcham
Camp, and at 10 a.m. we left by train . . . We arrived at the
Outer Harbour and we then marched to the wharf. It was
impossible to pick out any people, as all we could see was a
wall of faces. After giving up my embarkation card at the
gate, we embarked on the A.73 SS *Commonwealth*, 7 000
tons – the name had been painted over. The deck Sgt.
showed us our "Possie" which was D deck, in the steerage
quarters, and when everyone had stowed their belongings
away, we were dismissed. It was then a rush up to the poop
deck, to get a "possie", just as the people were let in on the
wharf. When the mater and Kath had located me, Kath
sent a streamer up to me. I cut a piece of the streamer for a
keepsake. Lill came afterwards and sent up peanuts and
apples. At about 1.20 p.m. our boat left the Outer Harbour.
I stayed waving to them until they gradually disappeared
from sight.'

On arriving in England he was sent to a riding school for
one week. When horses were issued, it was found that only
one Australian had not been on a horse before. 'He was a
Melbournite, so he was nick-named Bobby Lewis, after a
well-known Victorian jockey. When grooming our horses,
Bobbie was next to me in the stables, and was having

trouble with his horse giving him sly nips, while my horse was quiet and easy to groom. This gave Bobby ideas, so the horses were exchanged. That morning we entered a very large closed-in building, with thick sawdust on the floor, for a riding test. With our 40 horses, the instructor ordered the troops to make a line of horses down the centre of the building, side by side. At that time the English Tommies were completing their test by going round the circle mounted on their horses. On completion of this they were lined up behind the Australians. The instructor told them mockingly to watch how the Australians can ride! On the order to the Australians to 'step forward all those that reckon they can ride a horse', no Australian stepped forward. The next order was 'All those that have been on a horse before, step forward', and they all stepped forward. He then yelled 'Mount!

'It was a thriller – when I was mounting, my eye wandered down the line of horses – all sorts of styles were being used; one with a small horse even carried out a hand spring from the back! On the order to dismount, some were correct, others cocked their right leg over and slid off, some put their arms around the horse's neck and swung off! The next order was that in the Army you do it all by numbers 1, 2, 3, etc, and had explained to us the procedure. The Tommies enjoyed the entertainment!

'Later a lecture on how to saddle a horse was given. We had a very efficient instructor, who was more sociable than the Sgt. Major at the horse lines. . . . To complete our riding schooling, a test was made in the large, enclosed building. When mounted we trotted around the arena in single file, and, without using stirrups, arms folded, with reins dropped on the pummel of the saddle, we had to complete our exam by going over a 3 ft. hurdle. Everything went along fine until the hurdle came up for Bobby. Unknown to us, he had a trick horse, and, on the instructor blowing a whistle, his horse stopped dead. Result – Bobby went over the hurdle without the horse.

'The English Officers were very good to us, apart from

the Sgt. Mjr. at the horse lines. He would come to our hut in the early hours of the morning, turn the lights on, and pull the blankets off the ones sleeping. He made everyone rise and groom the horses before breakfast. Andy, always our spokesman, thought it would be a good idea to stop this nonsense. We planned that action was to be made when the Sgt. Mjr. was half way in the hut. Loftie who slept by the door would put the light out, and the remainder were to throw their boots at the Sgt. Mjr, then cover up and shield themselves from flying boots that missed the target. A miracle worked – and Sgt. Mjr. did not worry us after that brain wave!

'The next school included lectures and practical work on permanent lines. With a pair of climbers fastened to our legs, we would climb poles in cold and frosty weather, and also learnt the right way to mend cable breaks and how to wire a test board. It was emphasised that we should never let the front line Troops down, and that we should remember the three C's – Courage, Co-operation and communications . . .

'Our stay . . . came to a finish after being put through a test on Permanent Line work (theory) and practical line work. The instruction received at Haynes Park was a wonderful experience for our future work. On Jan 13th we entrained back to Hitchin. . . .

'Every day it snowed and, after stable work, we paraded for drill and physical exercise in the parklands. One elderly man would appear from a distance every day and inspect the troops. He thought they were perfect when doing their neck exercise. Unknown to him it was smoko time and the troops formed rings playing two up – hence the apparent neck exercises as they watched the coin spinning!

'The Sgt. Mjr. asked me to take on driving until more drivers arrived. I named my two wheelers "Splinter" and "Rowdy", after the two bullocks at home. They were pretty slow, so I invested in some common lollies for them as a change of diet, which speeded them up. When out exercising the horses one day, the Sgt. Mjr. rode up to me, and said he had never spotted the two horses so close to the front before. It was a work of art driving them on the icy roads. . . . The Sgt. Mjr. ordered me to take Splinter and Rowdy and go out for a load of wood. The axemen sat in the back and another Aussie named Doc drove the leaders. On our way, looking for fire wood, Doc and I spotted a most beautiful house . . . some distance from the road. We decided to go through the large entrance gates at a trot, where a private road led us to this large building. Being dinner time, the G.P. waggon was left at the main entrance to the building, while Doc and I put our horses in a really flash stable. The others had gained entrance from household servants, who were the only occupants in charge of the premises. Noticing a dead limb on a tree in the parklands, the servants allowed the axemen to cut it up for firewood. We saw deer and pheasants etc. living in the area. The property was . . . Lord Lucan's Estate and named Wrest Park. Unfortunately Lord Lucan was killed in an aeroplane in France during Nov. 1916. . . .

'On Feb. 17th, it was flag day for the citizens of Shefford. The Aussies held a fancy dress procession for the occasion. I drove "Splinter" and "Rowdy" in a bridal coach and pair, the coach being 120 years old. I was dressed up as an aboriginal, with straw hat and clay pipe. Frank was the bride and Os the bridegroom. The Aussies raised 50 pounds that day. One weekend, three of us hired bicycles and journeyed to Bedford.

'I was now a cable hand on a draft 110 strong being sent to France. We were separated from the others, and, parading in full marching order, we received our pay books and also a green disc with name, number and religion, then some "leg-pulling" by the adjutant, re. splendid chaps and a tip top draft. On leaving Shefford, the residents gave us a wonderful send off. . . .'

21
Somewhere in
France

Private Vic Graham was 'outraged' when, newly arrived in
France on 25 April 1916, he saw a copy of a German
newspaper found on a German prisoner. 'They alleged that
with the arrival of Australians in France "it was regretted
that the noble sons of Germany should be pitted against
such filthy human refuse, the descendants of convicts and
blackguards who were transported to Tasmania by England
in earlier times",' he wrote.

After eight weeks re-training in the desert, the reinforcing
of decimated battalions and the actual doubling in numbers
of the AIF between the withdrawal from Gallipoli and their
re-entering the war, the Australians sailed to France. They
had recovered their health, their wounds had been patched
up, and now it was Europe – where the *real* war was.

> Come cheer up brave Anzacs
> You're off to the war
> You'll soon meet your comrades
> Who've gone on before
> You'll soon be in Flanders to fight with the French
> Then, never look back but go forward and trench.*

There was very little chauvinism written from the
trenches. I have come on only two letters that could be
construed as 'bull-dusting' and even these were not
exaggerations so much as aberrations: the two soldiers I
have in mind were telling of factual occurrences but in
'gung-ho' terms as if to impress the receiver of the letters. In

* Published by Dinsdales Pty Ltd Melbourne.

each case the recipient was someone they had known back home who had not enlisted, and both writers appeared to be attempting to deny the accusation that they were 'six bob a day tourists' by stressing the dangers they ran, the wounds they received. But if the participants were not bull-dusting, then much of the world back home was scarcely surfacing through a sea of sentimentality, grand gestures and, in the case of much entertainment, cashing in on every facet of the war. The end of Gallipoli and the beginning of France gave rise to an explosion of song and verse. Some of the better known poets, men such as Hugh McCrae who should have known better, wrote far lesser poems than the despised doggerel of the rhymester in the trench. Christopher Brennan concludes his quite awful 'Lions of War' with:

> . . . to stride the road of victory to the end,
> and smite to hell you ravening bulk of sin –
> humble and proud, we greet and claim you kin.

Vance Palmer wrote:

What went ye forth to seek? Strange sights in a far street?
No, not for this a thousand roads, Have felt your marching
  feet.
What went ye forth to guard? An Empire's glittering pride?
No, not for this your blood gushed out, upon that dark
  hillside.
But free at your own hearth, and dreaming nought of harm,
Your eyes with horror saw the flames leap from a Flemish
  farm.
And Evil's shape grew clear, And Truth shone bright as
  day
When the black guns of Prussia blew, Your boyhood
  dreams away.

And from T. W. Heney we have:

> These even as their fathers, with their blood
> Consecrate our Flag. How shall we recompense
> The Perished promise of their golden youth?
> How save by Love, and love unto the end?

'A British Officer' according to London *Punch*, December 1915, referred to Australians as 'The bravest thing God ever made', and a poem appeared under the title: 'The Australian'

> We know – it is our deathless pride –
> The splendour of his first fierce blow;
> How, reckless, glorious, undenied,
> He stormed those steel-lined cliffs we know!
> And none who saw him scale the height
> Behind his reeking bayonet-blade
> Would rob him of his title right –
> 'The bravest thing God ever made!'
>
> *W. Ogilvie*

The fledgling Returned Soldiers' League in Sydney brought out a booklet of remembrance on 25 April 1916, in which the opening quatrain speaks of Mother, as of Homeland, particularly England.

> They owed their mother such a love
> That only life could pay
> Who to Gallipoli bequeathed
> The Freedom of their Clay.

But the women writers knew which mother mourned the laughing boys who had had donkey races and scratched their names on the pyramids of Egypt. Of all the women poets touched by the war Mary (later Dame Mary) Gilmore wrote most trenchantly.

> Gallipoli
> Had he never been born he was mine:
> Since he was born he never was mine:
> Only the dream is our own.
>
> Where the world called him there he went;
> When the war called him, there he bent.
> Now he is dead.

He was I; bone of my bone,
Flesh of my flesh, in truth;
For his plenty I gave my own,
His drouth was my drouth.

When he laughed I was glad,
In his strength forgot I was weak,
In his joy forgot I was sad
Now there is nothing to ask or to seek;
He is dead.

I am the ball the marksman sent,
Missing the end and falling spent;
I am the arrow, sighted fair
That failed, and finds not anywhere.
He who was I is dead.

Dowell O'Reilly wrote:

The Mother

He was all I had to give: Now, life has nothing for me;
For my heart lies in a nameless grave on far Gallipoli.
Why should I dry my tears, or talk of Victory!
For my heart lies dead in a nameless grave on far Gallipoli.
God guard all mothers' sons fighting for liberty
But my heart lies dead in a nameless grave on far
Gallipoli.

Dorothea MacKellar wrote a desperate stricture:

What does the World our mother remember while empires
die?
Honour and dreams and courage, and everything else goes
by
Lost in the dust of her going, lost in time's whelming seas:
Mother, forgetful mother, you shall remember these!

There was another side to war. Girls who were just
reaching womanhood were aware of it. Wolla Meranda put
it plainly, painfully, as early as 1916.

They will never come back – our stalwart men!
They will never come back – our splendid men!
And Beauty weeps in the land of the morn
For the flowers of love that will never be born.

And one remembers Amy Lowell's 'Patterns':

For the man who should loose me is dead,
Fighting with the Duke in Flanders,
In a pattern called a war.
Christ! What are patterns for?

Some poems, 'horribly stuffed with epithets of war', come from the Anzacs but not nearly so many as from the pens of the poets cashing in on the war back home. C. J. Dennis was a fine example of this. He has Ginger Mick killed off at Gallipoli thinking it would make for better sales and for further poems as 'The Sentimental Bloke' consoles Mick's widow, 'Rose of Spadgers'. Later, his returned 'Digger Smith' is the epitome of topicality masquerading as poetry.

The fighting men didn't think of themselves as poets; they merely found rhymestering a less embarrassing way to record their tears, toils and horrors and the jubilation of comradeship. Some, like the 7th Battalion, published their own little booklet, each 'poem' referring to the region where a company was formed. Every Battalion could boast songs similar to those in the Seventh's little pink-covered book but mostly the versifiers at the front were reflective.

Remember, Lord, Australia's sons tonight.
Be Thou their refuge in the darkest hour,
Be Thou their stay;
Stretch forth Thy hand, show thine almighty power
In Thine own way;
Thou didst on Gallilee reveal Thy might –
Oh! comfort, Lord, Australia's sons tonight.'
        (Anonymous writer from France, to be sung
        to the tune of 'Lead Kindly Light'.)

They cut out, and pasted in, and laboriously copied by hand poems about Australia, Australians and the war, and although a rough pattern of their selection is repeated in the collections almost *all* the poems are at variance with their own modest written records and with their often stated denigration of war. An exception is the original poem of Private Vic Graham who survived Mouquet Farm. He was to write:

> But of war, when all is torn or rent,
> When life is finished and blood is spent,
> Is there no better brighter way
> Than forfeit lives as devilish pay?
> For devil he must surely be
> To claim lives of our heroes to pay the fee.

In France the killing went on, and on, and the living survived under conditions that can scarcely be imagined because our imagination always stops at the impossible.

'I suppose', said Jim McPhee, 'we didn't really live. Our breath came, but that is the only resemblance.' Like all men who returned from France he spoke of another thing. 'Our bodies – some hobbled with trench feet, some had toes off with frost-bite; some shook with trench-fever – a sort of rheumatic fever that weakened the bones and joints; many had sores that wouldn't heal, all had lice; many had running noses and eyes long after they'd come back from treatment, from being gassed, and almost all had experienced shell shock to some degree – the slightest being the shakes, or bleeding from the ears, ranging to complete dementia. But that other thing that happened that you remember when you've forgotten all the bodily pain, none of us have been able to adequately explain this to anyone who wasn't there; there are no words for it; comradeship, mateship are not really what we experienced, it was . . . brotherhood. My own brother Vic was with me all the way from Gallipoli to 1917 in France when he was killed and we were awfully close but I've seen, and known, plenty of relationships in France as close as that with fellows who hadn't met before the war. I've even experienced this myself. It's something to do with having to rely *completely* on one another in life, in wounding, and even in death, that your mate – whoever is near you at the time – will see to your people, your kids, wife. I don't like to talk about it now because I don't think it can be explained.'

(On Anzac eve, 1976, the Melbourne *Age* published an article in which it was stated that this special thing was, in fact, 'sublimated homosexuality'. Surely there can be no greater evidence of the inability of any who were not with them to understand the relationship that these men knew.)

Roy Rankin wrote to his mother who had expressed a wish to send a gift to the *mate* he always mentioned in his letters: 'You want to know who is my chum, but I can't tell you for whoever I was on post with, or whoever I shared a dug-out with, was my mate. You see it is hard for any two to stick together and the whole platoon are mates.'

22
Fromelles

The French army, battered in a manner that had not before been seen in warfare, was in danger of becoming exhausted at Verdun. Driven out of 'impregnable' forts by the Germans the men still fought tenaciously from bomb craters in the ground and the enemy could make little headway against them, but their desperate defence could not hold out forever unless the Germans were harassed and deployed elsewhere. And so, on 1 July 1916, the Battle of the Somme (named for the nearby Somme River) began, an almost entirely British enterprise and one where more men were killed or crippled and there were more mental and emotional casualties than anywhere else the British nation has gone to war. In Australia in 1978 there are still men who are in hospital from that time. I have visited patients whose periods of lucidity are interrupted by weeks and months of terror, fear that pushes them over the lip of sanity.

The Australian introduction to the Somme was the most brutal experience they had yet met: Fromelles, named for the nearby remnants of a shattered town, was to be the Lone Pine of France.

As though to show them what their fate would be in the remaining years of the war, Fromelles was hideous. The Australians, many of whom had never been in a battle, were not ready. They said they were 'ready and anxious' but enthusiasm is not the same thing as being thoroughly prepared. The allocation of artillery and ammunition was questioned but was said to be 'ample'. And there was 400 yards of No Man's Land to cross at a spot called 'The Sugar

236

Loaf'. (Military experience has since proved that attack formations should not have to charge more than about 200 yards across open country.) To help the infantry get across this twice-the-recommended attacking distance, it was decided they would begin the charge while the artillery barrage was still going on. As with so many battles there were many generals vieing with one another in what in a later age would be called one-up-manship. Some declared that there was grave risk of disaster, one admitted that the operation was no longer urgent; Generals Birdwood and Brudenall White were said to be 'acutely anxious' about the whole project 'but had no power to intervene'. It would be a joint 'hop-over' with the 5th Australian and 61st British Divisions attacking. As it turned out it was to be a venture that caused Australian troops ever after to distrust and view with disdain the new 'Tommy' as a fighting unit.

The Australian 5th Division set off on 15 July on the forced march to the assembly line through crowded communication trenches, pushing their way forward for two days and two nights without sleep; before slumping to the ground on arrival they learned that none of the artillery, trench mortars or ammunition, not even they, the infantry, were in their final position. Rain fell, the heavy guns were unable to be manoeuvred into place, mist concealed their targets. Then one general asked another if the battle could be postponed; this was agreed to and the troops were awakened, some being sent back behind the lines to rest. One general now asked another if the battle could be cancelled altogether; but the other said no.

On 19 July the men moved up once again, in bright sunny weather, 'in fine fettle' and at 6 p.m. the general advance began.

While in the attacking trenches waiting for the word to 'Go!' the left flank (the 8th Brigade) had been so heavily shelled by the Germans that several hundred Australians had been killed or wounded before the 'hop-over'. Worse, their own artillery caught them and killed them. Then, as they began their run, Germans outside the area of their attack shot them down. These 8th Brigade men had had no experience of battle except for their march to the trenches and their wait in them during the past two days, but their training stood, as did their determination, and they took the first trench, the Germans fleeing before them. The order had been to 'take the third trench and hold it as front line', but now, surrounded by ditches, shell holes and the haze of shell smoke, the leaders realised that a mistake had been made. There was no third trench – or if there ever had been it was now part of the morass of watery slashes in the land. They therefore decided to settle their men in what they called 'the first and second ditch' and the men, over their boots in water, began to fill sandbags.

Across in the centre of the field, although none of the groups could see one another for the thick smoke of the artillery barrage and burning farm-houses, the quarter-mile-wide No Man's Land now held the dead, wounded and the survivors sheltering in watery ditches from the furious rifles above them. The distance across was so great that Brigadier-General Elliott reported that his 15th Brigade attack appeared to have succeeded, because the Germans were no longer firing. He could not see his riddled brigade in the tangled rank grass. The lines that had followed the first attackers thought those first men must be waiting to make the final rush – then they, too, met the tempest of machine guns and rifles and, as they went to earth, saw the dead and dying around them in the grass and ditches.

The British troops to the right had not been successful and now those men on the far left who had looked for the 'third trench' were exposed to fire that later surrounded them. All senior officers in the 53rd Battalion (of the 14th Brigade) had been killed or wounded. Young Captain C. Arblaster then organised the defence of the beleaguered battalions.

While these movements were taking place, across on the right the British 61st Division decided to capture the Sugar Loaf, where No Man's Land was a quarter of a mile wide. They sent word to the Australian 15th Brigade, who had originally failed, to help them.

At 9 p.m. as arranged the 58th Battalion (15th Brigade) charged the by-now even more heavily defended Sugar Loaf, but the British 61st Division had cancelled their plan and the 58th had begun their attack before the belated message arrived. Like the first attack, this failed and more men died.

Back on the left flank, young Arblaster, who had taken charge when all the senior officers were killed or wounded, was strengthening his advanced line when suddenly he saw 'spiked helmets' (the Germans) moving along the 'first trench' between his position and the Australian lines. He was now encircled but he organised such a counter attack that no more enemy could get into that 'first trench' although he could not dislodge those already in. From the Australian line all that could be seen were white flares curving through the dust and smoke and the sound of bombing. 'From that corner the call for bombers never ceased,' wrote C. E. W. Bean. 'Captain Murray, farther along the front would nod to one of his officers to move off with their men into the inferno. Of every ten men that went barely one came back. Troops firing to their front were being shot from their rear. Finally, having held the Germans until early morning Arblaster decided that the only remaining chance of saving the position was to face to the rear (towards the Australian trenches) and charge that portion of the Germans who were holding their old front line. He lined his men out, distributed bombs, gave the signal, and then led the charge. Heavy fire immediately broke out. Arblaster was mortally wounded, and the line fell back to its trench.'

More Germans ran into the trench that cut the beleaguered men off from the Australian lines. There was only one thing for it: they must attempt to run back through the Germans to the Australian trenches and by 5.45 a.m. on the day following that long night the last of them to succeed reached their own breastworks and were dragged down into the 'trench'.

Those men still out in enemy-held territory were now ordered to 'withdraw'. They set off singly and in twos and threes at 8 a.m. Left to command the rear-guard was a massive Queenslander, Captain Norman Gibbons, a man 'of great height and strength' who held off the Germans until the brigade had all got away from the trench. He was the last to leave, going down a communication trench that had been dug across No Man's Land during the night. This trench was clogged with wounded and dying men, it was impossible to move without crushing them, so Gibbons climbed out to give them relief and as he climbed the Australian parapet he was killed by a German bullet.

Other parties still cut off behind the German lines fought on, but there was no way they could be rescued, and the last man firing was heard at 9.20 a.m. All reports, diaries, letters and tape-recordings of the survivors of Fromelles tell of one thing: the scene in the trenches where wounded and dying were piled up. There never was, before or after, such a scene for Australians. The 5th Division had lost 5533 men, 400 of these prisoners, as well as many wounded still out on No Man's Land. The British 61st Division lost 1547 and the Germans in the vicinity of 1500 – all in forty-eight hours.

Opposite the Sugar Loaf the greatest number of wounded lay on No Man's Land.

The New South Welshman, Sergeant H. R. Williams (56th Battalion), wrote a touching – and damning – record of this tragedy and it is interesting to compare this battle-ground with Gallipoli. On the peninsula there were no civilians, shops, drinking or entertainment centres. While awaiting their turn to move up to the front at Fromelles some men of the 56th Battalion 'entered an *estaminet* and found the place crowded to overflowing. Madame and her assistants were hard pressed to cope with the rush. All talk was of the "stunt" and the women of the *estaminet* knew the details as well as we did. We were only about three miles from the front line. We stayed in the *estaminet* for some time and then strolled back to our billet. As parade time came all was bustle'.

The peasants hoeing the mangold fields watched them pass without ceasing their work, tilling the crops on the edge of the battleground under the arch of the shells already beginning to fall on trenches the Australians would occupy. The Germans knew that a division new to the Western Front was coming into the line: 'refugees' sent word, enemy airmen spotted the white horse new to a certain paddock, the washer-woman's habit of spreading her linen in a field suddenly became a message of coloured cloths placed by '*franc-tireurs*', selling information to the enemy.

The bombardment was meant to break the spirit of this new division. The genuine inhabitants knew this, as they also knew more about the attack than the Australians who at that period of the war were never given details 'for fear of information falling into enemy hands'. The French knew that the Germans were in possession of a copy of operation orders before the battalion commanders themselves had received them.

The men moved off to the trenches with bees humming in the drowsy sunshine, smoke rising from cottage chimneys, past a crucifix in a brick shrine. Shells fell among them as they marched.

Their leader, Captain Fanning, was known to be one of the hardest of martinets but also one of the most sensible. There is no record of his men being anything but well-informed and so disciplined that if it was possible to live through such a time their training would assist them to do so.

This was the first time into battle for many of the men. Sergeant Williams recalls, 'We entered a shallow trench, here we sustained our first casualties. The first experience of shell fire, the shattering of the trench breastworks, the concussion of the exploding shells and the smell of high explosives are still vivid in my memory. . . . At dusk, the order came for us to move up to the front line. The German shelling and machine gun firing had now reached a terrific volume. The trench had in places ceased to exist as a defined work; the bodies of dead men lay thickly along its length. The German shells still sought this sap and blew great craters along its length as we struggled through, trampling underfoot the dead who cluttered it. All the while we were losing men. Some of the wounded lay in pools staining the water with their blood.

'Dead men, broken trench material, shattered duckboards that tripped us as we passed, the smell of the fumes of the high explosives and the unforgettable odour of death made this trench a place of horror.'

So they 'marched' to battle lines. A gas alarm was passed down and on went the vile-smelling gas helmets. The heat of their heads soon clouded the glasses and they floundered through the mire and fell over the dead in the shattered trench, partly blinded. At one stage Williams and his mate Alex O'Rourke, in their semi-blindness, got out into the open through the shattered side of an angle in the broken trench and had eventually to remove their helmets to find their way back.

Williams writes bitterly of the non-existent trench the men had crossed No Man's Land to find, and of the 61st Brigade, the British. 'There can be no excuse for the way our troops were misled on the very vital point of the situation of the German second line of defence.

'In the din, concussion and horror of it all we went about our jobs as though stunned. I suppose the numbing concussion was a good thing in that it dulled our senses to the horrors about us. Captain Fanning was constantly along our line and walked about talking to us as though not a shell were falling. His conduct was a wonderfully steadying influence.' This battalion was a supporting one, and spent the night trying to get bombs, ammunition, wire and sandbags up to the besieged battalions but many were killed *en route* and they and the material further clogged the narrow shallow ditches used as trenches. Their wounded, staggering back, told of the hopeless task of attempting to hold a position where the Germans knew the ground so thoroughly that their bombing parties were appearing 'from everywhere'.

These support trenches had their own horrors, even though the concern of the men was with their friends in the encircled area. Beside Williams a man was knocked down by shrapnel. 'He raved like a lunatic, calling out to his mother to shut the gate and other nonsense until, exhausted, he moaned in a way horrible to hear.

'At last daybreak came and in its light we saw the battle-field in all its ghastliness. In the long rank grass that covered the No Man's Land of yesterday were lying the dead and wounded. Many of the latter were trying to crawl back to us, and in doing so made a target of themselves for the machine gunners. Among us were many of the wounded from the attacking battalions, their uniforms caked with mud and blood from their wounds.' He watched the run across the open by the remnants of the 14th Brigade. 'We were powerless to assist them, and had to watch them shot down at point-blank range. Regardless of anything else we stood up on the fire-step to assist this race with death. It seemed an eternity of time before the lucky ones reached our parapets to be pulled in by willing hands. No sooner was our field of fire clear than we blazed into the Germans who had lined their parapets to punish the retiring troops. Few of the rearguard escaped. Many of them disobeyed the order to save themselves and continued to fight in the German line to give their comrades a chance to retire.'

By 11 a.m. both sides had fought to a standstill and not a gun was being fired. The men looked about as if waking from a nightmare. 'All faces ghastly white showing through masks of grime and dried sweat, eyes glassy, protruding, and full of that horror seen only upon men who have lived through a heavy bombardment. We realised in a dull way that we were hungry and sat on the remnant of the fire-step and munched bully-beef and biscuits. Then Peter Hughes and I went along to a dump to get a tin of water. Our path was strewn with dead men lying mangled and huddled in the ruins of bays or along the shattered duckboards. We reached the dump and helped ourselves to a gallon tin of water which had been used for petrol and tasted through the water. On our way back I stood on a corpse and to my horror I recognised the man who, on my first night in Liverpool camp (NSW) had spread his blankets beside me.'

Williams had again seen this man, now a lieutenant, when they were in Paris. 'Now he was lying alongside the duckboards practically cut in two.'

Out in No Man's Land the wounded were crying out for water and for help. 'One man almost in front of our bay crawled inch by inch towards us, drawing a badly wounded pal with him. He got within a few yards of our parapet when he was fired upon by a German sniper. The two then took shelter in a shell hole and called to us for water. A bottle was filled and heaved over the parapet to them. One of them called that they would wait until dark before moving again. There was another man I could see in a slight depression working with his entrenching tool to build head cover for himself. Most of these we got in when darkness came down. Then there were others who had lost all sense of direction and seemed not to know which was the German line and which ours. One man we saw crawl towards the German line and, within a few feet of it, was bombed by them. As soon as darkness came parties of us went over with stretchers and worked all night collecting the wounded. Within our trenches the wounded were now moving more freely. Some of them had been hit the day previously but because of the heavy shelling had been left in the front line. My pal Fred was a walking wounded case, hit in the back by shrapnel. He paused to say a few words to me and asked if I'd heard anything of another mate. Alfie came, with his hand and knee bandaged. He crouched as he walked and did not stop to speak as he went past. I watched him being picked up by a stretcher party and he waved his hand to me as he went around the traverse.

'The following morning broke with the usual hymn of hate, artillery, machine-gun and rifle fire. Then there was a heavy ground mist and both sides were silent as though they were weary from the watchful night. Suddenly a cry, so clear and unexpected that it made me start rang out: "Stretcher bearers! Stretcher bearers! Come on New South Wales!" Despair punctuated the words. It was a man we'd overlooked in No Man's Land and though unable to help himself he was conscious enough to know that there were men ready to chance their lives in an endeavour to rescue him if he was able to guide them to him. Company Sergeant-Major Dykes, my pal Jimmy Sowter and two others went out with a stretcher. After a time we saw them picking their way back over our parapet and we eased the stretcher down into the trench. He was a sergeant of the 14th Brigade. A machine gun had made a wound in his hip so large you could have put your fist in it. While he had lain unconscious flies had blown his wound. With ashen face, clothes soaked with blood and mud, he lay face downwards on the stretcher, shivering in the raw morning air. He said he'd been hit on the Wednesday afternoon during the initial stages of the advances, had lost consciousness, and could hardly believe this was now Friday morning.

A farmer, Lieutenant S. Fraser of the 58th Battalion, wrote: 'Some of these wounded were as game as lions, and got rather roughly handled; but haste was more necessary than gentle handling . . . It was no light work getting in with a heavy weight on your back, especially if he had a broken leg or arm and no stretcher bearer was handy. You had to lie down and get him on your back; then rise and duck for your life with a chance of getting a bullet in you before you were safe. [That] foggy morning in particular, I remember, we could hear someone over towards the German entanglements calling for a stretcher bearer; it was an appeal no man could stand against, so some of us rushed out and had a hunt. We found a fine haul of wounded and brought them in; but it was not where I heard this fellow calling, so I had another shot for it, and came across a splendid specimen of humanity trying to wriggle into a hole with a big wound in his thigh. He was about 14 stone weight, and I could not lift him on my back; but I managed to get him into an old trench, and told him to lie quiet while I got a stretcher. Then another man about 30 yards out sang out "Don't forget me, cobber". I went in and got four volunteers with stretchers, and we got both men in safely. Next morning at daylight, whilst observing over the parapet,

I saw two figures in their shirts and no hats, running about half-way between our lines and the Germans. They were our captains Cameron and Marshall, hunting for more wounded.'

Sergeant Williams's company was relieved during the night. Two of their mates had spent the day 'working like horses carrying out the dead. Alex, mellow with rum now, bustled about in the darkness getting his kit ready; he became highly indignant when he couldn't find the pick that he had brought into the fight! The relief completed, we began to file away towards the rear. It was a beautiful moonlit night. There was a shy bushman ahead of Peter my mate and me. He had been near to collapse for the past twelve hours. Like a sick dog he had spent the day in a little dug-out unable to eat, refusing to speak to anybody. Halfway down "Brompton Avenue" trench his slung rifle was caught by the wire cutter attached to the muzzle in a telephone wire. The sudden check almost dragged him off his feet and appeared to make him panic-stricken. He plunged and pulled like a steer in a wire fence; his mad antics threatened to brain the man behind him. After he calmed down Peter and I released him and he scampered along the duckboards to catch up, with hunched back and flogging equipment. We laughed. But the poor chap was dead in a couple of days from pneumonia.

'As daylight was breaking we halted to allow stragglers to catch up. Then in column of route we moved into the village, which was just astir. This was Saturday morning. Surely it was longer than last Wednesday evening that we left here to take part in the battle? How different we were now. We entered the fight with the spirits of a well-trained team taking the field for a hard game. Now we felt old and broken, hoping only to fall to the ground and sleep.

'Such are my memories of the costly blunder called the Battle of Fromelles, the bungling and waste of brave men's lives. Some of the battalions were nearly obliterated.* I

* A battalion strength is 35 officers, 970 other ranks, usually battle strength is around 850 men.

have heard this claimed to be the heaviest casualty list of any British Division during the war in the same space of time.' Here he repeats that the English 61st Division lost only 1 547 men.

'Can the XI Corps Staff [English] absolve themselves, when the 61st Division had failed to take the Sugar Loaf, and when the initial attack of the 15th Brigade's right battalion had been almost swept out of existence by the fire from this strong point on their flank, of committing the 15th Brigade to the attack again on the assurance that the 61st Division was to make another attempt on the strong point – whereas the 61st failed to make the attempt? The 5th Division were sacrificed on the altar of incompetence.' The official war history states, 'The impression already created in the AIF, that the new British armies lacked something in fighting capacity, was noticeably strengthened by this episode.' Williams has the last word: 'At least by their gallantry and tenacity they [the 5th Division] proved in those bloody hours that they were fit to rate with the best fighting divisions on the Western Front. Men who had fought on Gallipoli from the Landing to the evacuation, admitted freely that Fromelles was the severest test they had seen.'

Two years later, when the war ended, some Australians visited this area.

'We found the old No Man's Land simply full of our dead [one wrote]. In the narrow sector east of the Sugar-loaf Salient, the skulls and bones and torn uniforms were lying about everywhere.'

The losses were so grievous that the battle was likened to the Charge of the Light Brigade at Balaclava in 1854 when, in that famous charge of 670 men, forty per cent were lost. The following figures give some indication of the tragedy of Fromelles.

The 60th Battalion had gone into the battle with 864 officers and men; at roll call only 1 officer and 106 men answered, roughly 88 per cent had been lost. The battalions that had fought on the flanks suffered as follows:

	Officers	Other ranks
31st Battalion	16	528
32nd Battalion	17	701
53rd Battalion	24	601
54th Battalion	19	521
59th Battalion	20	675
60th Battalion	16	741

The 5th Division had lost in that one night 5 533 officers and men, of whom 400 had been taken prisoner and marched through the streets of Lille in order to impress the French, but these people rushed out into the streets in sympathy and tried to give the prisoners chocolate and cigarettes.

Sergeant Stevens of the 58th Battalion was now in France and still following the infantry, with his box of records. There were other occupants in the trenches besides the men. 'The rats are worse than they were before and they have sprint races on us when we lie down to sleep.' He was accurate in his predictions when that July he anticipated 'a big sick list for Australians. We'll never stand this cold weather. They say the winter starts about December but this is quite enough for me. If I can see the winter through I'll be doing better than I thought I could. Blankets are not taken up to the front line. The men are suffering from exposure in this cold wet weather for there is no shelter. The mud is over knee deep in the firing line.'

23
Beaucoup Australie,
Fini Pozières

In War, the first casualty being truth, Army Headquarters reported Fromelles as being 'some important raids'. Never again were British communiqués the matter of faith with which Australian troops till now had invested them. The 'important raids' captured 140 German soldiers and put the 5th Australian Division out of action for many months.

But the fight that was to be perhaps the hardest the AIF suffered was only a few days off. The 1st, 2nd and 4th Australian Divisions were now marching up to the Somme through Picardy. They passed through Albert. 'Hey! Look at Fanny Durack!' they shouted when they saw the gilded statue of the Virgin hanging head down from the cathedral. (Fanny Durack had swum for gold at the 1912 Olympics and brought her medal home. She was the world's champion diver.) They passed the gleaming chalk craters pocked by shells, moved up Sausage Gully crowded with guns and reserves, through white chalk and clay, until they reached the narrow front line that was more like a ditch dug for drainpipes. This was the jumping off point for Pozières, the village that was now rubble. The diaries of men in the battle area give an indication of the carnage. Stretcher bearer Vic Graham, arriving some days later, asked about the peculiar odour in the air. The French answered, *'Beaucoup Australie. Fini Pozières'*. His group went on up through the dead, both Australian and British. 'Into this inferno of galloping mules bearing wagons of wounded, past the tram lines carrying wounded to capacity, we picked our way. Pozières, the town, has disappeared. Rubble desolates its site, trenches and the remains of their attackers and defenders are littered as far as the eye can see. We are asked to help bring in wounded who have been laying out in the field for two nights. It is by the dark hours we toil yet most times it seems a charmed life, for though Fritz flares light everything as day and his shells burst about us, we continue to bring our mates in. For two nights we thus work and complete the assignment with the loss of only 2 of the 6 bearers. We rejoin our company in the line and hold off against a projected counter-attack for the remaining period in the remnants of a trench bearing many dead of a previous attack . . . burying bodies up to 2 weeks dead.'

For three days the Australians had been bombarded to such a degree that it was always after said to be more severe than the Verdun or first Somme battle bombardments.

The 1st Division had lost 5 285 officers and men. The survivors were relieved on the fourth day and came out 'like men who had been in hell. They were drawn and haggard and so dazed they appeared to be walking in a dream and their eyes looked glassy and starey', wrote Sergeant E. J. Rule. 'They were strangely quiet, far different from the Australian soldiers of tradition.'

The 2nd Division relieved them. The battle plans were for them to advance for twelve minutes before the artillery fire descended, forcing the Germans in the front trenches to shelter. They were seen by the sentries, and 'pinned to the ground' or, as the statistics showed, 3 500 were killed.

The difficulty of finding a way through the dark in that shattered area (a daylight advance was out of the question) was such that 'the windmill' was fixed on as a landmark even though this, by now, was beaten down by gun-fire.

That low mound is still there, in 1978. On it is a small plaque that states: 'The ruin of Pozières windmill which lies here was the centre of the struggle in this part of the Somme Battlefield in July and August 1916. It was captured on 4 August by Australian troops who fell more thickly on this ridge than on any other battlefield of the war.'

For seven weeks they steadily advanced in the Pozières sector, the only part of the fighting along the Somme that did so.

In a letter home, Lance-Corporal Arthur Foxcroft speaks of Pozières: 'on 23 July we captured the village of Pozières and went through a rough four days and nights all without sleep. The taking wasn't so hard . . . but consolidating our gains is terrible because they know to a nicety the position to shell us and they rely on their biggest shell, 9.5 inch, which throw up a mountain of dirt and bury you. We have nearly all had a turn at being buried, some several times, and if you are not noticed at the time you are almost certain to have found your grave. I will not detail it for it is too horrible but as our artillery is more dreadful than their's they must have suffered properly, in fact we saw proof of it when we got amongst them, some of them are so demoralised by our guns and by our bombardment preventing them getting their rations they just staggered into our trench and some cried like kids.'

Later he goes on to Mouquet Farm. 'If you are killed you are left there and your pockets or disc are not even looked at and you are known as dead by being missing at the assembly after coming out of the trenches after being relieved. If [bodies] were buried they would only be rooted up again by shells – for as far as you can see all around us to the horizon is torn up, over and over again. When we get the Hun a good way back the cleaning up parties will bury the dead and pick up all the material off the field.'

Daily he wrote up his diary, even at Pozières and, later, at Mouquet Farm.

'*August. Tues. 15* Moved off 9 a.m., marched through Warloy to Albert, camped for tea, and then moved up into Long Gully (Sausage) where the 15 500 Guns were, when we attacked Pozières. Camped in shell holes for night.

'*Wed. 16* Moved off 4 a.m., went through Old Pozières to position as close supports at Mouquet Farm. Poor trenches, no shelter, enemy shelling us from three sides. Rotten. Enemy pelted us with shells all way up.

'*17 August.* Had rough night last night, had to go into front line, standing to all night expecting Huns to attack, some men in trenches for their first time, had job to keep them awake, difficult work sending messages along line as shells were causing casualties, only Corporal Weir and myself left out of our Companies N.C.O's to attend to ration and ammunition parties etc. Had to dig half buried dead out of trench and build up parapet before daylight. Roy "Bluey" Wilson had head blown off; Sergt. May blown to pieces, what left of us is very tired.

'*Sat. 19.* Standing to all last night, we took bit of Huns' trench last night. Was cleaning mud off rifle at dawn when I was wounded by "Whizzbang", 13 lb shell, in left shoulder, face and left hand. Had awful time getting back to dressing station. When going through narrow trenches, one did not know whether the man he trod on was asleep or dead.

'*Mon. 21.* In a tent which holds 40 beds; good number of our lads here . . . Had hand dressed. Was marked for "Blighty".'

Private Vic Graham met a mate from another battalion who had survived the second attack at Pozières, and this man advised him to go AWL if he got a chance, as he said there was little hope of returning if one went in a second time. 'I went on to the battle at nearby Mouquet Farm on 26 August and here was wounded and taken prisoner.'

To each variety of projectile that killed they gave a name; there were Flying Pigs, Stokes, Plum Puddings, Pineapples, Minnies and Whizzbangs. 'Things get pretty warm,' Tunneller Victor Morse wrote.

Lance-Corporal Roger Morgan at the 2nd Battalion aid post in July 1916 during the battle of Pozières wrote, 'It is marvellous how the men stand the agony of their wounds, many shot to pieces but never murmur, others, when forced to cry out apologise for it. One old chap when he was dying kept saying "Stop the bleeding boys and I'll get back home to the missus and kids". I'm afraid they won't see him though in this world. Eventually all were carried back or walked. It is awful to see crippled men staggering back with the help of a shovel, stick, anything, just crawling along until either they reach help or fall exhausted on the road, some to be picked up later or buried where they fall.'

At another post Private K. S. Cunningham wrote, 'There is nothing quite like a stream of wounded passing back. A man with a broken arm supports on one side a man with a flesh wound in the leg, another with wounds in the feet hobbles on a pick handle. There are always a majority of walkers although when a stunt is on many walk who should be stretcher cases. At one time when the rush was worst, the stretchers were lined up three abreast for almost a hundred yards along the road. Cases kept coming through in a constant stream. Our dressing room was a place made in the bend of a road with room for one or two stretchers.'

The 14th Battalion Medical Officer, Captain R. C. Winn, wrote of his aid post at Pozières. 'The entrance was choked with wounded, many of whom would be wounded afresh or killed outright while being attended to. Our dug-out rocked with concussion. Many were brought in who had been out for days before being rescued. Some of their wounds were crawling with maggots but looked clean.'

Sergeant F. T. 'Theo' Ford of the 4th Field Artillery: 'At Pozières we fired so much ammunition we ran out. "I'd like to give the bastards a few more," one of the gunners said as we all crouched down under the bombardment the Boche was putting on to us. You couldn't see left, right, back or front for the haze of metal flying. Suddenly there was a shout for everybody to unload the ammunition! We raised our heads and there was Paddy Drew charging up with a limber of ammo. Paddy had driven his team through one of the worst bombardments that war saw. "I knew you'd need it," old Pad said. He was later killed. He got the M.M. for bringing the ammo. up that day but he deserved it when you saw what he drove through.' Theo was just a boy. 'You were pretty busy at such a time and if you could think of anything other than the gun you were thinking of a bullet. Thinking of it hurts.'

In the midst of every man trying to kill another, Lieutenant

Cherry and an officer who was leading the German attack in that neighbourhood were shooting at one another from neighbouring shell holes, each endeavouring to dodge the other's shots. It happened that they rose together and fired simultaneously, the German hitting Cherry's helmet, but being mortally wounded by him. The Australian presently went over to his dying opponent; as he bent down, the German took some letters from his pockets, and in good English asked him to promise that, after submitting the letters to the censor, he would post them. On receiving this promise, the German handed them over, saying as he did so: 'And so it ends.'

Trooper H. H. Moule from South Australia was taken from the 3rd Light Horse in Egypt and sent to France in 1916 and thence to Pozières as a stretcher bearer. 'There's not two bricks sticking together here. Supposed to be forty odd men buried underneath the dug-out we are in.' They began to dig. 'We unearthed another poor chap, half of him missing. Then pieces of flesh were picked up all over the place – one box of pieces is supposed to be the remains of four chaps. The men on the digging worked like Trojans all day. During the day they managed to cut through to one dug-out and rescued six chaps, four were OK and looked happy enough, two were bruised and we carried these away on stretchers. In the evening a dead chap was found.'

Stretcher bearers continually saw the real horror of war. 'At Zonnebecke', Jim McPhee said, 'we were close to the trenches. The boys lit fires to boil billies and down came Fritz's shells and men just buried were blown out of their graves.' Jim and his brother Vic were now together in France. 'Brothers didn't say anything heroic or anything to one another when going into a hot time, just cheerio, or see you later, but my brother Vic did do something when the call for bearers came this day.

'He grabbed a stretcher with his carrying mate – and then he turned, and he looked at me, that's all, he sort of looked at me when he was going out that time. They brought his body back next day and they were very good.

They dug a grave for Vic, a proper grave, and a Chaplain and the boys got a wooden Celtic cross from somewhere and some railings and they painted the railings black and it looked very nice indeed.'

The mud that stayed on every soldier's memory of France was a new experience after the sands of Egypt. Moule was sent off as a runner to inform aid posts of a move of relay posts for bearers. He waited until dark. 'It took 1½ hours to get to the first post what with shell holes of water and barbed-wire entanglements. Reached destination safely. Then had to go across to the Culvert. Had to run, then stand still like a statue as a star shell went up, then run like blazes, stop, wait for the next flare, then run again and so on. It seemed like hours [I] had the rest of the journey on my own. I struck duckboards, but Fritz had knocked parts of them to bits. Fell head over heels twice, lost my tin lid in a shell hole full of water, didn't attempt to recover the helmet, just said a few things to myself and made off again. At times I thought I was on the wrong track it was that dark, couldn't distinguish a thing around you, couldn't see where you were putting your feet, just felt my way along the boards.

'Second cropper happened soon after the first – you should have seen me – mud from head to feet, I did look a trick, caused great amusement when I lobbed in our dugout – got a knife and made a start scraping the mud off my face and hands, then my clothing.'

It was the one part of the battle line which the Germans had been free to bombard at will and the figures tell of the cost. On that crowded mile the three Australian divisions lost 23 000 men in less than seven weeks. In only twelve days the 2nd Division lost 6 848 men and when brought back a few weeks later lost 1 268; the 4th Division lost 4 649 the first time in and 2 409 the second; the 1st Division, brought back a second time with reinforcements that brought the battalion up to two-thirds strength, lost 2 650. Individual battalions' losses were tragic. In two days the 48th lost 600 of its 800 men and the 45th, 350.

The survivors knew that their constant advance while the rest of the Somme was deadlocked was a notable achievement but their losses and the knowledge that they had been mis-handled embittered them. No special effort had been made to ensure greater loss to the enemy than to the Allies. The intensity and duration of the bombardment over the forty-nine days was such as to surpass any that came before, yet they held every trench once it had been firmly captured.

'We tried to believe that someday we would be out of the mud, someday we would fight in the open. We tried to convince ourselves that Autumn would make an end, but the war seemed eternal and the Hun was still strong and fighting well. We came up to Bapaume past a bank now sprouting green and covered with the grey and frozen bodies of British and Australians, and of very many Germans, witness of the bitter fighting to and fro. White skulls perforated with bullet holes lay here and there,' W. H. Downing wrote.

Many of the ex-Gallipoli boys 'died game'. Roy Rankin was wounded after a comparatively happy time in France. Before the raid that proved to be his last he wrote of leaving his French friends – gendarmes, factory workers, children and old people – 'It was quite a sad parting. We had made so many friends'.

The last three letters he wrote were from a bed in the Military Hospital in Colchester, England. 'I was hit through the spine, and was as helpless as a baby, having only the use of my arms. . . . Since I found it very awkward writing on my back, and the Sister was so kind as to offer to write for me, she is finishing this letter . . .' There are only two more letters, the last being written on 5 September. 'Just a line to let you know I am still progressing favourably, although not yet strong enough for the doctor's examination of the spine. I have not received any back letters yet, but am going to get the 'Australian Lady' to shake up Headquarters again for me. There are well-to-do ladies comes round every week, and will get everything a chap asks for. I hope you were not anxious when I missed last mail. With best love, Roy.'

Private Rankin died five days later on 10 September 1916.

Drivers were said to be a law unto themselves – as well as holding the record for the most scorching tongues in the army. Phillip Herbert, a limber driver with the 10th Battery of 4th Field Artillery, kept a tiny diary in which he detailed their movements. It certainly shows a life different from that led by the other men. They sailed for France with 600 horses on board and moved up to Messines on 5 July, ready for the great bombardment of that area.

On 8 July they 'Brought the battery out of action 10 o'clock in the morning and travelled about 15 miles and got to St Omer at 7 a.m. very tired after our nights route march. Entrained for Amiens.' They moved daily, sometimes twelve miles, sometimes fifteen. On 30 July they went into action at Pozières. 'My birthday. Terrible dose of guns about our position. Mick Farrell and Keith Howe wounded, 2 horses killed and three wounded.

'*16 August*: Came out of action after 17 days at Pozières and are now in tents, quite a change after a star-spangled roof. *23 August*: Back into action again after a good spell. Taubes dropped bomb on wagon line and knocked out 46 drivers and killed several horses.'

He and his horses moved from one awful battle to another. '*22nd October*: Came out of action from Ypres. To Amiens, then Albert. *30 October*: Came into action on the Somme.' He lists six men killed, four wounded in his battery. '*4 November*: Having a rotten time. All pack work with the horses on account of bad road, mud up to our knees.'

When the Naval Bridging Train was disbanded Private Thompson (whom we first met at Suvla Bay) joined the 4th Division artillery as a gunner and went to France. 'We were "mobile artillery" and went wherever there was pressure. Six horses hauled our 18-pounder guns, six hauled our ammunition wagons, others our supplies. In time, so many horses were killed by shell fire that they sent us mules. Horses were valuable. There wasn't anything they could replace the men with so we stayed. The mud along the Somme was so bad that if a horse got off the corduroy track across the morass it flounded into mud and slurry up to its belly and we had to shoot it. It was awful. There was always someone trying to get replacements for lost horses. Fellows would pinch horses from other fellows' teams . . . We all did it. We used to ride our horses back for water. They were ploughing through mud . . . When we got our horses back we'd have to scrape them down, the mud hung like armour on them. It was awful there for horses. Wet and cold always, and up to their shanks in mud all the time. Lots of them just died.'

Throughout the war the Australians had a reputation for bringing their equipment out with them even in retreat. 'Many's the time we've got the sudden order to get out and get the guns out with us. Then it's every man to the wheel. You'd see blokes leap up like circus riders, always three men rode, and lead another horse of the six horses that pulled the gun limber and also the communication wagon but you should have seen them go when ordered at the double. Once I remember, the Portugese-held part of the line broke and suddenly the Scots began racing past us. "Jerry's coming!" a Scottie yelled at me. "Jerry's coming." We didn't take much notice but then we looked around. Jerry was coming alright. He was nearly here! I had to race to get the drivers. "We're nearly surrounded". I shouted "S.O.S." . . . to get them awake and then we limbered up and did we go!

'You could always find a gunner in a room full of sleeping men. You only had to call out "S.O.S." and every gunner in the place would jump up.

'Only one time did we have to leave our guns. We were swamped. Had to desert our guns. We'd charged through at Bapaume and then the tide turned and we just had time to remove the breach blocks and go for our lives. But we got them back in a short time.

'There were some awful things in war. One day I got really frightened. It was the only time I ever got frightened. The howitzers were behind us. We were under fire and then I saw a hit on the howitzers. We were pretty busy with our gun; a shell fell among our horses. It was awful. Then I turned and I saw through the smoke, I thought I saw, some black thing, a big black thing. I kept looking back when I could. It was a blob, flapping, between us and the howitzers. It was a shapeless black thing, flapping. It frightened me. So I ran over, ducking and weaving, till I got close. And it was a man, blackened, not a bit of flesh not burnt, rolling round, waving his arm stump with nothing on it. That frightened me. Really frightened me. I got wounded after that. I think it was because of that.'

Since 1 July 1916 the fighting had been continuous, giving no time to take precautions against the coming winter. When the weather broke in October the troops had behind their front line seven miles of wild, churned-up moorland, devoid of shelter. The Germans, at this time, were not so hard hit. Their mud was in a narrow strip; in fact, grass-covered slopes led down from trenches they occupied, and behind them nearby there were towns, including Bapaume, which accommodated several thousand troops in its cellars.

On the British side, the seven miles depth along the front was a morass. In some camps the men were ankle deep, in others knee-deep in mud. The few country roads that might have serviced the troops gave way under the strain of heavy traffic. Not even these broken tracks existed for the last two miles over which all the carrying must be done by men and animals. It was unspeakably exhausting. The removal of the wounded called for four or five relays of stretcher bearers working six or eight men to a stretcher.

Most of the trenches were now reduced to slimy ditches and, apart from the actual front line systems, were hardly used, the men preferring to drag themselves over the open beside them. In the dark, men straying from the slippery track fell into shell holes and often the deep pits almost met lip to lip. Often the men were pulled out of the mud minus their boots, and animals that became bogged had to be shot.

Because of these conditions men in the front trenches were unable to exercise, and from standing hour on hour in icy slush hundreds were put out of action by 'trench feet', a form of frost-bite which often ended in gangrene and the loss of toes or even feet. For those three months, before the frost and snow hardened the ground, the Australians exhibited a depression that not even their awful casualties had brought on them.

The mud was eventually attacked. 'Duckboards' were laid across the morass and light railways were pushed forward, warming clothing and gum boots issued and special food containers were designed to keep food hot. Whale oil was rubbed into the feet, but the men believed puttees were the main cause of trench feet, the tightness of the bound woollen strip cutting off the circulation of blood to the feet. Their remedy was to leave the puttees off and tie sand bags round their legs. These had the added advantage of being easily replaced, so were thrown away when wet or muddy and clean dry bags tied on in their place.

From April to December of that year the Australians had 87 862 casualties on what was now called 'the Western Front'. The violence of the shock to those at home when these figures were released, had the effect of damping the euphoria Gallipoli had left on the country. For such a small population – less than 5 million – to read 43 068 names on the casualty lists during the two months of July to September alone, was a trauma.

Officially, this 'wastage' had not been expected and by mid-August it caused crisis: the battalions still in training had been bled of their half-trained men, the organisation of getting the wounded and sick away was crude – and remained so for the remainder of the year – and over-crowding back at the hospitals and convalescent camps in England was eased only by returning to France those men 'fit' to be sent. This last of course helped meet the demand for more men to replace those killed at the front, and Colonel D. W. McWhae in command of the AIF reinforcement depots in England has written that the depots consisted of a 'proportion of convalescents considerably greater than the reinforcements'. Simply, the medical services were being imposed on to 'maintain' the battle replacements to as great a degree as the training battalions.

One of the men who lived in the mud in France and wrote a book that is the Australian equivalent of *All Quiet on the Western Front* was W. H. Downing of the 15th Brigade. In his *To The Last Ridge* he describes the coming to Montauban in 1916.

Men reached the front line in a state of indescribable exhaustion, 'with their reserves of strength poured out before the duties of the line began'.

'There, dead lay everywhere. The deeper one dug, the more bodies one exhumed. Hands and faces protruded from the slimy, toppling walls of trenches. Knees, shoulders and buttocks poked from the foul morass . . . We were soaked from head to foot (the feet that were never dry all that winter) with sweat and icy mud. . . .

'A greatcoat, wet and muddy, weighed forty pounds or more. Soaked equipment laden with one hundred and seventy rounds of ammunition and two or three bombs bore like the load of Atlas. The rifle-sling over the chest, when the rifle was carried diagonally across the back, strangled our panting breath. If hung from the shoulder, the strap repeatedly slipped to the fore-arm, the butt bumped awkwardly against the legs, and fell continually in the mud . . . rifles became entangled in the thousands of old telephone wires festooned across and along the trench in a mesh of tentacles which reached out and grasped the labouring men, became entangled in the equipment, knocked helmets in the slime, caught men under the chin and tripped their feet as they lifted them within the mud. The way was complicated by coils of barbed wire unwound beneath the surface of the slush.

'Short men fared badly. Eight yards a minute would have

been good going for a fresh, strong, unencumbered man . . .
it frequently took a full hour for a hundred men to pass a
given point. Parties met and jammed in the narrow saps . . .
It was almost impossible for two men to pass. . . . It was
dark as the unlit corridors of Eblis. Absolutely nothing
could be seen except by the blinding flash of shells, the
flicker in the sky of guns along the hills, the dazzling flares.
These left baffling mirages of colour on the retina, preventing
the eyes from becoming accustomed to the gloom.

'They fell full length often. There was a foot of slush on
the changing surface of the clay. The sound of the wrenching
of their boots from its grip was like the tearing of sheets of
cloth. They were weakened by hunger, shattered in nerve
by the continued barrage. The rain poured in torrents. . . .
Some were forced to crawl. No matter how overcome, few
dared rest. . . . because they might be unable to move again
– might fall asleep and perish before morning.

'They were often bogged and helpless. Artillery mules
were used to drag them from the shell holes. Getting the
mules out was a harder matter. Many had to be shot.

'Companies took twenty-four hours, without halting for
rest, to reach Montauban. The weaker men and those who
had lost their way – an easy matter, for there were no landmarks – did not rejoin for days. . . .

'It was five miles to the camp, and there were no duckboards. It was mud, mud, mud all the way. . . . Battalions
were reduced to one-sixth their strength by frost-bite and
trench feet.

'In that dark winter the armies thought mud, ate mud,
lived in a sea of hundreds of square miles of it. Europe
failed many times to break the hearts of the men of the
Antipodes, but was never nearer succeeding than here. . . .

'Ration parties lost their way or got hopelessly bogged.
. . . Sometimes they all but wandered into the German
lines. On one occasion a party was captured, bogged and
lost in No Man's Land. Their German captors, equally
bemazed, conducted them within our lines, and in their

turn were taken. Many Germans were captured by wandering into our trenches, but there was scarcely one such case in the whole of the AIF.

'On being relieved, the parties, six at a time, filed through the pitchy night across the bog, crouching while machine-guns rattled and the bullets hummed past, standing like statues as the white and brilliant flares popped, then roared and curved, making the night like day, and fell and burned on the ground in white smoke. Then blackness and on they struggled, feverish with anxiety to get away. At long length they reached the slippery duckboards that tipped beneath their feet and shot them into shell holes, with missing boards that entrapped the feet, and great gaps where shells had blown the causeway to the winds. Now and again shells crashed in red flame and fragments whirred through the air. Artillery roared without ceasing . . . After hours, they reached Delville Wood, or Switch Trench near Ginchy, or "B" or "D" Camps in Bernafay Wood – altogether pitiable, with bare feet puffed and cut by the duckboards, or swollen so that the boots had to be cut off them – weak and weary, caked with mud in various stages of drying, as in a cocoon – soaked, except their hands and faces – filthy from toes to hair – sometimes half naked. They came walking, or were carried on the backs of staggering mates. They rested a few days, were (possibly) given a bath, cleaned themselves, and went back to the line.'

They fought back and forth over the same ground until it was churned to slurry. The minewerfers,* shrapnel, bombs and decaying bodies had pulverised and fouled it; when the rains came and stayed for months the earth just fell apart. It was an assault for which nature had no remedy; the soil would hold together no longer. It was not so much mud, as decayed, unnatural earth.

'Golly!' wrote Norman Mills in November (he had come from a very wet place himself – Omeo, in Gippsland), 'You

---

* Trench mortars.

ought to see the mud. Just imagine ground that has been churned over and over to a depth of about six feet and then soaked for months in rain'.

'The mud was so deep we could not dig trenches because the walls slipped down as fast as we dug. We dug backwards and forwards over ground that had been fought over a dozen times and old trenches had collapsed and it was hopeless. The ground was pretty flat, low-lying and of course we could be seen. The Germans had advanced at one hell of a pace early in the war and had built magnificent cement pill boxes – some of which held hundreds of men, but we couldn't do this. Later, we had one big place and a few smaller but all back behind the front line. Well, here we'd be, digging, and you'd come on something that gave way in a different sort of way than the rotten soil and you got so that in the end you knew a body before you saw it and sometimes didn't have to see it because it went out with the mud. But it was no use. We never did get a good trench system going; we relied on breastworks – sandbags sloping up to give us shelter above earth. Even then we were up to our ankles in the front line.'

The artillery, in crushing the enemy, crushed the land over which its own infantry would cross. In dry weather the shell holes were easily passed but the autumn rains turned it into a greasy bog. All men speak of the mud's tenacity.

The Australians had gone into the trenches with no time to prepare the ground. Not only the trenches but the tracks leading to them were, in many parts, impassable. The tracks would not support lorries to bring up gravel or timber for repair: any strength in the tracks must be preserved for ammunition lorries. On their way up to reserve trenches behind the front line suction of the mud was such that for a six-mile journey nine to twelve hours were allotted for getting into position.

For the battle of Flers the troops had such a journey through the mud that they reached the front line half-exhausted; many sank down to their hips in the slurry, and many were late. Some had been shelled on the way there by the enemy and had to disperse. They were then unable to assemble in No Man's Land. The leading waves of the 1st Battalion 'had to bridge with their bodies the top of the trenches while the supports crawled in to assemble beneath them'. The artillery barrage had begun and by now was creeping back over the German lines to enable the troops to gain the front trenches of the enemy but the men, because of the mud, were unable to keep pace with the creeping barrage. Some reached the objective but later were ordered to retire when it was seen that the partial gains could not be held.

Sergeant Stevens's task was to remain in a position where returns and information could be sent back to him by runner from the firing line; he then consolidated them and forwarded them on to Brigade HQ. He also received telephone messages which were delivered to him by signallers. At the close of October 1916 'a runner arrived from the line at 12.30 a.m. The battalion are moving out tomorrow. This runner had been on the go since 9.15 – it took him over 3 hours to come the 4 miles from the line, that gives an idea of what the ground was like. . . . Had to send my 2 runners out with despatches at 1 a.m. and was awakened again at 4 a.m. with more despatches.

'Our A.M.C. came today for a Red Cross flag for waving purposes to see if Fritz will stop firing on stretcher bearers when they are taking wounded away. Our boys had a rough passage back last night for they had a heavy barrage to go through. Impossible to know casualties yet as impossible to get in touch with front line during daylight.'

Then, on 26 November 1916, the 'battalion moved back to Switch Trench Support line. The boys are cutting up badly owing to severe conditions. About 20 men straggled back here on their own accord. I did not know what to do with them as they were done up. Paraded them to 59th Bn. Medical Officer and a few sent to hospital. Got in touch with C.O. who told me he was sending down to collect the stragglers. After tea my friend R.S.M. Harry Sutton arrived to escort these men back. He was settled [exhausted] so we got him to bed and fixed him up for the night.'

The following morning Stevens went with the Regimental Sergeant-Major and took the 'stragglers' back to Switch Trench. 'It is about three miles through what used to be dense woods but only a few stumps now remain. Where there are no duckboards the mud is awful. All the way the ground is torn to pieces, shell holes being one against the other – not a place which has not been shelled. All holes were full of water, most of them frozen over on top. . . . some . . . contained water stained red which meant some soldier had made his grave there. Cold and foggy. Reached battalion, at work trying to make a shelter of some kind. Great number of men hobbling about through having trench feet. Started on my journey back by myself. I had to watch myself for aeroplanes were being fired at and shrapnel was falling all around me and very close.

'*29 November*: Battalion moved up to front line again – many men going to hospital sick and with trench feet, 150 have gone during past few days. Up to now we have had 47 casualties – 7 killed, 2 men were killed only 100 yards from me today from shrapnel.'

They march off again. 'I did well but my feet got bad and for the last 3 miles I had to get along somehow.' And then, St Vast, where he was to be billeted. 'This would do me till the end of the war.'

In fact he went back several times, in between battles, until the end of the war, being given a warm welcome each time and questioned carefully about the fate of other boys whom the town had billeted. While in St Vast he had occasionally to go to Amiens, a nine-mile journey. For this he usually tried to find a horse, for otherwise he had to walk there and back. He went to Albert, and promptly drew a diagram of the falling virgin, 'Fanny Durack'. 'It's a most marvellous thing how it does not fall down.'

Then he is back at his post. While summarising his diary one realises how rarely he was able to get to bed before 1 a.m. any morning – and many days it was 3 and 4 a.m. When they move up to Bapaume he fills pages with description of the sight that met his eyes: 'Many bodies are lying about simply left where they fell last, but steps are being taken to bury them. It seems incredible that a week ago no one dare show himself for fear of being picked off and today we march over Fritz's trenches in fours. It is amazing that once we passed over Fritz's old line instead of mud we had green grass under our feet and roads in splendid condition.'

His next joyous news is 13 May 1917: 'our battalion have done a marvellously good piece of work in taking a big slice of the Hindenburg Line at Bullecourt. Our casualties amount to 233 all told which is rather heavy but considering the work done we got off rather lightly.'

And so it goes on. He makes his home from anything at hand, once a piece of tarpaulin stretched over some tree stumps, another time, 'made a shelter out of boxes of ammunition with a tarp for roof. Bad luck if a shell lands near'.

Private Fred Walton had jotted down some 'snippets' of conversations he'd heard. 'We'd had a few days in billets, out of the line. Then "Forty men wanted for a raiding party". A little natural shyness, then, "Go on, put me down," from fifty men. On the way out from the "tour of duty" we talked. "Fancy Harper being killed." "Yes, his brains oozed out for a couple of hours before he died." "Terrible bloody game this!"

'We'd arrive at Supports. "Three men this way! Not four men. Eh? – alright five men. Hurry up!" We were directed to a dug-out. Stayed together always until one went west and then another.

'Four days of shells, gas and fatigue. The battlefield was an awful sight, apparently deserted, but men were like rabbits up here. There was a subtle smell of decaying bodies.

'Moved back a bit. In a dug-out. Had a light. Then, Hummm, Hummm, the minnies were coming over. "Get the light out!" "You've got the wind up!" Bang!! The light went off, also a man's hand still gripping two or three cards.'

Battle on battle, name on name followed as inexorably as death followed life. Back home in Australia the newspapers headlined towns that had never before been mentioned in that country.

In Western Australia they spoke of Bullecourt and the 'Joan of Arc Battalion', the 48th, so named because many of its leaders were of the Leane family – 'made of All Leanes'.

When the attack was made on the Hindenburg Line at Bullecourt on 11 April 1917 it was known that the great belt of wire protecting the Germans had not been cut. There had been no artillery barrage because, for the first time, a new weapon was to be used. The men were lined out in front of their trenches during the night, lying on the snow, watching for tanks, the new invention behind which they would go into action. By 7 a.m. the pasture was littered with the hulks of the machines burning all over the battlefield. Only one reached the German line. They had been made of steel too thin to withstand gun fire, moved more slowly than walking men and could not travel in the blizzard now sweeping over the area.

It was now broad daylight and the Germans knew all, could see all of the attacking force. Bringing their guns to bear they cut off the Australians' retreat to their own (Australian) lines. No ammunition, supplies, messages or reinforcements could come to the exposed infantry. Terrible fire was sweeping the ground, the air was hazy with lead but some made a dash for it and a few got through. Last on the ground were the 48th with part of the 47th Battalion. It fought on until the artillery, at last permitted to fire, brought its barrage down on them under the impression that all Australians were out of the sector. 'At 12.25,' the official history records, 'a full hour after the other troops, with proud deliberation, under heavy fire, picking its way calmly through the wire, helping the walking wounded, its officers bringing up the rear, the 48th Battalion came out.'

Captain A. E. Leane was killed as they got through the wire, another Leane had been killed earlier in the day.

It had been a place of terror. The enemy fired shells at

single men hurrying back behind the ridge, they fired shells at stretcher bearers. Day and night, backwards and forwards, the fighting raged. The deep trenches the Germans had built, now occupied by the Australians, rocked continually to shell fire. 'One heard men squealing like trapped rabbits,' wrote Reg Mills.

'Day by day we dragged ourselves from under the heaps of burnt clods flung by shell-bursts into the trenches and wiped the shattered flesh of comrades from our faces.' The finest soldiers of two great nations came together in that charnel-house; were slaughtered in thousands; riddled by bullets; rent, mangled, twisted and tortured by shells; suffered thirst, hunger, the heat of striving in battle at noon-day, the horror of dreadful nights, the frigid misery and the weariness of soul at daybreak; the torments of hell under fire; wounds; the loss of brothers and comrades; the frightful sounds and sights of death and agony; the nausea, the unutterable suffering of mind and soul and body that comes from the frequent tension of waiting to attack, and from nervous strain, long and unrelieved; the noise, the wailing, the silences – till life was hell and death a fearful thing.

This lasted for five weeks. There were trenches where the struggle never ceased, where bomb fights raged for hours of every day. These trenches were filled with corpses, over which men trampled and stumbled and fought like demons until the enemy were driven back a few yards and a sandbag 'block' could be made in the trench. And then the enemy would come again in force and drive us away; and so it would go on now one side, now the other, driving along the trench until its men and its strength and its bombs were exhausted, and then being driven back in turn.

Scraps of shattered bodies obtruded from the obscene earth. The country became more and more abominable, more and more desolate. Steel helmets, rusted rifles, parts of equipments, broken iron, dead men.

This battle further shook the Australians' faith in British command – and it would be a full year before they would again put faith in tanks. The 4th Brigade had 2 339 casualties out of the 3 000 men engaged. They had achieved the unbelievable: for a time they had seized a part of the 'impregnable' Hindenburg Line and that without artillery help, but the miscarriage of yet another ill-planned scheme was a staggering blow to them. Within a few days they were back – to 'Second Bullecourt' and this time they not only took a section of the Hindenburg Line and held it against seven general counter-attacks and twelve minor ones; from 5 May to 17 May they were mentioned almost daily in the *British Bulletin*, often as the chief item. A French journalist cried, 'The Australians have again captured the British communiqué!' But the 'first' and 'second' Bullecourt battles had cost the AIF 10 000 casualties.* The remnants of the battalions were now to be 'rested' – three weeks behind the lines and, with luck, leave to 'Blighty'.

* C. E. W. Bean. *Official History of Australia in the War of 1914–18.*

24
Blighty

Take me back to dear old Blighty
Put me on the train to London town
Take me over there, drop me anywhere

they sang, as they crossed the channel on leave. 'We looked more like country bumpkins in town for the first time rather than soldiers,' young Will Dodds wrote to Glennie in a twenty-eight page letter describing leave in London after 'a spell in the trenches'. 'Got into Peel House. A cubicle each, to ourselves. I tell you Darling that is very nice, and clean sheets and the very best thing that happened here was the hot baths. I had two in four days.'

Roly Mills wrote, 'On reaching Victoria Station an Australian sergeant . . . gave us particulars of how to get to headquarters where we have to report. The first thing to do was to get my pass registered, then I was given clean clothes, had a hot bath, and was set!'

Reg Mills (not related to Roly) came to Blighty direct from the trenches: 'After getting fixed up in London with all new clothes − as the old ones were torn and in an awful mess, blood and everything all over them owing to just coming out of the line − I started off for Scotland.'

The following compositions tell their own story. The first is a printed memo to be read to every soldier going from France to England on leave (*circa* 1917).

'Complaints are still being received that Australian soldiers on leave in England do not salute officers in the streets. This is, of course, not only contrary to orders, but

271

gives a very bad impression, as people in England judge the smartness and soldierly bearing of any troops very greatly by their manners in the streets; and this matter of saluting is the most obvious and noticeable test that comes within their daily observation. . . .

'Officers will be instructed, when in England, to take the name of any man failing to salute, and report him to A.I.F. Headquarters. Any man so reported will lose the balance of his leave, and be at once returned to duty. It must be impressed on all officers that it is their duty to report these cases. The reputation of the A.I.F. is suffering more than those serving in France understand or appreciate, through the slackness of certain men in this respect, and all must do their utmost to get this set right.

'This order will be read out by the Officer in charge of leave men, to all parties before entraining.'

The next is the song the troops sang in reply (to the tune of 'Sweet Betsy from Pike').

He went up to London and straight up he strode
To Army headquarters on Horseferry Road,
To see all the bludgers who dodge all the strafe
By getting soft jobs on the headquarters staff.

Dinky-di, dinky-di
By getting soft jobs on the headquarters staff.

The lousy lance corporal said 'pardon me please'
'You've mud on your tunic and blood on your sleeve
You look so disgraceful that people will laugh,'
Said that lousy young corporal on headquarters staff.

The digger just shot him a murderous glance
And said, 'we're just back from the shambles in France
Where whizzbangs are whining and bullets are flying
And brave men are dying for bastards like you.'

'We're shelled on the left and we're shelled on the right
We're bombed all the day and we're bombed all the night
And if something don't happen and that mighty soon
There'll be nobody left in the bloody platoon.'

Dinky-di, dinky-di
There'll be nobody left in the bloody platoon.

The story soon got to the ears of Lord Gort
Who gave the whole matter a great deal of thought
And awarded the digger a V.C. with bars
For giving that corporal a kick up the arse!
Dinky-Di, Dinky-Di, for giving that corporal a kick up
    the arse!

One of the most admired officers of the 1st AIF, Colonel
(later Brigadier-General) H. E. 'Pompey' Elliott, has written
a clear appraisal of the Australian soldiers' attitude to
discipline. 'In the confusion and noise of battle he (the
soldier) learns little of what is going on save in his immediate vicinity. He must, therefore, place implicit trust in his
immediate superiors who direct and control the fight while
it is in progress. Such confidence is readily given by the
Australian soldier to those worthy of it, but none is readier
to discover and disdain those who prove unworthy.' He
speaks of their 'intelligence and initiative in battle' and the
need previously to inform an Australian soldier of the
reasons for an order being given. 'Sir John Monash achieved
a great deal of his supreme success as a commander by his
issue of orders, whenever possible, in time to ensure the
most thorough and careful explanation of them before the
men entered the battle zone at all. Under our previous
commander this was not the case.

'As a result of General Monash's decision, the loss of
officers and N.C.O's in the course of the fight had little or
no effect on our men gaining their objectives. There was
always some intelligent private who would assume command and carry on in the light of the knowledge previously
imparted to him.

'In action the Australian invariably accorded a cheerful
and implicit obedience to those whom he knew and trusted.
But he demanded elbow-room for his inventiveness, and
reserved the right to use his commonsense.'

Now and again one discovers stories about saluting in

the men's diaries. On his first leave to Blighty from France – six days – Sergeant Phillip Herbert and his artillery limber-driver mate ran into trouble regarding saluting. Phillip's diary for 13 June 1916 reads: 'Harry put in Hotel de Clinque for not saluting a general. Was in for 25 hours (Boshter time).'

Trooper Moule, after Bapaume, was 'walking up the road when I passed Gen. Birdwood. Course we slung him a salute and he returned it with his'.

The South Australian, Eddie Johnson, tells of when he was convalescent at Le Havre and, with other diggers, going for a walk on the beach. 'All of us were wearing the regulation blue suits with golliwogs pinned on us. While sitting down a Portuguese Officer passed us, then turned and came back and wanted to know why we had not saluted him. To our surprise a Queenslander jumped up and said, "Salute you! catch this" – and to our amazement he spread-eagled the officer on the beach. We Aussies jumped up and scattered in all directions for the Y.M.C.A. Later, on asking the Queenslander why, he said, "That's the crowd that raced the civilians out of the line, when Fritz advanced during April."

'This saluting business reminded me of a story going around in France of how a General came on an Australian in a trench, all on his own, smoking a cigarette, with his rifle some distance away. The General said "Who are you?" the Aussie replied "A bit of a soldier, who are you?" The General, sensing a bit of humour, said "A bit of a General". The Aussie then said "Hang around a bit, till I grab the gun and give you a bit of a Salute".'

Sergeant 'Harry' Kahn, 28th Battalion (WA), remembered in 1977, 'Salute? of course we saluted, didn't mind at all and did it with complete satisfaction to the lower echelons if the officer was known to us and known to be worthy of it. It wasn't a popular pastime and we didn't see the need for it. We were not permanent soldiers, only war-time soldiers. We thought it was more unnecessary.'

In London, Private 'Marty' Berry, on last leave before

departing for France, wrote: 'Ena took me to a Revue, *The Bing Boys*. I must say I felt rather like a fish out of water because these English people talk in terms of majors and colonels. At the Revue we were in the best seats and there were colonels to the right of me and majors to the left of me and I bet they were wondering at the presumption of a mere private to intrude into such society. They put us on a level with the English Tommy whereas there is a tremendous difference – at least we think so.'

In May 1917 the *English Review* published 'The Bush-rangers' by Herbert E. Palmer.

As I was walking down Oxford Street
Ten fierce soldiers I chanced to meet;
They wore big slouch hats with khaki sashes,
And talked like the angry guns, in flashes.

And my friend said to me 'They come from Australia
Villainous fellows for War's regalia.
John Briton keeps a tobacconist's shed,
And twice they have held a gun at his head.'

Well, I would have given all I had
To have gone with the lot of them, good or bad,
To have heard the wickedest say 'Old fellow!'
And staunched his wounds where the black guns bellow
I would think it a merry thing to die
With such stalwart comrades standing by.

One of them had round eyes like coals
True parson's quarry when he hunts souls.
The brawniest made my heart turn queer;
The devil in hell would have shunned his leer.
And the tallest and thinnest bore visible traces
Of his banished grandsire's vanished graces.

But all the lot of that swaggering ten
Were terrible, fine, strong soldier men,
Oh! all the Germans in Berlin town
Couldn't put those ten Australians down.

Those lucky enough to have 'addresses' to visit in London found, as they said, 'a home from home'. Eddie Johnson from Hughes Park had an 'address'.

'I travelled to London for my leave and headed for Mr Holden's and found no one home. Having been told how to get into the house, if at any time no one was home, I put my fingers in the letter box hole of the door, pulled a string and the door opened. I hung my overcoat and hat on a peg, and stoking up the fire, I decided to read a paper. It was not long before Mrs Holden arrived. During tea time she informed the others of the incident, and everyone had a good old laugh.'

This lad and his mates were not lacking in the initiative that Australians were being credited with. 'Owing to possibilities of leave, Jimmy and Sgt Hill, Peter McKenna and myself had thought of one way to obtain some money for the intended trip. A hall was hired for a boxing gala. Jimmy challenged Holder, a chap from a Pioneer Battalion, and won in 5 rounds. Peter and Sergeant Hill boxed against other opposition, while I was doorkeeper at 3 francs a time. The proceeds were shared equally between the 4 of us.

'One night I slept at an Australian Hostel near Australia House. When going to bed, I noticed that the digger in the next bed put a leg of the bed in each boot, so I did the same. Next morning, while walking down the Strand, a digger approached me, and said he was on his last days leave, broke, and could I give him 10/-? I fell for it, but afterwards thought that if more were on this racket, the old money would be light on. Shortly afterwards another digger approached me, so I got in first and asked him for 10/-. He said, "Sorry, 'Snow', get on the other side of the street, I am doing this side".'

Harry Dadswell had a warm welcome at an 'address' in Scotland. 'I got on the flying Scotchman and went to Miss Sanderson's, a relation of Weir's [his mate]. I walked in the building and thought I had to go up two stories. I was going past the first, when an elderly lady came out and said, "Come right in Laddie. Sit ye doon the noo. Take your coat and boots off, are they wet?" But I thought them better on. "Hae ye ever had meal cake?" I said no. "Weel ye'll hae some right noo." She got tay and cakes. After I'd been there half an hour, answering questions, she said, "And what might your name be?" I told her and she said, "I thought you'd be the right boy". "What if I hadn't been?" I asked, and she said, "Ye'd be just as welcome Laddie".

To the men in the trenches, leave to Blighty was overdue. 'Expect Blighty leave soon', Reg Mills wrote home, 'and hope to have a good spell. I feel aged now. These last 3 years have put 10 years on my life and many others are in the same plight. Have had a rough time lately.' Reg had been wounded on Gallipoli and again in France. 'It is over 12 months since I came to France and feel equal to a little dissipation now.'

When his leave was up he wrote again after visiting relations in Scotland. 'I was sorry to leave them and the girls (5 of them) all had a good cry when I left. I had a great kissing match and as I am not used to kissing girls I can tell you it was good practice.' His brother Norman had leave earlier and 'saw *Maid of the Mountains*. It is pretty'.

It was the London of Harrods, Horseferry Road, Piccadilly, The Palace, and advertising girls in music shops singing the latest songs. For a few weeks they forgot, as far as they could, everything about the front, but there was one task most had to perform either for themselves or for enquirers back home: they must try to find out from AIF headquarters the fate of a relative or friend.

'Went to headquarters to enquire about Austin', Alice Kitchen wrote. 'Found he died of wounds on 24th.' My father said, 'I had leave to London. I went to Horseferry Road to try to find out about Jackie Pierce [his nephew and friend of the same age] and brother Dick. I'd just missed Jack. He'd been wounded on two occasions, patched up and sent back into action. Dick had been patched up as much as he'd ever be and packed off to Australia.'

Lieutenant Athel Collum of Brisbane, writing home from England on 28 December 1916 said: '*London leave . . . .*

destroys a man's character first "pop" unless he has some [spiritual] help to fall back on. When a man goes on leave here in England he is issued with a "Dreadnought" and instructed how to use it. A "Dreadnought" is simply a box with two tubes of ointment in it. One to use on the penis before having connection with a woman and the other to use after. What's the use anyhow? Even dropping out all moral considerations the scheme (in my opinion) doesn't work. What man, after having been on a ship or away from any woman for months who, if he decides to have to do with a woman, will think in the heat of the moment of using the "Dreadnought"? Witness the percent of VD patients here. I cannot give you figures but I am quite satisfied in my own opinion that there are more VD's in proportion here than there were in Queensland where a man's honour was the only thing we depended on to keep him straight. . . . I am and always have been far from the narrow path and some of my past life is very black and smudgy but . . .' He goes on to suggest soldiers should be lectured on drunkenness and 'sexual matters'. 'I cannot think whose idea the "Dreadnought" is but it seems to me that the authorities are making a terrible mistake in "recognising that sexual intercourse is a necessary evil".'

This soldier is adamant that recourse to the sacraments of the church will assist men who are tempted. 'Be perfectly clear of this point: I am not one who should speak of this fault in others. I certainly was never meant for a "celebate" but I have a great advantage over many in having those two helpful sacraments to fall back on.'

Their time expired, they tramped to Victoria Station about which Richard Smith wrote, 'The trains are lined up every night, one for the nobs, six or seven for us'. The 'nobs', senior officers, travelled first class, had dining cars and bar service; the troops were packed ten to a small third-class compartment. 'You can't get near a lavatory,' Richard writes, and perhaps his realism and comparison with the comfort and attention given to the senior officers reminds us that these latter knew no more of the tragedy

and the horror of the front line than did the civilians of
Mayfair, Montreal, Kings Cross or Yarrawonga. Their
isolation made for complete segregation.

His leave now over, Eddie Johnson wrote: 'We crossed
the channel to Dunkirk, and, after entraining in open trucks,
I tried to get some sleep. It had been very cold, and the
snow had frozen. There had been an accident with two
leave trains at Tournai, and, whie hanging around outside,
off the train, a Scotch chap did a standing jump over the
railway lines. It was not long before a Canadian did the
same thing. An Australian Officer said, "Come on Aussies!"
I surveyed the jump – the railway lines were well above the
ground – then jumped over safely, with the result that 3 of
us were in a competition. After all the odds on had been set,
the competition commenced. I fluked a win, and an
Australian Officer handed me 20 francs, which I busted up
with the boys in our truck at the next canteen.'

Reg Mills said 'my holiday is now ended and I have had a
fine time. I will be in the mud tomorrow night. [He was – in
the battle of Poperinghe.] We passed many hospital trains
on the way up through France.'

Blighty leave might be finished, but they would get the
odd leave pass to a French village after a 'stunt' was ended
and during the winter.

The mud ended in January 1917 when the temperature
dropped to 29 degrees below zero. It was the coldest winter
Europe had known for twenty years. Some men had no
blankets when they moved into the line but later they were
provided with Australian-made sheepskin jackets. 'The
bitter wind cut straight through them,' young Downing
wrote, 'Lobbed here, 3 a.m. yesterday. No blankets. 25
degrees frost. Feet aching. Hardly bear to stand on them.
Lousy. Thoroughly miserable. Had four trips to the front
line last night [with] duckboards, timber and iron sheets
for dug-outs as well as shells for a mortar barrage. Evans,
Smith and Reid killed just in front of me. Poor old Smithy
wouldn't let us touch him. Scarcely stopped screaming
until just before he died. Williams stopped a bit in the guts.

Went off on a stretcher. Duckboards covered with ice. The stretcher bearers slipped and fell with him.' Then, in his diary we read, 'How long, O Lord?' It was the cry of thousands of men at the end of 1916. 'No mail for 6 weeks.' It was the point of lowest ebb for the Australians over the whole four years. 'We just go into the line again and again until we get knocked. We'll never get out of this. Just in and out, in and out, and somebody stonkered every time. Australia has forgotten us and so has God.'

They did not expect to get home, they expected to 'leave our bones in France'. Leave, even a few hours duration to a French village, was a time to grab at the life their youth had never known and their future appeared to deny them.

> O the dalliance and the wit,
> The flattery and the strife,
> And the wild kiss, when fresh from war's alarms.*

* Quoted in a diary.

25
One In Every
Ten

Veneral disease is traditionally associated with war. In March 1915, before the troop left Egypt for Gallipoli, some cases were sent home to Australia on the *Ulysses* as she shuttled back to take on more reinforcements, and 450 cases were sent to Malta. On 27 April it was decided to return all cases of venereal disease to Australia since it was necessary urgently to relieve hospital pressure. (Their foresight grimly warned them that they would soon be needing every bed they could get.) The absurdity of this action is evident: of the 261 cases that left by the *Ceramic* on 4 May, the majority were said to be 'well' on arrival in Australia. By August 1915 conditions were deplorable. As all cases were to be sent to Australia, there was no local treatment until it was arranged that no cases be returned to Australia unless they were incurable or very intractable.

Throughout the war veneral disease remained a problem. It was the most difficult casualty to prevent, the most troublesome to treat, and the most productive of absence from duty. From February 1915 to February 1916, 5 924 Australians were treated at the Detention Barracks, Abbassia, Egypt, with an average stay in hospital of thirty-five days. Of these men, 1 344 were returned to Australia. Every counter-attraction was tried to 'abate the violence of attraction' towards the source of infection, but the only one fully effective was removal from the sphere of influence. In the middle of March 1916, 2 000 cases were being treated. When leave to Cairo was stopped and the training camp moved to Tel El Kebir, the number dropped the following month to 914. After the departure of the troops for France the problem didn't lessen, it merely changed its address. The Light Horsemen who remained to fight in the desert were treated now at a single centre and here the records show that the average proportion of the force constantly under treatment for venereal disease was 1.13 per cent, the highest at any time being 2.35 per cent. From September 1916 to June 1919 2 607 men were admitted to hospital from a total of 23 000 men in Egypt, a proportion of 11.3 per cent, almost double that of the British troops there. The cause of this ascendancy is believed to have been the Australians' higher rate of pay.

The cost in time away from units was severe:

	Proportion: %	Average days in hospital
Gonorrhoea	58	53
Syphilis	15	47
Chancroid	27	23

Risking the approbation of the ostrich-like population at home the medical teams had taken action and distributed self-disinfection kits to men as well as giving prophylactic treatment. Specially trained orderlies gave 51 205 treatments.

A series of lectures were given by chaplains on ethics and by medical officers. 'This action', states the official history, 'was not followed by any appreciable decrease in the venereal rate'.

In France, the situation became even more chaotic, like everything else in that shapeless battleground. The fetish that had kept the reproductive functions of man a 'mystery' to generations of otherwise sane people affected even the medical profession, with the result that they had entered the war with little knowledge of the treatment and science of preventive or curative medicine for this oldest of soldiers' diseases.

At the war's end the official history admitted, 'It is necessary to face the truth that in none of the dominions was the proportion of admissions to hospital less than 100 for every 1 000 soldiers. The Australian was among the highest'. Yet for much of the time the best the army could do was to practise prophylactic blackmail by means of naming the disease a crime and by exposing the 'sin'. The entering of the name of the disease in the pay book had little effect other than of a heavy 'loss ' of the books. The men knew by then that the essence of war is violence and that moderation in war is imbecility.

In the case of Australia and New Zealand the circumstances were special. Hundreds of thousands of young men in their prime had been brought 12 000 miles from their homes and kept under conditions of great restraint (and frequently of great danger and hardship) with occasional intermissions of leave with money to spend, no home ties and few morally restraining influences.

The medical authorities behaved wisely, humanely, scientifically and sympathetically. They overrode any suggestion that prophylaxis tended to encourage 'illicit' intercourse, and that if they initiated men into the knowledge of methods which later might be used to prevent conception it could be a vital matter to Australians whose essential need was population.

They opened 'early treatment' depots and provided condoms – 'french letters' – or prophylactic outfits. At the 'Blue Light' clinics no names or inquiries about identity were asked and the depots were open day and night. Good, straight-forward advice was printed and distributed about the type of 'bearer' to avoid. The pamphlet ended with these words: 'It is frequently necessary to report to a Blue Light Depot for under the stress of circumstances you may not have been able to carry out exactly the method of using the outfit and within the time limit laid down. However, do the best you can and don't be shy of hurting anyone's feelings by using the 'Blue Light' outfit. Probably more than your feelings will be hurt if you don't.'

The men responded well to the offer of assistance. During

the nineteen months ending December 1918, 235 277 soldiers went on leave accepting 171 277 instruction cards and 142 609 prophylactic outfits. At the end of their leave 168 563 attended for prophylactic treatment, 12 128 attended for abortive treatments, and 8 173 were reported as cured after showing signs of the disease.

The scientific enthusiasm, earnest endeavour and high standard of clinical work performed by the medical officers and staff of the Australian Dermatological Hospital was one of the unsung services of the war.

The most striking experiment in the treatment of venereal disease took place in Australia, at Langwarrin outside Melbourne. The first 366 VD patients were sent there in March 1915 from Egypt. The numbers rapidly increased, the punitive aspect was accentuated and, until August 1915, Langwarrin was treated as a 'prison' hospital with the patients herded behind barbed wire and 200 militia men as guards. The round tents were old, leaking and unfloored and, in the wet weather, damp and muddy. For bedding, the men had only blankets and rubber sheets; they were dressed in oddments of uniforms and plain clothes. The small medical staff found it impossible to treat the men adequately. There was no local water, all water being brought by iron tanks to the railway and then carried by water-cart to the camp: the lack of bathing facilities implied habitual personal uncleanliness. The attitude of the public and the authorities towards the men was that they were 'untouchables'. Naturally, the men were disgruntled, spiteful, and insubordinate. Recovery under these conditions was slow and, for some, impossible. It can be imagined what those unhappy men had to endure until the conditions were remedied.

The change came about through two men, a 'young, hardworking soldier' Captain Conder, the camp commandant, and a 'wise and humane old soldier', Brigadier-General R. E. Williams, commandant of the district. These two men shared the belief that the patients would be restored to health and self-respect by improving their treatment and environment and converting the 'prison' into a hospital. The tents were struck and replaced by wards; they bored for an adequate water supply and erected furnaces for hot as well as cold showers. In this same building was a large irrigation room in which ninety-six men could be treated each ten minutes. They laid out lawns and gardens, concert parties came regularly, sports were held and to complete the break from 'prison' the military guard was removed. In an attempt further to help the patients, who were without pay, the men themselves were invited to act as hospital guards and orderlies and could therefore earn 5s. 0d. per day, 1s. 0d. of this being paid while in VD camp, the remainder of the daily allowance on their return to training camp, cured and fit for duty. The following figures show how the work of these two humane officers restored men's self-respect and contentment after suffering 'the banal tragedy, the human cruelty' of this ancient disease:

AWL	*Deserters*	*Offences dealt with during year*
1916:926	1916:88	1916:1 487
1917:199	1917:22	1917: 497
1918: 33	1918:nil	1918: 108

From March 1915 to June 1920, 7 242 patients passed through the hospital. More than 6 000 patients discharged from Langwarrin went overseas on active service; they won 400 decorations, including a VC. It was a triumph of science and sympathy over righteousness and hypocrisy.

The total incidence on 330 714 Australian embarkations works out at 150 per thousand. This is precisely the official figure for the Canadian Forces; the New Zealand figures were in the neighbourhood of 130 per thousand embarkations. British figures are far lower owing to the relative frequency with which the men were able to take leave to their homes.

British troops	1915	1916	1917	1918
In Britain	23.51	29.73	31.93	33.36
In British Expeditionary Force	29.65	18.23	25.60	32.36

Australian troops In Britain				
(at H.Q. or on leave)	134.05	148.1	129.2	137.12
In BEF	58.7	72.6	59.6	63.65

Americans, whose Expeditionary Force imposed the fiercest punishment for contracting venereal disease, nevertheless found VD one of their most serious medical problems of the war. According to the American official history of the war, out of 3 515 464 'admissions to sick report for disease' in the American army, 'respiratory' diseases came first with 26.63 per cent of the total number of men in the army, or 1 in every 3.5 men. Venereal disease, 357 969 or 1 in every 11 men, was responsible for the next largest number of admissions.

The French figures for 1916–18 were 83.19 per thousand; the German, 82.2 per thousand 'on establishment' and 110.3 'on actual strength'.

The figures prove but one thing. 'War is Hell,' as General Sherman is reported to have said. In every force venereal disease came very high among the causes of army casualties and 'wastage'. The human male was the same man no matter which side misfortune had placed him in this most awful tumult that a generation had to live through. In *Man and Superman* George Bernard Shaw has these words: 'when the military man approaches, the world locks up its spoons and packs off its womankind'.

From June 1917 to June 1919, 272 980 Nargol and Blue Light outfits and 196 825 condoms were issued from AIF depots in Britain; and 422 887 men reported for 'early' treatment.

The wastage, not of men as men, but as men to put back

into battle, was of concern to the authorities. The average stay in hospital was 52.2 days for syphilis alone. With 52 538 admissions to hospital from 1915 to 1918, the concern can be appreciated, but perhaps the figures for venereal disease will make more human the men over whom an unwanted halo has been placed. Perhaps these figures will show more clearly than any other that a man involved in the heat and effects of battle, of murder and sudden, unexpected death, especially in a war such as this one was, must behave differently from the same man in peace time. He is chained to a treadmill till death or wounds rescue him. His sordid task begets sordid passions. War is soldiers, and soldiers are men whom we send to battle, encourage to loosen the primitive instincts and to concentrate these instincts into a blood-lust: if a soldier does not take life he is of no use. Given the hypocrisy and double standards of the age, these truisms could not be faced and along with the horrors of a war that he could not erase from his mind, many soldiers must have suffered damnable torture of the spirit on returning to civilian life, where they knew that added to the banal tragedy was social cruelty that could affect even their future wives and children. One old man said to me, 'You always knew those "friends who stayed at home" were waiting for any evidence of any infraction you'd been involved in. Only in this way could they excuse their reluctance to fight for their country. Yes, I pity those poor boys who came home with V.D. behind them: they'd have to watch out for the rest of their lives because these sharks who didn't go never give up, our presence amongst them is enough to make them uneasy, fearful of their past decisions, and this fear comes out in disdain of us when we meet for a drink on Anzac Day, of our reunions, our nostalgia.'

While recording the statistics of venereal disease in the armed forces it is necessary to comment, for comparison, on civilian figures in this country both pre-war and during (but not affected by) the war.

In May 1916 a report was tabled in Federal Parliament and printed in Parliamentary Papers from the Committee appointed to consider the *Causes of Death and Invalidity in the Commonwealth from Venereal Diseases.*

'In 1904, of the result of 100 consecutive *Post Mortems* held in the Melbourne Hospital signs of syphilis were found in 34 and doubtful signs in 19 others,' they reported. They learnt that in 1908, at the Australasian Medical Congress in Melbourne, Dr P. B. Bennie had reported at the special meeting concerning syphilis that 25 per cent of the sick children in Melbourne were 'tainted' with syphilis and 10 per cent of *all* children in that city were 'syphilised'.

As an experiment in determining prevalence the confidential notification of syphilis was attempted in Melbourne for the twelve months ending 31 May 1911. 'Five thousand cases were reported . . . only about half the practitioners making reports.' (An optician gave the Wasserman test to 500 patients attending his eye clinic and found 14 per cent with direct evidence of syphilis.) Of 100 consecutive child mortalities at the Children's Hospital, Melbourne, *post mortems* showed that 44 infants who died within the first twelve months of life were diagnosed as syphilitic.

The report showed that in the Royal Prince Alfred Hospital, Sydney, gonorrheal infection was three times as prevalent as syphilis. 'Mr Clubbe, FRCS gave evidence that at the Children's Hospital, Sydney, every year there were about 500 children suffering from gonorrhoea.'

If any further evidence were necessary to show that Australia was not the 'cleanest land on earth', as C. J. Dennis put it in 'The Battle of the Wazzir', it was the reference in the report to '. . . the utterly ungrounded superstition that congress with an innocent child banishes venereal disease. Horrible results of this belief are not unknown in Australia'.

In 1915, night clinics were opened for venereal disease at the Royal Prince Alfred Hospital, Sydney. On 11 January 1915 only three patients came in, but by the end of the year 2 279 had come forward for treatment; and in addition to wards for men and women eighteen new beds had been provided for children between the ages of three and eight years suffering from congenital and other forms of syphilis. In 1914, thirty-four children under the age of one year were admitted with the disease to the Children's Hospital, Sydney.

At the Tenth Australasian Medical Congress held in Auckland, New Zealand in 1914, a percentage figure was stated that was later to be precisely the same as that given for men in the armed forces. 'It is fairly certain that 12 to 15 per cent of the population of London, Berlin and Paris are syphilitic and a much larger number are gonorrhoeic. There is good reason for thinking that Australian cities are affected to much the same extent. There are no other diseases which cause so much loss to the community.' The Congress produced figures to show that 7 189 deaths in Australia in 1914 were attributed to syphilis, and this did not take into account abortions or still-births. (These statistics were arrived at by way of a schedule applied in Paris in 1910 to ascertain the number of deaths attributed to syphilis, and other deaths a percentage of which was believed to have been caused by syphilis.) There was a large trade in proprietary medical 'cures' and chemists advertised openly that they could 'cure' the disease.

The Report to Parliament concluded: 'At least half the spread of syphilis is due to clandestine prostitution. The danger lies where it is not suspected. Any control of brothels should be under the ordinary police regulations.'

26
The Rose of
No Man's Land

There's a rose that grows, in No Man's Land
And it's wonderful to see
Though it's bathed in tears, it will live for years
In the garden of my memory.
It's the one red rose the soldier knows
It's the work of the master's hand.
Mid the war's great curse
Stands the Red Cross nurse
She's the Rose of No Man's Land.

No Man's Land was a place that altered its contours in each
man's mind. For many it was the grey land of pain, that
arena that a man could not, *must not*, by the rules of the
game speak of. Across this parade ground marched the
women who enlisted along with the men and who followed
close behind when they advanced. Brisk, brusque Sister
Alice Kitchen was typical of the tough, well-trained nurses
who were accepted for service and who went to the front.
The song 'Rose of No Man's Land' may seem too simpering
and sententious to describe those remarkable women with
their skill, efficiency and resilience, until one reads their
diaries. Only there do the hearts of the women show.

Alice Kitchen had set off with the first convoy in 1914,
sixty-four years after Florence Nightingale led the first
nurses on to the battlefields of the Crimea and only a few
months before Nurse Edith Cavell was shot by the Germans
in France for assisting wounded soldiers to escape. Whereas
history has chronicled the deeds of men at war since the

beginning of recorded time, little has been written about these latter day women who nursed men from the worst battlefields soldiers have known.

They had left Egypt with relief; on 5 April 1916 they arrived in Marseilles and 'went on deck in time to see the Chateau D'If as we passed it: and the morning mists round Notre Dame De la Garde. Afterwards we moved in nearer and passed a transport full of Australian troops who gave us a welcome. We are to split up into 5 parties and go to different parts in North of France. One to Rouen, one Étaples, one to Havre — and Samsing and I to Boulogne: to work in Imperial Hospitals.

'In the meantime we are to stay at the Hotel Requia; 117 women was rather an invasion . . .

'*April 10th*: 'Evacuation [of Marseilles] took place at noon today. . . . We went off in batches to a special train . . . loaded . . . with food and rugs and etc. (contrary to orders of course) no parcels or suit cases allowed as we would be sitting bolt upright packed like sardines for 2 whole days . . . We went through . . . green fields and all in the glory of spring, fruit trees laden with bloom, pink and white: yellow and purple iris growing wild in the grass, and cowslips and violets among the grass on the banks. The fields plentifully sprinkled with daisies and buttercups, grey olive groves and young vines. A lovely day . . . heather on the hills, sun on the sea, "Fair France" deserves her name. At Arles the children cheered us and waved to us and wanted our badges as "Australie Souvenirs". Everyone greets us kindly and cheerfully.

'*April 12th*: Arrived at Rouen in a perfect deluge of rain and drizzle, sloppy underfoot, roads like porridge and cold and chilly. Found we were to go to Boulogne on a supply train rather crowded, no corridors, no food arrangements and the possibility of a very long time in the train. We got a bit to eat in a bag and set off at last nearly an hour late starting. 8 p.m. *April 14th*: Had a long and miserable journey mostly spent crawling along the lines and in shunting. 10 hours at Abbeyville! We were ravenous. . . .

we arrived at Boulogne about 7 p.m. nearly 24 hours journey – our 16th day of travel.

'*April 15th*: On duty. [This was a British hospital.] I am in a surgical ward and we are billeted in an empty hotel nearby. It is bitterly cold here and we are thankful to have some winter clothing to put on. The wards are pretty and in beautiful order, red blankets for quilts, red screens, waxed floors, gorgeous flowers and kindly sisters, good orderlies and patient sufferers. So many awful amputations and injuries.

'*April 18th*: An awful day, the wind is wild and tears the doors out of your grasp and the breath from your body almost and the air is icy. Each ward has a nice coal stove and some comfort. . . . The patients' food is excellent and they lack for little that will aid their recovery. Some lady in England keeps the place supplied with the most beautiful flowers, carnations, tiger lilies, tulips, narcissus. The orderlies are fine workers and no trouble.

'*April 19th*: Had a half day off so we went to Wimereux to the Aust. Voluntary Hospital. Most of the patients there are wearers of the Kangaroo feathers. Met a man who came out on the *Benalla*. We trudged along the muddy roads through a couple of smelly villages with little old houses which seemed, for the most part, to be almost deserted, so little sign of life about, few children, no men. Beyond, the French sentries in their little straw sentry boxes guarding the bridges and the roads etc. Got back in time for dinner. A good many of the patients went off to "Blighty" and the ward is light, but so many broken bodies, so many limbs gone.

'Anzac Day. It scarcely seems a year since that dreadful landing at Gallipoli. L[ord] Dudley is inviting all Australians to a sort of bunfight. It seems queer to celebrate what must be to so many a day of National mourning in such a fashion. To so many in Australia it will only be a day of grief. This morning a German airship flew over the place and much excitement prevailed. 40 or 50 shots were fired at it but it sailed soberly on. About 4 p.m. the same one or another like it appeared again and we had the performance repeated.

'*May 2nd*: Got in some gassed men last night. There is a constant stream of patients who go off to England almost daily from here.

'*May 3rd*: Our half day. . . . The lilacs and laburnums are coming into bloom and the trees in the gardens and lanes a mass of soft wavy leafy greenness . . . the grass is thick with golden buttercups, ferns, solomons-seal and orchids and yellow iris and sprinkled with daisies . . . like a lovely carpet and the ponds covered with water lilies in the silent woods. A scarlet butterfly fluttered round us; the wild strawberries in bloom and the ragged robins and monks-hood clustered nearby. In the deep and quiet woods the ground was quite blue with hyacinths and I could not walk in some places without standing on some. . . . We heard a cuckoo calling insistently all the time we were there and behind it all the far-off sound of guns.

'*June 3rd*: A very large convoy of about 100 in today, very busy. Germans have nearly wiped out the Canadians at Ypres, and many regiments suffered badly. Heard dreadful news of an immense naval battle in the North Sea and loss of about 14 ships and many officers and thousands of men. May their souls rest in peace! Don't know whether it was a victory or not, if so a costly one.

'*June 5th*: Hear the Germans are trying their best at Verdun to get through, and it seems the naval battle was a victory for us, the enemy losing many more ships than we did and forced to go back. still the loss of life and ships was dreadful. It seems to have been a dreadful affair. Tonight a rumour is current: Lord Kitchener has been lost on a torpedoed ship . . .

'*June 7th*: The news of Kitchener's loss is too true. He was going to Russia on the *Hampshire* (which escorted us from Colombo to Egypt) . . . England's loss will be very great. There seems no one to take his place. The outlook seems depressing on top of so many naval losses.

'*June 8th*: A year ago since Samsing and I joined the

Gascon for a 6-month cruise in the Mediterranean where our life was so strenuous but so interesting, but so sad, memory clings to the sunsets and sunrises at Anzac and Lemnos, to the beautiful but barren Grecian Isles, the lovely Mediterranean . . . and Algeciras, and one I can but try to forget: the days full of heat, work and misery and all the heartbreak it meant for those at home so far away. And all for nothing –

'This has been a busy week, the Germans doing havoc at Ypres. We have had a large convoy of Canadian regiments in. About 120 this week, being the largest here for over a year. . . . [but] it is not heavy compared with Egypt or the Dardanelles.

'*June 13th*: . . . Getting in such lots of Canadians from Ypres [the second Battle of Ypres] so many lost limbs, poor men. All wounds here in France need to be opened up and drained. Such lumps of metal fished out of their anatomy, huge fragments of broken, sharp-edged shell and shrapnel, which makes one shudder to hold it tightly in your hand. There are many eye cases – so many with eyesight gone for ever. The saddest ones of all. We had no half-day off for a fortnight, each day is full of work and a convoy in every night – and nearly every day are evacuations to England.

'*June 27th*: Samsing, and others gone to a Casualty Clearing Station at Poperhinghe tonight. Some day we will be shot off too. The expected rush has not yet come yet all leave for Sisters has been cancelled. The Russians still progress if all the papers say is true.

'*July 2nd*: Orders to go back to Rouen, then in less than an hour had orders to get on to the train at 2.29. They say the casualties are pouring into Rouen in thousands – the great offensive has begun. *Rouen – July 4th*: We arrived at 2 a.m. – and an ambulance met us and we finally got here about 3 a.m. . . . All along the line Ambulance trains passed us laden with wounded and even ordinary trains full of walking cases. At the Boulogne Railway Station they were pouring in in thousands. At least 80 trains had gone through since morning. Reinforcements also pouring through to take their place. May it end in peace! The men seem optimistic, but then they always are when anything is doing.

'*July 5th*: Yesterday we went on duty. I to a section which had been medical. Was very tired having had very little sleep but the wounded were constantly pouring in and constantly being evacuated. They must have had over 20 000 through Rouen already. They come in, get washed, fed and dressed and then go on to Blighty, none go to Casualty Clearing. Everything here is beyond description and like several pig styes, one feels helpless to deal with such a situation, no order, no organisation – no anything that makes for efficiency. [She was *always* critical of Australian hospitals such as this one.]

'*July 6th*: There is no competency anywhere – the tents are separate, old, leaky and dirty. The rubbishy equipment should have been burnt when leaving Egypt. One feels ashamed to belong to such a muddle. There is a great expenditure of effort, for no result. No water laid on hot or cold. All has to be carried some distance. The orderlies were good enough boys but now rendered useless – slow, uninterested in nursing, no efficiency anywhere. It would make the Angels weep to see Australian money wasted so. It surpasses my wildest expectations. The last notice on the orderlies' list of work reads thus: "Orderlies will assist Sisters in lifting and changing helpless patients. In no other respect shall they have to do with the nursing of patients". Most of the girls looked tired and pasty. All who returned hate the place. Those who never were away think they have done marvels and resent any remarks and nothing upsets them more than to speak well of the British Expeditionary Force Hospitals. The arrangements for serving meals are disgusting and good food is spoilt by the Sister or orderlies having to hack off a joint all the food for sometimes 60 men – with knives like hoopiron – potatoes out of a billy, likewise pudding, no hospital trays, no way of keeping food hot in the meantime. The M.O.'s are well aware that none of us rejoiced in coming back. The girls resent the fact that at one time the M.O.'s had 22 batmen between them while the Sisters have to do everything but stretcher bearing.

'*July 7th*: Heavens! How it rained today and torrents of water everywhere. Rivers were running along the road near the quarters and swamps and pools everywhere, ankle deep under the Sisters' shacks and tents, solid streams poured and one wonders how long they will last out in this unhealthy spot. In the ward tents, it also poured in everywhere. *July 11th*: The girls look played out. It isn't much wonder: run down to start with and then to come to the damp and cold and hardship and even drag the heavy men off the stretchers, undress them, carry screens, water and a good deal of dirt and discomfort and not even a warm bath after the day is over.

'*July 15th*: Getting busy again. At night in the stillness we often hear the distant boom and thud of the guns. One night we had no lights at all owing to a scare about Zeppelin raids. Many patients in and out daily . . . more beds put in "with power to add to the number" – everyone tired. In a few months time there will be few of the original staff left so many are getting done up. Sister Jacobsen ill and off duty and has to go to England. Supposed to have a patch in lung not cleared up. She has been ill since we came back, but no notice taken . . .

'*August 9th*: Convoys in and out with a stream of sick and wounded men. The great offensive movement was late in starting this year and few anticipate that this year will see the close of the war. Another winter of cold and misery seems to be before these nations.'

Alice now followed her Sister Samsing to an Australian Casualty Clearing Station. 'During the night the train bumped a good deal and evidently has no Westinghouse brakes on – and pulled up, and let up and down crowds of troops; poor creatures, how many of them will ever return? . . . One of my patients among them . . . spoke to me at the station. I went on through Boulogne and up to Calais which was to me – a town with 2 church spires and a station yard. A Scotchman gave me hot water for tea.'

After a further twenty-four hours in a train she arrived at the station nearest her destination, where an ambulance awaited her. 'I had a motor drive of 15 miles by the canal banks some of the way, passing several hospital barges which looked nice and would be easy travelling for the wounded. Arrived here in time for dinner in the mess tent. Found I had a nice comfortable room and a good French bed in a nice house with a lovely old garden. Hear the guns booming and see the flashes of shells and rockets etc. Passed a large aerodrome on the way and saw one buzzing overhead.

'*August 21st*: Found a pretty full ward where Samsing and I work together. All seems so peaceful and homely. The Hospital is part of a Sacred Heart College with a Chapel attached and part still used as a boys' school where the youngsters play about the yard. . . . We carry our gas masks with us everywhere we go in case of accidents.

'*August 23rd*: After 8 p.m. Samsing and I went for a toddle down the road in the dust. A tiny little chapel in the street was lit up, it was only the size of a church porch and on the roadside the villagers congregated and said the Rosary in French. It looked so nice and homely and sincere and you felt that the people here still cherish the faith of their fathers. When we got back a heavy gun fire was going on and we listened for about an hour to the guns and watched the flashes in the sky. Tanks, aeroplanes and anti-aircraft – it has been going on for 2 or 3 days all around and many troops are about in the cobbled streets and eating and drinking in all the little shops, cafés and restaurants. . . . Tonight is the night for the attack. At least we have heard so for the past fortnight and probably Fritz knows all about it also. Hear that at the great offensive movement there were 30,000 Australian casualties and out of that very many died.'

By September she comments on 'little patches of frost on the grass in the morning . . . this all too short summer is drawing to a close and no prospect of peace'.

'. . . So much gun firing going on: it seemed louder and

heavier than usual. A soul-shaking sound in the night. Was wakened in the early morning with it and lying in the dark, with windows falling with the concussion, and flashes like wild lightening in the room, my heart went out to those poor lads who were in the thick of it, and I felt I could understand a little how unnerved they must get with the terrific noise and the awful sights . . .

'*September 11th:* Gradually filling up again. One poor man came in with spinal injury and perhaps lung or stomach as well. Father King brought Father McAuliffe to see me and we were pleased to meet again [Alice had shopped for this priest when he was on Gallipoli and procured 'altar bread' for him at Malta].

'*September 12th:* Being off in afternoon I went for a walk down the village street passing a transport column – mules, and waggons of all sorts about a mile long. Such young boyish faces some of the troops had, most looked grim and silent and serious and seemed to have lost all their reckless gaiety – they rarely spoke even to each other, and only occasionally to the children playing about the footpaths or smiled at some girl or woman, looking on in idle curiosity in the doorways. I found the little cemetery where a portion is set apart for the A.I.F. soldiers. It is a pretty, peaceful spot enclosed by very tall poplars all round. Its paths bordered by primly cut cypress trees. The French graves are nearly all marked with a crucifix monument large or small and many glass cases with wreaths of bead work or coloured china flowers. Ours are in rows with neat brown wooden crosses with the names and particulars: already about 120 of our men are buried there. In four large green patches lie many bodies brought from Neuve Chapelle buried together in a long trench. A soldier making borders ot white picoties told me many things about them all and it is something to know that as far as possible they are taken away from the scene of action and buried decently and where in times of peace, if it ever comes, some sorrowing women can come and see their last resting place. Here and there a larger cross or a plain white railed fence denotes that "someones" comrades erected it to his memory.

'*September 25th*: I am to depart tomorrow for Rouen or Ruin as the boys call it. . . . Bade farewell and regret that I shall not be able to see again the flights of aeroplanes coming home at night like a flight of homing birds. . . . 4 officers travelled with me, so I was not able to get a rest or sleep. [26 September] Arriving near Rouen we saw a train load of German prisoners, all such young boys. The day goes well with us just now, successes on the Somme and 5 000 prisoners and many guns.'

By now winter was well upon them, and the long hours and heavy work began to tell on the women. Her diary speaks of 'wet drizzle and miserable day. Paddling about in the rain doing surgical work with macintosh and umbrella is anything but comfortable or satisfactory and the detached tents make the work harder than it need be'. And each day she says 'Very tired'. On 19 October it was two years since their departure from Melbourne on the *Benalla*. One of the sisters died from pneumonia and kidney complications, two more were unable to go on leave because of U-boats in the English Channel and the closure of the port at Le Havre.

'Two years since we all sailed out of Albany Harbour,' Alice Kitchen says on 1 November, All Saints' Day. The wildflowers and greenness of May have been replaced by frost and ice, and the water is frozen in their rooms. By 12 November they had 'A big convoy of Australians in, mostly trench feet and sick. Very cold and bleak; everybody getting chilblaines and red noses and feeling the cold . . . a constant stream [of patients] in and out'. 'God help the poor men in the trenches and at the front,' she exclaimed on the seventeenth. 'Every bed full and the ports closed and no evacuations.' There were icicles on the thermometers in the wards, the ice was thick on the fire buckets – and still there were no fires except in the sitting room. Snow began to fall, and 'the whole place was covered in a beautiful mantle of white snow as dry as sugar – bitterly cold and so we have put on gaiters, mittens, mufflers and knitted jackets and everything warm we possess. Rain fell later and made it all slushy. Hear some reinforcements are expected to arrive anytime, not before they are needed. *November 19th*: Reinforcements not yet here: some sisters are working 5 and 6 days without a break and no hours off. I have every 3rd day for a half-day which means we work 2 days and a half without any time off.

'*November 21st*: The whole of France seems to be coughing and blowing its nose: felt like "flue" all night and cold all day. Went to bed last night with 3 hot bottles. The shacks are cold and damp and no fires anywhere for us. Sister Samsing has a sore throat. *November 29th*: Our pneumonia boy very bad and likely to die. Felt nearly demented with the cold icy wind and general miserable feeling. Coughed like a sick cow and after dinner hastened to bed with 2 hot bags and everything I could pile on top of me.'

When she eventually went on sick parade she got a cool reception. The sisters may give gentleness and attention to the men but should not expect too much themselves. By 5 December she was suffering from 'a wretched cold and a maddening cough and asked if I could see Matron. Was told a few home truths about my age etc. [43] some of which I knew and some I didn't believe'. Within a few days, age or not, both Alice Kitchen and the younger Sister Samsing were bed-ridden. 'Samsing and I are both at the hospital for sick nurses. They can't say I'm "swinging the lead" as they put me off duty themselves.

'*December 10th*: Had a miserable night and still no voice and only a cough and a squeak. Sr. Ross and Carlile came to see me bringing flowers and wattle from Miss Finlay. Snow drifting softly down. Matron R. expected and so kept the bed tidy, being told she didn't like Australians. Her dislike seems based on our independent-spirit (which applies to men as well as women), our so called easy times, having so much time off-duty – so much salary and the fact that we are supposed not to kow-tow to the military authorites and perhaps take no notice of rules! Our faults seem to be legion in her eyes. However she did not call on us. My voice not much better and I shudder at the thought of pneumonia or lung. It is taking so long to clear up.

[She remained ill, 'cough foggy and damp' and records the names of many other nurses invalided out. Still she cannot speak.] '*December 17th*: The loss of a voice is rather a worry especially to a woman used to airing her opinions. Marked up for evacuation to Blighty. Feel as if I were deserting Samsing in all her worries but have no choice in the matter. *December 19th*: Sister Rogers and Sister Curtis came in today as patients, with Broncopneumonia. *December 20th*: Got my "Blighty" labels and went off at 10.30 a.m. via the *Aberdonian*. The snow was on the ground and the trees and looked pretty, yet I left with tears in my eyes and sorrow in my heart for somehow being a failure at Rouen. Everybody was most kind and nothing was missing that could make me more comfortable and happy – and every care and attention given to every sick sister.

'The trip down the river was pretty and went to bed after dinner and so kept warm. The matron was most kind and attentive – we reached Southampton early and disembarked about 11.30. The sheds looked comfortable and roomy and dry and all the stretcher cases were in a large walled in place with coconut matting all over the floor and stoves to warm it while waiting. Train left at 12.15 and got to London at 4 p.m. – or thereabouts and I was put in a motor and brought to St Vincent Sq. Everything here is just the thing – like a £5.5.0. hotel room, peaceful and quiet, a radiator, nice furnishings and food and the usual kindness that the B.E.F. just lavish on one. I shall always be grateful to them for their kindness to strangers. Don't know what the next move is – Perhaps more laryngoscopes and mirrors etc. though am constantly assured it is nothing chronic. At any rate there are points about leaving the fair land of France as a patient. Everything has been done for me – luggage looked after, nothing left to chance or even to myself and I have been spared much bother and discomfort.'

27
Kangaroo Feathers

Some men I sought, some came to me. I thought I had not seen Rex Hall before he came to give me his diaries. 'Do you go to the Anzac Day march?' he said. Of course — nowadays, that is. 'I led the mounted Light Horsemen this year. I was in the Camel Corps most of the time, at the first war, with Gallipoli and later the Light Horse charge to Beersheba with Allenby thrown in.' 'Wait,' I said. Enough is enough. What historian could hope to meet in one man an Australian Camelier, a legendary Light Horseman, a survivor of Gallipoli and one of the horsemen wearing their kangaroo feathers as they ride at the lead of Australia's biggest Anzac Day gathering?

Rex Hall had been the little boy who was fourth on the pony to school in the bush and who, at ten years of age, used to ride with the district mail-bag five miles before breakfast.

Although some men who could not ride did get into the Light Horse, they were in the minority. Most were horsemen born and bred to the saddle from farms and outback stations. Some took their own horses, others were issued with mounts. From the 1850s on Australia was prominent in the remount trade — particularly to India. The thoroughbred element in Australian remounts gave them a stamina and spirit that was invaluable, and the trade became one of the allies' main sources of reliable horses. During that war 121 324 top quality horses were sent overseas, 39 348 to the AIF and 81 976 to India. Like their riders, these horses took part in the last great cavalry charges the world will know; if their riders were known as tough men the horses matched them. They endured times of hardship such as few animals could do and still be serviceable. As the mounted troops advanced over the Sinai Desert into the Palestinian plains their labour was immense. They became painfully wasted from lack of water and food, yet all the mounted men noticed that they remained alert 'and utterly dependable'. Their courage never wavered, neither did their stamina. They were superb. 'Once you got a good waler you looked after him,' Rex Hall knew. The waler took its name from the state that first bred these tough remounts – New South Wales – but later they came from all states. My mother, who was raised on the steep hills of Gippsland (Vic.), has told me of buyers coming regularly to the farm. 'They liked our tough riding horses, we used to have them up and down the hills all day after cattle and they'd never give up.' As explorers in Central Australia found, they are superior to camels in the desert, travelling at a greater pace and going as far, provided water is obtained for them. As well, Australian walers progressed from a walk to an easy, level canter ideal for heavily laden troopers. (The traditional cavalryman's charger went from a walk to a trot, thus increasing the noise of the approach of the troops and making for greater strain in riding.)

Horses were used for mobility only. The men dismounted to fight, except for the few dramatic charges they made leaping across trenches. The chief value of the horse under ordinary conditions was that the troops arrived at the scene of battle relatively fresh as opposed to the infantry who were invariably fatigued after long marches. They could also cover country impassable by mechanised means. Four cavalry divisions once covered over 300 miles of country totally unsuited to motorised vehicles in twelve days and took the enemy by surprise.

The Corps was the largest body of mounted troops the modern world has known. Unlike the mounted regiments of other nations, they carried rifle and bayonet and were not issued with swords until 1918, towards the end of the war.

In the Australian equivalent of cavalry both horse and

rider were likely to have taken part in many bush race meetings and were used to anything at all. They travelled well. Lieutenant C. R. Morley of Tweed Heads, NSW, wrote home, 'Bosker wasn't it? Our horses came over very well, only lost 7'. Morley was aged twenty and did not want to die. 'I don't care if we stay here [Egypt] till the end of the war because if we get to Europe there is a chance of us getting shot but if we stop here our only chance of snuffing it is of old age.'

When he arrived in Egypt Morley was sent to an officers' school. 'All the officers and NCO's here are old cavalry men, and call us gentlemen and to tell the truth I'm beginning to wonder if I really am.'

The Australian Light Horse and the New Zealand Mounted Rifles (most of whom had served as infantry on Gallipoli) were mounted again on their return to Egypt and formed into the Anzac Mounted Division, for most of the time under Major-General H. G. Chauvel. The division remained in Egypt with British yeomanry and a brigade of camel troops. 'We volunteered for the camels,' Rex Hall says with some amazement. 'We were mainly Australian volunteers from the Light Horse.'

Almost 1400 Australians served in the Imperial Camel Corps. Like the Light Horse, it was a body formed for purposes of mobility only – the riders dismounted and fought as infantry when attacking. It was a cosmopolitan force, almost half of it being Australian, with some English, New Zealanders, a Scottish machine-gun company, the Hong Kong and Singapore Mountain Battery (Indians) and a Welsh field ambulance. They were mounted on light, thoroughbred riding camels, bred in the Sudan and bought by the British for £15 each.

In 1916, after the infantry's departure for France, the Turks tried to strike across North Sinai to capture the Suez Canal. They were held and beaten by the mounted division at Romani on 4 August 1916. This was the beginning of a campaign that lasted until the Turks were beaten in Sinai and Palestine and sought an armistice on 30 October 1918.

The battles the boys wrote of in their letters home were at first successful – Magdhaba (23 December) and Rafa (9 January 1917) – after which the enemy retired to Gaza and Beersheba in southern Palestine where they had established a defence line thirty miles long. The next two battles were far less decisive. Led by Chief-of-Staff Murray (the man who had held the Australians in disdain because of their 'lack of training and discipline') the first attack on Gaza failed because of the lack of water for the horses and the second failed because of leadership. The British Government now placed General Sir Edmund Allenby and Lieutenant-General Harry Chauvel in command and on 31 October Allenby attacked, this time with infantry around Gaza and mounted troops inland about Beersheba. It was here at Beersheba on 31 October 1917 that the 4th Light Horse made the magnificent cavalry charge that will be recorded as among the greatest in military history.

The mounted force had ridden through the dark of night and by dawn were in position to attack. All day the Turks strongly resisted until it was late afternoon. Beersheba had to be taken by nightfall – the watering of the horses made this essential for they must get to the wells of Beersheba. Chauvel knew that the Turkish positions to the south of the town were not protected by barbed wire. He decided to send the 4th Light Horse in on a desperate bid: they would go in as cavalry, not dismounted as usual but on their horses, using their bayonets as weapons. 'Australians had never ridden any race like this,' the official history records. 'The Turkish gunners saw them coming and opened up with shrapnel but their pace was too fast for the gunners.' After galloping for two miles the Turkish machine guns began firing, then, as they got nearer the trenches, the Turkish rifles opened up, 'dangerous at first, but wild and high as the Light Horse (who could now see the trenches) approached'. They came on at a hard gallop, leapt the trenches, dismounted, and turned on the Turks from the rear with rifle and bayonet. The garrison, astounded, surrendered. Other riders galloped on to the rear trenches where parties of bewildered Turks surrendered to single horsemen, while yet other squadrons galloped hell for leather on into Beersheba and the day was won.

This demonstrated once and for all that Australian (or Dominion) troops, when led by their own officers, have an initiative unknown to the cavalrymen of old, for while galloping in formation they fanned out across the desert without waiting for an order when the Turkish artillery opened up on them, galloped on, and closed up again when nearing their objective and swept through the Turkish positions.

Within a week the whole front, including Gaza, collapsed. On the last day of the skirmishing, Lieutenant Reg Morley, now aged twenty-two, was killed at Sheria.

Young Morley wrote regularly to his parents of the battles he was riding in. The letters stopped in November 1917 and in their place came one from a comrade, Captain J. Boyd. 'It is with sad heart that I write to tell you of the death of Reg. He was wounded about 3 p.m. on 8 November during an attack on Tel Aba Dilahk, 15 miles east of Gaza. All through the day he had led his men splendidly, taking all sorts of risks and exposing himself first when danger threatened and in one instance, early in the morning, was one of the four that moved forward and remained unwounded. In the early afternoon the squadron moved forward and carried a ridge formerly denied us by the enemy. Reg was advancing along the ridge with his troop and all firing had practically ceased and Reg was sitting up looking into a hollow and I was walking towards him and was only a few yards away when he was hit. He was very cheery and suffering no pain. I remained with him until the ambulance took him and now understand he died during the night at the Light Horse Field Ambulance Station. I feel poor Reg's death and miss him very much. He was my especial pal ever since leaving Enoggera and never again can I have such a mate. We shared many dangers on the battlefields. He and I made an arrangement before the battle started that in the event of either of us "going under" the other was to fix up his effects. I will see to this and will visit you on return.'

By February 1917 mounted troops had driven the Turkish army from the Sinai Peninsula, and, four-fifths of these men being Australian, there was a call for them to be sent to France to fill the gaps left after Pozières. It was then that General Sir Archibald Murray, who had earlier criticised the Australian troops as being 'undisciplined, poorly trained', wrote, 'I cannot spare a single man. These Anzac troops are the keystone of the defence of Egypt.'

Their next foray was Palestine.

Rex Hall, aged nineteen when he embarked in 1914, was a typical Light Horseman. Dismounted in 1915, he had gone to Gallipoli where he served in the medical corps on board the *Galeka*, arriving in Anzac Cove after the massive Turkish attack of 21 May. 'Our operating theatre to which I had been allotted was a sorry sight with serious cases lying around on tables and benches, a dozen surgeons operating under most difficult conditions for sixteen hours without a break, snatching a meal when they could until every one of the 400 wounded men who came aboard that first day was treated. A Turk with a shattered arm had it amputated at 4 o'clock in the morning.' He saw a lot for a young country boy.

Arriving on shore on Gallipoli in early August he heard a thing that shocked his innocence. 'I learnt that in planning an attack the authorities calculated the proportion of expected casualties, to the strength of the attacking force. For example, if 50 000 were in the attack we could "afford" to lose 15 000 and planned accordingly.' He arrived in the middle of the string of battles that included Lone Pine, The Nek and Chailak Dere.

Back in Egypt Rex remounted and shortly after was seconded to the Imperial Camel Corps. He remained with the 'hooshters' until April 1918 when the camel corps was disbanded, its members forming the 5th Light Horse. Rex, still in his early twenties, took part in the battles that drove the Turk out of Palestine and Syria and put Turkey out of the war. He held the rank of Captain and later Brigade Major. He revelled in the antiquity of the land he rode by camel or by horse.

'We fought over the ancient cities of Biblical times. We took Ramlet and Ludd . . . took 350 prisoners at these native villages that once had been prominent centres. Ludd, on the plain of Sharon, ten miles from Jaffa is where St George is reputed to have been born and buried [and in 1972, the scene of a massacre at its airport]. Ramlet, now a squalid village, was once the centre of the Crusaders' battles and King Richard had his seat here in 1191. Amman, where we rode in 1918, was the Philadelphia of the olden times. And Tel Aviv – well, when I think now of that city of half a million Israelis and then remember the few native shanties that were there when I rode my camel through it in 1918!

'We rode on Samaria, the old Northern Kingdom of Israel, founded in 887 B.C. Its great palaces and large water cisterns were destroyed and built again by Alexander the Great, then by Herod. It is claimed to be the burial place of John the Baptist. We rode to capture Nablus, the ancient Shechem – it was here I was handed the keys of the city, being in charge of the victorious troops! They were very heavy and I took them away spread over the pommel of my saddle. We rode on Jerusalem, past Nazareth, over the mountains of Moab, and Baalbek where I was virtually Military Governor for a time amid the Greco-Roman ruins.'

Not all the troops were so enthralled by the biblical history of the stony, dry desert lands. 'We were camped three miles outside Bethlehem in March 1918, and gave the troops leave to visit the city. By 11 a.m. an irate staff officer had hurried out to tell us our troops were playing up. Immediately we rode in to see what it was all about. Along the road we passed several men in various stages of inebriety, but when we reached the scene of the trouble – the Church of the Nativity – we found the troops had been sold the local brew of "Arack", a potent drink that acted quickly. To relieve them of "backsheesh" the men had been encouraged to go over the church and several were shown into the Grotto of the Manger. There one viewed, through an alcoholic haze, what was explained as the light of the manger that had been burning for a thousand years. He said, "Well, it's bloody well time it was out," and out it went. Simultaneously, a secret bell chain had been found by another. That tolled, plus the extinction of the lamp, caused alarm and consternation and fear of the end of the world amongst the congregation.

'That incident roused the ire of the c-in-c and questions continued for months. It was a file two inches thick when I saw it last and nobody ever did find out who blew the light out.

'After a rest of a few days we moved on. Approaching the Holy City the column of camels, four abreast, stretched for about a mile and a half. As they shuffled along their riders were silent, appearing to sense the solemnity and to respect the sacredness of the city when one man, possibly still suffering the "overhang" from Bethlehem, fell off his camel. His language, as reported to me, was hardly in keeping with the sanctity of the Holy City.

'One saw funny things. On the way to capture Damascus we had French colonials, Algerians, as drivers. A funny lot. If one driver had an urge to go behind a bush he'd just pull his cart up and block the rest of the column. I saw my Transport Officer, Vic Allen, riding along the mile and a half long column of carts trying to get them to move along. He was hitting the drivers over their heads with his hat and swearing loudly. "Those silly bastards don't know a word of English," he said to me.'

Sister A. E. Cocking, when an elderly lady, dictated her memoirs of the days she spent nursing the Light Horse and Camel Corps troops. 'We were kept busy in the hospital, convoys of wounded and sick came down from the desert. Just before General Allenby replaced General Murray the Gaza stunt was fought and our soldiers and the Welsh unit were badly beaten, the killed and wounded were great. Our hospital was full of wounded, as were the tents and improvised hospitals – I remember that convoy from El Arish, the wounded coming down to us in the little train, covered in dust, bearded and lousy, we just had to cut off their clothes, give them a wash, clean dressings and pyjamas. Many died before we could tend them. For three days and nights we nursed them, the theatre was going night and day – there were many amputations – the shrapnel wounds were awful. Reinforcements of nurses arrived from Australia – we had two days off and spent them in bed.

'During the Palestine attack the soldiers' wounds were slight but many were ill with malaria. I pitied the camel corps out in the desert with those camels; the soldiers got very sore hands and gastric trouble, good food was hard to get . . . Most of the officers had a turn in hospital either sick or wounded.'

'The crossing of the Jordan' was the moment the riders had been waiting for, the 'relieving' of Damascus. They had the Turks on the run and they knew it, but they also knew the survivors would fall back on Damascus in the hopes of continuing the fight from there, so it was to be a race. That they would reach the ancient city first they never doubted: their morale had never been higher than when they rode out of camp at 6 a.m. on 27 September 1918 to ford the Jordan and take Damascus. As with other individual incidents this last evolved into a controversy that is unlikely to be officially solved: who 'took' Damascus – the Australian Light Horse or Lawrence of Arabia and his Arabs?

Rex Hall is one of many students of that campaign – who also took part in it – who heaps scorn on Lowell Thomas, the American journalist who created 'the romance under the caption "With Lawrence in Arabia".' 'I do not for one moment denigrate the good name of Lawrence nor detract from his leadership in the "Arab Revolt" in Arabia in harassing the Turks, blowing up trains etc. but when it came to cooperation with Allenby's forces, the Arabs under Lawrence had . . . nuisance value only.' Other observers have commented that Lawrence was a myth, not a legend and his Arabs 'as soldiers, they were figures of ridicule'.

Twice Lawrence's Arabs had failed to arrive at allotted positions, during attacks – even when the battles lasted for three days they didn't arrive – and now, when the Light Horse had surrounded Damascus and were still fighting the groups of Turks and Germans, attempting either to get into the city or to escape so as to reform and later re-take the city, Lawrence led his Arabs into the city, firing guns and shouting, and demanded King Feisal's right to rule Damascus.

At this time, 7 a.m. on 1 October, the 10th Light Horse entered the city from the west intending to head for the Aleppo road to cut off this outlet from the city. The civilian population ran out into the streets to greet them, 'uttering frenzied cries and chants' Colonel Olden of the 10th wrote. 'The women leant from the windows of high buildings, raised their dark veils and called out, "*Meit allo wesahla!*" [a hundred welcomes]. The cry was taken up and carried along the line of march in one continuous chant.' At the Hall of Government Olden and two officers dismounted and entered to where they were told the governor awaited them. 'Inside the splendid room a large gathering, clad in the glittering garb of Eastern Officialdom stood, formed up in rows, quiet and dignified. Behind a table sat the Emir Said, grandson of the Sultan of Algiers. He had been installed as Governor by the fleeing Turks.

'In the name of the City of Damascus I welcome the first of the British Army,' he said through an interpreter. Olden asked, 'Does the city surrender?' On being assured that the city intended no further opposition, he asked what then was all the firing in the streets? 'It is the civil population welcoming you.' Olden told Said to have the shooting stopped as it might be misunderstood. 'You need not fear,' the Emir said. 'We have expected the English here and have prepared for them.'

Olden remounted and led his men off to where he had been ordered on the Aleppo Road. 'The march now assumed the aspect of a triumphal procession, the dense masses of people rapidly becoming hysterical in their manifestations of joy. They clung to the horses' necks, they kissed our men's stirrups, they showered confetti and rose water over them; they shouted, laughed, cried, sang and clapped hands.' In the midst of all this an airman who had been brought down and captured ran up. 'Thank God you're here at last,' he cried. 'Where are you going now?' 'To the Aleppo Road,' he was told. 'Right! I'm coming with you!' He grabbed an Arab pony from a native, leapt on it and rode off with the Light Horse and within an hour was fighting side by side with them against the German machine gunners and Turkish infantry, helping to keep the enemy out of the war 'while Lawrence and his rabble galloped up and down the streets of Damascus firing their rifles into the air'.

They fought and harried all that day. From 27 September to 1 October they had had only one night's sleep. For a fortnight they had followed and attacked Germans and Turks, preventing them from reaching Damascus. Since leaving the Sea of Galilee, 250 miles as the crow flies, it was estimated that they had ridden upwards of 400 miles. On this last day they had ridden and fought over forty miles.

Exhausted, they lay down to sleep at 10 p.m. unaware that they had fired their last shot in the war on this, the day Damascus fell.

Before they left for home arrangements had to be made for the disposal of the horses: they would not be returned to Australia. There were plenty of rich Arabs and Syrians anxious to buy them but the Light Horsemen had seen too much of their cruelty to animals. The troops raised such an uproar at any suggestion that their mounts be left at the mercy of the Arabs that the authorities decided to destroy them. A final race-meeting was arranged, the brave horses that had crossed deserts were given their final gallop, and the day after the races they were taken out onto a high plain and shot. 'With our horses gone, our camp seemed gloomy and depressing,' Olden wrote. 'They had been part and parcel of our very lives all these years and now – the death sentence.'

The Light Horse gained their swords – and lost their reputation – at Surafend, now Sarafan, a small native village. Having fought with rifle and bayonet so long, the issue of the traditional cavalryman's weapon in mid-1918 was an anticlimax, although they were reported to have become skilled 'overnight' in its use. But Surafend would remain on the record for reasons other than gaining a new weapon.

After the Armistice in Europe, Australian troops were still used to 'maintain order' in Egypt during the 'Arab uprising'. The story the men tell is that a New Zealand trooper – a sergeant – was disturbed from his sleep and, as he jumped up, was shot dead by an Arab who was thieving. The troops, a mixed bunch of Australians, New Zealanders and Scots, raided the village in their anger and undoubtedly killed men there. One report states that they threw villagers down a well and rolled a large grindstone down on top of them. Their excuse was that they were sick of the natives stealing; for five years they'd put up with their small private possessions from home being stolen as well as their uniforms and gear, were weary of their men being ambushed and killed while the authorities 'did nothing'.

The morning after the punitive raid General Allenby was told. He blamed the Australian Light Horse and demanded a parade during which, among other things, he called them murderers. All leave was to be stopped, all men on leave were to be recalled and all recommendations for honours and awards were to be withdrawn.

Rex Hall, on his way on leave – the special leave granted to men who had been overseas since 1914 – was angry. 'I am still,' he said in 1978. 'Only a few men took part in the raid and the rest have been victimised, left without honours or medals, unhonoured, unsung.'

Perhaps no other incident during these five years demonstrates so sharply the absurdity of 'a state of war'.

Early in 1918 the Imperial Camel Brigade was disbanded and the Australian members formed into a new Light Horse Brigade (the 5th). The abandoning of the 'Hooshter' Brigade meant the end of one of the most interesting groups warfare had known; had they been other than Australian they would have been termed exotic or romantic (like the Foreign Legion) but such tags never sat easily on Australians.

High cockalorum and traditions that have become an absurdity were occasionally still practised in the officers' mess – even in that of the Imperial Camel Corps. Rex Hall tells of one such tradition and its sequel.

'Each week we had a formal mess night. At one of these there was an unpleasant incident for one officer. Captain George Smith of New South Wales appeared in Mess with his Sam Brown belt on. That being a service *faux pas*, for which the offender may be called upon to shout for the Mess, Captain McCallum, a solicitor of New Zealand rose – "Gentlemen, mine's a liqueur".

'George had been imbibing rather too freely. He showed and expressed his resentment, and continued for the next week to ignore McCallum, until the eve of our departure for the war front.

'George came round the mess table and said to Mac: "I'm sorry old chap about the other night; tomorrow we leave for the front; some of us may not come back; let us shake". That they did. Two months later, almost to the day, on 9 January [1917] in the battle of Rafa our Corps had two Company Commanders killed, they fell almost side by side and within a few minutes, Captain George Smith and Captain McCallum of No 12 and No 15 companies respectively.'

The battle that Rex spoke of was one that proved the worth of the Camel Corps. Nine companies, after a march (or ride!) of thirty miles, attacked the Turkish garrison at Rafa. 'Here our mounted mobility proved again its value in being able to strike quickly some thirty miles from base and retire with all dead and wounded under cover of darkness. Sand carts and sledges moved the wounded to the railhead and then the train took them back to Port Said and Cairo.'

It was said that there was a voluntary and unwritten law in the Light Horse that no sound man should allow himself to be taken prisoner, and no wounded man should be allowed to fall into enemy hands. In the two-and-a-half years of their campaigns in the desert, only 73 Light Horsemen were captured by the Turks. During that period they captured 40 000 Turks.

28
The Shellal
Mosaic

During the second attack by the Light Horse on Gaza a quite startling discovery was made in the Wadi Guzzi. With the Light Horse was Queensland's Padre Maitland Woods, Senior Chaplain to the AIF in Egypt, an Oxford man and Greek scholar still in touch with his old professor at Oxford.

Writing from Palestine to Colonel Padre Garland in Brisbane, Maitland Woods tells of shell-fire exposing one of the major archaeological finds in the world at that time. 'It proved to be the floor of a church built in A.D. 622. The Earth was cleared entirely off, which had laid on it for 1 200 years, and General Clayton sent me over to see it and report, I offered to remove the Mosaic by a long and tedious process, but I was refused permission. However, by devious devices, I obtained permission from the Higher Military Command in Palestine to get to work. I have been working with a squad of engineers for over a week now and the Mosaic of Exquisite beauty and magnificent colour is gradually being placed in 62 flat boxes 4 ft by 2 ft each. My work has been constantly interrupted by the visits of Generals and others. Six motor cars of them came out here yesterday (I am living on the site) and all now are convinced that a most priceless piece of early Greek Christian art will be added to our possessions in this direction – I have been to Cairo twice to obtain materials, and so far the work has cost me considerably over £30 – I have trained my workmen (English Engineer Soldiers) so that we have not had an accident so far – At the East end of the Church where the

Altar stood, was an inscription in Greek which (translated) runs somehow like this:

Sign of the cross ┬ and he provided bountifully for the building of this Church (broken off) He who was the most saintly of us - - - George. The beloved of God - - - - - Founded in the 622nd year after --- (Christ?)

This inscription (Mosaic) I took up and warned the watchmen to dig most carefully with their trowels – what I expected happened – *We found the bones of the Saint lying feet towards the East* – These I reverently placed in a casket as they had lain there 1300 years you can easily realise that some of them were as delicate as the wings of a butterfly. Now my friends the Generals are being exercised in their minds as to what is to be done with such a priceless piece of Ecclesiastical Beauty – the Senior General suggests a Committee meeting of us all – as you no doubt have already surmised – there is Australia – New Zealand – and England to be considered – and they will have to face the awkward fact that it was my energy and determination to say nothing of ingenuity which has recovered the whole of this Mosaic – which, for its period, is one of the finest in the world – what becomes of the Pavement I do not mind – I will willingly bear all the expenses of removal, and make no claim on the large coloured portion – But I *do* want (1) the wonderful Greek inscription in black and white marble mosaic (a photo of which I intend to send you); (2) the Relics of the Saint (George of Shellal) and I want to place the inscription and the Relics in Brisbane Cathedral under the Altar there where they will be a fitting witness to the bravery of our Anzacs in Palestine and a link between our Holy Catholic and Apostolic Church in Queensland and the Church (alas! now extinct, since it was destroyed by the Mohammedan invasion of the 8th century) in Southern Palestine.

'Will you please with Canon Bones if possible, lay these facts before his Grace the Archbishop of Brisbane and ascertain whether these Holy Relics would be accepted by the Cathedral chaplain, and duly placed in site – Mind you – I haven't got possession of them altho' everything is at the present time in my keeping – and I hold a written authority from the G.O.C. in supreme command to me to "remove the Shellal pavement" – which is now known to the troops here as "the Shellal Mosaic". But I have every confidence that I can persuade them that a Museum is *not* the proper place for the memorial Tablet and the Relics I could I suppose send them to Queensland, but I would much prefer to bring them myself . . . I am sure you have read this letter patiently through and understand how I feel towards dear old "George. The most saintly of us all, who generously built this Church" as the inscription reads – and how he wished to be near the Blessed Sacrament – he was a fine strong hefty fellow – and a bit of a fighter too, for one of the arms was broken and had set beautifully.'

On 15 June he could write to Padre Garland: 'At last I have finished . . . The whole pavement is up – and packed in boxes (51 of them!) and a tractor is coming from General Russell to take it to the railway. I am dog tired after 12 days of incessant work (32 men were on the job!) but forward you these photos'. And just over two months later he was able to inform his 'dear old Padre' that the 'Holy Relics and the pavement are now in the Anzac Kit Stores in Cairo (with a guard on them).'

'Maity Woods' was very popular with the troops and they took a pride in assisting with the lifting of the pavement. The mosaic floor was of an old Greek Catholic Church. Worked in marble cubes it measures thirty feet by eighteen feet. In the centre a chalice is surrounded by a grapevine and two crosses in a vibrant green. There are animals – tiger, elephant, stag, rabbit, peacocks and flamingoes – all worked in scintillating colours, baskets of figs and a bird in a cage: in all, a wonderful and artistic piece of Christian work of the 6th Century A.D. (British Museum archaeologists fixed the date as A.D. 561.) The pavement was transported to Australia and is preserved in the Australian War Museum, Canberra.

29
The Boys in Blue

When Sister Kitchen was on the hospital ship *Gascon* she had been shown over one of the submarines of the day after taking a load of wounded from Gallipoli to Malta – and marvelled. 'It is a marvellous and complicated mass of machinery inside and yet everything seems to work by the touch of a hand on a wheel or screw and looks so simple. We saw all the torpedoes and the means of firing them was explained to us; and looked through the periscope and saw the *Gascon* outside and the people on the wharf quite distinctly and also it was explained to us just how the submarine was sunk under the water [diving]. When on business bent, the periscope is never allowed up above the water longer than 3 seconds, which seems very little time in which to take all the bearings sufficient to do their deadly work. They never chase a vessel only lie in wait for them and when a torpedo is fired into a vessel they just clear out quickly and never show up above water. When you see how little space they have in which to live and sleep on the floor except the Captain and one other whose bed is a drawer you realise that they could rescue none, not even themselves if anything happened to them. They can stay under water about 40 hours without discomfort or fresh supply of air; carry no medical dressings or stores except for burns; never go down more than 20 feet at a time and then only about 60 ft altogether.'

Primitive as the controls were on this newest of maritime novelties, there was a waiting list of hundreds of men anxious to transfer from the conventional ships to *AE2* when she was towed behind the second convoy of the AIF to the Mediterranean.

At 3 a.m. on Sunday, 25 April 1915, the tiny vessel entered the narrow Dardanelles Strait, creeping along seventy feet down (their gauges cut out at 100 feet) beneath the mine-field.

For an hour they moved ahead, with the 'damnably continuous rapping and scraping on the hull of the boat by the mooring wires of the mines, held taut by the buoyancy of the mines themselves overhead. Choose the wrong moment to rise for observation through the periscope and you choose a moment to hit a mine, so you choose to observe as few times as possible. Try to forget the result should one of those wires catch on a projection of the boat's side. Twice something hard hit the boat's bows and rattled away astern. Once something seemed to catch forward and remained knocking insistently for several minutes before it broke away', the Captain wrote.

As there was no precise method of calculating their speed, the distance travelled was unknown. Currents swept them around and at no time when they put the periscope up were they where they had estimated. Worst of all was the uneven sea floor. Constantly they ran aground. 'From 70 feet we suddenly run aground at 8 feet. Which means much of our ship is above water and now we see we are surrounded by boats converging on us all guns firing,' observed their captain, Commander H. G. Stoker, D.S.O., R.N. Time and time again they manoeuvred the little ship back into deep water. They sank a cruiser and were in danger of being rammed as she sank. They had been told to penetrate the Dardanelles and cause havoc amongst enemy shipping, and while the troops landed on Gallipoli they did just that. When the shipping in that narrow, walled-in strait forced them to dive for the last time, they lay on a mud bank at seventy feet hearing the search for them go on overhead. Every now and again they heard and felt the sweeps knock their little vessel but go on without recording their presence. When darkness came, they surfaced, 'the crew swarmed on deck, eager for the clean night air after having passed the only 24 hours of their life without sight of the light of Gods day'. They must recharge their batteries, re-adjust their lost diving trim and signal the fleet that they had successfully got through. Their radio receiving gear was out of order so they were unaware whether their message had been received. (It was not till three and a half years later, when they were released from P.O.W. camp, that they learned that the message had been relayed to the Council of War being held on the *Queen Elizabeth*. The matter under discussion was whether to hold on to or evacuate Gallipoli, less than twenty-four hours after the Landing. The news that a submarine had got through the entrance to the Dardanelles was a major point in deciding to hold on.)

They passed on through the strait, firing a torpedo at another cruiser, and eventually reached the Sea of Marmora: they were through the Dardanelles.

They had no guns and only a limited number of torpedoes, and since their instructions had been to prevent the passage of enemy troops to the Gallipoli Peninsula, they attempted to 'frighten as much as possible'. Sometimes during the following day this consisted of surfacing near a group of fishing boats while the fishermen begged for their lives, calling on Allah! 'We let them return to their villages with tales of the coming of the British fleet; the morale effect would all help. And so, in this pleasantly interesting manner we passed the afternoon,' Commander Stoker wrote.

But next day, terror struck, the little ship herself ran amok beneath the water, refusing to respond to control. First her bow would swing up and they would shoot to the surface; then her bow would incline and they would sink eighty, ninety, a hundred feet down where the gauge cut out, down to where the pressure would cave her walls in. Eventually, on one of the crazy leaps to the surface, the enemy shot a hole in her stern sticking vertically out of the water. Before she sank the men leapt overboard – to three and a half years in P.O.W. camps.

The experiences of naval men were as varied as those in the army. W. T. 'Bill' Divers, a strong union man and prominent socialist, was an example. Bill, when he was aged fifteen, in 1909 had agitated for a rise in pay from 5s. 0d to 7s. 6d a week for delivery boys at MacRobertsons' Australian chocolate factory. They got the rise but Bill was sacked. Looking for work, he went to sea in 1910. At the outbreak of war Bill rushed to join up and from August 1914 he was on – and in – the most dangerous waters. He served on HMAS *Boorara*, HMAS *Barunga* and HMAS *Moorgate*, all of which were 'flattened' as Bill puts it by the enemy.

'Hell! We once were going along in the *Boorara* minding our own business about a hundred miles from Lemnos when the Gallipoli stunt was on. All of a sudden a damned big thing comes straight at us and rams its big ramming bow fair through us – it was a French ship, or rather an old German ship, the *Kleber*, that the French had collected, old enough to have a ram that could've demolished a fort. Well, we were in the *Boorara* and this fellow decides to back off. Well, seeing that he'd made a hole in us as big as a block of flats our Captain hails him and asks him not to pull out until he'd got off the Turkish prisoners and their guards who we were carrying to Egypt and some of the crew. So these men clambered over onto the armoured-cruiser – damned thing – Anyway, a lot were got off and then *Boorara* looked to be about to go so the rest of us hopped off into HMS *Doris* which had rushed up. . . . After a while *Boorara* was still afloat so the Captain took some of us and we steamed her slowly and eventually reached Lemnos where we beached her.'

This ship was later refloated, taken to Naples for repairs, and then back onto the shuttle service to and from Australia with troops. There was such traffic on the seas in those war years that in August 1916, when she took troops from Brisbane and Sydney, the congestion was so great at Bordeaux that she had to wait thirty days before a berth could be found for her.

'I spent the war years (that war, anyhow: I was in the air force next war) zig-zagging. From Australia and back again we zig-zagged the whole way. No wonder there were so many collisions at sea.'

The *Boorara* was attacked by a submarine which blew a hole 40 feet by 22 feet through her port side. This time she saved herself by calling for help. Five trawlers took her in tow and, while sounding in her hold showed water rising fast, the crew stayed aboard pumping.

'There wasn't much monotony you know,' Bill says about his war on the smaller ships.

For men serving in the Grand Fleet it was different. Unaware that the world would never again see such a body of ships that centuries had built into the greatest maritime power history had known, they nevertheless were aware that the Grand Fleet had a tradition that set them apart from other men.

'Of course we were proud that HMAS *Australia* was flagship of the Second Battle-cruiser Squadron,' my father told me. 'But I can't recall any of us admitting it.' He said that when the call came that sailors were to respond to with 'God Save the King!' the lower deck response was, 'Bugger the King!'

But as for glamour, that was reserved for the rare times of leave. My father had 'long' leave once (three weeks) in all his years in the North Sea and twice was put ashore in hospital. 'When we picked up a bit they'd take us out on route marches to toughen us up and we saw the countryside and of course there were nurses to play tennis with and go for walks so we looked on that as leave. But "leave" at the places we sailed to – what could you do?'

For the rest of the time it was a routine whose dreariness, for young boys, can best be illustrated by the charts marked with the route taken by HMAS *Australia* over the years from the Firth of Forth in Scotland or Scapa Flow while they patrolled the North Sea or sailed on a raid to the Skagerrak. For all these years their task was to keep the German Fleet bottled up and unable to break through.

They were in the very centre of war, but of actual fighting and a visible enemy they saw not a trace. Their days were spent in a prolonged chase of a foe believed to exist somewhere, over seas peopled solely by traders and fishermen (though strewn here and there with submarine-made wrecks). 'Sometimes', my gun-layer father told me, 'we'd be stimulated by the Admiral's signal to prepare for action. Into the turret with its four foot thick walls we'd scramble, the trap-door would be fastened over us and I'd scan the seas in the hope that at any moment enemy masts might slide upwards from where the horizon dropped – then, an order would be snapped, sharp commands, and we'd return to one or another of our undesired harbours. Our days were ages of uncomprehending disappointment.'

But then that, as the official historian of the Australian Navy points out, is 'the real naval war, with Trafalgar and Jutland but episodes neither inevitable nor even probable'.

So my father, the young bushman from back of Tanjil Bren, who from the age of 12 had cut forests for railway sleepers ('all the Smith boys were born with a broad axe in their hands' the old man at the 'Back to Neerim South' had said) spent his years from seventeen to twenty-one on the 'high seas' of which songs are made but which, in reality, were a wearying repetition. His work was interesting, but being a bushman he speaks little of it and I do not know how a lad who left a one-teacher bush school at the age of fourteen was trained to the precise work of a gun-layer. 'Our gunnery officer had us at it all day – it was the whole of our work; those of us who were gun-layers had few other duties and these were connected with the gun and its turret.' The thick wall protected the gun crew from much of the explosive noise. 'You would be deafened on deck.' Much of the time he was homesick. He didn't drink, but he did learn to gamble. 'Crown and anchor men were in every mess. Ours had a "cockatoo" outside the door with one end of a piece of string in his hand and the other end tied to the operator's ankle. When an officer appeared, the "cockatoo" tugged the string and in two seconds there was no sign of the game. One man would shove the board up his tunic, another pocket the crown and anchor pieces. The operator of course pocketed the spondulics [cash]. These fellows were enormously wealthy. Men would gamble the whole of their pay away on a game and then borrow against their next pay. They'd gamble anywhere, when things got hot in the mess they'd carry on the game down in the heads [lavatories]. I didn't have much to lose because I'd allotted most of my pay to my mother back home.'

It was an existence completely alien to the big, noisy bush family life he had known in the forested mountains, and along with many others the strain affected him.

'The German submarines were terrible, for us, the Allies, that is. We had the German fleet bottled up but for a long time their submarines almost had England in a state of seige. There was the distinct danger that she might be starved out. We saw the effect at sea and knew that we would be a prize worth fifty of the smaller ships we saw sunk. We zig-zagged non-stop; the men out shovelling snow off our decks – we had snow for months at a time on patrol up north – found it hard to keep their feet with our cork-screwing round. We were returning to our home port one day and were told to line the decks to salute the *Hampshire*, as it passed with Kitchener on board. He was going to Russia on the route we had swept clean. Two hours later we were mustered and told he was dead. A submarine had let us pass because they were awaiting bigger fish altogether. Some people said his trip was "advertised" by his enemies in the war council because they wished to rid themselves of him but of course we knew nothing of that.'

This constant awareness of unseen danger, the incessant preparations and perpetual readiness for actions that were never fought, untiring strife with one of the stormiest seas in the world and a climate that to Australians seemed almost perpetual winter, wore down even that resilient young sleeper-cutter and he was twice put ashore to hospital. 'Lots of us got sort of run-down, heart racing, hard to find our pulse – all sorts of tiring things. You collapsed with it.'

It was perhaps the oldest of war-wounds, known in the past as 'Soldiers' heart' and one of the commonest causes of hospitalisation from the trenches.

> Sing us a song of the Northern seas,
> (where the ship's police and the gunners breeze)
> of sights and frights and Jack's delights:
> The pudding and beef and gravy.
> Sing us a song to clearly show
> That the boys in blue are the ones to know
> While they wait like hounds for a skulking foe,
> Sing us a song of the navy!
>
> *J. M. Ryan*

'My old school teacher used to write to me from Neerim South, he wrote to all his boys at the war. By jove I used to look forward to hearing from him. I got a feeling of what was happening in Gippsland from him. I've got a card still, for Christmas 1916, and he says, "There are plenty of sad hearts over here" and I knew by that the boys from the hills back of Warragul must have got it bad in France.

'One of my nieces wrote for Christmas 1917. I was in hospital with an injury then. She said, "During this Christmas-tide I will think of you on your bed of agony". It might seem silly now but it was the only way the people back home could try to understand what was happening to us. And for us there were lots of times when Neerim South, Tanjil Bren, Fumina and Darnum seemed something I'd only heard about, read of, dreamt of, but the ship was real life.'

My mother told me of the end of HMAS *Australia*. 'It was 12 April 1924. We'd read about it in the papers. Under the terms of the Washington Treaty the nations were to disarm. This day they towed the *Australia* out through Sydney Heads and sank her. Your father didn't say anything. I don't know what he thought. We all thought it was awfully sad. Even though I hadn't known him during the war I was proud of the HMAS *Australia* like everyone else. But he said nothing.'

The Australian Navy was only seven years old at the end of the war and already a veteran. Fear of its ships had driven Admiral von Spee's squadron from the Pacific, its units had sailed the North Sea, the Mediterranean, the Indian Ocean and the Atlantic, and had patrolled the Malayan and African coast. One of its submarines had been the first to get through the heavily-mined Dardanelles.

This navy had scarcely completed its first training when it steamed into the Pacific to war on 6 August 1914. It had had a long struggle to come into being but because of this, when war broke out, its ships were as modern as any afloat, in particular its dreadnought battle-cruiser HMAS *Australia*. The newspapers of the day published little about them – the Navy is rarely 'hard news' but a 'sailor boy' was a big catch for girls and, as children, my mother never let us forget that she had caught one.

30
The Circus

Among the ephemera contained in collections of letters and diaries of the men, folded between the pages of a small diary, was 'a piece of the wing of an aeroplane shot down near our trenches'. Written on the fabric was, 'You can see why these machines are not much good in the rain'. In another collection an airman in France complains, 'I could not go up today. It is raining and that would damage parts of the machine'.

Russell Ince, whose family's well-known business in Swanston Street Melbourne consisted of sewing stripes to jackets of servicemen and mounting service ribbons, was a Fabric Worker in the AFC. 'I looked after the fabric, the linen. Stretched it over the frame of the wing – look, you stretched it to the degree that you could push it down, in the centre, the depth of your three middle fingers. Then I doped it. Doped it with sago. Mixed a pot of sago and painted it on the wings to give it body. I couldn't look at a sago pudding for years after.'

The concept of the aeroplane was so new that many men had not seen one before they went to the war. Chaplain W. F. Shannon wrote home from Egypt in 1915, 'This afternoon we saw an aeroplane fly just above the hospital. It went alright, and the people around here who had never seen an aeroplane were amazed. We could distinctly hear the whizzing of the propeller as it careered over the roof of this big building. Probably these sights will be common enough after the war is over'.

The genesis of the Australian Flying Corps was at Point

Cook (Vic.) two weeks after war was declared, when four pupils began a course of flying instruction. Among the aircraft they were to learn on was a Blériot monoplane similar to that which crossed the English channel in 1909, and two Deperdussin monoplanes that 'fiercely resisted any attempts to get them off the ground'.

The four trainees were seconded from the AIF; for the duration of the war the Air Flying Corps served as part of the AIF, its men wearing the same uniforms as the army.

In April 1915 the British Government asked whether Australia could supply flying personnel for service in India and this request was met the following month by the despatch of three officers and 45 other ranks comprising a unit known as the First Half Flight. The men proceeded to India, thence to Mesopotamia (now Iraq) where they served against the Turks until the latter part of 1916.

When the mechanics (who had never seen an aircraft close up) got to Mesopotamia, they found they knew as much as the similarly inexperienced English mechanics. There were two Farman Shorthorn aircraft presented by the Rajah of Gwalior and they trundled along at 40–45 m.p.h. They had no machine guns, only 2-pound bombs and these they dropped by hand; the air crew were armed with revolvers. Here, as well as the problems with the aircraft itself, the men had to contend with intense heat which created air conditions that made flying hazardous, dangerous but decidedly interesting.

They were quickly in action, and on 30 July had their first casualty with Lieutenant Merz (one of the original four trainees) being forced down among well-armed and hostile Arabs. Merz and his New Zealand observer, Lieutenant Burn, were never seen again.

The planes this Half Flight used were totally unsuitable. Even if they could be coaxed aloft in the hot air of the desert they threatened constantly not to stay there long. The men had to contend with sand, lack of replacements, poor equipment and the heat on their long reconnaissance flights over enemy territory in unarmed, slow and unreliable craft.

One man, Williams (later Air Vice-Marshal Sir Richard Williams), had to drive his Shorthorn aircraft along the ground like a motor car for twenty miles after it refused to remain in the air. He passed close to a heavily armed Turkish post but trundled steadily on towards where the only other plane then in the force was waiting with the men. Later, in November 1915, T. W. White set off to rescue the Chief-of-Staff of Mesopotamia, Major-General G. V. Kemball, whose sea-plane had been forced down. He landed amid rifle fire from hostile Arabs and then found that the extra weight of Major-General Kemball was going to mean another drive home along the ground. He was saved from this by the timely arrival of an Indian cavalry patrol who took his passenger off his hands.

White had only a short time left before his war ended in a P.O.W. camp. On 13 November he volunteered for a round trip of 120 miles that could be termed a suicide mission. His instructions were to cut the telephone wires near Baghdad, the city then being held by the Turks. The flight would be possible only if there were no head winds, the plane performed faultlessly and the Turkish gunners didn't shoot him down as he flew low over their heads. He carried with him petrol and oil for the return flight.

He carried out his mission and cut the wires while Turks and Arabs rushed up firing, but he had damaged a wing of the machine. Once again he tried to make a run for it like a motor car across the sands, but the snapping telegraph wires ensnared his plane and he was captured.

During the three years of his captivity White kept diaries, stowing them in the soles of his boots to avoid confiscation. The boots are now in the Australian War Museum, Canberra.

When the Turks pushed the British back, the Half Flight, with its single remaining aircraft, travelled to Egypt and there reformed. Of the nine airmen taken prisoner in Mesopotamia only four survived the rigors of the P.O.W. camps.

By September 1916 there were four squadrons formed.

No. 1 Squadron remained in Egypt and the other three went to France.

Those in Egypt began with BE2C aeroplanes, claimed to be quite comfortable because of their built-in stability but totally unable to take swift evasive action, making them conspicuous death-traps. Another drawback was the lack of synchronisation that would enable the machine-gun to be fired through the revolving propeller blades without shooting holes in them. The armaments consisted of a Lewis gun operated by the observer who sat up front among the wires and struts and became known as 'Fokker Fodder'. If bombs were carried, the weight was such that the observer had to be left behind and the pilot had to operate the Lewis gun as well as lean out to drop the bombs. Devising effective mountings for these guns consequently took up much of the spare time and initiative of both pilots and ground crew. As well as the BE2C they flew a Martinsyde. The idiosyncracy of this machine with its Beardmore engine was its habit of blowing back through the carburettor when the throttle was opened after idling, thus risking fire. Rigger Tom Mahood recalls that he had more work to do with planes catching fire than repairing crashed machines. 'Because they were so likely to catch fire the pilot would land over the far side of the field and immediately put the motor off. Our job was to run over, to wind the propeller to start them again and then run across the field to the hangar, holding on to a wing to steer the thing.'

In those early days of the war German air-power was superior to the British and the less suitable of the unsuitable planes were sent to areas considered to be less pressed by the enemy. Consequently, the Australians in Egypt had plenty of opportunity to experience the most terrible of them. They were restricted to photography, reconnaissance and bombing across the desert and rarely took part in aerial battles because they couldn't catch the German planes.

They lived with the ever-present danger of being forced

down in the inhospitable land, miles from their own lines among hostile Arabs and armed Turks. Because of these factors they attempted some of the most daring rescues – resulting in the only V.C. to be awarded an Australian airman in World War I. This was granted to Lieutenant Frank McNamara when he rescued Captain D. W. Rutherford whose BE2C had been brought down near a unit of Turks who were moving up swiftly to capture him. McNamara, seriously wounded by a bullet from the ground, swept down and landed near Rutherford who hung on to the superstructure while they roared away, trying to take off. But McNamara, weak from his wound, was unable to control the plane with Rutherford hanging on and it crashed. The two men set fire to the wreck, ran to Rutherford's plane which McNamara managed to get off the ground and flew the seventy miles back to base.

Some pilots after being forced to land began the long walk home. In March 1917 Lieutenant J. V. Tunbridge was tramping over the desert when Lieutenant P. W. Snell sighted him from the air and picked him up. On board, as well as the two pilots, was Snell's observer, making three altogether, yet even with this overload Snell got the machine off the sand into the air.

Snell attempted another rescue a few days later when he located Lieutenant L. W. Heathcote on the ground but this time he could find nowhere to land and Heathcote was taken by the Turks.

The Captain Rutherford once rescued by McNamara was again in need of a 'pick-up' when his plane was shot down by ground fire, but Lieutenant F. W. Haig's plane crashed while attempting to land and rescue him. Both men were captured and became prisoners-of-war.

The heavy and accurate ground fire was as great a danger as the primitive machines and enemy aircraft. Captain Williams, while landing to rescue Lieutenant A. T. Cole, had a near miss from ground fire that whistled by him. Cole later took part in a pick-up when eight aircraft were returning after a raid on Jerusalem. A plane was forced down and Cole and another went to rescue him. Cole, after take-off, watched the rescue plane itself come down and he once again landed to go to the rescue, but this time his own machine was damaged and the three pilots set off together on the long walk home through unfriendly territory. In this perilous race against the desert and the twin enemies of Arab and Turk the three men were rescued by the Light Horse galloping over the sands: an irony when one recalls that many of the AFC enlistments had come from the Light Horse. It was said that horsemen, having good hands, control and quick reaction, made good pilots.

Aerial photography demanded conditions that made survival tenuous for the air crew operating the camera — often one man, the pilot. Straight and level flying was necessary; any evasive action under attack would ruin the plate. Not for these men the spectacular circus sorties high in the clouds. In Egypt in January 1918, Lieutenant L. Taplin was attacked while on a photography reconnaissance mission behind the Turkish lines just when he was busy trying to repair his aerial camera and had spread parts on the cockpit floor. For a time he had to leave the camera, meet the enemy, break off the engagement, and only then return to re-assembling the camera and continue his mission. At this time in Egypt the AFC had received Bristols which had a range not before available to them. With this aircraft they were able, in a two-week period, to photograph 500 square miles behind the enemy lines.

A roll call of No. 1 squadron, AFC, serving in Egypt, would be answered by men whose names later were heard often in Australia. (Sir) Ross Smith, pilot of the first plane to fly between England and Australia; (Sir) Hudson Fysh, the founder of Qantas Airways; (Sir) Lawrence Wackett, Director of the Commonwealth Aircraft Corporation; A. Murray-Jones, Chairman of de Havillands (Australia); (Air Marshal, Sir) R. M. Drummond of the post-war RAF; and (Sir) Richard Williams who commanded the squadron in 1917. McNamara joined the RAAF when it was founded in 1921 and rose to the rank of Air Vice-Marshal. T. W.

White, after escaping from a P.O.W. camp in 1918, returned home and became the Hon. Sir Thomas White, M.H.R. Ernest Percival, who left the Light Horse in Egypt to fly in France, later made one of the most efficient small planes in use for decades, the Percival Proctor, along with seven other models of popular light aircraft.

Australia was the only Dominion to form its own Air Force during World War I but from the beginning of the war keen young Australians, fretting at the delay, had paid their own way to England to join the Royal Flying Corps or the Royal Naval Air Service, as did Bert Hinkler, who became a well known post-war ace. In 1916 there was a call for 200 volunteers from the AIF in Egypt and France to join the RFC as pilots – Charles Kingsford Smith was one who joined as was Granado Foreman. An undated, unidentified newspaper clipping records this latter man's service:

'Gallant airman Killed
Died on active service, July 14, 1917

'Lieut. G. W. Foreman, 23 years of age. Enlisted February 12, 1915. Left Melbourne in charge of reinforcements for the 5th Battalion. After serving in Egypt was transferred to Salisbury plain where he was engaged in training fresh troops.

'Transferred to Royal Flying Corps. Received 3 months instructional training course. Learning the mechanism of 12 different machines he obtained his commission. He left England for France on May 2. His machine was hit several times in France and he was twice compelled to land. Born at Poowong Lieut. Foreman was well known in that district.'

The letters to his sister 'Lizzie' are packed with detail. The ties of Empire are strong, as he finds when he visits English relatives. 'Aunt Louisa . . . knows more about our relatives in Australia than I do. I have been told a lot of funny things about various people in Australia. She is always so pleased to see me and thinks that the Australians are so good to come and fight for them.'

His letters invariably mention girls. From France he complains 'but I only took her out a few times!' about an English girl writing to him of marriage. Later: 'It does not matter where one may go, London, Bournemouth, Plymouth, South Hampton or any other place, there are girls to burn. As a parson preached on one Sunday sermon he said "The girls are suffering from hysteria" of course we giggled. I mean the men in the ranks did.' When his sister sent him a snapshot taken with a girl friend he quickly asks, 'That girl friend of yours I have never seen her have I? What's her name again, Day or Kay? I can hardly understand your writing. Anyway whatever her name be remember me to her. I might come back and see her one of these dark nights.'

And he sent pages of news of what he saw, heard and did. 'I am sending you the latest and most popular song in London at present time. I wouldn't be a bit surprised if you already have it in Melb. It is from the best show in London the "Bing Boys". I am greatly impressed with it. The name "If you were the only girl in the world". Let me know if it is already out in Melb.'

In January 1917 he wrote to Lizzie: 'I did my solo flight today. That means, of course, that I went up in a machine alone & flew about. The first flight like this is generally sensational for one feels quite lonely so far up in the air among the clouds. . . . I immediately took off, not thinking of danger etc. It did not take me long to climb up to 1000 feet. The thing kept on going up and up so I thought the best I could do was to cut out engine. My first thoughts were "I am up a long way, how the dickens am I to get down", however, I glided down to 500 feet and discovered that there were too many machines in the way for it was necessary to land on top of one of them so I then put on the engine and circled round again. By the time I got round all was clear, so I said to myself "here goes". Cut off the engine, dropped the nose and got my correct gliding angle. The ground seemed as if it were coming up to bump me so I flattened out and hit the ground nice and lightly. Hardly felt it. I suppose you will wonder why I thought all these things. Well this is it; lately people have been playing circuses with machines and crashing them also bumping themselves a little. Monday being an exceptional good day for flying this is what happened. A lot were passed to take their solo. First one officer did a silly thing he landed on his nose (nose of machine I mean) result crashed machine and ambulance took him away. Next just in front of us he started to climb too steep, result engine slowed down and machine lost flying speed and he tried to turn in this stage and machine side slipped coming to ground wing tip first. Machine came to pieces like paper. I will never forget sight. The officer walked out of debris as if nothing happened. The instr. in my machine called him over and roused the very life of him out, let alone the shock he may have got from crash. He was made to get into overalls and clean up mess. . . . Later on another man was landing too flat and also crashed. He walked home all right and went up in another machine. Now imagine me with instructor sitting in this machine ready to take off. I might say I had the "wind" up slightly. . . . I even thought I was going to break an undercarriage for I started to drift while landing. . . . however I corrected it before touching the ground. . . . since I have told you so much I must explain reasons for mother might want to read this letter and feel rather anxious. In first place they are men on their first solos and get the "wind" up when in the air. I don't, but always feel calm. These crashes are silly mistakes, so don't worry. It is quite safe if one is careful. It is quite as safe as infantry in trenches. This job is much more exciting and more interesting than the foot sloggers.'

In February: 'Flying very slack lately on account of wind you see. I must fly a very light machine before I finish and this cannot go up in rough weather like the heavy fighting buses. The heavy machines go up in all weathers except wet for it spoils various parts. However, I think I will be in France for April and seeing the battles from the air. Don't imagine it is a cold foot job for it is far from it. There are more decorations won in Flying Corp than any others.

'One has not only Archies to contend with but opposing machines with Machine Guns. Of course engine troubles and other accidents are thrown in. We call the anti aircraft guns "archies". It is rather awkward when engine blows out when a few hundred miles over enemy line.

'The last few days we have been without machines. All been crashed by learners, none killed though. . . .'

Within a few months he was in France.

'Tomorrow I expect to fly right alone over front for many miles to get used to the country etc. before actually going across the enemies lines. The enemy are now rather good with their anti aircraft guns so must avoid them if possible.'

With only two months left to live, he replies to one of Lizzie's letters: 'You say you would like to come for a joy ride in an aeroplane with me. I would be delighted to take you up for it is a beautiful sight up above the clouds, especially just as one is breaking through them after being down below in the rain. It is just like a sea of gold and silver for the sun is shining up above as if it were a bright day down below. I am sure you would find it so strange at first. You would look down and wonder what was keeping us up. One has very little sensation of forward movement since there is no ground to be rushing by. No wind is felt when behind the wind screen but as soon as one puts his head or arm over the side he wonders what has struck him. Of course we get used to all these things.

'Last night we received orders to go over the lines and while climbing to get our height clouds came up so then no earth could be seen. It pleases one greatly when a coloured light goes out from leading machine – wash out. That means to go home and land. These clouds that came over looked beautiful from above as the sun was then just going down.

'Nearly everytime we go over the lines generally "Archie" [anti aircraft guns] puts a few holes through our plane or shoots off a few wires. . . . When shells are bursting all round like going through a swarm of bees one gets the "wind up" a little and often think about two miles is a long way to fall all at once. However this does not worry us much. Up to present have not been in aerial battle with Huns. . . .

'I am fed up of this wandering life. Never have a permanent friend who I can knock about with. You see I am always shifted about. Of course it is the same with all in the R.F.C. yet one gets to know quite a lot of people. The officers in the Flying Corps are all a fine lot of fellows and always looking for plenty of fun. . . . When not actually over the lines we have quite a joyous time in the Mess. Of course we must not drink or smoke much as it does not agree with the air.'

At all times his homesickness crept through his letters. Once, after receiving a family photograph, he wrote, 'I notice one of the family is missing'. 'You can't imagine how near it made me feel to home. I now have it pinned up over my table in my cubical and can tell you I am often gazing at it. You look quite well and innocent. It is the first photo I have seen of my people since being away from Australian shores. It gives you an idea how well I am pleased with it, I dreamt that you six as in photo were going for a holiday up to Scotland with me.

'I often long to take a trip back home. It is now going on for two years since I left. I am thinking seriously of transferring to Austn Flying Corps but all same I don't think British Government will let me go. I think I will try when I get my wings or after being in France for some time.'

When he learned of his mother's fears for his safety he wrote: 'It is our great worry here to think of our people at home being over anxious of our safety etc. It is a lot of rot really.

'I am sorry I had such little leave in London before my departure for I am sure mother would have liked another photograph of myself wearing wings on my left breast etc. But if I ever return to London I will carry out same.'

But of course there was no photograph. The life expectancy of these young pilots was said to be three weeks on 'active service'. He was killed on 14 July 1917, eight weeks after arriving in France.

For more than half the war the Germans' aircraft were superior to those of the British and as late as 1917 the technical superiority of their adversaries' craft took its toll of the Australians as well as the other allies. On 8 July 1917 three Australian pilots with their observers were out on reconnaissance in their slower machines when two German scouts attacked them. One pilot, Captain C. A. Brookes, spun away to avoid the attack and the wings of his Martinsyde were seen to fold up and the tail to fall off 'and the broken machine went down like a stone'. One plane made for home but the third, flown by Lieutenant C. H. Vautin (previously Light Horse), was driven to the ground by the superior manoeuvring power of his opponents and Vautin was taken prisoner.

The fight led to an odd (for these times) exchange of letters. Two days after the battle Lieutenant G. Felmy, perhaps the most affable fellow the Australians ever fought against, sent a letter by 'aeroplane messenger' to say that Brookes had been killed and buried with military honours and that Vautin was well and would like some of his kit sent to him. He said he had shown Vautin around Jerusalem and enclosed two photographs of himself and Vautin taken together. In the dropped bag was a letter from Vautin to be sent back to his father.

On the following day, Captain A. Murray Jones (later M.C., D.F.C.) flew low over the German lines and dropped Vautin's clothes and letters from home to the German airmen waiting for him on their aerodrome at Huj. Murray Jones waved, the Germans waved, and the young Australian flew back to his own side of No Man's Land unmolested. A week later a message bag was dropped from a German plane over the aerodrome with a letter for Captain Murray Jones. From Felmy. 'All Dear Sports,' he wrote. 'My joy was very tall to receive your many letters.' He says Vautin had 'talked very much of Murray-Jones. I hope to fight with this sport more oftener. He is a very courageous man. We have feeled it in flying and when he came to drop the things to Vautin so down (perhaps 100 feet).' He said he would like his Australian address to write to him and a photo of him, and ends: 'With sportly respects, G. Felmy Offt.'

Arriving in France in the heat of the Spring offensive of August-September, the AFC were sent to the Somme, to the area dominated by Baron von Richthofen's red circus, the outstanding formation of the German Air Force. Day after day the war-weary diggers in the trenches watched their own flying corps above. 'They might have been watching our planes,' Tom Mahood says, 'but you couldn't begin to understand how our fellows felt about the men on the ground: nothing could stand in the way of assisting them. You'd see pilots land really knocked out with weariness but as soon as we'd run out to them with cans of petrol – one in each hand – they'd be off again to try to ease the weight off the men in the trenches.'

This fraternal pride between the airmen and the infantry was simply welded, the AFC were still technically members of the AIF who watched and knew of the dangers and skills of the men above as the airmen themselves knew they were operating 'in support of the finest assault infantry in France'. In the final months of the war the pilots were scarcely out of the air in daylight hours and said they felt ashamed to be on the ground when they saw the advances made by the infantry after the attack on the Hindenburg Line.

That the men in the trenches appreciated their skill is shown in many letters. Reg Mills wrote home in October 1918, 'I often go over to the Aerodrome close by and watch the flying experts doing all manner of tricks. They are wonderful now. What they do is really marvellous. They are as good in the air as birds. An interesting entertainment.'

The AFC were now flying their splendid Sopwith Camel aircraft – Private George Jones (later Air Marshal Sir George Jones, D.F.C.) had actually been a member of the Camel Corps in Egypt when the call came and he swiftly left the desert camel for the Sopwith and with it brought down seven German machines.

These planes, designed by Sopwith in 1917, had a 130 h.p. Clerget engine, a big, powerful motor for those days. It could climb to 10000 feet in 12 minutes with a full load and could fly at 113 m.p.h. at that altitude. A later model driven by a 150 h.p. Bentley rotary engine carried two Vickers and one Lewis gun and a later one still, the Snipe, had a 200 h.p. Bentley, could climb to 10000 feet in 9 minutes and 20000 feet in 27 minutes, and could fly at 100 m.p.h. at any altitude and 121 m.p.h. at 10000 feet. This was a remarkable performance for the period.

The German plane designed by the Dutchman, Fokker, could rival more powerful planes in its ability to avoid a stall at low speed. Powered by a 160 h.p. Mercedes engine, its 14 minutes for 10000 feet was not as good as Sopwith's Camel. The circus built around Richthofen performed with Albatros Destroyers, their 130 m.p.h. powered by 225 h.p. Mercedes-Benz engines. The Pfalz with a speed of 110 m.p.h. had the advantage of a flying endurance of two-and-a-half hours.

By the end of the war pilots had come in from the cold and were sheltered by the fuselage, the old wires and struts were out of sight, but they were still without head cover; the wind, sky, clouds, fog and sun were reminders that they did battle with the elements as much as with their mortal enemy. They sat in their Castrol-oil-smelling cockpits amid a roaring mass of air that tore at everything around them, and twisted and banked and dived to avoid the sharp crackle of machine guns sounding like the harsh ripping of canvas behind their backs when their leader rocked his machine back and forth – the signal to follow him into action.

It was in September-October that the legendary air battles took place. 'The sky was literally filled with air battles,' the soldiers wrote. 'There were planes fighting wherever you looked.' Before 8 a.m. on 16 September, in three separate battles over a two-hour period, Squadrons 2 and 4 had met with and defeated 'a whole covey of Fokker flights'. Each was out looking for trouble. 'After breakfast the Australians were in the air again and fought the whole day until nightfall.'

Life expectancy was short for the pilot and observer. Lieutenant A. L. D. Taylor brought down a German Pfalz with a Lewis gun on the day the famous Red Baron was killed and four weeks later died in a fight with the red tri-planes. His Flight-Commander, E. J. Jones, was wounded but managed to get the plane to base: he was the third Flight-Commander to have been wounded in one month – Captain Ralfe had died and Captain Duigan had been wounded twice within three days.

During the year they fought along the Somme the Australians destroyed 276 German aircraft, losing 60 aircraft themselves in combat. The cost of the war to the AFC was 78 pilots and observers killed, 68 wounded and 33 taken prisoner. As P. J. Taylor (another whose name was later indelibly linked with airways) said, there was no great difficulty being accepted as a pilot in 1916 when he enlisted, owing to the heavy casualties inflicted by the superior German machines on the obsolete craft the RFC and AFC were then flying.

The ground crew were instructed in the rigging of a machine, splicing and sail-making techniques, as well as instrument and bodywork repair, engine running adjust-ments and handling the machine. Tom Mahood recalls that the mechanic in charge of working on a machine always went up in it afterwards to 'try it out'. 'One day I was up, I said to the pilot "Where are we?" He said, "Over the German lines." I said, "There's nothing wrong with this engine, you get me back quick!"

During the latter part of 1918 when the fighting was keenest, the 3rd Squadron was called on to take ammunition and supplies to a beleaguered group of Australian soldiers. Russell Ince made a parachute from linen. 'I hadn't seen one but I got to work on my sewing machine in the workshop and it turned out well.' Tom Mahood describes the mechanics of the drop. 'We cut down a petrol drum and fixed it to the under-side of the plane where the bombs would hang ordinarily – planes by this time were getting sophisticated and carried two bombs – anyway, we fixed the parachute and ammunition and stuff in this drum and bound it in with a great big rubber band we made. It was crude but it worked. All the pilot had to do was pull the bomb-release lever and as we had this attached to our contraption the rubber band dragged off, the goods tumbled out and the parachute opened. It worked and that's all that mattered.'

Lloyd George, speaking to the Vote of Thanks to the Flying Service in the House of Commons in November 1919 said of these airmen: 'The heavens are their battle-fields. They are the cavalry of the clouds. High above the squalor and the mud . . . their struggles there by day and night are like a Miltonic conflict between the winged hosts.'

It was surely an unfortunate, injudicious eulogy. If the infantry were in 'the squalor and mud' it was where Lloyd George and his War Cabinet had put them. That they had placed the airmen in 'the heavens' did not elevate them above slaughter.

Few massacres in history exceed that of 25 September 1918 when, between the hours of 6 and 8 a.m. airmen 'ceaselessly bombed' 3 000 Turks fleeing through a narrow defile off the Plain of Armageddon near the River Jordan. The official history states that those not killed escaped to the desert to die of thirst or to die of the Arabs. The Turks were fine soldiers and were carting 300 guns and 600 camels with them – a strange appositeness to the proud boast of Australians that they always brought their weapons out with them no matter how severe the fighting. The official air historian, F. M. Cutlack, in his *Australian Flying Corps*, says that 'the retreat of the Turkish 7th Army was closed'. In a mass they were trying to escape up an old Roman road with 'steep hills on one side, and a sheer precipice into the Wady Fara on the other'.

Two Australian airmen found the fleeing army shortly before 6 a.m. on 21 September and sent a message back to the aerodrome by a wireless specially fitted to the machine, reporting that the enemy was trying to escape, that 800 horse wagons and guns and a mass of cavalry and other troops were packed along the few miles of narrow road. (It was no tactical error that sent the Turks this way: Allenby's army was moving in for the kill and they knew it and took what route they could.) Cutlack writes that the two Australian planes attacked the troops on the precipitous road, 'made five direct hits with their bombs and fired 600 machine-gun rounds into the confusion. That was the beginning of a massacre'.

'By 6.30 a.m. the first three Australian bombing machines sent out in response to the wireless message arrived, bombed the column and raked it from end to end. A British formation followed and repeated the attack. All day long air raids were maintained by available machines from all squadrons. Towards noon the columns under punishment at that place included thousands of infantry and cavalry as well as transports. No. I (Aust.) Squadron made six heavy raids during the day, dropped tons of bombs and fired nearly 24 000 machine gun rounds into the struggling parties in those terrible valleys. Yet this was only half the ammunition expended for the British squadrons attacked this road with another 3 tons of bombs and 20 000 machine-gun rounds. The panic and the slaughter beggared all description. The long, winding, hopeless column of traffic was so broken and wrecked, so utterly unable to escape from the barriers of hill and precipice, that the bombing machines gave up all attempt to estimate the losses under attack. The passes were completely blocked ahead and behind by overturned waggons; men deserted their vehicles in a wild scramble to seek cover; many were dragged by the maddened animals over the side of the precipice. The

Turkish 7th Army as a fighting force was destroyed. In all the history of war there can be few more striking records of wholesale destruction.'

Had Lloyd George possessed the honesty of a General Sherman he would have known that 'War is Hell' whether in 'the squalor and mud' or the battlefields of 'the heavens'.

31
The Red Baron

To understand what some believe to be the pertinent evidence of the following controversy it is necessary to remember that, in the aircraft involved, the pilot could shoot straight ahead only – he could not shoot to either side or to the back of him. His machine gun was synchronised to fire between the blades of the propeller. Another point often overlooked is that these dog-fights rarely lasted more than ten minutes but were of a rare intensity.

The great 'circus' fights were a willing and thrilling spectacle and men on the ground stood with necks craned to watch. Indeed, it was often unnecessary to crane one's neck as the fights were at little more than eye level. The two opponents flew straight at one another and then the formations split up and it was every man for himself. One has written, 'You fly round and round in cyclonic circles. Here would be a red Hun machine, then a flash of silver as one of my formation would whizz by. All the time I was in the same mix up myself, every now and then finding a red machine in front of me and getting in a round or two of quick shots. There was no need to hesitate about firing when the right colour flitted by your nose. Firing one moment, you would have to concentrate all your mind and muscle the next in doing a quick turn to avoid a collision. Then your gun jams, and you have to zoom up and fuss with it to put it right.'

It was a fight like this the day the 'Red Baron' was killed. The legendary Baron Manfred von Richthofen, like many Australian Light Horsemen, had transferred from the cavalry

346

to the airforce and by this day had brought down eighty
Allied planes – 'a world record' both sides claimed for him.
His squadron was unmistakable: Fokker Triplanes, painted
red. It was 10.45 a.m. on 21 April 1918 and while the two
groups flew at one another the Australian infantry on the
great natural grandstand of Morlancourt Ridge were
spectators of one of the greatest air fights of the war.

Taking part in the circus up aloft was a young Australian,
Lieutenant May, of the RFC. May, being inexperienced,
had been instructed not to go into action unless he was in a
position to down an aircraft, and if attacked to head for
home. It would have been the shock of the day had May
known that the red triplane that dived on him was that of
the feared Red Baron, but all he knew was that he was out-
manoeuvred by the red circus and his guns were jammed.
The official history of the war in the air describes what
then happened:

'Suddenly the watching gunners of the 53rd Australian
Field Artillery Battery, 5th Division, near the crest of the
ridge, saw two whirling and twisting forms emerge from
the haze where the popping of the machine-guns had been
heaviest. Then one machine dived for the ground with the
other on its tail. They darted about wildly for a few seconds.
Suddenly the pursued aeroplane, evidently in desperate
straits, made straight for the crest of the ridge near the
battery. The gunners saw that it was a British machine and
its pursuer a red triplane.'

The Lewis gunners at first could not fire because the
machines were flying so low that the fleeing British plane
blocked the gunners' sight of the German. The German
was firing but the other was not, nor did he attempt to turn.
(May later explained his dilemma: he had no room to
manoeuvre so close to the ridge and, with no weapons,
knew his only chance was to dash behind the home lines.)

'The machines flew on right overhead, careless of everything else except their own duel, and at this point, at about
a hundred yards' range, the artillery Lewis gunners and
other machine-guns from Australian camps on or behind

the crest opened fire on the German. Splinters of wood were seen to fly off immediately from near his engine. The triplane wobbled, side-banked up, swerved across to the left in a half-circle, obviously crippled, then dived straight into the ground about 400 yards away and was smashed to pieces. The Australians into whose territory it fell discovered from the watch and papers on the dead pilot that he was Richthofen. No. 3 Squadron saved his body and the remains of his machine that evening and buried him a couple of days later.' Captain A. R. Brown of the British squadron 209 claimed to have shot down Richthofen, and undoubtedly he had followed him down for some distance, firing at Richthofen while Richthofen fired at the Camel (May's plane). It is equally certain that when Richthofen passed over the Australian bivouacs there were only two machines in the picture – the Camel fleeing and Richthofen following and firing. There is abundant evidence that these two machines were the only ones near the scene of the shooting, and this testimony seems decisive.

The controversy has gone on for sixty years and much evidence has been gathered from Australians who saw the action. Gunner (now historian) Eric Harding, who at the time had been in hospital having his leg amputated, has made a study of this evidence and in 1976 he stated: 'In the interests of historical accuracy it would be reasonable for the Royal Air Force to withdraw their claim.' Brown had died – he was a sick man for weeks before the fight and had taken little part in the use of the claim for propaganda. The name of the Australian whose shot was the fatal one is generally believed to be Cedric Popkin of the 24th machine-gun company. Popkin also was dead when historians began to gather and sift evidence.

As Harding says, it is only in respect of historical accuracy that there is any reason to continue the claim. The three points not taken into account when the British made their claim was the distance at which Brown broke off his attack on the red triplane and where it crashed and the location of the wound in the Baron's body.

The body was taken to No. 3 Squadron and there it was inspected by Colonel Barber (later Major-General Barber, C.B., C.M.G., D.S.O., V.D.). At that time he was Deputy-Director of Medical Services to the Australian corps.

'When I arrived I saw an orderly washing the body of a dead aviator. When I learned that it was the body of the famous German "Ace" Richthofen I made an examination of the body. The report that it was riddled with bullets is absolutely incorrect. There was one bullet wound only and that was through the man's chest. The bullet had passed completely through the heart and chest and from its position, I formed the conclusion that it was fired from the ground and struck the airman as he was banking his machine, because the point of exit of the bullet was three inches higher than the point of entry.' (That Captain Brown was behind and above when in pursuit of the red triplane has never been questioned.)

All this of course was a later point of dissension. On 21 April, as Major (later Major-General) L. E. Beavis commanding the 53rd Battery said, '. . . hundreds, perhaps thousands of eye-witnesses could see with their own eyes that Richthofen was not shot down by one of our fighters'. The strangely undramatic rites that precede even the most dramatic burial were taking place.

Fabric worker Russell Ince, 3rd Squadron, AFC heard that 'one of the red planes' had been brought down and a tender was being sent to bring the body in. 'By the time the tender got in we'd heard it was Baron von Richthofen's body and that an Australian machine-gunner had got him. The plane, they told me, was badly smashed, but I noticed that the Baron's body was alright. We laid him in the hangar on a sheet of galvanised iron and we put another over him – we didn't have anything else you see. Well, later a doctor came to examine the body and we undid the trouser buttons to remove his clothes and there were 5000 francs there. We reckoned that he must have carried the francs in case of being shot down over France and needing cash to buy his way home. Anyway, we handed that up to the officers, we had to, and then we saw the wound. It was only one as far as I saw, one bullet hole. It could only have been fired from the ground. There was no way it could have been an aerial shot. Well, the next time I saw the body was in the coffin. Corporal Sammy Kitto from South Australia was what they called a wood-worker, well, he made the coffin and I was detailed to help him, I sawed odd ends of wood up for him and things like that and then I painted it. There was no paint to hand except what we used for camouflage, a water color, green, so that's what I painted it with. When the body was placed in it we screwed the lid down.

'Then we were asked to volunteer to be part of the burial party. Well, no man in the army volunteers more than that once [when he joins up] if he's got any sense but we thought they'd be taking him to Abbéville and we'd have a three day break so we said yes, but what happened was he was buried near us and we had a mile march to the grave yard. That's all! I was one of the firing party who fired a salute over the grave. There were big beautiful wreaths of flowers on the grave when we left but next day they'd all disappeared, been tossed away by the French who hated all Germans. No one I ever spoke to there mentioned anyone but the Australian machine-gunner having brought the red plane down. There was never any talk at that time of any doubt at all.

'We got a piece of aluminium and we made a disc of this and Harold Edwards, a jeweller from Bendigo, inscribed on this all about him – Richthofen. Our propellers in those days were four bladed and of course they used to get damaged a lot so we kept a lot of spares. We took one of these propellers and cut two arms off it and made a cross out of it and put this aluminium disc on it and took the cross up to the grave the next day.'

On 19 November 1925 Richthofen's body was exhumed and taken home. The private train carrying the new oaken coffin was met at the border by crowds of silent, bare-headed Germans. En route to Berlin the train 'became the object of veneration all along the road to the capital where it was met by a torchlight procession which escorted the coffin on a gun-carriage to the Berlin church where the body lay in state for two days'. The *Berliner Zeitung am Mittag* reported, 'Princes and princesses of the old empire that is gone followed common citizens of the new republic in the crush of humanity that came to pay homage to the bier. Eighteen silent flying men, sombre knights of the air, in black leather helmets and jackets, formed the final guard. They were survivors of the Red Knight's war days. Throughout Germany, flags of the Republic hung at half-mast, and in many places the old Imperial flag was flown. It was the most largely-attended funeral that had ever been held in the capital. When the body was being lowered at Mercy cemetery, Hindenberg tossed the first handful of earth into the grave and the old war-song of the Empire "Deutschland uber Alles" rose from 500 throats to the accompaniment of martial music.'

32
The Butchers'
Picnic

'Marty' Berry is completing his signals training in England before leaving for France and the 'bullet with his name on it'. He writes home to his parents: 'About six weeks and we are right for "The Butchers Picnic" – pretty ghastly isn't it, but that's what they call the Front over here.'

Theo Ford was training in England too. 'Another month and you'll be fit to kill,' the artillery officer told him before he left for France.

There was no longer any innocence, any ignorance left; they knew what war was about.

'We're none of us the same,' the boys reply.
'For George lost both his legs and Bill's stone blind;
Poor Jim's shot through the lungs and like to die,
And Bert's gone syphilitic.'*

A Queenslander, Oliver Hoskin of the 9th Battalion, had marched down Brisbane's streets on his way to the ship only one year ago, 'my uniform fitting where it touched and me thinking I looked so good I could eat a German a day. Then I heard a woman in the crowd squeal, "Look at that little boy!"' After twelve months of 'The Butchers' Picnic' Oliver would no longer be thought a 'little boy'. Like Richard Smith, who 'was looking in a tin mirror and didn't know for a while who I was looking at', Oliver Hoskins's boyhood had been blown away.

* Richard Smith copied this poem, 'They' by Siegfried Sassoon, into his diary.

'We all have lice,' Richard Smith wrote. 'The big-wigs say we are "pediculous" and that only means lousy. They're on us from head to foot. The German prisoners tell us they're all as bad.' And Roly Mills says, 'We had 2 flannel shirts and the one I was not wearing I washed. It was a frosty night and I hung it up and it was frozen so solid I hit it with a stick and the sound echoed off and icicles tinkled off and I thought "that's the end of the people who have been living with me" but sure enough, as soon as my body warmed up after I'd put it on me, out they came. You couldn't get rid of them.'

The most painful malady was 'trench feet'. 'There's no wound worse than trench feet. The ball of your foot swells up very painful and red and it gives you no rest even at nights.' A black and spreading mortification followed and first the toes, then feet, were amputated. 'I remember Billy Edwards,' Miss Flora MacDonald of Kerang (Vic.) recalled in 1976. 'He took his boots off to show us when he got home. Where the toes had been were a couple of stumpy black bones.'

The men were ordered to rub their feet to revive circulation, but there was nowhere to sit in the trenches and they were knee-deep in mud. Their hands were filthy and there was nothing to wipe them on that was not filthy also. At first whale oil was used at Regimental Aid Posts, then camphor, but the only effective cure was dry feet. There was such 'wastage' of fighting men from trench feet that 'the big-wigs', as Richard would say, had it designated as S.I.W. – self-inflicted wound – in an attempt to make men take greater care.

Among the slang terms the men created was 'a Blighty' (not to be confused with 'Blighty' which simply stood for England.) To 'get a Blighty' meant to receive a wound that would necessitate your being sent to a hospital in England, therefore away from the trenches. Some men were said to have been so overwrought with the constant battles that they 'gave themselves a Blighty'. Sergeant Harry Kahn believes there were more rumours than actual cases of men giving themselves 'a Blighty'. 'There are many apocryphal stories, tales of the odd man welcoming a "Blighty". I admit that I would have loved to have had a "Blighty": I used to think when my morale got a bit down that I would welcome [one] but I don't know to what degree I would have done so.'

It was the more minor irritations that wore them down. 'Baths were haphazard affairs. Depended where you were,' Harry Kahn says. 'There was an old dye works at Armentières. The troops got in the big vats and clothes were put in other vats in big steam baskets to get rid of the lice . . . the clothes came out sadly creased and funny colours. But it was good to have clean underclothes and deloused uniform.'

Even items issued for their own safety were tiresome. At Fromelles on 15 July 1916, Sergeant Stevens (58th Battalion) wrote: 'Wakened early with the cry. "Gas! Gas!" Donned helmets. . . . later . . . we had to don our gas helmets again, this time for our own gas which was passing over our lines to the enemy. It is very uncomfortable wearing these helmets for one must breathe through the nose and out through the mouth in which is a rubber tube which will only open on being blown through – air cannot pass in. Air can come through the material as the latter is saturated with chemicals – purifying the air as it comes through.'

It was little wonder that Chaplain W. F. Shannon found his church services were poorly attended. 'Indeed, the men generally take little interest in things religious. Neither the war nor their wounds seem to make any impression on them spiritually.' However, he does note on another date that a dying boy was murmuring over and over, 'Tell Mother . . . going home tomorrow . . . for Jesus sake . . .'

The men were now 'on the Somme', or 'the Western Front' as the newspapers wrote of it. The Somme is a sluggish stream that rises near St Quentin, flows south-west, then north-west for a distance of 220 kilometres and empties itself into the English Channel. This swampy waterway split into numerous streamlets which flowed between chalk plains and watery meadows. The Romans had built a causeway astride the river 1 500 years before and across this Henry V managed to get his troops before he fought the battle of Agincourt in the fifteenth century.

It was along this swampland that most of the Australian battles were pitched. They got to know its own peculiar mud and its chalk pit. 'O Chalkpit,' wrote Vic Graham, 'Can you talk? I've talked to you so often. I wear you, I shelter in you.' This snowy white chalk made concealment of trenches impossible. They flung camouflage nets over the dross thrown up from their digging but the pristine glow of the chalk stood out like the lines of a tennis court.

The 56th Battalion had been at the Battle of Fromelles and now, in November 1916, Lieutenant Williams describes how they marched off to the Somme. 'At last we turned to the left from the road, and sank to our knees in the mud. Not a shelter of any kind was to be seen. "Where are we going to sleep?" piped a voice from the darkness. "Right here in the mud," said Captain Fanning in an angry voice. It was our bivouac.'

Next morning they set off for their posting, the front line, past the rubble-heap that had once been Montauban. They marched through the ravages of other battles. 'We came upon a sight that must have made the angels weep,' Lieutenant Williams wrote. 'Delville Wood, or Devil's Wood as the soldiers called it. Shell fire had torn its great trees into blackened jagged stumps and littered the ground with the trunks and branches. Trench systems had criss-crossed through the wood, separated in places by only a few feet: huge shell craters pock-marked the ground, many of them partly filled with greenish water, and the desolation was completed by a carpet of rotting corpses of the men who had lost and won the wood. British and German lay there unburied. The ground was littered with equipment, rifles, cartridges and all the other debris of an untidy battlefield.

'The tide of battle had now rolled on, leaving Delville Wood to its unburied dead. Our little party was very silent as we picked our way through it. Forward we went to a hollow devoid of cover where our field batteries were firing at full pressure. Coming towards us over a low rise were many walking wounded. We came to a trench and struggled along it, sometimes knee deep in the stinking slime. Turk Lane. Bodies of dead men were lying on the parapet throughout its length. 'A boyish looking Tommy with white face, staring eyes and blood-stained tunic came along and asked me to light his cigarette and if we were going to the front line. I said yes, and he said, "My God, you're going to hell up there". The bottom of this trench was so slippery we had to catch hold of both sides to lever ourselves along.'

They met some of the Manchester Regiment huddling exhausted in the trench and the sergeant gave Williams a full jar of rum. 'I entrusted this along with my overcoat to a lance-corporal with strictest instructions that he was to sit on the jar of rum and if he valued his skin not to lose sight of it!'

The shelling from both sides was very heavy all afternoon but at dusk the Germans lashed out with a barrage that tore the sector into an inferno. While this shelling was at its height an English officer came hurrying along the trench and addressed Captain Fanning. 'Colonel's compliments, sir, and will you relieve the Front line at once?' 'My compliments to your colonel,' replied Fanning. 'I will relieve the front line when it is dark.' In a few minutes the officer returned, 'The colonel's orders are that you are to relieve at once.' 'You tell your colonel from me to go to hell. I will not take my men over the top to go through this barrage when it is still light,' Fanning snapped, and he did not move his men until darkness would shield them.

'We began to dig even before the Manchesters were out,' Williams recalled. 'Captain Fanning walked along the company front and to each group said, "Dig like hell tonight boys. The deeper you are tomorrow the safer you'll be."'

It was at this time that Williams discovered that the barrage had 'rattled' his corporal who had promptly forgotten both the rum and the overcoat, and of course the rum was never seen again.

That day Fanning and an English officer took a walk along the top of the trench in full view of the enemy to mark positions for the attack. Later Williams saw Germans doing the same thing. It was apparently an unspoken agreement that only when an attack was on would anyone who couldn't get along the slimy mud of the trench be fired on. But the interesting thing is a remark Fanning made that night to Williams (who had accompanied him on the walk and was in no way composed regarding the experience). 'Captain Fanning said to me, "I was glad when we had finished that walk this afternoon Sonny. A German with half an eye could have seen we were officers by our sticks and trench coats. As an English officer set the fashion I had to follow in all details."' No attack was made but the barrage was nerve splitting. 'While the barrage was at its height a swarthy-skinned youth from the Australian outback came along the trench at a trot. He had two shrapnel wounds in his head and one in his arm. He was quite delighted. "This will do me for my cut," he said and left us at a trot with the blood running down over his shoulders.'

They dug out a 'Tommy' soldier who had been buried alive since the night before but the worst experience of that barrage was the Englishman who had enlisted in the AIF and now was stricken with shell-shock. 'He had been wounded at the Battle of Fromelles and had rejoined us only a few days before we took over this sector. Bent double, sometimes on all fours, the poor chap came along the trench foaming at the mouth and babbling insanely. It was hard to recognise in this awful wreck the tall, straight young Englishman who had been with us since the early days in Egypt. He was the most pitiable sight imaginable. He never came back to the battalion.'

Leaving the trenches for an attack was strangely calm and business-like. Usually two or three men assisted one another. When the order was given to hop over one of the men 'legged' a mate up onto the parapet; once up, the man leant down and took the hand of the first man and hauled him out; they then leant over and were handed the bags of bombs or the ammunition or whatever they must carry, hauled that man out, and lined up ready for the command 'Go!' John Masefield's words were as true for the Western Front as they were for Gallipoli. 'All along the crumbling line there came a whistling and a crying. The men of the first wave climbed up the parapets, in tumult, darkness, and the presence of death, and having done with all pleasant things',* they advanced across No Man's Land.

In this way began the Battle of the Somme.

The men continued to write verse on a variety of themes.

If Dreams Were Only True

Last night I had a funny dream and dreamt to my delight
I had ten thousand blankets to keep me warm at night
I dreamt there wasn't any snow, or rain or sleet or mud
And saw a German shell descend that proved to be a
    'dud',
I dreamt I saw a big QM who didn't drink the rum,
And a great big Gotha overhead whose engines didn't
    hum;
I thought I saw Old Bill himself, digging in a trench
And heard our own interpreter really speaking French.
I dreamt I played the Good Old Game, won five bob on
    the crown,
And saw our anti-aircraft guns bring a Hun plane down;
And I thought I saw a Driver who really couldn't swear,
And got a shirt from 'Divy' baths, clean enough to wear.
I dreamt I had some money, fully twenty pounds,
And came upon a village that wasn't 'out of bounds'.
I dreamt I saw a real M.P. who hopped the bags with
    dash,
And a soldier on a base job, who wasn't very flash;
I dreamt we'd really won the war and finished Bertha
    Krupp,
And my blankets weren't inhabited. 'Reveille' woke
    me up.

A. N. Shuttleworth

* John Masefield, *Gallipoli.*

The humorous verse is far outweighed by the serious, contemplative, and often homesick poetry.

Lindenow (Gippsland)
If freedom of flight to my soul be given
I know of a surety I must go
To the nearest approach that I know to heaven
Home, Australia and Lindenow.

Frank Westbrook

O, on some morning dateless yet
I shall steal out in the sweet dark
And find my ship with sails all set
By the dim quay-side – and embark.

Private R. Smith (copied in his diary)

Lady knitters were slipping notes into the neat toes of woollen socks and children at school were being encouraged to write to 'our brave soldiers', like young Norman Bass of Diamond Creek, Victoria.

Dear Soldier,
How are you today?
I think you might be lonely so this is to tell you that I am thinking of you. I am 8 years old.
At school we sing a song about our brave soldiers and ask God to send them home to us again. Thank you for fighting for us I pray for you each night.

Sister Kitchen was still in hospital in England on Christmas Eve 1916. Despite general debilitation from her months in France and the illness that robbed her of her voice, she is as abrasive as ever. Her memory that night wanders back to the first Christmas Eve in Egypt, when 'Capt. J, Mrs White and Capt. E. and I sat under the sphinx and wondered if those at home were thinking of us'.

For almost a month she recuperated, going on short trips into the city 'a pale-faced crook, an unedifying spectacle in the awful grey uniform, my voice far from musical'. Eventually, she was discharged from hospital by the 'kindly courteous senior medico. For manners, deference and consideration to women, especially nurses, commend me to Englishmen. What a contrast to some of our medicos!'

Sister Samsing joins her and they are sent to a convalescent house where they slowly recover strength and begin their sight-seeing again. 'Coming back from town I got a nice fall in the garden without any trouble as the frozen sleet on the ground .is hard and glazed and like walking on plate glass.' An Australian soldier saw her. 'He was recovering from a nice "Blighty", one in his foot.' They travel to Scotland and immediately are hailed as 'Aussie Lassies'. 'A Captain was most charming to us when we asked for travel permits. Said that before the war Australia and New Zealand were just names to him but not now after Anzac. He arranged matters for us right away.'

She writes thirty pages about Glasgow, Edinburgh, Inverness, heather, hills and hospitality. By 12 February her leave was up and she and Samsing reported back to London and Alice was 'told off for Harefield', the Australian General Hospital. In the evening, the two friends went to see *Chu Chin Chow* with Oscar Asche, a native of Geelong.

Within five days she is complaining characteristically of 'the usual Australian muddle puddle; untidy show, lazy patients sitting round the fires smoking and skiting all day, and making cross-stitch belts. Too lazy to empty their own ash trays. No one seems to worry about dirt or disorder, the idea being that men cannot be both happy and tidy at the same time . . . there is no comparison between the work here and in France. The men here are mostly up and about'.

That they sat around the fire is not surprising when she records on 12 April that the morning newspaper reported the winter of 1917 as the longest for 840 years, 'since 1 Nov. 1076 to April 1077 – and ours began in October with storms and is still going on'. ('That winter in France the moisture in our bread became ice crystals and we made crunching noises as we ate it,' remembered stretcher bearer Jim McPhee. 'We melted syrup from a black block.') She is tired and the war has been long, but there is no sitting before a fire with needlework for her. She is heartsick with having seen too much, and weary with having done too much. Still she walks the woods at every opportunity and discovers churches and buildings. 'Walked to Harefield church, most interesting with many monuments, brasses and tablets, one rather pretty grave being that of an officer (General Goodlake) who was awarded the first V.C. ever awarded . . . In a corner of the graveyard lie all the men who die here; many are marked "Anzac". It is known as "Anzac Corner".'

Anzac Day comes round once more, but this year 'there was no official celebration. We had a memorial service in the little church where some of the "Anzacs" are buried, the only fitting way to spend the day'. The next day she writes of the submarine menace: '55 ships have gone down in the last week. Potatoes have quite disappeared from our menu. Today some four–five hundred women in a queue trying to buy potatoes.'

Then, on 29 April, 'Spring is here at last. Daffodils blowing everywhere. Boys preparing for Australia tomorrow. Went to Selfridges for tea but found it hard to get anything to eat. Food is evidently becoming scarcer. 51 ships sunk this week. King's proclamation made today advising people to be frugal. Every day the papers are full of food warnings and threats to do away with pet shops to save food. Am making a red rag cape being determined not to spend 5/6 on a thing I have to wear to please a certain party. We nurses and patients went for a picnic down to the Goodlakes' place – the original V.C. people – a lovely home on the bank of a little river with sloping lawns under spreading chestnut trees; just budding. "My word", one of the men said, "wouldn't it break you up if you owned a place like this and then had it all destroyed!" Memories of that Fair France laid waste and desolate and its soil drenched with the life blood of nations no doubt were in his mind.'

By 23 May Sister Kitchen mentions the Big Push and its effect – her ward has been turned into a surgical one, and she is working late. 'So many bad cases and only a "plumber" to assist me. The M.O. says he ought to be good at the joints. There has been a big air-raid at Folkestone or Dover, 70 killed and 200 wounded by the large number of bombs dropped on the town. A busy day, our light work is over and we now "don't have time to spit". One of the sisters left for France – perhaps her departure will increase a little our scanty food supply for there is rarely enough to go round and a second helping almost unheard of. There is a note on the biscuit tin for night duty staff "One biscuit to each sister and 6 over for the 5 a.m. team before going on duty".'

'Haig's big offensive yesterday,' she announces on 7 June. 'They could hear the guns in London and Dover. We went to Richmond. The lawns smooth and green like billiard tables and everywhere the little punts and canoes were being made use of – so often by the "Boys in Blue" [the blue walking-out hospital suits] with the girls. *July 1st*: So many in everywhere and so many bed cases waiting for the boat which we hope will go soon. Only 6 mugs to 22 patients. Went to town, saw the Queen driving along Victoria Street and . . . the top of a pink flowered toque through the crowd. After a lengthy survey of all the exhibits she . . . decorated a soldier in Blues, admired the woolwork banner which 12 of them surveyed with pride in their own handiwork – an appeal from the men at the front, to "look after our children in our absence".

'*July 3rd*: . . . The place looks like a drunkards' home with kits scattered everywhere, with no one to do anything, and even find it difficult to find a man to hold a splint up while the dressing is done. No patient who is left here is able to do the smallest thing; if able to walk about they have a wing gone, or they are on crutches . . . it is a struggle to get the dressings done. All the sisters look tired out . . . I feel beaten at the edges and frayed to a frazzle. At dinner we were asked to have our photo taken. On an especially busy day we always have our photos taken or a linen inventory and we always must look pleasant at both . . . Up at 5 a.m. tomorrow to get the hospital ship patients ready for the *Kanowna*. They say the Russians are retreating.'

By the end of the month she is back on night duty,

dealing with haemorrhages and heart attacks, her life 'reduced to bed and route marches . . . the weird nights go on as usual like solitary confinement'. '*August 1st*: In the night a sudden memory assailed me: I heard the East a'calling. All at once a vision of those first days at Mena House rushed over me and I felt how I should have loved to have been back there on one of those lovely mornings and look out through the sunshine to the top of the pyramid sticking out of the rising mists. If only I could recapture all the beauties of that past time, see the faces again that are gone, and start out on this campaign again with all the ideals and beliefs we once had and with the knowledge of all the after events and the power that knowledge would bring.'

It was claimed that the Australians commissioned officers from the ranks more than any other army. When the opportunity came these men were given a course at an officers' training school. Young Lieutenant G. W. Harris of the 12th Battalion who had long ago written from Gallipoli 'I wish this blessed old war would end', was one of these men. Two 'pips' had not destroyed his boyish fun. From 'Somewhere in France' he wrote: 'I used to wonder what it would be like under fire and I know now. It's rotten . . . But I'm pleased I've not shown the slightest sign of a white feather all the time I've been on Active Service.' By November 1916 he was at Bisley, the officers' college. 'We're treated as gentlemen here and it makes a wonderful difference. We have ripping meals and don't have dinner until 7.30 so you see we are some swank, eh what?' The real business is never forgotten, even with such levity. 'Hughie [brother] has arrived in England. He seems older but of course active service makes one older in many ways. I'm afraid you won't find the frivolous youngster that left Western Australia when I return. I've managed to recover some of my old spirits again so perhaps they're not quite gone.'

Harris had been wounded at Gallipoli but was back in the trenches six weeks later. In 1916, as a Lance-Corporal, he held a captured pill-box with eight men and two machine guns for sixty-eight hours without food or water and under heavy fire. When relieved, only he and one other had survived. He was commissioned in the field and sent to Bisley where he qualified as a machine-gun specialist. When the big offensive began and the Hindenburg line was broken at Bullecourt, he led his men forward. Keith Murdoch, correspondent at the time for the Melbourne *Herald*, wrote a despatch: 'Lieut. Harris of Claremont (W.A.), died gallantly at the extreme objective 5 May, 1917. He was one of 15 cousins serving with the A.I.F. of whom four were killed.' The young lieutenant, it was said, was killed 'while trying to rescue one of his men while returning through our own artillery fire'.

Sergeant J. Stevens, Orderly Room Sergeant, Headquarters 58th Battalion, persistently and consistently refused a commission. 'I'm alright as a sergeant,' he confided in his diary. 'Lieutenant is alright but it's rather late in the game for me to start field work now when I've been doing clerical work so long.' What surprises us in his diaries is not so much that he held out against firm pressure to accept a commission, but that his work as orderly room sergeant required, and was given, vibrant initiative, long hours, danger and hardship. He documents the day-to-day life of a fighting battalion.

He had gone to France in 1916 and marched for three days, carrying his pack like every other man in his infantry battalion, until they reached 'the Front'. 'Had hard stones to march over so feet got very sore.' On the way to Fromelles, 'Had to march in small parties of 6 in file, machine-guns were playing everywhere. Had a couple of dangerous spots to traverse but did it safely.'

He cycles often when the battalion is relieved and occasionally goes back behind the line. 'Every evening for this week we sit in front of a nice big fire in madam's kitchen and she makes coffee for us. Madam lent us a blanket each on our way back to the firing line.'

When Christmas came and they were again out of the

trenches, 'Madam roasted our duck for us and cooked vegetables in a fine old-fashioned way. Dinner was such a success that all that rich food was too much for us and we felt a bit off later. Hope next Christmas dinner is in good old Australia.' (That was Christmas 1916 and his next Australian Christmas was not to be until 1919.)

There was no rest, although actual battles were delayed because of the weather. Early in 1917 he was 'Passing through lovely country even though it is winter and the trees bare. I stood the march well until the last three miles when my feet packed up but I got along somehow for the remaining miles.' Next day he was off again. 'Rather a good day for marching. We were up early and did 12 miles to St. Vast by 1 p.m.' Then his typewriter broke down so he walked the nine miles to Amiens for a new spring and then walked back. It rained the whole time. As for Amiens, 'The majority of the girls of whom there are many are very pretty. . . . We are moving back to the trenches on Friday and expect to be there 6 weeks.' So the 58th set off again. In three days they marched three stages of nine, eight and six miles carrying full packs and blankets over wet roads and through driving snow.

On reaching their bivouac, an acre of mud in which they were invited to make themselves at home, they moved immediately into the trenches. 'Shelled in afternoon.' Here rations were hard to come by. 'Had a damper tonight for tea – flour and water cooked in a pan. Very heavy but only food we had.'

One of his tasks was to record battalion casualties. On 23 January, one week after they 'went in', the battalion 'came out of the lines'. 'Our casualties during this time were 3 killed and 12 wounded.' (This was a 'caretaking period'. Soon his entries would be multiplied by one hundred.) He records the small items that added to the discomforts as the winter came on heavy. 'The ink in our bottles is always frozen and we have to melt it. The air cuts right through me. . . . Did not get to bed till after midnight last night. Despatches from Brigade coming in late. Up at

4 a.m., on the march again at 8 a.m. carrying blanket and pack.'

There were times when he must go back behind the lines to 'check battalion records' with the colonel. Anything could happen on such a trip. After walking, then hitching a ride in a van that broke down. he got a lift in 'a bonzer car' and 'sat well back with a rug over my knees. Just the thing!' That night at Rouen 'the colonel's batman and I shared a big room with two beds in a most beautifully furnished room in a most fashionable hotel. Got in among the white sheets and thought of the beds I had been having – on the floor between dirty blankets in a corner where the cold air comes straight through the cracks off the snow which I can see while in bed and the times when I had newspapers for mattress and blanket or the times on wet stones in the Q.M. store. (Many soldiers say it takes some time to get into the way of a soft bed – but not me!)' He makes the most of this luxury. 'Slept in till 9 a.m. this morning and had to go without breakfast to dodge the colonel.' After 4 a.m. reveille this was indeed luxury. He goes to the opera – and other places. 'Some of the things that are staged in Paris would not be permitted in Australia being rather on the "warm" side. At the Folies Bergere women are there as much as the men, and all drink and smoke.'

After a dreary trip riding in motor lorries and wagons and walking he 'arrived back in camp'. 'It was a very nice week. I wished I could stay a month'. Once more at his 'desk' he works through the nights until 1.30 a.m. and sometimes until 2 a.m. Every time the unit moved up to or back from the lines he had to 'pack [his] boxes and set off with the records'. Sometimes six men carried his most precious box, on other occasions he got the whole of his goods on a wagon while he himself invariably had to march in full marching order.

He is the perfect recorder. Emotion rarely shows through his lines, and then it is mostly pride of his battalion that escapes him. In October 1917 at the Third Battle of Ypres (Passchendaele, the Australians called it): 'Very busy still.

Tomorrow another big phase of this attack comes off, the 1st, 2nd and 3rd Australian Divisions and an N.Z. Division jump out. We are standing by in reserve. The Australians have added greatly to their fame for their recent successes. Our Brigade has done very well and have been congratulated by the C.-in-C., British Armies, and every British General; 58th Battalion are now termed the "Stonewallers". Very heavy bombardment all night and this morning.'

33
Wipers

In the eleventh century Ypres was the greatest town in Flanders and some of the beautiful buildings of the Middle Ages were still standing when World War I began. The beautiful Cloth Hall, a rich Gothic architectural jewel, had been battered to rubble by early 1915 by German gunners with high-explosive shells. It became to Australian soldiers as famous a landmark as the diving Virgin of Albert.

Ypres is only a few miles from the French frontier and for 800 years it had sustained many sieges, many occupations. (It had been attacked by the British in 1385 and again in 1680.) By 1905 it was described as a phantom town, a cemetery, deserted by commerce but carefully guarding the great buildings erected in its years of prosperity. The best known of these had been the Cloth Hall. By 1916 there was scarcely an Australian soldier who did not send home a postcard of the ruins of this building.

In the closing months of 1917 the third battle of Ypres saw a watershed of men affected and changed by the years of war and the ceaseless, un-human life. They knew the name of the city but not its pronunciation and called it – sometimes wrote it – Wipers. 'No battle in the war could compare in dreadfulness,' the German official monograph stated. 'This battle in Flanders was the worst of the war, so bloody.' It comprised eleven full-scale attacks, five of which the Australians spearheaded. (The Canadians were the spearhead for another four.) The Australian casualties were 38 000 in eight weeks and this caused an insoluble problem of reinforcements. The battles, according to a German authority, 'wore down the German strength to a degree at which the damage could no longer be repaired'.

Most Australians call the battle Passchendaele because it was in this area they fought. Others call it Menin Road because it was along this road (which led into the ancient city) that they tramped to their various areas. The road became the *via dolorosa* along which men limped, were wounded, died and despaired. Almost one million men were 'lost' in this Third Battle of Ypres, half of them British (including Commonwealth) and half German, and the eight offensives in the mud made 'Wipers' a name to make men shudder. 'After Wipers I knew I'd get home,' Thorvald Kook said, 'To live through Passchendaele was to come out the other side of hell.'

Neither side knew exactly what it was fighting for, nor even the confines or content of the contested territory. They just ranged backwards and forwards over the churned-up, sickened soil.

The third battle of Ypres has been called 'the greatest battle of materiel in history'. The British had a gun to every six yards, the French one to every two-and-a-half yards.

The Germans had built small concrete forts, known as 'pill-boxes', and with their four-foot thick walls could shelter numbers of men until the artillery barrage had passed, when they could rush out and attack the attacking infantry. To combat this, a 'creeping' artillery-barrage was introduced with the infantry following close behind the artillery as it moved across, so that they were able to surround a pill-box before the Germans could emerge. Some had only a door at the back, others were loop-holed to enable machine guns to fire from within, and around these fighting became particularly fierce.

On 22 April 1917, Eddie Johnson's name had been 'called to pack up and report to 1st Division Headquarters, near Bapaume, their position for the Bullecourt stunt'.

'Baizieux, near Amiens, was the town allotted to the 1st

Div. Sigs., and our time was taken up with intense training for the forthcoming autumn offensive . . . the 3rd Battle of Ypres.'

'On Sept 19th 'S' Department left Dickebusch, bound for Halfway house (a large dug-out in the line). The day had been perfect when leaving, but towards evening a steady rain was falling, and the surface of the battlefield changed from dust to mud. Owing to weather conditions etc, the previous cable line had badly deteriorated and had to be relaid from Halfway house to Hooge Crater. It was a very important line, and would be used by Brigadier Bennett at Hooge Crater for the hop-over, during the Ypres stunt the following day. It was situated close to the front line.

'At 3 p.m. the artillery opened up with a terrific bombardment . . . Having arrived safely near Halfway House, we dismantled the 4 cable reels, and in a hurried departure the drivers and cable waggon returned to Dickebusch. Then, 10 signallers were detailed to lay 4 lines about 40 yds apart to make a ladder line to Hooge Crater. . . . We received a light bombardment from Fritz, but completed the line by approx. 11 p.m. Overnight we continued parading our line and mending any breaks.

'During the morning Lieut. Neale informed us that our objective had been gained by 7 a.m. . . . The following day 2 lorries left at 9 a.m. taking 16 men for buried cable work and also some of our Officers to Lieut. Ferguson's funeral . . . After the burial the 16 buried-cable boys with Lieut. Neale left by lorry for Ypres. From there we brought our gas masks to the alert, and headed by foot down Menin Road . . . We arrived at Sans Souci, another German Pill-box, situated near Polygon Wood, and in front of Westhoek Ridge. It was slow getting there, with mud up to our knees. Six of us stayed at Sans Souci, we formed the breakdown gang, while the others went to test strips. . . .

'It was on Oct 25th, at 8 p.m., when Lieut. Neale paid us a visit, and while he was with us, Fritz lobbed a shell near the side of the pill-box, rocked it, and put the candle out used for our test strip. Next day 3 of us went back to Frost

House for more cable. On arriving back, a Fritz shell blew the sand bags from our window, rocked the pill-box and put the candle out for the 4th time. An officer nearby sent a runner down, who yelled out, "Is anyone still alive in there?" We filled sand bags with porridge-mud to block up our window again. Our Pill Box had railway lines holding up approx 4 feet of concrete blocks for the roof, but the water still dripped in. We had duckboards on the floor to keep out of the water, and erected ground sheets to the ceiling to catch the rain drops, but some mug would knock his head into the ground sheets, and you would be lucky if you did not get water down your neck.

'In the early hours of the 28th Oct. Cpl. Noel was on duty (test strip). The others were sitting or laying on the duck-boards, in readiness to go out on the lines when required. Word was given to put gas masks on, as Fritz had mixed gas shells with a bombardment of high explosives, and then one gas shell arrived near our door. We all showed signs of being gassed. After a hectic night my eyes started to close and burn in the corners. I indulged in a series of bouts of coughing and sickness. On Oct 30 I was told to go and get my eyes dressed and bandaged at the 2nd Brigade. An AMC soldier told me vomiting would help. He placed me with others in a single file and then told us to put our paws on the chap in front. Like this, blind, we scrambled along duckboards and stopped at a dressing station then were put on a horse-drawn ambulance, later changed into a motor ambulance near Ypres. We arrived at 2nd Canadian Clearing Station, and after being inoculated etc, I was placed on a stretcher, undressed, washed, eyes dressed, had a terrific headache, was then placed on an ambulance train.

'Then my days were a repetition of doctor's visits, eyes burning pretty bad, eyes dressed twice before dinner, eyes dressed before and after tea, indulged in coughing, restless-ness, throughout the night, lost my voice to a whisper (later I was to receive a letter from Australia. It had been stamped 4.11.17 and signed "deceased" at the 22nd G.H.B. where I was still alive). A Scotch chap in the next bed informed me that the night sister had sat alongside me, and that I had been delirious. He wished me luck, and mentioned that the last that occupied my bed had passed out from gas. . . .

'In the early hours of Nov. 7th I was told to dress for Blighty and be ready in one hour's time. my togs being socks, pyjama shirt and pants. cardigan. a tie, cap comforter. a small bag for my pocket things, with a Blighty label pinned on me. A nurse assisted me, then we were driven to Étaples in a Motor Ambulance. . . . From Étaples we trained to Calais, went up the jetty by train, were placed on a ship by two German prisoners, and then went across to Dover. . . . arrived at Whally in Lancashire, and placed in F3 ward, Queen Mary's Military Hospital. . . .

'When I was marked fit, I headed back to the 1st Div. Sigs again [and] received news of Sans Souci – Sgt. Miller had received a D.C.M. apart from his M.M., and had been sent to the Officers' School in England. Cpl. R. Noel had for a short period stayed on duty at the test strip in Sans Souci Pill-box, waiting for a relief party. while the other five had evacuated gassed. A high explosive shell shattered the Pill-box while he was inside. He had then been invalided back to Australia . . . it could have been a lucky break for the other five that were gassed. One of our Sigs, stationed at 2nd Bde, actually saw him arrive at the A.M.C. He said his hair was all singed and blood was coming from his ears. He had crawled out of a small hole from the smashed-up Pill-box, and was shouting "'S S' blown up!"'

'Just one day on Menin Road?' I asked Jim McPhee. He got out his diaries.

'September, 1917. Swung down carrying wounded to Hell Fire Corner and on to Menin Road under the pounding artillery. Things could not possibly be worse. Up the corduroy track, packed with walking wounded and Hun prisoners from Polygon Wood. We all threaded a tortuous course through the horse and mule transport pouring up the cranky, shell-torn road. A splendid team, killed overnight, formed part of its foundations in one part. Returned from a

carry we were told off to report to the regimental M.O. at
the advanced battalion line – I surged inwardly.

'Down the slope of Belvaarde Ridge we trudged after our
M.O. through the crashing batteries in the valley, and on to
Westhoek Ridge, down its slope to Nun's Wood Valley and
up the next ridge with earth and smoke spurting. Bock, one
of our bearers suddenly sang one of our ditties:

> Good-bye General Birdwood,
> Farewell Godly too
> Ever since we left Australia
> We've been mucked around by you!

and then he cursed the day he'd left Australia.

'What remained of the guiding tape brought us to some
of the 13th Battalion on the crest. The ground appeared to
be sewn with dead. Suddenly all eyes were drawn to
Polygon Wood, ominous, blasted and gaunt, not a kilometre
away, into which descended a deluge of shells. Gloomily
we felt that the Boche's metal was not the inferior stuff the
London papers had tried to make us believe. Machine-gun
bullets swished savagely and I was blinking – uncon-
sciously I think, blinking an SOS to Heaven!

'We reached the advanced dressing post pretty exhausted.
There the M.O. and dressers of the 15th Battalion coolly
dressed outside what wounded wouldn't fit inside. Khaki
and grey dead looked up. We took refuge in a sap and
whizzbangs smashed part of it and dazed us. A nearby
heliograph flashed and under the same heavy fire two
bomb-laden diggers crossed to the front line on higher
ground, with an assumption of carelessness that thrilled
us.

'One of our squads met with trouble, so, with some
battered square-heads in tow, three squads shouldered
stretchers in good heart till we struck a worse belt of fury,
the stretcher wobbled, and we stumbled. A Fokker dived
and its machine gun spat at us. Bock fell. We examined
him and decided to return later to bury him and the patient.
Mechanically we went on.

'Then at 3 p.m. a deathly quiet came over the front. We

quickly crowded all the wounded we could push in to the post, and as we got the last into cover the storm broke, the Boche's counter-attack rose to tornado pitch and lashed the country furiously. Fatty staggered in with the news that number three squad had been knocked out. Two of us left now. The M.O. urged a spell. "No sir," replied Fatty. "We're still home on the pig's back."

'A Hun took Bock's place for a carry and we worked quickly till nightfall. The eerie Jack-o-lanterns of No Man's Land dazzled and left a deeper gloom, through which we blundered into entanglements and cursed. A bearer stepped into a shell hole and down the wounded man toppled into foul mud. A great radiance flamed red in the sky above Ypres. Someone said it was an incendiary shell. To some of us it was heaven sighing over the ghastly loss of life on the battles of Ypres and it left us chilled and full of dread. At midnight we crawled into a deep pouch in the ground and before the last man slept the bright-eyed rats appeared in search of food.'

Downing, too, wrote of Menin Road and of the weariness: 'We had a feeling of sinking through space. Men fell silent, or spoke casually, or made surly jests according to their natures. Bodies lay here and there. No one spoke of the task before us. Time dragged on. Despair, hope, despondency and resolution fought for the possession of each soul. Despondency and resolution remained. There was a lull in the shelling. The moon was hidden in clouds. From the darkness all around came the tinkle of harness, the oaths of drivers, the clink of picks and shovels as the artillery pulled into place and dug positions. Wheels made no sound in the dry and crumbled earth . . .

'At ten o'clock came a sudden order to move. . . . One addressed one's friends in a low voice as they went by, each man's scabbard, entrenching helve, and wire-cutter swinging and clicking against his shovel and his rifle butt. They passed like black shadows. One took one's place and moved along.

With infinite caution we worked along the German wire,

one man at a time. We found a body sprawled across some strands of wire. When would we be like that – so shrivelled, so grey? Sooner or later, for it appears there is no way out, except by losing a limb. Rats ran away squeaking. Bang! A flare fizzled upwards. We lay flat. We saw the dead man's face. It was a poor beggar reported missing after the raid a week ago. One arm hung down, the hand lightly touching the ground. All the fingers were gone . . . gnawed off. Bot cut the string of his identity disc and took it. We moved on.

'Suddenly the sergeant stopped and clicked his tongue. We all dropped into shell holes. Figures of men loomed through the darkness. By the faint light of a distant flare we saw them. One – two – five – eight – eleven – fourteen. They wore helmets like coal-scuttles. We lay still, our nerves on edge. One repressed a mad desire to yell. They passed within inches of us, several times brushing our faces with their boots. One of them stood on Graham's hand.'

Orderly Room Sergeant Stevens lamented: 'Cannot get any particulars down from the line about casualties . . . We now learn that Fritz counter-attacked this morning and pushed back the Tommies on our flanks but our A and C companies turned them back on our sector. [Next day] Reports are that half our battalion have gone west but can get nothing official, all communications cut off. Shelling has been most terrific. Early tomorrow the stunt takes place and is to be a hop-over on a twenty mile front and will be the greatest bombardment of the war. It must be hellish in the front line.'

And the following day he enters: 'Bombardment intense. A lot of our battalion wandering back here and nobody seems to know where they should be. Hop-over, all objectives were taken but with big loss. About 1000 German prisoners marching down look a motley lot. Advanced 1100 yards but Tommies didn't do their part and now there is a big salient. We can get no information of casualties and every-thing seems to be upside down.'

Eventually he learns of 290 casualties from his battalion

of 800 men. Sometimes his 'little home' is bombed, twice at least he had to make a desperate run for safety. Two men were hit beside him, 'one badly. One of his legs being smashed and broken, the other leg being blown right off. His cries were pitiful. I am going forward to the line with the battalion tomorrow'. His 'desk' sits wherever he can put it. Once he was in the middle of a field. 'There was nowhere else I could go.'

They sang a song to the tune of 'Send me to Sleep':

> Far from Ypres I long to be
> Where German snipers can't get at me
> Damp is my dug-out
> Cold are my feet
> Waiting for whizz-bangs
> To send me to sleep.

Then there was the professionally written

> Here we are! Here we are! Here we are again!!!
> We're fit and well and feeling right as rain
> Never mind the weather, now then altogether!
> Hullo! Hullo! Here we are again!

And psychology in those days was said to be in its infancy!

Around about this time the term 'Digger' became common usage. It had been used among the miners in some units but it was from the New Zealanders, who took it from their country's gum-diggers, that the Australians adopted the term and in time 'it spread like a crown fire through the A.I.F.'. Theo Ford remembers that 'by the end of 1917 we were all, Aussies and En-Zedders alike, calling one another "Digger".' The term was taken up by the folk back home and the men were happy about this, whereas the English soldier 'never liked "Tommy" because it carried the "Superior person's" view of his attributes'.

Nursing was 'not much fun', as one of the girls wrote, and Alice Kitchen at the army hospital at Harefield knew it keenly when she wrote in November 1917: '[Sister] McCarthy died today, being unconscious most of the time. Three years today since we left Albany. How far away it seems. Today met Captn. Bennett from the 8th wearing "the Blue Badge"* and he came to Paddington with us. Two of my patients nearing the end. The ward seems quiet after the bad cases are at rest. The others are still awaiting the Hospital ship daily. The mornings are cold and freezing and getting more wintry . . . getting ready for the evacuation . . .

'*Nov. 25*: Got up at 3.30 a.m., as the boys are off on the *Karoola*. Such a relief to see them start. Then we came over to cold porridge and bread or dry toast and dripping and "burial" jam.'

The cold this winter seemed as intense as that of 1916–17. 'All the taps are frozen up – no gas for some time, no cold water anywhere – thermometers frozen into glasses and the medicine glasses frozen into a solid block of ice. Absolute misery for most of the men. Shortage of fuel very tiresome.' But by Christmas Eve a thaw had set in and 'the snow is gradually melting and the lake unfrozen'. Once again she remembers the first Christmas abroad and notes that this is now the fourth away from home. They decorated the wards with 'greenery and dangling yellow apples and a fine Xmas tree decorated with crackers and flags etc. Wards 13 and 19 had permission to dine together but both scornfully refused the offer and preferred to "ate" by themselves. We had a fine dinner for them. Roast turkey and pork, green peas, potatoes, plum pudding and custards etc. nuts, prunes, apples and champagne cider. Also a nice tea and all enjoyed themselves. I have 3 wards on my own. Staff shortage acute.'

And so the pattern continually repeated itself, with no resolution to a final shape, merely a crocheting of design because the materials were at hand. Over and over the

---

* The blue band around the arm of the hospital walking out 'suit' signified a wounded man. Londoners called it 'the blue badge of courage'.

entries fill the pages – 'Hospital Ship due; patients left this morning; cleaning up after evacuation; wards filling up; wards full; someone dying; someone limbless; someone eyeless; hospital ship due; getting patients prepared for evacuation'; as fast as the beds were cleared the war machine churned out replacements and the diary repeated itself: 'another amputation, another abdominal'.

Alice Kitchen was now in her forty-fourth year and for four years had worked hours and laboured harder and seen sights that few men or women could have so ably survived. In between, whenever she could snatch an hour of sanity, she wandered off and was her own woman, roaming the woods, gathering flowers; buying knick-knacks everywhere; her diaries contain notes of what appear to be no less than 83 separate items she bought, from brass trays to glassware, pictures and needlework. While at Harefield she scarcely missed one notable theatrical event of the day from *Dear Brutus* and *Maid of the Mountain*, to *Samson and Delilah*. She 'did' the palaces, castles, ruins, cathedrals, monuments, entertainment centres and the general sights with an enthusiasm that would have disabled many a tourist. But overall the pages reveal one awful gulf: she never regained the buoyancy of those nationally youthful days of the First Convoy, when a whole young land had cheered them on their way. Gallipoli stripped that page right out of the diary of her life and we can tell by her rigidly non-subjective lines the numbing numbness of the whole heart of the woman when she repeats over and over again, 'saw a boy of the 8th today', 'a boy of the original 8th came up and spoke to me'. The torn and battle-stained pennants that these remnants represented were all that remained of the one glorious, vibrant moment in her life and the life of all those who embarked with her on what had been a wild unhesitant pilgrimage to parade the mettle of a young, untried country. It was no longer untried, unsung; it had made its historic point and would be entered in the lists of the heroes, listing not the leaders or individuals but the group. As with 'the Three Hundred at Thermopylae' the remnants that Alice

Kitchen pained for would be listed by the collective term, 'Anzacs'. But the making of history does not repair the damaged heart and the nurse was sick with the weariness of memory.

Physically, she was no worse than the other nurses. She writes often of the illness, the hospitalisation, the 'boarded back to Australia' of nurses who, to a reader of her diaries, are only names. But her age was against her and she knew it. Matron Gertrude Moberly wrote to her Peter: 'I was dreadfully shocked when on the last hospital ship going back to Blighty I saw a young A.N. Sister (and so pretty she looked, with her fair hair plaited in two big plaits, sitting up in bed, softly singing to herself). Matron told me she was quite mad; the awful sights had turned her brain, and I wondered how many more would share her fate. . . . I feel, and see red, when men in high positions glibly talk as though these frightful things do not exist. How would they feel could they see their own beloved daughters driven mad by sights that no girl should see?'

In the summer of 1918, Alice Kitchen noted that 'Sister Bowman [is] ill, left for Australia today. Saw her off. Poor Sister Dickenson became very ill during the night and was taken to the Sisters' hospital this morning and died in the afternoon. It seems too dreadful to realise . . . Terribly tired: everybody depressed. We can scarcely realise what a dreadful happening all this last week has been. Samsing still in bed ill. I went to bed early. *June 25th*: Very tired. Samsing going to St Albans today to rest. Dickenson was buried today. A long day on. I am quite a war widow having lost my companion! The wards get heavier and there are to be no days off till after the boat goes. Frightfully tired with the work and the after effects of influenza.

'*June 28th*: Ran to the woods before going on duty to gather an armful of green boughs and blue bells for the wards . . . violets from their mossy beds and the fern fronds that are springing everywhere; buttercups are out, lilacs in bud and wallflower scent everywhere.'

Human nature being what it is there were always girls, though some men's letters make one confused. Young Roly Mills answered his sister's query as to 'whether a chap has opportunities of meeting girls over here' with 'There are few chances. The girls here don't have anything to do with soldiers as a rule. Anyhow, there are very few a chap would fancy. They are mostly rough and ready farmers' daughters'. He was then in Flanders, where he wondered if the people were poorer and less attractive because of the long German occupation.

Later, he was able to write that his last spell out of the trenches was spent at Warloy-Baillon 'and I was able to see my friend again, who wrote to you when we were there in the summer. They, Mlle and her mother, were always very good to me. Whenever I had a feed of eggs or coffee they would absolutely refuse to take any money'.

Roly moved to another part of the front and Mlle promised to prepare some French lessons for him. Tucked in his wallet when he returned to Australia at the war's end was a small sheet of paper with the following phrases in English and French.

It is very cold in the trenches.
Are you free on Sunday?
Where do you live?
How many sisters have you?
Will you be free tomorrow evening?
I hope to see you again.
No, I am not married.

He never saw the girl, Léonne, again. When he returned from his next 'stunt' he found the village bombed to the ground. With difficulty he found what had been his friend's home and, searching among the ruins, found the remains of a slip of paper with his name written on it. That was all. (The author has met his daughter, born long after the war's end to the Australian girl he met on his return. The daughter's name? Léonne.)

There was little relief for the men. 'It is three months now since we have been in action. The longest spell our division has ever had. In a few days time we expect to go in again though.'

Roly wrote to his brother George on 28 April 1917: 'What did you think of the last big stunt at Arras? 15 000 prisoners and 200 big guns in a few days. It looks as if the Hun is just about done. If we can do that at Arras there is no reason why we can't do it anywhere now that the rough weather is just about over. . . . We are still looking forward to a good long spell when we get out which won't be long now. Perhaps in less than a week. The Australians have had about the toughest job of the lot during the winter with very short spells. . . . The worst part of the whole front to look after and that is the Somme. No doubt you have read in the papers about the Huns retreating. . . . The lads have had a fairly exciting time keeping in touch with them. The English papers say he left 1 500 dead behind but I believe there were close on 2 000. . . . Yesterday when I was out patrolling one of our telephone lines I saw a few of them lying in shell holes. One of them was quite a youngster. He couldn't have been more than 17. It will give you an idea of how Germany are off for men when they bring lads like that into the firing line. Of course there are many lads in our army about that age. But I think there are more youngsters among the Huns judging by the prisoners I've seen working on the roads.'

With youth on his side, Roly was liable to forget the bad days. He once commented that the cold was better than wet weather, quite forgetting that on 27 January, only three months previously, he had written, 'These last few weeks the cold has been almost unbearable . . . one continual frost. The snow is still on the ground and of course all water frozen hard. Whenever the cooks need water we have to set out with a pick or axe to break the ice which is on the shell holes of water. It must be over 6 inches deep. Our rations are always frozen hard before we get them. Bread and cheese, jam and tins of milk. Today, coming up here, the water in our bottles was frozen into one solid block.

'I am always fit but the other day I had a pretty severe

attack of cramps in the stomach caused through catching cold while waiting for a bath. . . . It didn't affect me until about 3 next morning. The doctor put a scalding towel on my stomach several times and gave me a dose of Castor oil. . . . That was the first bit of misery since I had jaundice at Lemnos.'

He spent some time as a D.R., a despatch rider, in France. 'It's not so bad. All I do is look after the horse and do a couple of trips every day to Division, about 4 miles from us. The horse I have is . . . very frightened of motor cars and lorries. The other day I had a pretty rough time with her. She took fright when a motor was passing and jumped in a ditch full of water on the side of the road and I didn't *get any fish* I can tell you [A euphemism for 'a wet bum and no fish'].'

All the men were great souvenir hunters, and Roly was no exception. He sent his young brother Ted a 'Hun cap' and a German five mark note acquired during the Passchendaele stunt.

He described the 'pickings' to his brother George: 'Some of our lads have been getting good souvenirs out of German dug-outs that have been blown in by bomb and shell-fire. What they do is to get to work with a pick and shovel and clear the dirt away from the entrance. There are always a few dead bodies in these dug-outs and in their packs and haversacks there are always souvenirs of some kind such as pocket-books, diaries, wallets, etc. One chap showed me photographs of Germans in their dug-out having a sing-song with all kinds of musical instruments and there were bottles on the table and glasses filled with what appeared to be whisky. They all had a bleary look in their eyes as if they were elephants trunk. Evidently it was a photo taken in the early stages of the war when they thought their comfortable dug-outs impregnable against any attack. There is a different tale to tell now. If you saw some of these German trenches George you would think it impossible to advance at all. In one trench close by there are, at intervals, solid concrete machine gun emplacements still intact. There are marks on some where 18 pounders have made a direct hit and still they are quite fit to be used. Of course the tanks were responsible for destroying a lot of these strong positions as they were able to get in close and pump the shells in.'

It was the hey-day of picture postcards and most soldiers' collections have their packet of silken, painted cards they sent home.

Corporal W. Fuller was aged seventeen when first he went into the trenches in France. He wrote constantly to his schoolgirl sister, Elsie. He sent her cards from Egypt, England, France and Belgium and had gathered some handkerchiefs, an apron and other souvenirs to bring home to her. Twice wounded, he died of 'Spanish Influenza'. He was aged nineteen when he was awarded the D.C.M. in June 1918 in France. The apron and other things of silk arrived after the news of his death and were never taken from the box which was packed away until Elsie died as an elderly lady. Among these silk cards and letters was an extract from the *London Gazette* dated 26 June 1918.

DISTINGUISHED CONDUCT MEDAL
No. 3809 Cpl W. R. FULLER, 21st Battalion, A.I.F.

For conspicuous gallantry and devotion to duty. On the enemy raiding our front line posts after a severe bombardment, he distributed his men in order to avoid casualties, keeping with himself two men and a machine gun. When the enemy were upon him the machine gun jammed, but he threw bombs until the gun came into action again. Though a shell landed in the post, wounding and partly burying him and killing one of the gunners, he maintained the defence single handed until he was again wounded. His courage, initiative and determination cannot be too highly praised.

34
The Dinki-dis

Young Matron Moberly, the daughter of a clergyman, continued throughout the war to write to her beloved 'Peter'. Her letters came with postmarks from the periphery of war, not the battlefield as did Sister Kitchen's. Nevertheless, she saw service in some strange and difficult areas. Leaving Australia in mid-1915 she spent the following year as matron at No. 6 Auxiliary Hospital for Officers, London. Then home to Sydney (for two weeks) in charge of the nursing staff on the transport ship *Euripides*; after that to Cumballa War Hospital, Bombay, then Colaba War Hospital. Next she was transferred to the hospital ship *Herefordshire*, then to the Persian Gulf, to Dar-es-Salaam (East Africa) and Secunderabad, India, where there was a 1 000-bed hospital.

She was awarded the Royal Red Cross (1st Class) and had the medal pinned on her uniform by General Birdwood. Her letters are lively, loving and bubbling with fun and warmth. In London she had her first experience of nursing the wounded Australians.

'A few days ago I could not help being amused by a visitor, Lady H—. She came to see the officers, and brought with her ever so many books, with coloured scraps for pasting in (the same as little children amuse themselves with). I was so flabbergasted when she asked me "would the patients enjoy having them to keep them occupied?" Fortunately she also had some packets of playing cards, so I suggested that they would be more acceptable, as the officers played bridge quite a lot. . . . I nearly dropped dead at the thought of the faces some of the colonels, majors, captains and lieutenants would present should I escort the lady, armed with children's scrap-books to their bedsides. . . . . I tell you it was no "laughing matter" for titled ladies to have such a false idea of the minds of our Australian men. . . .

'Did you know my brother Will and cousin Tom are both expecting to leave Aussie about the middle of December? I pray that God will bring them back whole, for to me, to be maimed or blind is a thousand times worse than death . . . Two such dear brothers, Peter, but oh, better a thousand times dead than the living death that so many of our dear boys are being called upon to live. I thought my heart would break, darling, when visiting the Sidcup Hospital re having some dental work done. I was shown over the wards . . . there were six hundred men, and not one of them with a whole face. Some had had as many as thirteen operations. I shall never forget.

'I was shown photographs of before and after operations; my stomach turned sick, and I left hurriedly and as soon as I was out of sight of the building sat by the roadside and cried and cried, for my heart felt like bursting, like my head. War! war! war! oh, I hate it – and the promoters of it . . . we see some awful suffering from shell-shock. One of the worst cases I have had so far is Lieutenant E–. For nights I sat with him, sometimes until two and three in the morning. What that boy went through God in Heaven and I only know; and Peter, dear, he has a little baby boy and a young wife in Aussie. At first we tried to treat him in the ward with others . . . I had been to the theatre with some of the boys, and was in mufti. On my return I was met by the night nurse, who reported to me of the shell-shock patient admitted during my absence. I went at once . . . he was sitting up in bed, his eyes staring into space. "Why," I said, "I have come to massage your forehead and send you to sleep". "Oh, have you?" he said. "And who may you be?" "I am the Matron." "Oh, no you're not, you are much too young; and besides, matrons are old, and wear hornrimmed spectacles." I assured him that "only a few were guilty of that" and "I was the Matron, dinky di". At this little word of slang he smiled, and putting out his hand, said "Put it there Matron" . . . He did not improve, so with the O.C's permission I had him moved into a big empty room on the same floor as my own, and attended to him myself . . . the nights spent with him were very tragic. I would be sitting quietly beside his bed, thinking he was asleep, when he would start up and scream out, "Oh God, the shells are coming" and turning to me would say "Quick, lie down for your life! Look, look, there they are, oh, God, can't you hear them? Down, down, down," and his voice would rise to a scream, the perspiration standing out in big drops on his forehead. Oh the sadness of it all! I would hold his hand and soothe him, and in a quiet voice would assure him he was quite safe. This went on for nights, and often far into the morning.'

On 15 June she received the news that she was to 'go to Aussie', in charge of patients and sisters on the *Euripides*, a hospital troop-ship, and she writes from Liverpool on 20 June: 'We are under strict orders not to talk, for (as passengers) we have Mr "Billy" Hughes, "Our Prime Minister", his wife and baby Helen . . . we are going via the Cape . . .

'Cape Town . . . this has been a most interesting voyage . . . It was our first night out from Liverpool, and I was doing my mile on deck when up marched the Prime Minister, and taking my arm, said: "And now, Sister, I want you to point out to me the Matron," so I told him sweetly "that he had hold of that lady's arm". . . . Well, he has his wits on the alert, for, with a very nice smile, he asked me "did I like reading?" and being answered in the affirmative, he went on to say "that I was just to help myself to any of his books", and I tell you, Peter, he had a cabin full, so that is the way in which my heart was won. Some of the lads dreadfully badly wounded, and several operations were performed; one, an urgent appendectomy. The O.C. operated at about 3 a.m. . . . I happened to look up, and there were many watching and keenly interested faces. The O.C., fortunately, was quite unconscious he had an audience. The walls of the improvised operating room only go up to within a couple of feet of the ceiling.'

On arriving in Australia she saw to the preparation of her patients for going ashore and then she went ashore herself – but only for a few days. It was not considered to be 'leave' and she had to work night duty at the military hospital at Randwick while awaiting her next ship which would leave in two weeks time. Once again, it was goodbye to 'Peter'. Now she was off to East Africa.

As the years wore on in war there were more patients and less ease for the nurses. 'I apply ice to my eyes, drink very strong coffee and tea – anything to relieve the agony of wanting to sleep yet knowing one must keep on and on and on. Deo Gratias. It is 7.30 a.m. and operations have been going on all night.'

As with other theatres of war, sickness vied with wounds as the major casualty. 'As I went my round in Secunderabad I could nearly always tell who would be dead of the black plague by evening. The Last Post was sounded on and off all day.'

She was awarded her RRC (1st Class) at the close of the war but only after the Principal Matron of the Australian Army Nursing Service (AANS), Miss G. E. Davis, took the authorities to task. She reminded them that there were 540 AANS serving in India. 'India has not been very generous with awards,' she wrote on 6 September 1919. 'Of 540 AANS personnel serving in India and on hospital ships only 7 awards have been made.'

35
Keep the Home Fires Burning

Keep the home fires burning,
Tho' your hearts are yearning
Tho' the lads are far away,
They dream of home.
There's a silver lining
Through the dark clouds shining
Turn the dark clouds inside out
Till the boys come home!

It is said that 'war knows no fury like a non-combatant', and Australia's two conscription campaigns ably demonstrate this. It was a time that divided the country in direct ratio to the binding mateship of the men at the war.

The *Bulletin* had launched into the fray with gory and grim cartoons by Norman Lindsay and David Low, and the Melbourne *Age* lashed out at those who failed to enlist as 'muddy-mettled wastrels who disgrace the country in which they skulk and shirk and play the dunghill cock'. Above all rose the tiny figure of Prime Minister 'Billy' Hughes. He toured the length and breadth of the land and breathed fire at every whistle stop, to no avail. Both the 1916 and 1917 referendums for conscription were narrowly defeated, but the damage to the country was vast.

The resulting bitterness split the Labor Party – Hughes, with his followers, took the name of the National Labor Party; it split religious groups, many Roman Catholics openly rallying to the Victorian. Archbishop Mannix, who was the country's most ardent anti-conscriptionist; and it split the country itself into bitter factions.

The artist, Ben Strange, beneath his famous cartoon on the 1917 conscription campaign in the *Western Mail* (WA) wrote *East is East and West is West*: Western Australia had voted *for* conscription, the eastern States against. Strange portrayed the West as a lion, the East with the head of a rabbit.

The Rev. Colonel Garland, writing from Brisbane during the first conscription campaign, clearly shows his hand. 'The call up of men under the Defence Act begins today. Camps are in Toowoomba, Rockhampton, Townsville, Maryborough and Chermside. If the men in these camps volunteer they are transferred to reinforcements; meanwhile they wait for conscription to be carried. Labour and Rome are up against conscription. Of religious opinion generally the Church of England, Methodist, Presbyterian, Congregational and Baptist so far have declared in favour of it. The unions have been called on to stop work for 24 hours as a protest against the men being called into camp but I think it will prove a fiasco. My only boy David enlisted after you left.'

He writes that there are good attendances at Army services 'except where discipline is slack'. He advises a lad who writes complaining that soldiers are made to sit in the back of the church in England that 'Customs differ in different places'.

'*23 Dec. 1916*: I have been made one of the three members of the State Recruiting Committee set up to obtain reinforcements after the Referendum was turned down. *2 Feb 1917*: I have been in Melbourne on recruiting business and now I am very busy trying to get recruits in Queensland. *Dec. 1917*: I am very sad about the refusal of Australia to say *yes* to the Referendum.'

Even allowing for the drop in recruiting that occurred in 1917, Australia had provided, per head of population, almost the same number as other Commonwealth countries, all of whom were conscripted.

Figures for the Two Conscription Referendums:
28 October 1916: '*For*' 1 087 557; '*Against*' 1 160 033
20 December 1917: '*For*' 1 015 159; '*Against*' 1 181 747
The Armed Forces vote was:
'*For*' 103 789; '*Against*' 93 910

This high percentage of men 'at the Front' voted against conscription for many reasons, ranging from 'nobody should be made to come to this', 'every man should be able to make up his own mind' and 'If they have to be forced to come they won't be much good over here'. Many had written home earlier criticising 'my friends who stayed at home' but just as many had written to say, 'Tell Bob not to join up. The game's up to mud'.

Lieutenant H. R. Williams (56th Battalion) had written, 'It was amazing to me that most of our men seemed resolved to vote "No". The main reason was the reluctance of the men (all volunteers and still willing to fight for the cause that brought them overseas) to vote in favour of forcing their countrymen to join up and help in the fight. It was typical of the Australian soldier that he would face all the dangers that came his way, but would not vote to compel others of his countrymen, who had just as much to fight for as he had, to risk their lives in the common cause.' And Eddie Johnson said: 'During a special parade one day, we were informed that voting on conscription would take place after dinner, and we were told to give it thought while having dinner . . . the conclusion from conversations heard was vote No – let people please themselves.' (Strangely, one of their best wise-cracks was about men who *didn't* enlist. They called them 'Would-to-Godders' from 'Would to God I could go to the war'.)

The more destructive the war became, the more people were fascinated by it. Scores of charitable organisations were set up to raise funds for anything and everything. The cost of the war in terms of money was great because the country had given generously. £274,378,624 had been raised in war loans; £13,802,301 by 'Patriotic' funds ranging from the Sandbag Fund to Xmas Billy Cans and Cheer Fund, War Horses, Belgian Nuns, Belgium Canal Boats and Tobacco for Troops Fund. The 'gifts in kind' ranged from motor transport to the comforters and 'arm stump socks' that ladies knitted.

Muriel Mills, writing to her brother Roly had said: 'I do hope you are still quite safe. A lot of the boys have come home and poor fellows they are such wrecks. Did I tell you what a great day Australia Day was here. It will always live in the memory of Australians. I think there was the biggest crowd that ever was in Melbourne before, and the wounded soldiers – well, the people fairly threw the money at them. It was great.'

This excitement contrasted sadly with the experience of the young boy 'over there'. When going on furlough in France young Roly had seen, 'at every village we passed, the people were out waving handkerchiefs to the lads, welcoming them home on furlough. It made me realize I am away from home to think that I was not going home like that. There is no place like home, as Mum always says. When we got to London and saw all the English Tommies meeting their mothers, sisters, brothers and friends, we Australians realized a little more that we are far from home.'

The South Australian Trooper H. H. Moule of the 3rd Light Horse was obviously delegated to write a thank you letter for gifts received, but for all that, his letter does give a spontaneous picture of the excitement when a parcel from 'home' arrived. He writes from 'Somewhere in Palestine' in June 1917 to 'Dear Miss Fenton', thanking her for socks and hoping he is not breaking rules by mentioning his unit by name, for he knows she will want to have news of the 3rd Light Horse, to whose comforts' fund she belongs. 'Our advance over the desert was hard and wearisome . . . We don't want to face it again but look back with pride on the work our horses did on that lonesome waste of some 100 miles in width. A good many of us would not say "no" to a spot of leave in Australia! I have been a soldier since 1914.

It is tough to have been invalided home from Gallipoli with enteric and returned here over 12 months ago to carry on with this awful affair, still, things are much better than this time last year.

'I wish to thank the ladies of our Trench Comfort Fund on behalf of the boys and myself. Although we are doing our bit every one of us recognises that our womenfolk are doing theirs grandly, in fact more than we ourselves as we do see the excitement and serious things of this war face to face, you never do. Everyone is more or less disgruntled and tired of everything then – word comes through that parcels or cases of gifts have arrived at the Rail-Head. A limber of camels is at once despatched and the Treasure carted out to the Regiment; in the meantime, everyone is asking, "is it true a consignment of gifts is coming out?" A reply in the affirmative soon brings a smile to their faces and we are again reminded of our friends far across the sea – the 3rd L.H. Comforts' Fund – then they arrive, are divided out, and a right royal feeling it is to insert the tin-opener into a new tin of *Australian* fruit. Perhaps a stunt is on tomorrow but suddenly everyone is in a good mood or, in other words, an army fights on its stomach and that's the way the women of Australia are making it very hard for Jacko in Egypt and the Hun in France.'

Some men were remembered by their civilian employers. Sergeant Stevens for instance, on the way out of Pozières, wrote: 'Received a surprise letter from Sargoods, London, to effect they have forwarded me on behalf of Melbourne house a parcel for Xmas and that they hold the sum of £5 for me – sent by Melbourne firm. It is very good of them.'

The activity amongst patriotic fund-raising and gifts-in-kind groups was feverish. The Ugly Men's Voluntary Workers Association (WA) raised £62,222 while the Whiteheads Creek Red Cross Society (Vic.) made 'a large number of articles for the boys' according to the local paper of this hamlet (the small town is no longer gazetted in 1978). In April 1915 the ladies' work is reported as follows: 'Mesdames Coulsen and Halpin 8 handkerchiefs each; Miss

Graham 1 balaclava cap; Misses Wall 17 pairs of socks; Mrs Wall 6 pairs of bootlaces; Miss O'Shea 1 scarf; Mrs Wales 6 pillow slips; Miss Roberts 3 shirts.'

Cholera belts were a favourite among the knitters, some turning out nine belts a month. Private Roy Rankin received a number of these and was provoked into saying to his mother, 'Tell Dulcie that it is very good of her to make me cholera belts but I have a couple already. But if they come I will be able to use these I have now as rifle covers. A pair of gloves or mittens would be useful as I lost what I had in the wreck.' Later, he writes to Dulcie telling her that the belt she sent is the 'best knitted belt I have seen but I do not think I will ever use one'.

In a scrap book of newspaper cuttings the total donations were underlined in ink by the Wall family: 'Walls, 58 pr. socks, Coulsons, 50 pr.' There were mittens, knee-caps, sand-bags, sea-kit bags, 'clean linen' and arm-stump socks. It was all very exciting, but as yet the casualty lists had not been posted up outside the newspaper offices, and the arm stumps had not yet appeared on the streets. One voluntary organisation that initiated (and maintain to this day) a beautiful monument to the men was the Lucas Girls.

These were staff members of the women's lingerie firm of E. Lucas and Co. of Ballarat (Vic.). Planting their first tree on 4 June 1917 and their last on 9 June 1919, 'The Lucas Girls' planted an avenue fourteen miles long containing 3 700 trees, 'a living monument to the 3 700 soldiers from the beautiful city of Ballarat who offered their services to the Empire for Active Service abroad'. 'The Girls', forming a committee, agreed to have a sum taken weekly from their wages to plant the trees and build an imposing 'Arch of Victory', and sixty years later the survivors met for the sixtieth year in succession to plan for the caring of the avenue for yet another twelve months.

The labour market was not affected for some, for others it was acute.

T. Millear, from Edgarley, a well-known sheep station in Victoria, wrote to the manager of Stud Park (NSW) on 16

October 1916: 'I suppose you will lose all your men of military age. All mine go this week and old James is only a make-shift and Wyatt is getting old but valuable all the same.' He mentions that the new man being sent to Stud Park was asking a wage 'higher than any manager has been getting'. 'This man seems active but is not young.' The Millear family had sent £500 to the Patriotic Fund on 20 August 1914 and, later, £1 000 to Matrons of Australian hospitals 'to treat nurses and patients'. As well, they donated 100 'Patriotic Rams' for sale in Brisbane and encouraged the agents, Dalgety and Co., to forego the commission on the sale.

It was the worst of times for the families who waited for news and yet one got a sense of industry and vigour, as though for others it was the best of times. Occasionally one suspects that the intense activity may have been more to allay boredom at home and that assistance to troops was fortuitous. On 28 December 1916, Lieutenant Athel Collum from Brisbane wrote to his chaplain: 'Letters came fairly plentifully from Australia at first but people soon seem to forget or get tired of writing to us.'

The effects of World War I on the civilian population of Australia were coming to light as late as 1976. In the *Warragul Gazette* (Vic.) on 20 july 1976, under the heading 'German Peer Featured in Our History', there was a report of a visit by the local Historical Society to the home 'previously occupied by the late Count Kellisch von Horn, one of Warragul's active civic leaders at the beginning of this century'. This gentleman had come as a migrant in 1895 to Buln Buln shire to avoid military training in Germany. He married a local girl and had children; although he was impoverished, he built up a solid reputation because of his hard labouring on farms in the area. When he later inherited the family title and income, he could afford to buy his own property and soon became prominent in civic affairs. With his fine horses, and later a chauffeur-driven car, he became a member of Warragul Shire Council (1907–15) and was Shire President (1910–11). He was president of the local agricultural society and of the West Gippsland Hospital and gave generously to all these and more societies.

Then came World War I. Count von Horn's income ceased, public feeling against Germans amounted to hysteria, and his services to the community were soon forgotten. Some councillors even urged that the furniture he donated should be burnt, and it is said that his photograph in the gallery of shire presidents was turned to the wall.

Abandoned by his one-time friends, he resigned from or lost his various public offices and left the district with his wife and family, never to return.

Now that sixty years have passed and passions have cooled, we can sympathise with an unfortunate man who certainly did not deserve the treatment meted out to him by those who had benefited from his generosity and his efforts for the betterment of the community.

(The following week this newspaper reported that von Horn had died at the onset of World War II. His family still operated the newspaper *Berliner Zeitung* in Germany, but the family title had lapsed when Hitler came to power.)

Across the land, German settlers were harassed. In South Australia the newspaper *Sud-Australische Zeitung*, which had been published since 1850 without a break, was prohibited under the War Precautions Act. In 1917 the House of Assembly resolved that the names of towns and districts of foreign origin should be altered. 'We want to remove all traces of the German element in South Australia,' said one member. Forty-two place names were changed: Blumberg became Birdwood; Bismarck – Kobandilla; Homberg – Haig, and so on. Other states followed the example. In New South Wales Germanton became Holbrook; German Creek – Empire Vale. In Victoria's Western District Hockirch became Tarrington; Germantown – Grovedale. Queensland exchanged Bergen for Murra Murra, Bismarck for McLagan; Tasmania changed Bismarck for Collinsvale, and in Western Australia Mueller Park became

Kitchener Park. During the war 6 890 'aliens' were interned. That some of these were decidedly hostile appears to be borne out by the fact that 5 276 were sent back to Germany at the end of the war in nine special ships during 1919 and 1920. By an amendment of the Immigration Act Germans, Austro-Germans, Bulgarians, Hungarians and Turks were prohibited for five years from entering Australia. The prohibition was lifted in 1925 for all except the Turks, and it was relaxed for them in 1930.

Under the War Precautions Act, 3 474 cases were prosecuted on 81 different charges ranging from 'wrongfully dying military overcoats' to 'Exhibiting disloyalty or hostility to the British Empire'. About 650 cases were prosecuted for 'Failing to register as an alien' and during the referendum on conscription a similar punishment was meted out to 150 cases for 'making statements prejudicial to recruiting' and an undisclosed number for 'tearing down recruiting posters'.

Lady Grace Weigall wrote to Mrs A. Bath from Government House Adelaide in 1920 and pointed out the extra hardship Australian women bore during the war. '. . . I am so glad that you have your son home safely. What a terrible time you must have gone through so far away – that to my mind is where you (Aust.) women suffered doubly here across all those miles of sea, whereas we women at home were able to see our beloved ones when they were invalided or home for a few days leave and my heart feels for all those who had to endure this suspense and agony of mind . . . these past five years.'

36
I Want To Go
Home

1918

Everyone had been away from home a long time. The horror was exacerbated by time and boredom. They wanted a change, like their song said:

I want to go home; I want to go home
I don't want to go to the trenches no more
Where whizzbangs and shrapnel they whistle and roar
Take me over the sea, where the alley-man can't get at me
Oh my! I don't want to die!
I want to go home.

But the war was not yet over. An attempt to break the stalemate was beginning, and Sister Kitchen confided in March 1918: 'The great offensive has started. God grant it may be a victory for us – though the casualties are bound to be awful on both sides. [Two days later.] The anxiety is great; we hear the British are retreating all the time. Whenever I wake in the night I wonder if we are still going back. How awful if we lost now and the road to Paris or the sea – open to the foe . . . A great anxiety overshadows us night and day . . . If only the line remains unbroken . . .'

Easter came with spring flowers – violets, forsythia and daffodils – and still the Germans had not achieved their aim, although in a week they had 'taken back . . . nearly all we have gained in 2 years – and are back beyond the Somme once more. Their casualties are said to be awful. We had stations [of the Cross] in Concert Hall. . . . We hear all the staff of a Casualty Clearing Station have been taken prisoners – sisters and all and still hear of dreadful casualties and further retreats . . . went to town on my own – first to Horseferry to enquire about Bob'.

The tired troops knew now that the ultimate was required of them. The text of Field Marshal Sir Douglas Haig's Order of the Day, 12 April 1918, was: 'Every position must be held to the last man; there shall be no retirement. With our backs to the wall, and believing in the justice of our cause, each one of us must fight on to the end.'

Sergeant Stevens, still trudging behind the infantry with his box of records, says: 'I suppose we always knew it would come to this.'

On 3 March 1918, 'at midday had a very narrow escape – a big shell landed 8 yards from me. It deafened me and covered me with earth but otherwise all correct'. (When the author met Mr Stevens in 1976 his deafness was still his only defect.)

By the twenty-fourth of that month this entry tells us several things that were in the forefront of the Australians' minds at that time. 'Receiving news from St Quentin way. Fritz made big offensive and I believe they are 6 miles behind Bullecourt now – and *what a cost to us was Bullecourt*! It is, I think, most unpromising. All leave is cancelled and men on leave recalled as well as all men and officers at schools of instruction are coming back to us. We shall be relieved here [Ypres] and be rushed down to the Somme – because we are Australians I suppose. Australians are put into every stunt that is going. Sir Douglas Haig has wired an order to every unit in the army to defeat the enemy's plans to crush the British Army. Fritz has put over about 50 divisions on one extensive front. Things are blacker than ever they were.'

They marched down through Armentières and Neuve Eglise, then were put in cattle trucks and taken further south by train. The train was bombarded on the way and hit, eighteen men being killed and eight wounded and eight horses killed. 'All dead men blown beyond recognition.' They marched twelve miles to the outskirts of Albert. 'It seems as if the Tommies are getting away as quickly as they can – in most cases leaving Fritz to collect their guns. Things are, indeed, very bad. All people here have vacated their homes. I am now in a little bedroom which is furnished as all such, with women's clothing hanging on the racks – they got away hurriedly. Feeling tired for I have had only 4 hours sleep in the past 3 days. Just received word from Brigade that Battalion is to move off in one hour for Corbie. Very hungry on track, nothing to eat. Marched through all the places where we rested in June and July last year. Finished our journey at 5 a.m. To my disgust I learnt that one of my boxes had been left behind so tired and all as I was I had to jump on a bicycle and ride back.' On his return he had to work on without sleep. 'Now 4 hours sleep in 84 hours.' There was one consolation. 'Roast fowls for tea. Fowls, geese, fish, wine, calves, etc. are now being eaten by the boys.

'*4 April 1918*. Fritz has driven the Tommies (Oxford and Bucks.) out of the line. Tommies retiring. Where possible they are intercepted by our officers and ordered back to the line. Fritz is reported to be coming over in large numbers. *5 April*: Tommies leaving lines in large numbers. Most of them grabbed and put on fatigue work for us.'

Eddie Johnson said about all this: 'On 11th April we left Bertangles at about 4 p.m. and marched to Amiens Station. While boarding the train, Fritz got 3 direct hits on the Station, killing and wounding some Australians. At daybreak the following day, we detrained at Hondeghen, Belgium. Part of the 1st Division had been here only a few days previously, and had many friends among the farm people and villagers. The enemy were steadily pressing onward, and as our troops advanced to relieve the tired British Infantry, which was holding against enormous odds, we passed many unfortunate civilians leaving their homes in terror, carrying such things as they could in their hands or in wheelbarrows. Their spirits were brightened when they saw that the Australians had arrived back. When it was known that the Germans had captured Merris and

Vieux Berquin, this meant the Australians had no front line, so we picked our own line of defence and waited for the Germans.

'Meanwhile we, the Sigs, began laying cables and maintaining them under the fire that only the men who were there could know. That day we arrived back at 2 a.m. after laying more lines. We must have walked approx 18 miles, so had a rest on a hay stack at one stage. When the 3rd Infantry Bde hopped over near Meteren, shells and bombs arrived fairly heavily, and when out mending breaks, a Fritz plane came along low and had an unsuccessful pop at us with his machine gun.

'We laid line to 1st Machine Gun Coy, approx 3 400 yds long. We found on returning that there was no room in the dug-outs, so we Sigs camped in a small house close by. Thus Cpl Hill (NSW), Tom Gorringe (Tas.), Monty Newcombe (SA), and I had a home of our home. We found a clock still working, a stove and also a little fox terrier and a pet rabbit. We were constantly out mending breaks in the lines.

'On one occasion a piece of hot shell sunk into the ground 18 inches in front of my left leg – another step and I would have copped it. However a piece of shell caught Monty and he evacuated to a dressing station. Following that misfortune Tom and I were coming back from mending lines, when a piece of shell shoulder high whizzed between us. Although we were only a few paces apart, it was a clean miss. Our Bde was relieved on 10 May. We had been on line work from April 13th. It was pretty solid during night time.

It was indeed, as Sergeant Stevens said earlier, the blackest time. 'Today got news Fritz has attacked and taken all the places we held when we first came to France 22 months ago – and now they are lost again. Something drastic will have to be done and done quickly.'

On 25 March the Press correspondents at their Headquarters in bomb-concussed Amiens had written in their communiques that they believed there was no British division between them and the Germans twenty-eight miles away. The people of Picardy, wily readers of the future, began to leave their homes. A big gun was firing shells into Paris from only seventy miles distant. The Australians, knowing the area and the people, were anxious to come south where they believed they could see a way this time to beat the Germans.

When they arrived by lorry, dusty and cheerful, the country people recognised them and began to unload their carts. '*Pas nécessaire maintenant*,' they answered the Australians who asked why. '*Vous les tiendrez.*' ('Not necessary now – you'll hold them.')

The reverse was said, over and over again by the retiring English troops: 'You'll never hold them.' The Australians realised that they were the only troops heading towards the enemy. 'You're going the wrong way, Digger,' shouted a British soldier, 'Jerry'll souvenir you and your bloody band.'

Some Australian leaders worried lest the remarks and the depressing sights of retreat would affect the men but they need not have been concerned. The Australians were confident. This, they believed, was what they had come so far to do, to beat the Germans. 'They were the first stubborn, cheerful people we had met in the retreat,' a British artillery officer told the Official War Correspondent, C. E. W. Bean.

'Fritz will assuredly make another drive for Amiens,' Sergeant Stevens wrote in April 1918, 'but he will meet a stone wall against the Australians.' That was no idle boast. On Anzac Day 1918, the young sergeant was bombed out of his bed at 3 a.m. but he had had 'a few good hours sleep' and well he needed it. '15th Brigade counter-attacked during night and regained the old line the Tommies had lost. Villers-Bretonneux was encircled and Germans in the village cut off.' He goes to within 200 yards of the village looking for Headquarters but couldn't find it. 'Lots of blown-out bodies lying around, mostly animals, gives the place the appearance of a very old battleground.

'*27 April*: Villers-Bretonneux is on top of a ridge which commands the country to Amiens. Our casualties for the past few days are 70, a good many are gas cases. Other battalions of our Brigade having many more casualties than us. All Brigade receiving high praise. Yesterday whilst on the march had another look at Amiens – from a distance. That grand old cathedral still stands out as a great landmark. Villers-Bretonneux commands all the country to and beyond Amiens.' They stood, this antipodean stone-wall, between Picardy and the advancing German army but in their opinion the war was not yet nearly won.

Battles repeated themselves, casualties 'occurred' and were entered in Battalion records, reinforcements arrived – or didn't arrive – and the remnants of battalions went yet again into battle. There were few deviations from what came to be routine, but one entry differs from the others: '*27 June*: Today a message was received from higher authorities that 3 British prisoners behind German lines had escaped and were expected to reach our lines tonight. The information was supplied by Frenchmen who had also escaped and arrived ahead of our boys. At about 8 p.m. the 3 reached our front line safely and they came and slept in my cellar. They had escaped 3 nights ago near Peronne and had been travelling through the night and sleeping by day. They'd had a very good passage through hardly being molested – more by luck than management. They looked awfully weary and haggard and told frightful tales of treatment, one was an Australian, the other 2 Londoners.'

When the tide turned Stevens was jubilant. 'Fritz has been getting a bad time lately especially on the Marne where the French, British and American troops have done a wonderful counter attack – captured 20 000 prisoners and 400 guns and advanced 8 miles on a front of 7 miles.'

Eddie Johnson had been gassed again and he spent some time in a convalescent camp at Le Havre before returning on 10 July and rejoining No 5 section. 'The Peaceful Penetration, which was pinching German prisoners from their front line day and night, for information – this being done by our front line troops, from April 14th to July 31st, on the Hazebrouck front – used to amuse the commander of the 2nd Army, Gen. Sir Hubert Plumer. On his visits to the 1st Division he would ask "What's this your fellows have been doing?" and would depart without comment . . . his shoulders shaking with suppressed chuckles.

'On August 4th the old chief addressed the 1st Aust. Division: "You are leaving my army. I am sorry that I cannot inform you where you are going or what you are going to do. I am sorry to lose you, but I wish you success. You know, gentlemen, that it is not my practice to make eulogistic speeches – there will be plenty of time for that after the war. At the same time I would like to tell you that there is no division, certainly in my army, perhaps in the whole British Army, which has done more to destroy the morale of the enemy, than the 1st Australian Division".'

Sergeant Stevens had more information, however, for in his diary of 3 August he says: 'I learned a secret today. We leave on Sunday night – secretly – early next week we attack along the whole of the Somme Front, there will be 5 Aust. Divisions, 5 Canadian (already moved secretly into this area), and a couple each of British and American and 10 French divisions. Thirty of our battalion went away today. They are going to be taken behind the German lines in Tanks during the attack and they will establish machine-gun posts.'

It was the attack of 8 August. 'Germany's Black Day', General Ludendorff wrote in his *War Memories*, 'The war must be ended'.

37
Never Forget
Australia

On 8 August 1918, three years after the battle of Lone Pine, the Australians attacked along a front that gained for them the love of a whole town – Villers-Bretonneux.

Having by now overcome their distrust of tanks, they excitedly moved up to assembly points to pass the big black mass of tank upon tank that would assist them.

For the first time, the five divisions of the Australian Army were going into battle together. Beside them were the Canadians. They were jubilant. The thick mist was worrying – they could not see twenty yards in any direction – but not enough to depress them. Each battalion moved to its tape and lay down, the men wet, cold, but elated. The 57th Battalion, afraid of losing its way, suddenly saw lights ahead – they were candles in petrol tins with holes punctured to form the numbers 57 to direct them.

It was to be a massive onslaught. Men were digging trenches, planes were trying to penetrate the fog, but no man had any conception of the immensity until, at 8 a.m., 'the mist lifted like a curtain, gradually disclosing a scene that will never be forgotten by any who saw it. The Somme valley came into view, the gentle sunlight, still tempered by the haze, bathing the wheat-covered spurs of the south. It was to these spurs and the plateau to which they rose that all eyes now turned. Across the summit of the Villers-Bretonneux plateau, until lost to sight, were scattered parties of Australian infantry, some still digging, others looking out from their new-dug trenches, others strolling or standing between the groups in the easy attitude by which

Australians were recognisable on all their battlefields since the first sunrise at Anzac. Behind them was every arm of the Fourth Army's offensive in motion. First were the infantry of the 4th and 5th Divisions. Beside them, or sometimes still filing across country from the nearest road, like elephants accompanying an Oriental army, were processions of tanks, sixty in all, many having their infantry colours painted on their sides or on plaques hung by chains from their fronts. Farther back in the gully about forty other tanks were assembling to follow and assist. Behind these, chiefly crowded along the road in the valley and the Roman road along the plateau, came battery after battery of field and horse artillery, chains jingling, horses' heads and manes tossing. Partly with these, and partly in streams across the open, rolled the ammunition and water-wagons. Parties of pioneers and engineers, who had pushed out along the roads as soon as the advance started, were still at work upon them, and others were making trench-crossings for the artillery. At 7.40 a.m. the first of sixteen armoured cars entered and tanks towed them over the hurriedly cleared debris. Behind them came motor lorries and even touring cars. On either side of that village the entire 5th Division was ranged in deep artillery formation. In the rear stood the whole 1st Brigade of cavalry in mass, with about a hundred tanks, mostly whippets, for the final phase. A great shout went up as some of the field batteries, allotted to help the foremost troops arrived at a gallop and in a few minutes their guns were banging, to the delight of the troops. In the opposite direction moved a few lame tanks and, along the roads, droves of prisoners moved wide-eyed through the throng, astonishment evident in their faces. The attacking troops were in grand spirits, the casualties were obviously few, the prisoners in thousands, and in most parts hardly a German shell had fallen since the attack. 'You won't see him, 15th, you won't catch him,' said men of the 42nd Battalion to those of the 15th who were now to pass through.

Not only British observers held their breath as the

pageant unfolded. As many of their historians tell, Germans on the hills north of the river and elsewhere gazed for a moment in wonder, as the receding haze disclosed this panorama. This was the sight that the French and British – and among them the Australians – had steadily looked for through four years of unbelievable trials.

To describe a battle clearly it must be done in detail and in comparison with other battles. For Villers-Bretonneux it is sufficient to listen to what the French had to say of the Australians' part in saving France.

On 7 November 1920, when interring the bodies of a French and an Australian unknown soldier in the cathedral at Amiens, the French Bishop said, 'We bow to you *messieurs les Australiens* for the magnificent deeds you did . . . In the whole of history we cannot find an army more marvellous in its bravery, and in the war there was none that contributed more nobly to the final triumph.'

Marshal Foch said, '. . . the passionate valour of the Australians served as an example to the whole world. That wonderful attack of yours at Villers-Bretonneux was the final proof, if any were needed, that the real task of the high command was to show itself equal to its soldiers. You saved Amiens, you saved France. Our gratitude will remain ever and always to Australia'.

At Villers-Bretonneux is the grave of Jack Pockley (Lieutenant John Antill Pockley) of the 33rd Battalion, the brother of that Pockley who was the second death in the Australian forces at Rabaul on 11 September 1914, a month after war had been declared.

Now, in the final year of the 'hate', the second Pockley was killed, and the letters home had somewhat similar news of the last day of each. The Dr Pockley killed in the Pacific had 'given his Red Cross arm band to a soldier taking a wounded man back to the beach thus removing his own protection', and of his brother Jack a fellow officer wrote home, 'When the stretcher bearers got to him he begged them to take another chap who was worse off than him, so he believed, but when they got back for Jack he had died of exhaustion'.

No man was safe but some were in units that were less safe than others. Signalmen out running lines or repairing breaks led a charmed life and their stories would 'fill a library' as red-headed Sapper Harry Dadswell said. In battle zones their lines were merely laid on the ground, to be used with portable telephones. Before an attack they must lay lines across No Man's Land. Their lines were forever being cut by enemy (and their own) fire.

'I was out on lines to the 53rd and then the 55th Bns. Things were pretty willing and the shelling heavy with a lot of gas mixed in. Humphries was killed and Young, Blackburn and Stone gassed and sent out. During the day the infantry threw a line along Fritz's flank on the side of Villers-Bret. and held him there. They gathered all the English Tommies they could and mixed them with our men. They fought well and many of our chaps said they were splendid soldiers, only needed leading. Some who had a poor opinion of the Tommies changed their opinions that day. One chap, typical of the Aussies, said: "I never had any time for the Tommies, reckoned they were hardly worth their tucker, but I'll take my hat off to those chaps".

(Harry Kahn believes 'the Tommy could take it. He could hang on. He may not have had the initiative the colonial troops had. We always believed we were the best and the New Zealanders second best and there were times when I privately reversed that order but I didn't say so publicly'. Sergeant Kahn was at Pozières, Ypres and the Hindenburg Line.)

'Brig. "Pompey" Elliot of the 15th Bde. organised the counter attack. His brigade went through our boys on the left side of Villers-Bret. and the 13th Bde. came in from the right side and retook the town early next morning. They restored the line and really saved the whole front, for if Fritz had taken Amiens he would have split the French and British armies and caused chaos. The morning of Fritz's attack I did what I like to think of as the best job I ever did, saving the lives of our 53rd boys. Sgt. Sheppard and I ran the line to the 54th and then as we reached their headquarters saw some shells fall on it, a fair way back. Next thing *our own* guns opened on the 53rd in some terraces about three hundred yards away. Some plane had given the wrong map location of some Germans. You could see the battery about a mile back on a flat plain. Men rushed the phone but the 54th line was broken. Shep said, "We have to get to the artillery and stop them quick. Will we go back on the 54th line?" I thought of those shells on the other side of the lagoon and knew it would take nearly ten minutes to get there. The 53rd line was shorter but ran right under the shell fire. I said, "Come on," and raced for it with Shep pounding behind.

'I got the line and shells screamed just above our heads. Bent nearly double we raced flat out. We could see the guns flash and would crouch a little lower and the shell would go past within feet of us. Shep said, "I hope they don't take us for Germans, or we haven't got a dogs chance". You could feel the hot air as the shells whistled past. Then I saw the break and grabbed both ends of the line and started to mend it. Shep had the phone and he teed in and called Brigade. When they answered he said, "Give me the artillery quick". The next second came a voice, "Artillery here", and Shep said, "For Gods sake stop shooting, you are firing on our own men". In what seemed only a second or two the last shells went over and there was silence. Then came, "Who is speaking, what authority have you for stopping the guns?" "Linesmen here, if you will hang on a moment we will have the line mended and you can speak to an officer," said Shep. I had the line mended quickly and then we went back to the 53rd. Five men were dead and seven wounded and the guns had just lowered their range. At first the shells were hitting the top of the bank and they just lowered the range so the shells went right into the dug-outs. There would have been slaughter if those guns hadn't been stopped. . . .

'My brother was badly wounded in that attack on Fritz. On the 26th I got orders to go forward to the 53rd Bn. While getting my gear and line ready at the rear of the chateau, a limber with our rations on pulled up in front and some men went to unload it. Down came a heavy shell killing both the horses and badly wounding the driver and Darkie, one of the sentries, and wounding three others slightly. I had happened to walk inside and Blue Mortlake one of our cooks who had been hit said, "Eh, you fellows, there are wounded men outside. Aren't you going to help them?" I rushed out and the first one I came to was Darkie. "The . . . all ran away and left us Blue." I glanced at the driver but his back was towards me. "Hang on Darkie," I said, "I'll get a stretcher and help," and raced back. I grabbed a stretcher and called, "Get another some of you chaps, Quick". One chap had his head out of the door, too frightened to go out. I just dropped the stretcher like a bayonet and lunged and he went out. I went to Darkie and with another chap, lifted him on the stretcher. We got his shoulders on and as both his legs were broken I gently worked a hand under his back, when he said, "Go easy Blue, there is a hole in me there". I managed to get most of him on and then said, "Hang tight Darkie, I've got to lift your legs". I did, with one quick movement and Darkie groaned. I was nearly crying. Darkie was a good mate and one I thought a lot of. Some others picked up the driver, but I didn't look, I'd had enough . . . They later told me the driver was Charlie Payne, a chap who went into Royal Park [Melbourne] the same day as I did. We had kept in touch with one another and as many of the old Royal Park mob as we could. They gradually had dwindled and a fortnight before Charlie had told me, he and I were the only ones he could find and believed we were the last of our first unit, not wounded or killed. To be so close to him, hit and dying and not recognise him was pretty tough. He and Darkie died that night, but I had gone up to the 53rd and relieved Weir [his best mate]. Of our old linesmen, only Cpl Browne, Weir and myself were left. Sgt Sheppard was given the M.M. He had richly earnt it and was given a commission and left us. . . . Another couple of our boys who were extra good were Reg Tannebring and Jim Davis. A few days later I was going along a line when, from a group of infantry, one called "How are your mates Blue?" I said, "Which ones?" "The tall thin boy and the fat one." "Oh," I said, "That's Reg and Jim. Sorry, but both are dead." They weren't surprised. "We wouldn't have stayed out working under the shell fire those boys did." That was pretty high praise from the infantry . . . While in those terraces we were watching Fritz shell the road and a strip of ground beside the billabongs. Suddenly along the road came an ambulance needed to pick up some wounded men in the battalion. It drove in under shells. We just looked on, helpless to do any thing. Shells fell short or went over it, burst in front and behind. How we admired the coolness of the driver. He didn't alter his speed, just a steady pace. They seemed to have a charmed life and to our amazement went steadily on. They reached a point with only a hundred yards to go to be out of the shelling when a shell landed on the bonnet of the car. It jerked and then rolled to the side of the road. Two men nearest raced down but both ambulance men were dead . . .

'Back at H.Q., on May 27th Fritz opened up at 3 a.m. He made things pretty lively with H.E. (High explosive) and gas shells. Sgt. McAllister and Drake were sleeping in an upstairs bedroom in a house, a gas shell came through the roof. McAllister reeled into our place, choking with gas and unable to talk. He just gurgled and pointed and we thought Drake was still in the room, so Jack Dawes and I raced in without our helmets. We got a mouthful of gas, shot down the stairs and put our helmets on and went back up again, but Drake had got out. The gas was phosgene and we were all sick, choking, when the Q.M. arrived with rum. We swallowed some and the fumes of rum and gas made us horribly sick and we vomited most of the gas out. After a couple of hours we only had a bad headache and didn't have to go out of action. Rum is the best cure for phosgene gas, but no good for other kinds.

'On May 31st we were relieved by the 4th Bde. and came out. We had been in action since April 5th and were tired and nervy, not the soldiers we had been . . .

'We went back into the front line about the time that Fritz started using ground shrapnel. The shell would hit the ground and not make a hole more than six inches deep and pieces of shell would go in all directions, sometimes plowing the ground a couple of inches deep or even just skimming it. How I dreaded those shells. If a shell was H.E. and one stood up, he stood a fair chance of being hit, but if he threw himself down and the shell was a ground shrapnel, he could be torn to pieces. One couldn't tell which it was till it burst. One could always pick a gas shell by the sound . . .

'The 53rd Bn. had a raid that went wrong, 33 men went over and 17 were killed and the other 16 wounded. They had a Dutch chap with them and he was always a moaning type and that day he had disappeared. They were pretty sure afterwards that he deserted to the Germans and gave them the plan of the raid . . . That night [22 July] our Lieut rang up. He said, "Would you like to go to the seaside? . . . Two men are to go . . . from our lot and you and Weir can go if you wish."

'We left as soon as our relief arrived, and travelled to near Le Tréport, a great holiday resort in peace time and we had ten absolutely free days down there, camped near Mer Les Bains. . . . 6th August we started back to our lines.

'As we got closer we saw large numbers of American and Canadian troops moving up to the line, so we knew something was doing. On the 8th a big battle started. Wounded started going through and reported our boys were doing well. More wounded coming in and wonderful reports. Instead of the 1 000 yard stunts of Doug Haig the boys had gone miles. Later wounded reported that they had gone 10 miles and were still advancing. Chaps who had said, "They could shoot me before I'd go in again," got excited. "Biggest battle of the war and we missed it!" . . .

'We got our gear . . . caught a rattler . . . and next morning we came past advance division through Villers-Bret. and then on to Warfusee, then we were back with our own Bde. again. Our new officer Lieut H. greeted us, "You chaps get your gear off. The boys are nearly run off their feet." We were back on the job . . .

'We had to take the line across a lagoon. All the top of the bridge had been removed and only the piers left. A single plank went from one to the next and so on to the other side. It was the only place one could cross for over a mile either way. Then when we finished H. left me on Brigade side of the bridge, to maintain the line from there to the battalion . . . six [other] men were left in pairs further back where there was unlikely to be any shelling. My mate Weir was taken back to get rations and gear. Early next morning, Sunday 1st September, a heavy barrage started on our sector. The line went almost straight away and I moved over the planks and mended it. Our boys attacked and I went out again. Fritz knew that was the only point men could cross and put a heavy barrage on the rise in front of it. I had a very rough time, I would mend a break and move to another, only to have the line broken behind me. I put in over an hour under that barrage. . . . as fast as I mended a break, the line would be broken behind or ahead of me and sometimes both at once. Suddenly out of the dust and smoke came my mate, "Ack" Weir, racing along and swearing like a trouper. It was the only time I ever heard Ack swear but leaving his mate in a position like that on his own was too much for Ack. Shortly after he arrived the shelling stopped and we got the line working and we went up to the 53rd. From one chap came a voice, "Hey Blue, what will you take for your good job this morning?" Then another, "I bet you will sell out cheap Blue." I said, "You take this phone and I'll take your rifle." One chap said, "You keep it. I wouldn't have it for ten thousand." We went on and started crossing the planks. There were still a few shells falling in the lagoon. I was rather nervous walking those planks, for if a man fell in the concussion would cripple him and he couldn't swim out. I was about halfway across when there was a roar. I squatted and gripped the plank with both hands. The shell was so close one could feel the hot wind as it went past and the next moment up came a column of water so close I could have touched it, and feet above me. I took one glance and forgot to be frightened and sprinted across those planks. Weir and I raced down the causeway only 10 feet wide. Shells landed among some infantry near the end of it and there were calls for stretcher bearers. We raced on and near a bank was a break in the wire. Weir gathered the ends, but I yelled, "Come on!" Weir called, "Come and mend this!" I just raved at him till he followed me to a shelter in the bank. A few shells burst then all was quiet. "Come on," he said. "Right oh," I replied and started back. "What ever is wrong with you?" a puzzled Weir asked. I'm quite sure he thought I'd gone mad. "Nothing now, everything is alright," and we reached the spot where Weir had pulled the lines together. There was a fresh shell hole. Ack stopped and looked at it and said, "You must have known something." "I knew we had to get away from there, and fast," I answered. Some instinct had warned me to leave. . . .

'I did another trip on the lines and things quietened down. Then I collapsed. . . . I lay down and just shook all over and had no control over my limbs at all. Weir carried on through the night and when I was much the same the next morning, he rang H.Q. and asked them to recall me. So I went back . . .

'Our infantry had been relieved by the 8th Brigade. Of 1 400 men who moved in two days before, only 200 were left. We were relieved and came to a reserve position; Fritz bombed every night. Many large fires were burning behind Fritz's lines as he destroyed stores. On September 5th we went to Hargicourt and saw our guns put a lovely creeping barrage on the side of a hill. A line of shells burst near the foot of the hill and then crept forward. A solid barrage of shells creeping ever up the hill, with the infantry following about 80 yards behind. Few Fritz could escape that lot and I didn't see any infantry hit. In the evening we were out laying lines. General Monash had charge of the advance and he drove us hard. Still, it was very successful and we were going forward all the time. In the morning Ack Weir and I moved forward laying lines to a report station. A large squad of Fritz planes were over, firing at anything with their machine guns. Later we moved forward and lay lines to a new position 6 kilos in front of Peronne. Next day we lay a line 4 000 yards to a new forward position and later took another 3 000 yards to the 55th Bn. This continual advance kept the linesmen very busy. . . . On the 29th there was a heavy barrage and the Americans attacked. They were still pretty new to the game. We marched through Templeux to a new position. . . . We moved forward at 4 a.m. and came through Hargicourt. Our brigade started moving up to the Yanks, who seemed to be in trouble. We came under machine-gun fire. The Yanks had rushed forward and left about 3 000 Germans in a long tunnel and after the Yanks got ahead, they came out and had the Yanks between two lots of them. We had run into these Germans where we didn't expect any, and there was a fair number of casualties. We couldn't use artillery at first, for we didn't know where the Yanks were, and Fritz took advantage of the confusion. The infantry gradually got a grip of the situation and cleaned the Germans up and joined the Yanks in front of Bellicourt [Bullecourt]. We lay lines to Bellicourt. The fighting was pretty vicious.

'We had several jobs of laying lines or mending them. I was still very nervy and jumpy from Peronne and darn afraid I may crack up altogether. On Oct. 1st our Brigade attacked again and cleaned up a lot of Huns. A Yank we spoke to, reckoned they were wonderful. We were kept busy on the lines. On the 2nd a chap came along and told us there was a corpse factory half a mile away. Harry Carroll said, "You're a liar. I've lived with Germans in South Australia and they are human beings like us and wouldn't do it." "Alright," said the chap. "Go and see for yourself." Weir was in charge, so he said, "Take charge Dads, Harry and I will go and if there is anything to see, you others can go later." When they returned I said to Harry, "Well, what is it?" He said, "My eyes tell me it is one, but my intelligence won't let me believe it." With another chap I went and we had no doubt. We came out pretty sick. There were two places. According to the chaps, one had been a cook-house and part of the wall had been blown in. They were certain it was nothing else, but the men who went to the one I did, found it intact and they had no doubt of its purpose. It was a horrible sight."*

The boy from the Skilly Hills, Eddie Johnson, arrived at Villers-Bretonneux late at night on 8 August. 'We found General Monash was in command of the five Australian Divisions, and the battle of Aug 8th had gone in accordance with his plan. The 2nd and 3rd Divisions reached their first objective while the fog still hung low. A second advance by the 4th and 5th Divisions threw back the German Line about 8 miles. The 1st Division was thrown in to continue the attack after an advance by the 5th Division. . . .

'Cpl Barnard and I looked after lines to 2nd Bde . . . Next day 2nd Bde was moving, so Cpl Barnard and I reeled up our cable and left for Corbie. After reveille we left Corbie at 7 a.m. for Morcourt to get 12 kilos of cable. We put it on a limber and the limber attracted barrage from Fritz and so we wasted no time returning. We disappeared down a dug-out. On returning to the top of the dug-out, we found that Fritz had landed a shell and banged up 8 kilos of the cable just brought in.

'Unknown to us, we were very close to the front line. After laying a line to 3rd Machine Gun Coy, it was learned at 2 a.m. that a limber was down the road with more cable. The driver had refused to come on, so we tramped to the limber and brought the cable to our dug-out. Before going forward to reel out the cable, Cpl ordered the two of us to move without speaking or making any noise, as we would

---

* While researching material for the book in this area, I was taken to a line of concrete pill-boxes in which the Germans had stacked the corpses of their comrades to the ceiling and had sealed the entrances. At the gateway to the mausoleum the explanation – in German and English – reads that this was done for fear of disease spreading from the dead when there was no time for conventional interment. One such pill-box may well have appeared to the Australian soldiers to be 'a corpse factory'.

be with the infantry before they hopped over – we would follow 10 minutes afterwards with the cable. There was a road raised about 9 feet above the level of the ground, with Fritz on one side and the Aussies on the other, and only the width of the road separated us. At zero hour our infantry appeared to light cigarettes before going over the top with their pockets full of hand grenades. While Cpl used the compass for direction, Davis and I followed with the cable 10 minutes after the infantry. Naturally we saw the results of war. All objectives were gained . . .

'Our infantry were still advancing and it was necessary to pack up and move forward. . . . Sept. 18 there was a light rain when our barrage commenced at 5.20 a.m. At 6.30 a.m., the infantry advanced. We followed 10 minutes later with the cable, Cpl Hill using the compass for direction. When stopping for a short break, to let our Infantry get further ahead, it was easy to witness a good view of the battle. On the left the 74th Division (Tommies) were having a tough stunt; one could see the steel glistening; while on the right, underneath a lone tree, was an elderly civilian, leaning on a long stick, motionless. Fritz had retreated, but he had held his position, while our boys had advanced.

'Booby traps were noticed on the way. Later, Field Engineers found quite a number on land just captured. The dug-out we intended to use for a test strip had a bunch of half-dead flowers in a vase on a table. Cpl Hill told us to get out, and he reported it to Lieut. Hetherington in charge of Field Engineers, who found it mined, ready to go off when the flowers were pulled out. Looking down at the land in front, one could easily see the long waves of dark wire in front of the Hindenburg Line.

'Everyone was thrilled – I guess so was General Monash – his plan had been carried out all along the Australian frontier. During this stunt our Battalions had been only at half strength, but had been amazingly effective. Unknown to us, it was to be our last stunt in the line.

'Having been relieved by other Signallers, the two of us headed back to Tincourt, H.Q. and received the delightful news that the 1st Division was going out for a spell, and would be relieved by the Americans. The Americans were easy-going chaps, and this helped to make a very good relationship with them. . . . When saying farewell to one he told me that before leaving the States their Officer had reminded them 'If you can do half as good as little Australia you will do'.

38
The Mutinies

Mutiny was one of the only two offences punishable in the AIF by death (the other was desertion to the enemy) but although almost the entire complement of seven battalions 'mutinied' in the strict sense of the term, no man was put to death.

As the second half of 1918 saw longer spells in the trenches and consistently high casualty rates, the men began to murmur. They had been four years away from their homeland and the impression was growing in them that, because they were so successful, the British Command was using them more persistently than its own troops and for tasks which the British were unable fully to perform. Numbers were declining fast.

Battalions were going into some of these fights 150 strong; one man wrote, '300 or 350 seems to be a big number in the fighting line nowadays. They are not as done as they were after Pozieres, but they certainly are feeling that "there won't be any dominion army left soon"'. Another man stated, 'There'll be no more AIF before long'.

It was reported that Monash had said that 'six days rest and a hot bath restores the elasticity of a division. The troops are not tired, only a little footsore'. Monash wrote in *Australian Victories* that the men should be called upon to 'yield up the last particle of effort of which they are capable . . . I was compelled to disregard the evident signs of over-strain which were brought to my notice'.

The General may have felt safe in acting as he did, but regimental officers were aware that conditions were approaching such an impasse that if errors were made again in ordering a prolonged effort the burden might precipitate a mutiny. Already several battalions had noted rumblings.

By 9 July 1918 Sergeant Stevens of the 58th Battalion recorded: 'There is a good deal of dissension at present in the Brigade, owing to long period in the line and hard time being experienced. I too, feel very dissatisfied.' On 3 September he writes: 'Our strength is now very low' and three days later, 'We move on forward tomorrow. All the boys full up and done up. Hope they do not refuse to go forward as 59th did yesterday'.

This was the first recorded mutiny in the AIF. The 59th Battalion did eventually go forward and after a week of heavy strain and non-stop efforts was relieved on 14 September only to be hurriedly recalled and ordered back into battle. This time they refused and were not to be persuaded, believing this to be the only way they could impress their exhaustion upon the authorities at Base.

Through lack of reinforcements – or enlistments – the Australian infantry was dangerously depleted. The fifty-seven Australian battalions were 8 500 men short and the drafts for the next four months promised only 3 000 men, scarcely enough to keep up the strength of battalions.

By 18 September the 1st Battalion refused the order to return to the line immediately after being relieved. The men resented it and said they were not getting a fair deal and 'were being put in to do other people's work'.

The official history states: 'There was widespread feeling that British troops had repeatedly failed to keep up, and that the Australians, as well as fighting on their own front, were sometimes called on to make good their neighbours' failure.' When the 1st Battalion went forward 119 men were absent, or, in other words, had mutinied. One officer was relieved of his command for siding with his troops.

At this time another action was ordered which doubled the dissension. Because of the decimation of the battalions by casualties, it was ordered that those battalions worst hit would combine one with another and so make their numbers up to full strength. This would of course mean that some battalions that had been in the front line since 1915 would now be swallowed up and lose their identity, the one over-riding thing that had kept the men going.

The 37th Battalion set the pattern for the run of mutinies that now followed. They agreed to attend the final parade and obey all orders except the last one: the order to march to their new battalion (and so disband their regiment). On 22 September they were assembled and, on refusing to march to the new battalion, were informed that they would be considered to be absent-without-leave. (The officers and sergeants had 'reluctantly' fallen out, to ensure retention of their rank.) The men then set to work to establish a strict military routine in the battalion, chose their own commanders to carry on in their officers' absence and maintain discipline. One after the other, battalions selected to disband took the same action.

Sapper Harry Dadswell recorded the story of the 54th Battalion.

'There had been so many casualties over the past few months that there simply weren't enough men to keep four battalions to a brigade, so it was decided to make only three battalions. The officers tried to break up the 54th Bn. and put the men into the other battalions. The men of the 54th objected and the rest backed them up. While the men were on parade, all travelling cookhouses were taken away and no rations were issued. All other units halved their rations and sent half to the 54th. All officers were withdrawn, so the men elected officers from the ranks and discipline was very strict under them. Then the men were drawn up on parade, with many of us from the rest of the unit looking on. The Brigadiers of the 15th and 8th Brigades addressed the men. The men told them to go home to their own men. Brig. Tivey told them military police and guns would be used on them, if they didn't obey orders. The rest of the boys chipped in and told Tivey, if any force was used on the 54th, the whole brigade would attack them. Tivey was only getting the men worked up and things could have got out of hand, when our Brig. stepped in. "This is enough men. You are on parade and under orders," he said. "Give me the roll." Someone handed it to him. He took it and called a man's name.

'"Pte. —— you report to such a battalion."

'"I refuse Sir," said the man.

'"Put that man under arrest," the Brig. said.

'"Pte. —— you report to a Battalion."

'"I refuse Sir."

'"Put that man under arrest."

'The third chap called was an older man. "Pte. —— you report to a Battalion."

'"Brig. how long can a man be away before you arrest him?" the old man said. "I didn't hear you, and I'm going A.W.L." He walked out of the ranks and the next chap looked at him and then said, "So am I Brig." The rest woke up and called, "We are all A.W.L.!" and just walked off and left the Brigadier standing helpless. This went on for two days. Then they decided to join the 54th and 56th Bns into one and each lot to keep their own colours. That was alright.'

The resisting battalions informed their General that they wished to go into the next battle; the 25th Battalion said they wished to be given the hardest task in the great attack they knew to be impending but they demanded to be allowed go in with their identity unchanged. After such a task, they vowed, 'there would either be no 25th left to break up, or they would leave such a record as would make it impossible to break them up'.

'Like Colonel [said those of the 25th to Colonel Davis] the 25th from the first has been built on *esprit de corps*. We have been taught that the regiment is everything. You have often told us that we must sacrifice everything for its honour. We have always obeyed you and we always will – in everything but what you now ask. We cannot obey you in this just for that reason – we would sacrifice everything for the battalion.'

It was a situation riddled with dangers. The Australian populace, who had been encouraged as well as the troops to identify with a battalion and its 'colours', would have without doubt mutinied in some form on the already troubled 'home-front' if the men were imprisoned or, for that matter, if the old, battle-stained battalions were disbanded against the survivors' wishes. The Australian Government had already said this must not be done. Field-Marshal Sir Douglas Haig, who had at first insisted on the re-organisation, was now prevailed upon to defer the disbandment until after the coming attack. The battalion history of the 21st Battalion records that the news 'was received with deafening cheers'.

The 119 men of the 1st Battalion were in a different category. To have charged them with mutiny, the punishment for which was death, would have brought not only the AIF but the Australian people and Government out in opposition, so they were charged with desertion. (The penalty was remitted six weeks later when the war ended.)

The 'mutinies over disbandment', as they were called, open up the militarily interesting question as to whether eagerness for military prestige could ever, as Monash apparently imagined, maintain the will to sacrifice life. He had worked his troops to the extreme limit of their endurance. He knew the German troops were in a like state and at such times victory often goes to the army that holds out longest: wars are won by men withstanding strain, toil and exhaustion in 'perhaps unbelievable degree and for an unbelievable time'.

It was the movement on the Hindenburg Line that took the heat off the affair of the mutinous battalions.

39
The New Never-Never Land

They advanced so swiftly that the medical corps had difficulty keeping up with the men. So many prisoners were taken they were utilised as stretcher bearers. Let Captain J. Connor, Medical Officer, 4th Battalion, tell the tale.

'*17 Sept. 1918*: After some days' relief the battalion went in again behind Templeux to join up for the attack on Hargicourt. *18 Sept*: I got some old French dug-outs as R.A.P.* close to the starting tape. No difficulty in evacuating stretcher cases as there were plenty of unwounded P. of W. soon collected round the R.A.P. I signed a chit to the C.O. that I had used 50 prisoners to carry wounded but I must have made use of a good many more. The wounded slacked off about 10 a.m., and I retained some prisoners-of-war to push my wheeled stretchers with stores, dressings and blankets towards the battalion objective at Hargicourt. This was quite against regulations of course – but perfectly safe. Discovered a good dug-out right of Hargicourt and located the battalion headquarters and the various companies. The ambulance loading post was immediately in rear of my R.A.P.'

Lance-Corporal R. Morgan, 2nd Battalion:

'*17 Sept. 1918*: Going into action tonight . . . Battalion strength now under 300. *18 Sept.*: Moved up after midnight. Hargicourt somewhere ahead. When passing a sunken road in single file a German bombing plane passed close

---

* Regimental Aid Post.

423

overhead. To see the whole line of men in perfect time bend over and lie against the bank showed collective common sense. My section established itself behind a bank 70 yards from a tape, where battalion is lying waiting for zero. A number of casualties occurred immediately prior to this. During the advance I was assisting M.O. to fix a Thomas splint when a salvo of whizbangs struck the bank – a flash of fire and all was blank. Later I discovered my steel helmet a battered wreck – the piece of shell incidentally taking a piece out of my scalp. Had slight concussion and a terrific headache. Had a nip of brandy and felt much better for same. Having tended casualties before zero, and those in the first few minutes of the advance, Doc. Rossell gave the word for our section to follow the advancing battalion. The movement forward of our particular section was like rolling peas down-hill; the infantry in front had cleared the roads in no uncertain manner and in attending to casualties we lost touch with battalion which was well ahead, and still going strong. Moved forward 3 000 yards and found battalion advanced troops were still 1 000 yards ahead. It was rather unusual during the advance to witness the batteries of 18-pounders galloping into action, all smiles as if going to a picnic. Mick Carter of 2nd Bn., company cook, salvaged an old German cooker and went into action well loaded with hot soup and other rations for his company. He managed to get well up towards the front line and delivered a hot meal. The troops would have decorated Mick with a V.C. had they had their way. Plenty of dead Germans in evidence, and prisoners moving back – poor beggars seem pleased to have been taken.

'Was resting alongside bank when for the second time I knew no more, woke up in an ambulance (motor), by which I was conveyed to Main dressing station, received attention including anti-tetanus injection . . . had a good meal in the transport lines and a sleep and returned to duty next day . . .

'*22 Sept.*: 2nd Battalion moving back into reserves into a wood behind Jeancourt and a sorry looking lot we are, haggard, drawn and war weary.

'*23 Sept.*: Relieved by American troops whose battalion being at full strength fairly dwarfs the shattered remnants of what was once a full battalion 1000 strong and is now only 200.'

The boy-determined-to-get-there, Norman 'Mac' Young, was now aged 19. He wrote his fifty-first letter home to his mother the day they took the outposts of the Hindenburg Line, '*18 Sept. 1918.* '. . . I am O.K. No doubt by the date of this note you will know what took place this day. Though it's only some hours since we attacked it seems as though I've lived through weeks and weeks. This was my first actual stunt with Fritz . . . We were successful in gaining our objective so it's pleasing in that respect. I had my rare smoke today. A choice German cigar which went well. Your loving son, Mac.'

The 6 800 Australian infantry took 4 300 prisoners and 76 guns at a cost of 1 260 casualties. At dawn the following morning, 19 September, they found themselves looking across at the Hindenburg Line. They had demoralised the German troops. 'Captured German officers said that their men would now not face the Australians,' the official War Correspondent wrote.

This reputation had not been gained overnight. As Sergeant Stevens wrote in his diary, the Australians, since March, had scarcely been out of the trenches except to go into attack. But this had also been the cause of their decimation and was the reason many battalions could put so few men into action.

Here at Bullecourt the then-promising young artist, Napier Waller, lost his right arm from bullets in the back and shoulder. (He later so trained his left hand that none seeing his work in Coventry Cathedral and the War Museum at Canberra could know of his loss.)

Norman Young wrote again to his mother on 25 September: 'The excitement of recent days has been tremendous. Look up the papers that refer to the stunt of 18 September and you will get a small – very small – idea of what we call "a hop-over" One must actually take part in the proceedings to know the sensations and feel the excitement of an attack.' He tells of the preparations and everyone wishing it were all over, mostly because of the endless details to be attended to. Then, 'We left our comfortable possies and marched the 10 km to the front line. It was raining. The trench was half full of slush. Everyone ready a little before midnight with our gear. It's marvellous the thoughts that pass through a chap's mind while waiting to take your place on the tape. Things that happened ages ago are all crowded up with more recent events and the excitement is that great that it is a hard job to keep still. The "hop" was timed for 5.20 a.m. and 10 minutes before the company was formed up on the tape. The "tape" is actually a white tape which marks the hopping off line and also enables the different units to be lined up properly so all go off from their appointed places at the right time. Crumbs, the minutes seem to drag while waiting for the barrage. All eyes are constantly on your watch and occasionally you'll hear the words "Two minutes to go!" then, "one minute to go!" Then, sharp to the second at 5.20 the barrage opens, first with machine guns, then our 18-pounders and heavies join in the din. It's like hell let loose because there's an 18-pounder every 25 yards of front sending out iron rations as fast as the gunners can pull the lanyards. On our particular sector were 70 machine guns increasing the noise.

'Behind these were the counter-battery guns – heavy guns whose business it is to prevent him putting over a barrage while we are advancing. The barrage fired for 3 minutes then it lifted 100 yards but it was on the tape I had the narrowest escape I shall ever have for our line was only 50 yards or so behind the barrage line and there is always the danger of a shell falling short; perhaps a faulty gun barrel or a defective shell, nothing else is the cause. However, our company was lined out, it was drizzling rain, we were all crouching on the ground feeling pretty wet and miserable for we were all loaded with gear. The barrage opened, and practically the first shot fell right on our line killing the O.C. and wounding 6 others. I am the only one of the 8 that remained untouched but if that wasn't a close shave I don't know what was.

'The barrage included a lot of smoke shells and what with that and the mist and the drizzling rain it was impossible to see more than 10 yards in front, and mud galore. Two or three times I got hung up in the barbed wire and only freed myself by ripping my togs at last. We hadn't been going long when two signallers were wounded. We had to take on their load thereby doubling our own weight of gear − by "our" I mean the remaining Sig. and me. On account of the mist etc. we lost ourselves but eventually arrived at the first objective after roaming about for a while. Then we hopped over and took the second objective and captured a lot of prisoners. Some of the prisoners were only boys and looked scared to death and they all seemed delighted at the prospect of being taken. By jove I was fagged by the time we settled down in our new possy. Crumbs I looked a picture with mud head to foot and clothes torn from the barbed wire. [He then names 'cobbers gone west' and others wounded.] War is a damnable business. There's no other word for it, the hardest thing being that so many of our lads go west, while others are left. I would like to say a lot more but I can't find words suitable enough.'

Roly Mills wrote to his brother George that September: 'Judging by a couple of letters I've received from poor old mum she seems to think that now I've been away so long, and wounded, I will be sent home for a spell. Not a bit of it. You see there are a lot of 1914 men to go first and I didn't leave until Feb. 1915. Anyway, the war will be over by then. This battle that is going on now will decide things one way or another.'

Towards the end of 1918 Monash believed the men needed a stronger stimulus than that of patriotism, God, King, Country and Empire. He told the official War Correspondent that he was going to appeal to them on grounds of prestige. He arranged for parties of British journalists and touring politicians to visit areas successfully

fought for by Australians. Britain had not wished to give
Germany propaganda material by admitting that the
Dominion troops had been dominant in the 1918 fighting
and this lack of mention of their part naturally made the
Australians disgruntled. In the 4th Brigade, which had
snatched a costly victory from the difficult situation left by
the failure of English troops on its left, a discontented
section was growling: 'Whatever we do they'll say they won
the battle: next time we'll let them win it.'

The *Australian Corps News Sheet* reprinted extracts
from the journalists' reports.

THE NEW NEVER-NEVER LAND

'Going through the Australian Army to their front on the
Hindenburg Line last week, one was overcome at times by
the illusion that France was, for the time being, peopled
wholly by Australians. Long before we came to Amiens the
slouch-hatted men of the Commonwealth appeared to
possess the whole countryside. Practically no other troops
were visible thenceforth to the St. Quentin canal . . . The
"Digger," with a permanent organisation, with five divisions,
handled as one unit in the same Army Corps, and under the
same General, are prone to regard themselves as essentially
it. It is a fine wholesome, stimulating belief, . . . and I must
say the "Diggers" I saw the other day kicking the stuffing
out of their part of Hindenburg's precious Line have as
much the appearance of being *it* as any troops I have ever
seen . . . Australian names, or numerous hybrid names like
"Roo de Kanga," are on the street corners . . . Australia, in
her history, will have no prouder story henceforth than that
of the almost incredible feat of arms by which Monash's
stalwarts won a bet for their commander by rushing this
formidable outwork with two or three battalions . . .'

Though Monash's plan certainly made the English a little
more aware of the part Canada and Australia played in the
war it is extremely unlikely that the troops gave a damn for
his cunning. They were done-in, 'stonkered'.

In England industrial troubles were making the leaders nervous of the effects an unsuccessful attack on the Hindenburg Line would have at home. The London Police Strike on 30 August and the Railway Strike on 24 September left the War Cabinet pessimistic. The Australian Government and people were equally on edge. All five Australian divisions were now weak and exhausted as well as being well under strength numerically.

Then came the one plan that gave optimism, hope and buoyancy: to replace the 1st and 4th Divisions two American Divisions would go into battle with the 2nd, 3rd and 5th Australian Divisions. The American 27th and 30th Divisions had not yet been engaged in a major battle but Monash was delighted to have them under his command. 'I had no reason to hesitate,' he wrote, 'measures were taken to supply them with any technical guidance they may lack.' C. E. W. Bean wrote, 'Everyone else felt equally confident. Compared with the Australian and most British divisions the American ones were completely fresh, and in manpower each nearly equalled two Australian Divisions. Each had twelve strong battalions of infantry and three times as many machine-gun companies as an Australian division and twice as many engineers. Their men had much the same physique and bold, free, aggressive appearance that marked the Australians: indeed their obvious affinity made this a particularly suitable combination. Most Australians felt as Monash did, that the fresh spirit and numerical strength of the Americans would make up for their lack of experience, and that in combination they and the Australians would strike a very formidable blow.'

40
Boys, You've Lost
Your Jobs

By October 1918 the '1914 leave' was being granted: a trip back home for all the 'originals'. Alice Kitchen was nearing her forty-fifth birthday, and in October she received six months furlough to Australia. But she turned it down 'as I had just heard all sisters at home were to be demobilised at 45 and matrons at 50. No one seems over anxious to take it and "Australia's appreciation" seems to amount to a polite way of asking us to go home and be scrapped. Having gone on so long I daresay we can go on a bit longer. At least I can – and mean to for the present . . . Samsing is going next week, and also Wheeler and others shortly. I shall be left utterly alone and have no friend.

'*Oct. 17th*: . . . Found Samsing was going off tomorrow. Helped to pack up the luggage and after afternoon tea we went for a little last run to town and we walked in the cool evening to Hyde Park corner and had a little yarn by the way. I had dinner with her and then said our last "goodbye" and have come to the end of our four years friendship, for a time at least; and feel that I am indeed alone. *Oct. 18th*: Four years tomorrow since we started out. What a long long time and what experiences! some good, some interesting, some most bitter. Some most disappointing and heart breaking. I woke in the night suddenly awake to the fact that I had no longer a companion.'

It was to be an emptiness that many – perhaps most – experienced, and possibly they would never recover from that severing of companionships that had in all truth been tried by fire. '*Oct. 30th*: My day off, yesterday 29th. There seems no one to meet now and a blank space in my life on this side of the world and it is horribly lonely.'

She then writes the three words that are the harbinger of the sinister days to come, the spectre that would accompany the peace: '*Influenza spreading everywhere.* Over 1 000 deaths in London in a week. Our wards are getting full; we heard tonight that Sister Walker died and Sister Quartermain dangerously ill.'

Quite unaware that they had fired their last shot in the war, ducked the last bullet and run from the minnies, the puddings, shrapnel and machine guns for the last time, men moved back and forth from front line to reserve and back to the line again. They swept up and, with a flourish that was like a brilliant autograph, took Mont St Quentin with the remnants of two of their worst-hit battalions: they still had élan, panache and drive as fighting men but each of them was war-spent.

Harry Dadswell was war-sick. 'Of the 1 100 men our brigade mustered for the last stunt only 180 came out. Many old men who had lasted the greater part of the war, died in the fighting near the end. I had a few days sick. Then, on Nov. 11th, I was out reeling up lines and far from well. Then we moved out, after packing up, and we were starting for the line again. Somehow I knew it was my last stunt, whether I was killed or not, I wouldn't come out with the boys. We got orders to wait and I was still feeling jolly depressed and dreading another trip in. The officer came out, "Take it easy boys, we don't know what's doing," and we all lay on the road side. At eleven o'clock he came out. "Boys you've lost your jobs. The war's over and you can all go back to your billets." The men just stood quiet and looked at one another, as though they couldn't take it in. One felt like crawling away on his own, the relief was so great. Some of the boys got drunk, but the majority just seemed stunned, as though they were afraid it might not be true. We were a quiet and subdued crowd.'

Private G. L. Hicks was in a German P.O.W. camp when

the end came. He had survived Gallipoli to be taken prisoner in France. '*Nov. 9 1918*: The revolution started here today but so far is a half hearted affair. A small party marched down the road to the town carrying a red flag. All the soldiers here have taken the badges out of their caps and their shoulder straps off. A train load of troops was sent from Chemnitz to Leipzig to stop the revolution, but on their arrival they threw down their arms and joined the revolutionists. The same thing has happened at Hamburg. Several officers here have discarded their uniforms.

'It is rumoured . . . there are no Germans in France now except prisoners.'

On Nov. 10 he knew that 'the German navy went out into the North Sea flying the red flag and gave themselves up to our people'. Later that day he wrote: 'We had a "peace" concert and dance here tonight. Wine flowed freely and most of the boys were very merry – a vast contrast to the Germans. Latest news tonight – rumour only – is that British troops have landed at Hamburg. *Nov. 11*: The terms I mentioned yesterday were terms for an armistice for 30 days only. Not peace terms.' (Marshall Foch, he had heard, had issued terms to the German delegates.) But by night he writes, 'It is reported tonight that Hindenburg and his staff have signed these terms'.

'*Nov. 15*: The prisoners here are in a very dis-satisfied frame of mind both French and British. Most of us think we should not be working but the interpreter here says we are not to be exchanged until the war is over.' They were working in a coal mine. *Nov. 22*: This morning the Germans made an attempt to drive us out to work with rifles and revolvers but of course were unsuccessful.'

On 29 November they were marched out of their camp and walked from 8.30 a.m. till 6 p.m. to another camp to await a train. They were to be repatriated. '*Dec. 3*: Today is my 23rd birthday so we celebrated by breaking camp and spent the evening in a town 5 kilos from here. Arrived back at 11 p.m. in a respectable condition.'

Then came the 'walks', the long journey home from camp to camp through a land in chaos. The Germans were unable to help for their transport system was wrecked by war and now by the peace that brought revolution as well as the return of their own troops. They had their own P.O.Ws to contend with and the thousands of allied prisoners spread in camps the length and breadth of the country. Private Hicks observed the comings and goings of men from various camps and the chaos. On the Danish ship that finally took his 'camp' away he wrote: 'Had bread and butter and eggs for breakfast. Dinner at 1 o'clock meat potatoes gravy bread and butter fruit and beer. We can go where we like on the boat. Had a good sleep last night, a bed all to myself.' From now until the end of the diary he described the meals. 'Arrived Leith, England Xmas eve. 25 Dec. Issued with new clothing and pay. Statements taken as to how we were taken prisoner. Went into town at night and had some whisky. Most of the boys arrive back very merry.'

Before the men left Picardy at the war's end, the Bishop of Amiens spoke these words to them at the close of a service in memory of the dead they were leaving behind on the Somme. 'As Bishop of Amiens, I owe you and your illustrious dead my heartfelt thanks because the land of my diocese has been your field of battle, and you have delivered it by the sacrifice of your blood.

'During the painful days of the invasion you made a rampart of your breasts, behind which you shielded and saved the last shreds of my territory. Later, when Victory at last began to smile upon our arms, the Australian Army distinguished itself by the audacity of its attacks, by its utter disregard of death, by its doggedness, and by the rapidity of its advances.

'In the name of my Clergy and of my people I offer you my heartfelt gratitude and admiration.'

The cathedral at Albert had been built not for the Virgin, who became the Australians' 'Fanny Durack', but for a four-foot high stone statue, 'Our Lady of the Sheep', which was discovered in the eleventh century. In March 1918, when it was apparent that Albert would fall to the Germans, the old stone statue was taken by the Australians to Amiens for safety. When it appeared that Amiens might fall it was taken to Normandy. But, as the Bishop said, the Australians saved the city and now the statue was back in Amiens awaiting return to Albert. During the service an Australian guard-of-honour stood with fixed bayonets round the statue they had saved. (The old relic was returned to Albert in 1919.)

Some of the devastated towns of France were 'adopted' by other countries. In Australia this was chiefly done by Melbourne and Adelaide. Melbourne adopted the village of Villers-Bretonneux; £22,700 was collected and spent largely in rebuilding the village school. The Belgian Relief Committee at Adelaide spent £36,000 in helping to restore a small town in Belgium which was re-named Sud Australie in gratitude.

In Villers-Bretonneux (pop. 3 000) the school children stand readily as an Australian enters and unselfconsciously sing 'Waltzing Matilda'. Above their blackboards is the inscription *Never Forget Australia*, and in the office is the Golden Book sent from Victoria and listing the names of the schools and individuals who contributed to the rebuilding of their school in 1926.

'This school building is the gift of the school children of Victoria, Australia, to the children of Villers-Bretonneux as a proof of their love and good will. 1 200 Australian soldiers, the fathers and brothers of those children, gave their lives in the heroic recapture of this town from the invader on 24th April 1918 and are buried near this spot. May their sacrifice bind Australia and France together in a bond of friendship and future esteem.'

You walk down Melbourne Street, and Anzac, just for the hell of it, but suddenly are assailed by the realisation that these children, and their parents, have remembered us, but we have long ago forgotten them and their town.

'I tell you', Norman Young wrote to his mother that November, 'it is hard to believe we shan't see the trenches again. But it's glorious to know next year we will see dear old Aussie once more. Get in a stock of shirts, ties, etc. mother and keep a good larder for I'm an eater of the first order now. Smiles are the order of the day here now and to enjoy a peaceful Xmas is delightful!'

Some spoke of the French *poilus*, those lads that many Australians wrote of as 'The French troops are always laughing as they tramp off. You can always tell, even at night if it's the Frenchies passing, they laugh and joke like schoolboys'. 'What must they think?' Richard Smith wrote. 'Their country is safe.' In his book *Gossip From the Forest*, Thomas Keneally catches the tenor of the weary *poilu* when he writes of the passing through the French lines of the Germans come to agree to peace terms in that train in the forest of Compiègne. Shrugging, the *poilus* looked at the low-ranking Germans. 'After four years they might have sent us faces that meant something.'

When the declaration of peace came on 11 November 1918, an exhausted member of the AANS, Nurse Alice Neville, did not record it in her otherwise detailed diary, for her patients were 'dreadfully ill. Epidemic Spanish 'Flue attacking everyone causing shortage of medical and nursing staff. Everyone going down like flies. It's cruel. Seem to do nothing but go on duty, get off at night too limp with no energy to wash or keep one's clothes in order'. In October she had written 'Sickness among M.O.'s, nursing staff and patients is alarming; almost impossible to cope with it. Matron ill. Poor old Minnie not well but keeps on duty as many others are doing until they drop down in the tents.' On 9 October we find the terse entry, 'Minnie ill'. And next day: '*11 Oct.* Poor old Minnie died. Several girls dangerously ill. Never will I forget these nights. The roar roar roar of the guns dreadful, firing incessant, the ground under my bed shook. Of a night can not sleep for overtiredness.' But by 6 November she records, 'Great excitement. Rumored peace has been declared'. On 20 November she has a day off duty at last and copies into the pages of her diary Robert Louis Stephenson's words:

> Then on the day of Solemn things
> The bell within the tower swings
> And just a wee bit nearer brings
> The quick and dead.

The armistice seems to have taken some by surprise, like the writer of the official diary of the 3rd Squadron, AFC, in November 1918.

'*10/11/18*: Owing to continued and hasty withdrawal of the enemy only one squadron maintained contact flying on an independant basis. Patrols were carried out all day but very little information could be gained and pilots made themselves acquainted with country they would possibly have to work over in the near future as the squadron is now 60 000 yards behind the nearest enemy.

'*11/11/18*: News was received this morning that all hostilities were to cease at 11 a.m.'

Norman Young told his family: 'Wild rumours were floating about early in the morning so the troops and civilians were getting excited. Anyhow, at 10.45 we received it unofficially and then the celebrations began. Our band played all the national anthems in the square, flags appeared as if by magic until it was hard to believe the place was the same. The French folk were excited and the troops, being used to various forms of excitement, never carried on at all, only the celebrated Australian thirst was made evident by the over-crowded estaminets. In the evening the village was lit up with electric light, the first time since the war and little kids marched round the town with a flag, a drum and a trumpet. At times a chap has to pinch himself to make sure it's not just a huge dream. By jingo's I'll have plenty to talk about when I'm sitting by the fire once more.'

Three days after the Armistice was announced Birdwood sent a memo round the troops containing 'a personal appeal to every single member of the A.I.F. in the full confidence that it will be met as every other appeal to face and tackle the strongest positions has ever been met by the Australian soldier. Never has the name of Australia stood higher than it does now throughout the world, thanks to the bravery of her soldiers, and it is up to every one of us to see that this is maintained, and that no reproach can be cast on the Australian Flag owing to any behaviour of ours.

'The time of demobilisation will undoubtedly be difficult and irksome – I fully realise what great personal self-restraint will certainly be required – but if each individual of us makes up his mind to do his best during these times, realising the good name we bear, I feel confident that all will go off well.

'I want you to remember that everything possible will be done to look after and help the troops during this period, while every energy will be strained to get men back to their homes as soon as this possibly can be done. You will have to realise, however, that there is a great shortage of shipping and that there must be a considerable inevitable delay.

'Play the game, boys, during this time, as you have always done, and add still more to the deep debt of gratitude which will always be acknowledged to you by the Empire and remembered by me as your comrade and commander.

> *In the Field,*
> *14th November 1918*   *W. V. Birdwood*'

From 'somewhere in France' (censorship was in force for some time after the Armistice: habit dies harder in the army than anywhere else) Norman Mills wrote home: 'If there were only some means of getting things sent away it would be possible to get dray loads of relics and souvenirs of every possible description.'

By this time the effervescent Gertrude Moberly had, like many other nurses, become exhausted through heavy work, long hours and having seen too much. Before leaving for Australia when the war was over she was sent from India to England where she worked at the Infirmary Operation Hospital, otherwise No. 2 A.A.H. for Limbless Soldiers, in Southall. In April she boarded the hospital troopship *Castalia* and was on her way home.

She worried about her relationship with Peter who had

patiently waited for her. She doubted if she could settle to 'the daily round, the common task. It is certainly not all I ask and it will be ages before we can take on love in a cottage with cheese and kisses'. (But she did. She married her 'Peter' Hogan in 1926 and recorded that she was content and happy.)

It is pertinent to remember that many of the ships these nurses sailed on were not covered by the articles of war as being Hospital Ships, entitled to sail under the protection of the Red Cross. As well, they were often but poorly fitted out to carry patients and always understaffed. Ernie Mack's letter of 1915, written on his way from Gallipoli to England after being wounded, put it bluntly.

'Today we are in the submarine danger zone but if we miss those articles we ought to be in Devonport early tomorrow morning. Of course it would be diabolical murder if a submarine sank us as there are just on 800 wounded on board and to unload them would take at least three hours. We are in an unfortunate position as this boat (which by the way originally belonged to Germany) is a transport pure and simple and is only nominally a hospital ship but it is subject to all the rules of warfare as if purely a transport. It is even against rules to hoist a Red Cross flag. There are six Doctors on board and eight nurses.'

With women leading the free-from-restraints-of-home life these girls did, there were bound to be cries of dismay from the narrow, bigoted, unimaginative (or too imaginative!) citizens back home.

A Queensland nurse, Edith Avenell, writing home from a hospital in France on 8 June 1916 had heard of unsavoury gossip about the girls overseas.

'I'm sorry to hear such scandal discussed about the sisters and the only sister I know sent back was because she got married without the O.C.'s permission otherwise the sisters are having a very trying time here. Our hours are fearfully long, from 7 a.m. till 8 p.m. on day duty and 8 p.m. till 8 a.m. on night duty. I should now be sleeping but we had a big convoy in last night, shocking cases, I simply ran for ten solid hours without a stop. As for the scandal, of course in Egypt we did go out and had a gay time when off duty during the latter part of our stay there but why shouldn't we? It gave our troops pleasure to be with us and much better for them than down the town with bad company. I think some people are jealous of the nurses being out with the troops.'

Canon David John Garland of Brisbane, who went to Egypt as 'Representative of the Church of England to enquire into the moral and social needs of the men', saw Australian nurses on their day off going around *English* hospitals looking for any Australian boys who might be patients. 'There were about a dozen of them and instead of going out for fresh air and amusement here they were going round looking for Australian boys to comfort them. One boy who is paralized badly and will only leave the ward when he is carried out for the last time could not talk much. A Sister just stood by him quietly and stroked his forehead and "crooned" in gentle words to him. I could have kissed her hand for the beautiful thing she did with it. There was a blind boy, they fed him with cakes they'd bought and held his hand and joked and "chaffed" him in such gentle tones and he smiled.'

Ethel Mary ('Effie') Hargreaves kept only a few letters of her nursing days. Perhaps they hold the sentiments she was most proud of, and in one case, that was of the man she held most dear. Her reference for entry into army service from Melbourne Surgeon W. A. James reads: 'She is as devoted to her patients as they are to her. I have always felt safe when she, was looking after my patients.' Her exit reference in 1918 when she was leaving the QAIMNSR for home was written by the Matron of the service and reads in part: 'I offered to get her promotion but she preferred to remain as staff nurse where she could give more of her personal attention to her patients.'

In 1918 the world-wide influenza outbreak struck the ship on which she was returning to Australia. A letter from the Directors of the Union Steamship Company of New

Zealand on 2 November 1918 gives an idea of the girl's calibre as a nurse.

'The commander of the *Niagara* and our manager in Auckland have brought under our notice the services rendered by you during the outbreak of influenza on the *Niagara*. From the information we have received from them we realise that your professional knowledge, your readiness and cheerfulness with which you coped with the situation were very great factors in keeping the outbreak in hand.' The passengers wrote to her: 'From Vancouver to Sydney your name will always be associated with our recollections of the voyage. We too desire to be held in your memory and we beg you will permit us to append our signatures.'

The final, small note, in her small collection of documents of those years, tells its own story. It is from Caterina Kerr-Wilson, superintendent, Queen Mary Hostels for Nurses, London.

'6 June, 1917. Beloved Dear Effie. I do not know when I have had such heartache for I loved your Jerry. We *can't* spare them Effie but when they go we give them cheers not tears. You must come here so that we may talk of him.'

In Australia it was said that every bell in every church was rung, all day long volunteers coming to take over the gay cacophony; flags flew mast high, bands appeared in the streets and people danced and sang and laughed. Bonfires were lit in the country, fireworks crackled and all sorts of processions went forth.

41
Part of the Price

The Australian casualties were higher in proportion to their numbers than those of any other portion of the British forces. This was probably due to the fact that the Australians were nearly all 'front line' troops, engaged throughout the war in heavy fighting.

Over one-third of the Australians (137013) were wounded in action; a surprisingly low figure of 4044 were taken prisoner. The percentage of deaths to battle casualties was 25.3 per cent. (These are the correct figures of 1931.)

The United States of America, with a population of 102017312, put 2040000 men in the field. Of these 51000 were killed, 234300 wounded, 4500 taken prisoner – a total of 290406 battle casualties. (Note: The USA War Department usually adds *all* deaths. For comparative figures [excluding USA] see Appendix II, Table 3: Casualties. This is of deaths from enemy action only.)

The one wound that terrified all men was to be gassed. The fear of this silent weapon did almost as much damage as did the actual gas. They were, to a man, terrified of it. The physical effects were bronchitis, emphysema, fibrosis of the lungs, asthma, vertigo, palpitations, pulse rate up to 130, vomiting, pain after food, streaming, painful eyes and temporary blindness. Although 16496 men were gassed, only 323 died before 1920.

These mists of death began in France on 22 April 1915 (before the Australians attacked Gallipoli). Near Langemarck, in Belgium, the Germans used poison gas for the first time. 'The diffusion of asphyxiating or deleterious gases' had been outlawed at the pre-war Hague Convention, but both sides were ready with stocks and a determination to use it. It was sent over the trenches, one side to the other, at any time the wind was favourable. Sometimes the gas swept down as the men went over the mud and into action. Oliver Hoskin was blinded as he got into No Man's Land. His mates rolled him in a blanket and put him by a bank and said they'd come back for him, and he lay there in his blindness hearing them all go away – and then the battle afar off, and then, nothing. 'I thought I would never be found.' But when night fell he heard them calling and he answered. They had crept out of their lines to bring him in.

'Our respirators – we called them "gaspirators" were simply chemically impregnated pieces of cloth kept in a protective pouch and we were informed that if the cloth dried out urine could revive the anti-gas properties in an emergency,' Jim McPhee says.

At first, the signalling apparatus for giving the alarm when gas was detected was crude. Gongs made from empty shell cases beaten on with an iron bolt, rattles, klaxons, anything to warn the men in the front line. Later, the British Strombus Horn which could be heard five miles away was used.

The first war wounded arrived in Melbourne on 18 June 1915. The military staff had not foreseen the interest the public would take in this and had the men who could walk march from the ship to the train, along with men returned for disciplinary reasons or for venereal disease, and the awaiting crowd, not knowing whom to cheer, remained silent.

Apart from wounding by bullet, bomb or shrapnel, there were gas and numerous psychological diseases that hitherto were unknown or not known in such numbers. Victims were always treated well but little research was done into the ailments until the volume of men out of action seriously affected the numbers needed to replace those killed. Humanitarian reasons may be given, but the cry for more and more men (particularly after recruiting began to fall dramatically in late 1916) accelerated medical research. Psychology was scarcely practised before World War I and many of the non-physical diseases were considered in the light of what we would later call 'bludging'. Many men suffered with what, before the war, had been termed 'Disordered Action of the Heart' (D.A.H.). This manifested itself in feeble and rapid heartbeat – with many patients a pulse of 130 – trauma, mutism. It was termed 'an aetiological conundrum'. During the American Civil War Da Costa had written, 'The irritable heart of the soldier'. It later became commonly known as 'Soldiers heart'. During the Boer War it was described as '. . . increased irritability of the vasometer system . . . their nervous systems generally seemed out of order and they could not stay long without shaking all over'. It was said that 'many men, through fear, fled into disease, even death itself'.

When examining the troops in the trenches who were reputedly 'fit', or at least had not reported sick, Colonel J. Purves-Stewart found 77 per cent were emaciated and anaemic. He says the rapidity and feebleness of the heart was most striking. Tachycardia, 'not due to sudden exertion or emotion', was found in 50 per cent and 74 per cent suffered from shortness of breath'. Vitamin B deficiency has as its characteristic symptom weakness of the heart's action, and General Howse had reported that 'men frequently faint at their post'.

There was 'war weariness'. In 1918 Colonel A. E. Shepherd (2nd Australian Division) recorded that 'many men in the battalions who have rendered excellent service have become war worn and of little use to the battalion'.

A common casualty was trench feet. This was caused by the damp conditions, the cold, and inability to get the blood circulating by moving around. 'You'd stand in the trenches, unable to move about for upwards of four days before being relieved. For the winter of 1916, '17, and '18, always up to your ankles – at least – in mud. Always cold, hardly ever a warm meal and often poor boots,' Sergeant Harry Kahn (WA) recalls. 'Trench feet – well this showed at first with your feet going wrinkly, soft, puffy, then red, the ball of your foot swelled up and was so painful you hobbled round. Several days of this and it would go black. Next thing the troops found they lost a foot, sometimes a leg. The puttees were bad for it. These strips we had to bind tightly round our trouser legs from knee to ankle restricted the circulation. Up in the front line first one man then another unwound them and tied sandbags around in their place. You could toss the sandbag away when it got wet and soaked with mud and put a clean dry one on in its place. Later the powers-that-be gave official approval for this.'

Trench Fever (Pyrexia), although not notifiable until 1918, was 'one of the most important causes of expeditionary wastage'. This term embraced many diseases from influenza, dengue and other virus diseases to typhus and other lice-carried diseases. Pediculosis, the body louse, is believed to have infected 95 per cent of the men with an average of 20 lice per man, although gross infestation 'reached as high as 1 300 to 10 000 counted lice as well as approximately 10 000 eggs on one shirt'. As well there were the itch mites that caused scabies and a pyogenic cocci that brought on suppurating sores and impetigo.

Self-inflicted injuries in France totalled 701, the majority of these, 388, occurring in 1918. (All were by rifle fire or exposure to enemy fire.) Sickness and accidental injuries totalled 437 819, of which 6 371 died. Hospital admissions for venereal disease totalled 52 538, or 84.79 per thousand of the mean average strength of the AIF overseas.

'Shell shock' accounted for many unnumbered casualties, such as men who remained huddled in dug-outs in trenches until the line was relieved. Stammering, loss of memory and temporary blindness afflicted those blown into the air or buried under soil following a nearby shell burst. Some trembled uncontrollably for some days. Shell shock became a term loosely applied to all cases of physical and mental breakdown within the battle zone without apparent wound.

42
Good-bye-ee!

There was a young Australian soldier climbing on the statue of Eros in Piccadilly singing:

> Who were you with last night?
> Out in the pale moonlight?
> It wasn't your sister; It wasn't your ma!
> Ah! Ha Ha Ha, Ha Ha Ha Ha!
> Are you going to tell your missus, when you get home
> Who you were with last night!

And up Oxford Street and along the Mall they were running, four abreast:

> Mademoiselle from Armentières
>   Parlez-vous!
> Mademoiselle from Armentières
>   Same to you!
> Who was the girl who lost her sheep
> Thro' singing this Chorus in her sleep?
> Mademoiselle from Armentières!

They tried to make a gay refrain from another song:

> Goodbye-ee! Goodbye-ee! Wipe the tear
>   Baby dear, from your eye-ee!
> Tho' it's hard to part I know, I'll be
>   tickled to death to go
> Don't cry-ee, don't sigh-ee
> There's a silver lining in the sky-ee
> Bon Soir old thing! Cheerio, chin-chin;
> Nah Poo Toodle-oo! GOODBYE-EE!

But it was of no use. The songs had been written to send them to war with a smile. 'Pack up your troubles in your old kit-bag and Smile! Smile! Smile!' and now, all those years, those trenches, those mates later, after the legs and arms had gone, after the gas they knew wouldn't kill for a few lingering years yet, suddenly the songs were a sharper and shriller knife in the wound than any German had put in them. Those most ingenuous examples of what we once were in this nation had sailed off with their artless humour and their boisterous larrikinism and four years later, as suddenly as we turn a page in their diaries, it had all ended, they had crossed the gap, not the step all pass from boyhood to manhood, but a gap so exclusive that no man who was not with them could span. And so, in the clamour and tumult of the victory bells, the trumpets, the laughter, they realised a quite chilling thing. 'That moment in time when we swept across that gap was in reality an eternity, the extent of which our loved ones will never understand, and we can never forget,' Sapper R. Dadswell wrote in his diary.

Sister Alice Kitchen wrote on 11 November in her hospital near London:

'We all are excited, the men's most ardent wish seems a desire to go out and get drunk. Should have liked to see London rejoice but was on duty. Sirens and hooters blew, bands played, men waved flags etc. The terms are very drastic and far reaching. They need to be. Standing by the door tonight I feel I could fully appreciate the feeling that inspired the "Song of Miriam": "Sound the loud timbrel o'er Egypt's dark sea" and imagined the Jewish maiden's song of victory and how they waved their banners before their King . . . I cannot realise that it is all finished, it has become so much a part of one's life these past 4 years. I longed for Samsing to be here for the end – as we began together – just for the Grand Finale. Everyone now is thinking of getting home soon.'

The following day she 'Went to London p.m. . . . A great crowd everywhere, but not any wild hilarity. Everybody seems to have gone out to see everybody else wave a flag and laugh! yet with it all, the Tragedy of War still seems to lurk somewhere close in the background. We are still too near all the great sorrows and heart-breakings to feel great rejoicings and one sees as many sad faces as merry ones. I felt more like weeping myself. The general feeling is relief rather than joy. All the women who have lost their sons etc. must feel relieved that at last it has been proved not all in vain . . . Let us imagine all that Great Company of the Fallen rejoicing with us and singing a grand chorus of Victory and of Thanks to God . . . The lamps are being scraped clean and we are getting more light in the streets at night [which] are thronged with people, the road so full of pedestrians that buses can scarcely crawl along among them, flags wave, whistles and trumpets blare, soldiers and sailors, WAAC's and Wrens arm in arm dance and sing etc. in the good old "Mafficking" Way. I should love now to be in Fair France – Lorraine or Alsace for choice. . . . how can anyone picture their feelings or their joy at the downfall of the Huns. One of the happiest faces I saw was a N.Z. without any legs being wheeled about in a chair down the Strand laughing and looking as pleased as if he were a king. He probably was at that moment feeling happier than either any king (except Albert of Belgium perhaps) or Statesman.'

On her next day off Sister Kitchen went to see the King and Queen attend a thanksgiving service at the Albert Hall. 'The flags of victory were flying everywhere in the cold grey mist. . . . The street was lined with "Sisters, WAAC's and Diggers and a few Civilians". We lined up along the footpath and then at 3 p.m. – along came just 4 mounted police – abreast who, as we stepped forward into the road, politely and calmly waved a mild arm to us to leave the way clear for them – the King and Queen and Prince of Wales and little Mary were in an open carriage, all looking well and happy – The King especially was all smiles; no style or fuss – just a homely family party out for a drive among their own people.

'*Nov. 20th*: Today the 1st portion of the German fleet was to be handed over. What a fine sight it must have been and what a humiliation for the Germans. Miss Samsing, and I feel bitterly alone.

'The Weather gets more foggy and wintry and damp. The work heavier. More bed patients and no hospital ship since I left Harefield. A notice up to the effect that any of us may be given 48 hrs notice to go to Australia any time. Everybody chatting over it and imagining themselves off this week. Perhaps I'll be among the next lot. Somehow if it were not for mother and the rest, Australia would never see me again, it has sunk so far into the background of my life I never feel like living and working there again. . . .

'*Dec. 13th*: Hospital ship crowd went. . . . the first . . . since July or August. Went to Woolwich to try and do a little Xmas shopping; everything very dear – no dried fruits – fresh fruit beyond moderate purses; jelly 10½*d* pkt (1 pt) apples 6*d* to 8*d* each. Arranged for some cakes to be collected later. Chocolates 4/- a lb.; even boiled sweets 2*d* an ounce and little choice.'

The war might be over, but its effects would not end for a long time; in the wards the terrible round continued, lightened a little by Christmas celebrations, although the spectre of influenza still hung over everyone.

'*Dec. 25th*: Xmas Day: my fifth away from home . . . The men had a fine dinner of turkey and pudding. We had ours last night. Soup, turkey, pudding, trifle, claret cup and all the etceteras. Much fun – Doctor Spowers and others put on Sisters' caps and foxtrotted up and down all the spaces in the interval. Patients also had . . . much fun with mistletoe and one of the boys dressed up as a Sister and took in the M.O.s. Capt. Proctor rose to the occasion and mid much embarrassment said – "A digger was worth kissing anyway". A letter from Samsing yesterday from the Cape – first since she left.'

A week later she comments: '. . . This expected transport home hangs like a gloom over some of us and I feel a cold chill whenever I hear the telephone ring in case it's my

horrid turn. . . . The last dance allowed takes place tonight.
I am not going . . . Staff dwindling off home already. "Flu"
is making another visit, one poor man arrived last night
and no notification of his coming and only by chance he got
a lift up in the car – was put on the D.I. list at midnight and
has been in a very bad way all day and looks like passing
away before morning. Four years out and having leave
before going home.' It is a month before she records this
man's death 'after a short and sudden double pneumonia',
and we learn from her diary that 'Things have been so busy
that this entry will be just a summary of events: my ward
was converted into an influenza ward and we are having a
busy time and no days off for the past fortnight. Everybody
is tired and there is no relief and "flu" all around. The men
die very rapidly, poor things, of Broncho-pneumonia. As
for returning to Australia: we hear all outgoing boats are to
carry a certain number of wives and kids and the Sisters
are to look after them. I pray heaven I may escape the brats.
[These were the ships taking 'war-brides' – 15 000 of them
– and their children, out to Australia along with their
husbands and other troops.]

'*Feb. 27th*: . . . A busy week with Flu. One man died
yesterday after a few days – he'd had 52 months service
and just going home. Most of the other girls have got their
leave fixed so I am going up to try about mine today.' The
next day she 'Spent day in various dug-outs of the A.I.F.
where I . . . stood with several diggers and waited an
eternity . . . I . . . interviewed Cpl. Jackson, a kindly and
courteous creature who worked the wires on my behalf up
and down every remote corner of the A.I.F. till closing time,
by which he came to the conclusion all the papers were
mislaid and I am to go in again today. I wonder if I shall be
sitting on the benches in the park next week!'

But the army hadn't changed, even if the war was over,
and after tramping around for a week she and another
nurse, Sister Young, decided to take a room for £1 a week
in Gloucester Street, and enroll for various educational
classes. The fear of returning to what she feels will be the

loneliness of civilian life drives her on to apply for, and get, 'educational leave' to attend the Royal Institute of Technology course on advanced nursing techniques, about which lectures she becomes increasingly terse. She and 'Young' 'poke around' a lot together. Young gets asthma – Alice Kitchen mentions that quite a few sisters were suffering from it – but it did not prevent their 'going to hear Melba – at Convent Garden'. After queuing for two hours, they saw Melba drive up. 'Everybody gave her a cheer and she stood on the taxi step and did hope they'd all be able to get in and she looked doubtful but they cheerfully assured her they'd try so she said "Good luck, I hope so – or God bless you all" or something of the usual "A.I.F." sort of thing. By slow and painful degrees we worked our way up the stairs and found a very full house but splendid view.' A week after the announcement that the Germans had sunk the fleet at Scapa Flow, the two women joined in the peace celebrations on 28 June. 'We stood in an enormous crowd for a couple of hours enlivened by a band and a few short speeches on the Victory Loan by Mrs Pankhurst, Lloyd George, etc. Clara Butt sang "Land of Hope and Glory". The flag was half way up the column and an Australian sailor on leave was bent on climbing up to the top with 'his own flag' – to hang out but it couldn't be done. However, 2 workmen on the platform hung it up a little way for him. . . . it was nearly 5 p.m. when the news came – there was a lot of cheering and anthems and homology by the crowd; which was not excited or wildly boisterous. Everybody seemed to have come out with his or her flag to look at everyone else doing the same. Some diggers and N.Z. were mounted on all the lions and looked quite at home there. On a lamp post in the Strand an Aust. flag flew and another flew on King Charles' statue put there by some soldier – the fountains played and everything looked bright.'

On Victory Day she got up early to see the procession. '*July 19th*: The Americans came first – then Belgians . . . then all the other nations in alphabetical order – British last – Navy leading. It was a fine affair – every regiment represented and I think all colonies. The march of the colours was a beautiful and moving spectacle. Clemenceau would describe it as "Victory shining in the folds of their banners" – laurel wreaths crowning them all – I did not know there were so many. There were tanks and trench mortars, anti-aircraft guns – territorials and QA's and WAACs, WRAFs, WRENs and labour battalions and V.A.D.s, all received their share of cheers. Foch got a great reception. What a proud man he must be and how happy!'

Alice Kitchen's long leave ended on 30 July and, on reporting back to the A.I.F., she learned that her 'fate was the *Kanowna* on the 14th'. But before the ship sails she is to have fourteen days leave in France.

For France and Belgium the privations of 1914–18 had not yet ended and too often the sights there shot her memory off into recalling those other days. The poppies that once delighted her, growing thickly among the waist-high corn, were now garlanding another crop and slipped into her diary's pages we find a poem written later, John McCrae's 'In Flanders Field', with two stanzas marked:

> In Flanders field the poppies grow
> Between the crosses, row on row
> That mark our place . . .
>
> We are the dead. Short days ago we lived,
>   felt dawn, saw sunset glow,
> Loved, and were loved, and now we lie,
>   In Flanders field.

'*Aug. 5th*: The train passed through Épernay and many other more or less shattered places. The farther we got the more devastated it looked. All too sad. Rheims is a mass of ruins – only 13 houses intact. . . . Looks as if an earthquake had shaken it down, only 4 000 people now live there (out of 14 000) mostly in cellars.

'Then in a motor lorry out through miles of barbed wire

entanglements enough to go all round Australia I think; Hun prisoners working at it and farmers trying to straighten out some of the ruin. The trenches are all overgrown with a mass of lovely wild flowers, poppies, cornflowers, and shrubs. Birds twittering and bees humming in the sweet scented air. "Nature going abroad with her pockets full of seeds and holes in all her pockets." . . . The road divides the German from French trenches. We wandered round for about an hour among the ruins but it was so overgrown I felt rather afraid of stepping on some of the souvenirs we had been warned so much about touching – several people having recently been killed.'

She resolutely tramped on, in and out of cathedrals, gardens, galleries. Many of the art treasures had not yet been replaced from the hiding places where they were secured during the war; 'the huns were told they had been sent to England'. Even so, Sister Kitchen must have managed to see as many treasures as any traveller since Marco Polo and fills dozens of pages cataloguing the masterpieces and her assessment of them before she returned to England and arranged her departure for home.

On 24 August seven sisters boarded the *Kanowna* at Tilbury to find Sister Kitchen's worst fears realised. 'Find we have a bombshell about an infant which an A.I.F. father is taking out and of course the Sisters are to be saddled with it.' They call at Southampton, then leave England on 28 August. 'I cannot yet realise that we are really going home at last – and wonder if we will really get there. Nor can I realise that I shall probably never see this dear country again. I offer up silent prayers that some day I may come back – if only to leave my bones here – or spend my old age here.'

The five years have told on her. 'The wards are as per usual – very A.I.F. – one darned muddle – more patients than there are beds for and all the walking cases dissatisfied at being expected to sleep in hammocks and unable to – consequently much shifting of cases – officers also very dissatisfied with their quarters. One Sister off duty invalided and 1 for the kid. I am doing the General Hospital and the sick parade and outpatients.'

The long hours of heavy and devoted nursing and the pain and heartbreak have hardened her. She resents the 'amount of pandering to this crowd of men'. 'Even a "conversational" section has been got up to arrange for an officer daily to go about the decks and talk to them. Patients all grizzling over food – nothing pleases them – tired of too much meat, etc. A concert tonight but crowded – our table companions not too pleased at hearing that there must be "2 Diggers dances to the officers' one" – and as the men have all the deck space they can get and part of the boat deck they have very little to grumble about – the Sisters are the only people not catered for except a brief corner – the men (officers) using the whole of their side for "Medicine Ball", cricket, etc. and play madly all day – also use most of the Saloon as a card playing and smoking room. If the weather were wet we would have to stay in our cabins.'

There is jubilation when the Southern Cross is seen on 28 September – the first time since 1914. When the *Kanowna* reaches Perth, she notes that it is the anniversary of that day five years ago when the little *Benalla* embarked on its great journey. On 20 October the ship docks in Adelaide and two days later we read the last entry: 'Tried to get everything straightened up and packed till late. Just before turning in I saw what I expect is Cape Otway light and the signalling station talking to us. This time tomorrow we will be home!'

43
So Ends the Bloody Business
of the Day

The enemy was down, the battle ended. In spite of their generals the men had prevailed. It is true that from the blood of battlefields sprang daisies and buttercups but the red rain that made that harvest grow was still to be measured.

The homecoming, the aftermath, was, as the war itself had been, a tremendous social cataclysm affecting every part of the national life.

The men had tasted wild fruit, had heard strange music. Now the time had come when they would go home. To return them to this most outlying of the Dominions would take 137 different ships sailing 176 voyages.

They brought back to Australia 18 000 wives, children and fiancées. A soldier watching the children embark at Dover remarked that 'the bird of war is not the eagle but the stork!' They left behind them 38 462 identified graves and 23 400 unidentified or unknown dead.

The task of bringing home the living now began. Australians were in France, England, Egypt, Palestine, Syria, Mesopotamia, Persia and Kurdistan, and Australian nurses, as well as being in many of those countries, staffed four hospitals in Salonika and ten in India. The Australian Government out of pride in the AIF wanted each regiment brought home intact, but the men believed that 'first come, first served', was the only fair manner of repatriation. Thus, the early enlistments would go first.

The men were to go off in batches of 1 000 – a trainload, shipload and battalion strength. Each batch was to have a brass band, education staff and recreation plans. No Australian troops had been sent with the army of occupation into Rhineland (except for a squadron of the AFC and a casualty clearing station). The AIF believed that this was because the British Command preferred to have more docile troops in the army of occupation. The divisions, while awaiting repatriation, therefore had the warmth and welcome of living among the friendly Belgians near Charleroi until the last of them were taken in May 1919 to England. Most had sailed for home by October and Richard Smith was able to close his diary: 'I smelt the gum leaves again and Christmas 1919 I was home!'

They left behind in France and Belgium friends they would never see again but with whom they had shared the most tumultuous, memorable years of their lives. Bertha Hennay, of Thuin, Belgium, wrote to Sapper Richard Harding before he left for home in 1919. (Harding and his brother William had fought at Ypres and William's grave – he was killed on 8 August 1917 – would be cared for during Bertha's lifetime.) 'Write at we a little letter,' she wrote in English. 'No forget Mrs Harding your letters there are always once large pleasure for me. Finische all us good friends, but it is promised, that we do write. If it is possible write at we before you go take sheep [ship] and when you arrived Australia.' Then, '*Recevez, Cher Monsieur Harding, de vos bons et sinceres amis de Thuin, notre plus affectureux souvenir, Bertha Hennay.*' (Harding named his home in Australia Thuin in memory.)

Norman Mills was billeted with a family whose father had been away since the beginning of the war. 'A few days ago he returned home on leave and of course there has been a family reunion . . . such a chattering you never heard . . . I kept my end up O.K. I supplied a little drop of rum for the coffee and madame had a tart . . . for that I also supplied the jam (*confiture*). These people have practically nothing left. Fritz requisitioned their blankets and other woollen articles, they are wearing slippers made from an old Fritz blanket which they managed to hide. A Fritz soldier sold

them a good blanket (not wool) on the quiet and the young
madame had a manteau made from it by a tailor. It looks
quite stylish. For illumination they had a dirty little slush
light so I give them a candle or two and some kereosene
whenever possible. They call Fritz "*le sale cochon*" (dirty
pig) and "*tête carrée*".'

His brother Reg, now recovered from his wounds, wrote,
'Tell Dave I am sucking away at the pipe and will pension it
off when the others arrive and will send it back for a
souvenir if possible. Tell him to start fattening the sucking
pig and turkeys and get a good stock of "the good stuff" in
as I am looking forward to an early return and will need a
good feed.'

(The girls of Picardy leaning on their pitchforks in the
ripened crop could still remember the clumsy '*Voulez-vous
promenade avec moi ce soir?*' but the tune that careered
through their capillaries was now the haunting '*Après le
Guerre Fini, Soldat Australie Parti . . .*')

The 22nd Battalion marched from St Vast (near Amiens)
to Charleroi to embark for England. Norman Young wrote,
'Left St Vast 9.30 p.m. Mutual regrets when parting from
friends who had shared their small rations and fires with
us. Marched until 2.30 a.m., caught train to Bertry. Lit
braziers in every truck – resourceful to the end – only food
or drink was hot cocoa from Y.M.C.A. from Bertry.
Marched 4 km to Bohain. Bohain had been occupied for 4
years by the Germans. The number of sad faced women to
be seen there is remarkable. We will never quite understand
the depth of misery plumbed by civilians of occupied
territory.'

The War Diary of the AIF on board *Suevic* on the way
home to Australia was typical of the farewells. Many
batches of returning troops marched through English towns
past cheering crowds on their way to the wharf.

'*23 July 1919*: at 3.30 p.m. the troops were given a
Farewell Address by the Lord Mayor of Bristol who wished
them all God Speed and a safe return to their homes.
Captain English commanding the *Suevic* also addressed

the troops and expressed the hope that they would all have a good time on the voyage. The ship pulled out from the wharf at 4.30 p.m. The Military Police on the wharf were given a rousing farewell by the troops on board. A very hearty send-off was given by the many ladies and gentlemen assembled on the dock, some of whom had come long distances to say farewell to parting friends.

'3 *August*: . . . The evening was clear, the Southern Cross being observed quite plainly in the southern sky. *13 Aug.*: Lectures on VD and their effects were delivered to all troop decks by the Senior Medical Officer and all ranks were warned against the conditions prevailing in Capetown. *7 Sept.*: Victorian Premier sends "a congratulatory radio message: Brave Diggers. Victoria welcomes her home-coming sons".'

Norman Young was on his way home by 10 August 1919. 'Now that the Southern Cross is visible to us one can better imagine that he is home. And yet even at this stage of the trip I sometimes think I'm dreaming. I'm conjuring up visions of how everybody will appear, and all sorts of things. I guess you'll notice a slight difference in this chicken, perhaps not in looks but in other respects. I can already see your smiling dials.'

They had gone ardent innocents. Few would have read Rupert Brookes' concept of war and soldiering, 'like swimmers into cleanness leaping', but they would have agreed with him. They had been schooled on heroic litera-ture and not until they walked on the 'sickly-sweet smelling corpses' in the mud of the Western Front did they meet their moment of truth. Once having faced it they could never go back, but the world they would return to was a stable world where values had remained unchanged for centuries.

Thus, their diaries were incomprehensible to their loved ones back home. As stated earlier, very few civilians appear to have read the diaries of their 'returned' menfolk. The men had gone to war for the sake of Honour and Glory, God, King and Country, and it was to be fifty years before these abstractions would be openly questioned and, where necessary, put down. That they had learnt that war was no longer, perhaps never had been, 'an armed version of the Olympic Games', was their moment of truth that would be wasted almost entirely in the oblivion they must assume if they were to be again assimilated with the people they loved, longed for, dreamt of, for four of the worst years man has known. Until the 1960s obscenity was prohibited in books, films, plays, radio and speech. In this way a complete censorship applied to all portrayals of war. Being the ultimate in obscenity the reality could not be revealed, therefore war was mythologised, conventionalised.

While many mouthed thoughtless chauvinistic platitudes, some, a few, were pensively frank. Nora McAuliffe's 'Anzac Ghosts' published in the *Bulletin* of 30 April 1925 is such a jewel.

> I do not know if I could trace
> The outline of one laughing face,
> Or tell what colour were your eyes . . .
> I have not spent my heart in sighs;
> From war's raw ends I've spun new ties
> Though one died nobly at Quinn's Post.
> I've not found the decade drear –
> I've laughed and danced and savoured cheer;
> I've kept no vigil for my dead.
> But if across my days chance led
> A soldier lacking joy, or bread,
> I've done my best to right his wrong.
> To you I hymn no paean, no song.
> The skies are blue, the years are long
> But Anzac's wife and orphan, too,
> Will stir my heart to spend and do –
> This is my monument to you!

Louise Mack's verse 'Bury it Deep' is an honest attempt at being honest.

Bury it deep, bury it deep
Never let sign of it upward creep
Over its grave with regardless feet
Dance, defying your heart's loud beat
Merrily fight through the tangled sedge
And merrily dance on the grave's red edge.

Bury it deep, bury it deep
Under the breast where the secrets keep
Over it pile, with compassionate hand
Clouds and fancies from no-mans-land.
Cover it over! They do not weep
Who bury it deep, bury it deep.

Private Hicks, who had 'walked' out of Germany, was back home in Australia, and on 21 May 'Irene' suddenly becomes 'Rene'. 'Went to the market with Rene. She and I went for a walk after tea.'

He is busy getting timber to build a house and looking for a mill; he buys a separator, then looks at houses for sale, writes daily to Rene and, on 28 May, 'wrote to Merritt, one of Ern's old mates'. He sets off to look at a house, takes ill and has to get home to bed. Receives a daily letter from Rene. 'Read it 5 times already and am still thinking.'

He spends odd hours in bed with sudden illnesses. Sees a doctor and is recommended for a pension. ('Heart bad again last night. . . . Tonight read all Rene's old letters and burnt some of them at her request.') He is now working on his new home every day, and at night going out to what he describes as 'evenings' at various neighbours' homes.

Homecoming, if not physically crippling, was emotionally exhausting.

'There were rich and sacramental things – the love of comrades, letters from home, the comradeship of those gone West, whom we do not at all times regret, for they still guide us, in whose arms they died,' Downing wrote. He then quotes:

> The goodliest fellowship of famous knights
> Whereof this world holds record. Such a sleep
> They sleep – the men I loved.

'I praise the men who are said to have won the war; also some others, not so well known, who had a hand in the matter, and who shared with me their food, their rum, their blankets and their money. I praise the memory of friends who sleep in France and visit me in dreams.'

Thorvald Kook (43rd Battalion) had written verse throughout the war and now, on his return, some lines tell of the gulf between these men and their old friends who had not been to war.

> So you're back again old chap I see
> But you don't seem the same as you used to be.

(Probably more awkwardness on the part of the speaker rather than any other thing, but the man from the trenches resented it.)

'I knew we were changed,' this man told me when aged, his legs bowed and 'chalky' from trench fever. His poems contained lines almost of wonder.

> Yet today we're talking and home again
> Walking and calling for drinks
> In civvies once more.

and,

> Do you remember?
> Those scenes of sadness
> To me like days of drunken madness
> That awful dilemma
> Looking straight at hell
> While we ducked from the bullet and screeching shell
> Do I remember?

Private Cecil Hitchcock had written in his diary on leaving for home in February 1919. 'First draft left for Australia and to the dead loneliness of civilian life'.

Harry 'Blue' Dadswell found the resumption of civilian life bewildering. 'We wanted to be civilians but found it wasn't so easy. Men would say, "Come and have a drink."

' "I don't drink thanks."

' "What and you a soldier!"

' "Have a cigarette."

' "Thanks, I don't smoke."

' "What, and you a soldier!"

'It kept on until that expression, *you a soldier*! started to get me down. I thought of the boys, some of the fine, clean-living boys you could meet anywhere. There were no canteens in the 1st AIF and about half of our unit neither smoked nor drank. The standards of behaviour and honesty were very high.

'Members of Parliament, ministers of religion, civic leaders, all had told us it was our duty to go to the war. Now we got a shock. One M.P. published a bit of verse describing us as paid murderers and describing the dead in such a way that must have horrified all those parents bereft of sons. We expected a storm of protests but there were none, so five local lads decided to act. They called on the M.P. and took him off to pour treacle over him and dust him with feathers. He was left at the local baths to clean himself up. The five were arrested, and heavily fined and dressed down by the judge, who would 'not tolerate that sort of behaviour from returned soldiers'. Not a word against the M.P. who called us murderers.

'Next I met a woman who taunted me with "going away for a real whale of a good time, some of you came a real thud". I thought of the boys on the troop ship. "That's the last time we'll see Australia." I wondered how people could imagine that we hadn't read the casualty lists, that we hadn't known we were to take the place of men killed or wounded, with the probable same fate.

'Then another shock. I was teasing a lively, cheerful young girl when she turned on me. "Well," she said, "I've never killed anyone!"

'Astonished, I said, "But neither have I."

' "What about the war?"

'I felt flat, like a pricked balloon.

' "I've been trying to forget that."

'She was instantly sorry but it left a query – *How* did civilians regard us?

'Through an accident it was brought home to me that civilians just couldn't or wouldn't think of what soldiers had been through. A fine young man, badly injured in a car accident, died. His friend was behaving hysterically, so I said, "Lad, pull yourself together. It is to your credit that you feel like this, but you mustn't let it get you down". He turned on me. "It's alright for you who've never seen anything like this in your life. You don't understand."

"What do you think happened in the war? Don't you think those men suffered pain too? I've seen many and helped to pick them up."

'He stared and then said, "Good Lord, I've never thought of anything like that."

"Well, next time you see an old digger drunk, don't be too hard on him. He might be trying to forget scenes worse than this."

'We were back in the community, a part of it and yet apart. There was a gap we couldn't forget and the others couldn't bridge.

'And so we remained – returned soldiers.'

The pride of the new navy, HMAS *Australia*, spent the last months of her North Sea war in the routine work and wearisome, unexciting but frightening protection of convoys and mine-layers. The nation were as proud of her work as they were of their soldiers' for it was known that the navy's blockading of the German Fleet had had perhaps a greater effect on the defeat of the enemy than any other action of the war.

At the close of it all she led the port division of the Grand Fleet at the grim pageant of the enemy fleet's surrender and then came home. Australia was very proud of her, their navy's first flagship, but not even to soothe their pride could she be saved. Under the Washington disarmament agreement among the nations she had to go. She was stripped of all fittings that might serve as mementoes – each municipality of Australia was given a photograph of her framed in the teak timbers of her deck – the remaining decks were strewn with flowers and, on 24 April 1924, she was towed out through the heads of Port Jackson, 'escorted by her comrades of the Squadron and saluted by a visiting light cruiser squadron, to a point 24 miles due east, and there in 150 fathoms she lies today'. 'This,' said the Prime Minister that evening, 'the first great ship of the Australian Navy was our contribution to the defence of civilisation. In her passing she symbolises our contribution to the cause of peace. We sacrifice her with a regret rendered poignant by the memory of her great service.'

These grandiose sentiments may have been splendid, except that by now those who sailed in her were too occupied trying to make the ends of life meet to weep for her. 'What did Dad say when the *Australia* went?' I asked my mother. 'Oh, he didn't see a paper for a day or so. He'd taken a job as a navvy on the railway up on the edge of the desert and all his energy went into keeping that. He knew he was lucky. He'd had odd jobs when he got back, the best one had been shovelling coal on the railway coal stage at Warragul, sixteen hours a day mostly, but of course he was still a very sick man and he got sicker so when he got on the railways he hung on to it. Within a few years, for every returned man carrying rails on the line there were five trying to get their job. I didn't need to read any war books, I learnt plenty from the diggers we brought in for a cup of tea and a bite as they humped their bluey through the countryside like a lost army searching for a leader.'

They were beginning to find that war never leaves a nation where it finds it and that when the hurly-burly's done, 'it matters little who lost or won', that the participating nations had been merely 'a file of marching prisoners chained together by treaty obligations' and stiff-necked pride and stupidity. Its causes, as President Woodrow

Wilson had said in 1917, 'were lost in antiquity'.

Yet they had gone, believing that the time had come for the laying down of lives for their land. To their children it was almost incredible; to their grandchildren, totally incomprehensible.

Glory had decayed long ago in the trenches and now there was the realisation that the land that they had been promised would be 'made fit for heroes' would become worse than they had known it, and the working man, as before, would carry his pick and shovel until he died – if he was lucky enough to be given work. 'Gunner' and 'Wingy' and 'Leery' (who was proud of how well his face had been patched up at Sidcup) were a spectral reminder of what 'glory' was all about as they carried their swags from door to door.

And yet, there was the other thing, the nostalgia that bore no name. They expressed it in that talk that they became known for, a sort of, to observers, silly badinage; their in-talk in digger-French, in 'Eggs-a-cook' jokesy terms when they exchanged quips about whizz-bangs and shell-holes, duckboards, Gyppos and furphies. For a time when they came back they had no way of contacting one another and then the reunions began and later the Anzac Day marches. Perhaps these marches were now the only infusions of adrenalin to a body that for four years had had to absorb such overdoses to survive that now that the drug had been abruptly withdrawn physically and emotionally an individual could not adjust.

'Ye that follow the vision of the world's weal afar/Have ye met with derision, and the red laugh of war?' Alfred Noyes asked. Yes, that too was to come. They would retreat further and further into their association for returned men as derision followed 'the red laugh'. They would be accused of going to war for self-seeking reasons, 'to have a good time', 'to get out of doing a days work', 'for blood-lust', a host of trivialities they could ignore because even they knew that 'every man thinks meanly of himself for not having been a soldier'. Most women believed 'it were better to be a soldier's widow than a coward's wife'. But the thing they could not bear was what they realised at the same time as their detractors learnt it, that it had been a war for no cause at all.

The men asked for work, any work. In their newssheet of December 1918, the 22nd battalion had presented a poem:

22nd Preferred

And if you want a slushy or a station overseer
and a tinker or a tailor or a snob
Or a 'andy bloke wiv 'orses or a mining engineer
We've got the very man to do yer job.
Butcher, baker, undertaker, and a Caf de Pary chef
'E is waiting keen and ready in the little A.I.F.
An', later when we land back in a mob
Per'aps we might be arstin' for a job –
So, we ask, what about it?

They ask that readers take up the motto – '22nd Preferred'.

The returned men had already learnt that they were only considered when needed as fighters. They had no say in the peace. Indeed, many were bitter about the harsh terms exacted against their old enemies. 'We never felt like that about them,' Richard Smith wrote. 'We could all have worked it out together, a real peace.' As for their return to civilian life, the passage of the Discharged Soldiers Settlements Acts in all states during 1916–17 began, according to economist Brian Fitzgerald, 'One of the most expensive and least profitable public ventures in Australian history'. The Commonwealth had guaranteed to meet the cost of settlement, but it was a débacle only equalled by the effect on the men who had tried to make a living from the acres.

With many others my parents had taken up 'a block' (in Victoria). Within three years they had 'lost' it. 'We couldn't keep up the payments,' my father said. 'And we had no money to stock it, or put up a proper house or fences or anything. Your mother and I worked hard enough at it, but that's how it goes I suppose.' When she was caretaker of Nowingi railway siding in Sunset Country, beyond the

Little Desert, my mother was approached by one of the soldier settlers from that wasteland. 'If you'll give us a ticket south from here for the missus and kids and me you can have the things in our house – we're leaving them there anyway.'

'A soldier . . . lived a few miles across the desert with his wife and babies, in a tent. She was a lovely woman. The babies were born in that tent. The family were in an awful way and he was a terribly sick man, wounds and shell shock made him often useless, but they both struggled on trying to make a go of it until the place was seized for debts. It was a rotten scheme.' (No man today farms those desolate acres that had been sold as 'land fit for heroes'.) Had they been to war before they would have expected nothing more. The English Tommy knew from past experience that all one gains from war are taxes, widows, wooden legs, and debt, and returning warriors should rust in peace or 'rot in hospitals'.

It is said that every hero becomes a bore at last. Few of these men had an opportunity to bore. Their country was sick of war, sick of the shortages, the restrictions and the dreariness. They wanted to hear no more of it. It was too late for the dead men to cry 'I gave my life for freedom – this I know; For those that bade me fight had told me so'.*

One comes away from the amorphous bulk of material written about that war with little respect for the leaders, the politicians and the military manipulators of young men. Biographers and eulogisers may praise or excuse these men but I have failed to find much evidence of any who attempted to avoid the war, to reduce the mortality amongst their men, or to end the holocaust.

Sixty years later John King recorded: 'They never gave the ranks much thought, nor instruction. They'd put you out in No Man's Land on patrol and if you got knocked off, that was that, but no one seemed to care or know what you were out there for. If the "heads" got their men killed or

* W. N. Ewers, *b.* 1885.

wounded that was that, they'd win the war or they'd lose it. They knew damned well they wouldn't lose it, as fast as they killed us off, there was someone coming up to take our place. There'd be four men and a corporal out on patrol. Many's the time we'd dive in shell-holes and watch the German patrols go by – and many's the time we've seen them dive and keep quiet when we slunk by. You'd always get a fight if you wanted it but even then we wondered what it was all about. As for the heads, whether they themselves knew what they were doing, I don't know.'

Long before they reached home the men were beginning to learn what Tommy Atkins had known for centuries: when the war ends, a soldier is little more than a pest to his mother country.

For months battalions were 'mucked about'. Sergeant Stevens, humping his full pack around France, covered up to fifteen miles a day as they marched from camp to camp. '*24 November 1918.* Arrived Ribeauville 1.30 a.m. dead beat. It seems scandalous that men should have to march such distances carrying full kit with blanket now that all hostilities have ceased. Even in the height of battle we would not carry a blanket but arrangements would be made to carry them on motor lorry. This march was accomplished with heavy pack, no one had a meal for 24 hours – It seems as if now we have finished the job any old thing will do for us now we are not required for the more strenuous work.'

On their new, 'going-home' suits they wore a narrow gold stripe on the left sleeve for each time they had been wounded in battle, one miniature blue chevron on the right sleeve for each year of active service and a red chevron for Anzac.

With a cryptic reference to his brother's birthday, Eddie Johnson prepared for home. 'Twenty-four years after the bull got into the underground tank in the Skilly Hills, my brother Chris arrived back from his Blighty leave. He was very excited to find that we would be on the same draft for Australia and our cousin, Arch Berryman, would be coming with us . . . I said goodbye to Mrs Holden, a second mother, who showed tears when giving me a hug and a kiss. She had lost her son Jack in this war, but had kindly accepted me in his place, as one of her family, during my time overseas. She had exchanged letters with my mother in Australia. To me her kindness was a wonderful experience, hard to forget. I arrived for the leave train at Paddington Station, and found that Mr Holden and Miss Holden . . . had taken time off to say goodbye.' Eddie, nearing home, was with the others on deck as they reached Fremantle, 'It is common to hear the troops saying, "Smell the gum leaves boys?"'

'A deafening cheer and boat whistles in full blast greeted us on arrival at Fremantle. We were back on Australian soil. Next, the Skilly Hills!' With two blue bands sewn on his tunic sleeve he 'said goodbye to the interstate boys and went down the gangway. Mother, Kath, baby Beth, Uncle Will, Aunt Ada, Arch's mother and father, Aunt Martha and cousin Doris were waiting. Then, we left for Bush Farm up in the Skilly Hills.'

He took ill while on leave from the after-effects of the two gas attacks he had survived and was put in hospital. 'Screens were placed around my bed, a doctor and 3 nurses arrived. The Dr. pushed a long tube in my back and pumped out a pint of straw-coloured liquid. He then enquired if I felt alright. A digger in the next bed said, "Say you feel crook Dig., and give it to me". They were handing me some brandy!' On 6 November 1919, 'I was handed a certificate that said I had served with honour and was disabled in the Great War. I received a small pension.'

Sergeant Stevens continued his meticulous diary to the end. '*9 April 1919*: Pulled out of dock at 3 p.m. Sailors of Dreadnoughts *Warspite*, *Ajax* and *Benbow* being lined up on their respective decks giving cheers as we left. Cheers also came from the torpedo boats and destroyers as we went along the Sound. The Devon people waving enthusiastically as we passed down as we went on our way to the open sea and home.'

Fremantle, the first stop, never failed the men. 'Boat and train whistles blowing furiously,' Sergeant Stevens wrote on 14 May 1919. 'Good many people on wharf. Great excitement. Made me realise that I am at last back in Australia. Had good smell of gum trees, as good as a dose of medicine.' And then, Home! '*22 May 1919*: Today is the day of days! Passed Queenscliff, Portsea and Sorrento, looked as beautiful as any place seen. I am pleased beyond words to be in my homeland again.'

Signalman Harry Dadswell found that the next week or two was a succession of seeing friends and relations and going to 'Welcome Homes' to various mates, then his own. 'Many mates were missing. Forty-five of us enlisted from home, all the unmarried men of the district. Of these, fifteen had died overseas and of the rest, only three of us had not been wounded. Several of those wounded died within a few years, of their wounds. We were proud of the district's record. We thought there would never be another war while the men who had been through it, lived.'

Some didn't leave until after the gathering of the Allies in London for 'Peace Week' in August 1919. Rowan Smith wrote home to his father, dismissing the great gathering as, 'Lots of Chows and Niggers of exalted station, Amurkans, Dagoes, etc.'

Back at Bush farm Eddie Johnson was given a Welcome Home in the Forresters' Hall. 'Mr Emil Sobers, who, when speaking, told us that he first saw Chris lying in a cane clothes basket when a baby. He also had memories of me singing a song, which went, "I'm a little soldier, and only six years old". He fizzled out on the second verse and Chris had to get him going by singing it with him while his mother played the piano.'

Standing by in ghostly battalions were their mates 'over there'. It was useless for the dancers at the victory ball to excuse their laughter by exclaiming, 'We're young you see!' for the returning men could hear the whispers of shadows round the wall. ('Ah,' said the dead men, 'So were we!') Young Love, aged twenty-four, who had adored his wife and baby. 'Everyone around me have been hit or killed. I escaped so far'; Carl and Ernek Janssen, aged 22 and 24;

Roy Bice who had wept when he left South Australia; Grubb, the young Tasmanian who flirted with a girl on the banks of the River Esk; Rankin himself. 'I think they'll soon send me home, mother.' Bruce Laugher, aged 22, of whom all that is left is 'Two photographs, they are the only ones taken of Bruce'. One was of the boy, the other was of his grave in France. He was aged nineteen, his sister told me. Gra. Foreman, the young airman who cried, 'I only took her out a couple of times!' when a girl wrote suggesting marriage. 'Poor old Minnie', who'd worked on in the ward until the night she died, because the wounded were coming in so fast. 'You couldn't forget them even if you tried,' Vic. Graham said. 'They came upon you at most unexpected times.'

'Oh, the useless slaughter of young men,' Theo. Ford, at eighty, says. 'The older I get the sadder I feel about the uselessness of it all, but in particular, the deaths of my comrades.'

'You ask me how these sights affected me,' said my cousin Jackie Pearce, when he talked with me just once about those years in France. 'Well, I wouldn't have known at the time. We never talked to one another about it mark you, but I reckon each of us had learnt from the first shock not to register [the sight] again. Except for a few chaps. And they went mad.' Jim McPhee told me, 'We thought we managed alright, kept the awful things out of our minds, but now I'm an old man and they come out from where I hid them. Every night.'

Léoné Mills tells of her father, now an old man, but in those days the boy, Roly Mills, who survived Gallipoli and then France. 'In recent years he's begun to wake in the night crying out. I don't know if he knows he does it. He'll shout out things. It seems he hasn't forgotten any one sight he saw or any sound he heard. By his cries in the night the sounds and sights must have been unendurable.'

On the more intimate level Downing wrote, 'There were uproarious functions in the mess, but the boon companions dropped off one by one – and sad was the meagre crowd that sat round tables that never seemed so large and empty as after a heavy "stunt".'

In every small town the squat stone monuments went up, some at crossroads where it is difficult to imagine a squad of men having lived at any time. For other wars a church, a hall, hospital or park would suffice but as the poet Geoffrey Page said, 'This war took stone'. Some commentators claim that these monuments are 'yet another example of Australians' wish to immortalise defeats'. No writer having a scholarly interest in the personal documents of men who served in that war and the women who waited could come to such a conclusion. They were more the symbolic tombs of an ideal.

'What price me now?' There is no way of knowing, for most of the accounts were never presented.

Appendix I

C.E.W. BEAN

For those researching this war one Australian stands out beyond all others, partly because of his skill in many fields but mostly because of his warm humanity. C. E. W. Bean, during the war, and until his death at the age of eighty-eight in 1968, recognised the import and impact on Australia of the vast panorama. He watched the first men come in from all corners of the Commonwealth to enlist, he was with them in the first camps, on the first convoy; he wrote communiqués home from Egypt. On 25 April 1915 he landed at Gallipoli, and left only when the Anzacs did. In France he followed each attack, observed each trench and battlefield. Throughout the five years the men were away from home he was talking with them, recording their experiences, their jokes, heart-aches and behaviour.

When the men came home, he stayed on. He went back to the old battlegrounds, to the Somme and Gallipoli, learning from the relics still scattered around those things that the soldiers could not know while hostilities were taking place. From this last journeying he gathered the material that later became the nucleus of the Australian War Museum, Canberra. The museum and the official history he was commissioned to write mirror the man; in both we see a desire to record the heart-beat of a nation. The museum is not one that may please the most aesthetic curators. Bean was not so much interested in the scientific, technological item as in the memorabilia of a human tragedy.

472

There is a bag of earth from Pozières where 'more Australians fell than any other place on earth'; there are some of the logs from Lone Pine; there are the very touching personal items he found on the dead still lying out on The Nek; scraps of Turkish uniforms from the dead at Chanuk Bair demonstrate the patched nature of the Turkish uniform. Some items he gathered only to illustrate the farthest point reached by Australians or evidence of their having fought – and died – beyond where battalion histories had recorded.

There are descriptive cards: 'Jan. 1919. Found on Dead Man's Ridge beside 10 Australian and 1 Turkish water bottles. Pieces of Australian rifles and bayonets found scattered about the ridge in front of Pope's Hill.' (The Light Horse had charged the Turkish trenches here on 7 August 1915, and were eventually driven back we remember, leaving their dead and bringing their wounded in under cover of darkness. We remember Nurse Kitchen on the hospital ship during August, 'The wounded say there are hundreds more wounded there and some have been lying out in No Man's Land for four and five days.') 'Boot from No Man's Land, Fromelles', is an example of the place being worthy of remembrance, not the object. There is a portion of a brick from the flattened Mouquet Farm, an improvised draughts-board found in Quinns Post.

Bean had contacted the Australian Flying Corps (then in Germany) and by 1919 they were searching for relics to send him. As a result Canberra is now said to have one of the largest German World War I collections in the world. Certainly the museum houses two German planes that are rare; the Pfalz is represented in some collections but the Albatros, the most common German fighter plane, is the only authentic Albatros in the world.

As well as collecting for a future museum, Bean collected souvenir items to be sent home to every small town or settlement in Australia. Even places where only two or three men enlisted have their memento. It must have taken ship after ship to bring these trophies back to Australia. There were twenty German aircraft, tanks, machine-guns by the thousands, Lewis guns, gas equipment, the wooden memorial the French erected '*Aux Héros Australiens morts pour la défense de Villers-Bretonneux 24–25 Avril, 1918. Les Habitants Reconnaissants.*' It was similar to the armies of old bringing back war trophies.

The war trophies record books record page on page of them – over 4 000 machine guns for instance. An allocation committee was formed after the war and trophies were allocated to various towns.

Had a museum curator gathered a collection it would have been different. Bean was an historian, and a rare one.

An indication of his energy and enterprise is the lamentable weakness of World War II material in comparison. Because of C. E. W. Bean, World War I is much more prolifically represented. Indeed, the Light Horse Battles of the Middle East in World War I are poorly covered because Bean was not there.

His magnificent volumes of the history of that first 'great' war are compulsive reading. Those familiar only with his *From Anzac to Amiens*, which is a précis of his larger work, can have no conception of the greatness of the man. Those who see the War Museum as being 'cluttered with trivia' and unlike the scholarly precepts most curators would prefer, have not understood that the museum represents the overall endeavours of Australia in war. Few military museums in the world are as moving as this one to those who know the story.

This writer is indebted to the man, Bean, as is anyone who searches for reality in the study of that time.

Appendix II

Table 1. *Recruitment in Proportion to Population*

Country	Total sent overseas or undergoing training as at 1 Nov. 1918*	Estimated total white male population at July 1911	Percentage of total white male population represented by total recruited
Canada	458 218	3 400 000	13.48
Australia	331 814	2 470 000	13.43
New Zealand	112 223	580 000	19.35
South Africa	76 184	685 000	11.12
Newfoundland	6 173	–	–
British Isles	4 970 902	22 485 501	22.11

Table 2. *Enlistments By States*

State	Enlistments	Approximate percentages	
		To total population	To males aged 18 to 44
Queensland	57 704	8.5	37.7
New South Wales	164 030	8.8	39.8
Victoria	112 399	7.9	38.6
South Australia	34 959	8.0	37.6
Western Australia	32 231	9.9	37.5
Tasmania	15 485	7.9	37.8
	416 808	8.5	38.7

* 81 per cent of the men were single, 17.38 per cent married, the remainder widowers.

Table 3. *Casualties*

Country	Total Casualties	Total Embarkations	Percentage
British Isles	2 535 424	5 000 000	50.71
Canada	210 100	422 405	49.74
Australia	215 585	331 781	64.98
New Zealand	58 526	98 950	59.01
India (native)	140 015	1 096 013	12.77

Battle casualty admissions to field ambulances from the AIF in France from April 1916 to March 1919, were:

	Number	% of Total
High velocity bullets (rifle and M.G. Fire)	48 309	33.93
Shell fragments and shrapnel pellets	72 513	50.93
Bombs and grenades	2 714	1.90
Bayonets	396	0.28
Gassing	16 822	11.82
Shell concussion, i.e. 'Shell shock'	1 624	1.14
	142 378	100.00

(Figures are not given for burial by shellburst, mines, etc. or burns from *flammenwerfers*, stated to be 'numerous'.)

Accidental injuries	15 648	7.30

Non-battle casualties including primary infections and 'infestations by living agents':

	Number	% of Total
Gastro-intestinal infections	1 558	0.74
Faucial and respiratory tract infection	41 300	19.49
The neurotomic ectodermoses	354	0.17
Rheumatic fever	239	0.11
Tuberculosis	602	0.28
Infections of eye, ear, nose	2 671	1.26
Septic pyogenic infections	11 888	5.61
The venereal infections	13 105	6.19
Transmitted through an insect or other host	4 244	2.01
Skin infestations	20 533	9.69
Specific wound infections	21	0.01
Pyrexia (Fever)	24 593	11.61
Helminthiasis (worms)	43	0.02

Bibliography

Most of the source material has been taken from contemporary diaries and letters and augmented by tape-recordings of the survivors' own accounts. Official histories of individual battalions, squadrons, ships, newspapers and periodicals from all states, dating from 1880 to 1939, were consulted as were ships' newssheets, battalions' roneoed newssheets and the ephemera published for and by servicemen, both official and unofficial.

Books

Allan, P. V. *The Thirty-Ninth*. Green & Sons, 1934.

Ashmead-Bartlett, E. *Despatches From the Dardanelles*. George Newnes, London, 1915.

Barrett, J. W. and Deane, P. *Australian Army Medical Corps in Egypt*. H. K. Lewis, 1918.

Baylebridge, W. [Blocksidge, C. W.]. *An Anzac Muster*. Angus & Robertson, Sydney, 1921.

Bean, C. E. W. (ed.). *The Anzac Book*, Cassell, London, 1916.

———. *Anzac to Amiens*. Australian War Memorial, Canberra, 1946.

———. *Gallipoli Mission*. Australian War Memorial, Canberra, 1948.

———. *Official History of Australia in the War of 1914–18*. Angus & Robertson, Sydney. Vol. I, *The Story of Anzac*, 1921; Vol. II, *The Story of Anzac*, 1924; Vol. III, *The A.I.F. In France, 1916*, 1929; Vol. IV, *The A.I.F. In France, 1917*, 1932; Vol. V, *The A.I.F. In France, 1918*, 1936; Vol. VI, *The A.I.F. In France, 1918*, 1936; Vol. VII, *Sinai and Palestine*, by H. S. Gullett, 1922; Vol. VIII, *Australian Flying Corps*, by F. M. Cutlack, 1923; Vol. IX, *The Royal Australian Navy*, by A. W. Jose, 1926; Vol. X, *The Australians at Rabaul*, by S. S. McKenzie, 1927; Vol. XI, *Australia During the War*, by E. Scott, 1936; Vol. XII, *Photographic Record of the War*, 1934.

478 *The ANZACS*

———. *Two Men I Knew*. [Brudenell White and William Bridges]. Australian War Memorial, Canberra, 1957.

Belford, W. C. *Legs-Eleven*. Imperial Printing Co., Perth, 1940.

Berrie, G. *Morale: a Story of Australian Light Horsemen*. Holland and Stephenson, 1949.

Berrie, G. L. *Under Furred Hats*. W. C. Penfold & Co., 1919.

Bourne, G. H. *History of the 2nd Light Horse Regiment*. Northern Daily Leader. Tamworth, 1926.

Bridger, T. D. *With the 27th Battery in France*. Sydney, 1919.

Burrows, W. E. *Richthofen: a True Story of the Red Baron*. Hart-Davis, London, 1970.

Butler, A. G. *Official History of the Australian Army Medical Services, 1914–18*. Australian War Memorial, Canberra. Vol. I, *Gallipoli, Palestine and New Guinea*, 1930; Vol. II, *The Western Front*, 1940; Vol. III, *Problems and Services*, 1943.

Carne, W. A. *In Good Company*. 6th Machine Gun Company Association, Melbourne, 1937.

Cavill, H. W. *Imperishable Anzacs*. William Brookes & Co., 1916.

Chataway, T. P. *History of the 15th Battalion*. William Brooks & Co., 1948.

Chauvel, H. *'Nulli Secundus'. The History of the 2nd Light Horse Regiment. Northern Daily Leader*, Albury, 1927.

Collett, H. B. *The 28th, a Record of War Service With the AIF*. Library, Museum and Art Gallery, Perth, 1922.

Commonwealth Bureau of Census and Statistics. *Yearbook*. 1926.

Cutlack, F. M. (ed.). *War Letters of General Monash*. Angus & Robertson, Sydney, 1934.

Cuttriss, G. P. *'Over the Top' With the Third Australian Division*. Charles H. Kelly, 1920.

Darley, T. H. *With the Ninth Light Horse in the Great War*. Hassell Press, Adelaide, 1922.

Davidson, F. *The Wells of Beersheba*. Angus & Robertson, Sydney, 1933.

Dennis, C. P. *The Moods of Ginger Mick*. Angus & Robertson, Sydney, 1916.

Der Rote Kampfflieger: Eingeleitet und Erganzt von Bolko Freiherr von Richthofen. Ullstein, Berlin, 1933.

Devine, W. *The Story of a Battalion*. Melville & Mullen, Melbourne, 1919.

Dinning, H. and McBey, J. *Nile to Aleppo*. Allen & Unwin, London, 1920.

Dollman, W. and Skinner, H. M. *The Blue and Brown Diamond*. Lowman & Cope, 1921.

Downing, W. H. *Digger Dialects*. Lothian, Melbourne, 1919.

Downing, W. H. *To the Last Ridge*. Australasian Authors' Agency, Melbourne, 1920.

Dutton, G. *From Federation to War 1901–1914.* In the series Australia since the Camera. Cheshire, Melbourne, 1971.

Ellis, A. D. *The Story of the Fifth Australian Division.* Hodder & Stoughton, London, 1920?

Farley, E. *The 38th Battalion AIF.* Bendigo, 1920.

Fitzpatrick, B. *The British Empire in Australia, an Economic History 1834–1939.* Macmillan, London, 1941.

Gellert, L. *Songs of a Campaign.* Angus & Robertson, Sydney, 1917.

Gibbons, L. P. *The Red Knight of Germany: Baron von Richthofen, Germany's Great War Airman.* Cassell, London, 1932.

Gorman, E. *With the Twenty-second.* Australasian Authors' Agency, Melbourne, 1919.

Green, F. C. *The Fortieth. A Record of the 40th Battalion.* Govt. Printer, Hobart, 1922.

Hall, R. *The Desert Hath Pearls,* Hawthorn Press, Melbourne, 1975.

Hamilton, I. S. M. *Gallipoli Diary.* 2 vols. Edward Arnold, London, 1920.

Hardinge, L. F. *William Morris Hughes: a Political Biography.* Angus & Robertson, Sydney, 1964.

Harvey, W. J. *The Red and White Diamond.* Alexander McCubbin, Melbourne, 1920.

Harvey, N. K. *From Anzac to the Hindenburg Line.* William Brookes & Co., Brisbane, 1941.

Henderson, W. G. *Foiled! The Enemy in Our Own Land.* Australasian News Co., Sydney, 1915.

Hogue, Oliver ['Trooper Bluegum']. *The Cameliers.* Andrew Melrose, London, 1919.

Hoyt, E. P. *The Last Cruise of the Emden.* Andre Deutsch, London, 1967.

Hohenzollern, Prince Franz Joseph. *Emden.* Herbert Jenkins, London, 1928.

Idriess, I. L. *The Desert Column.* Angus & Robertson, Sydney, 1932.

Jauncey, L. C. *The Story of Conscription in Australasia.* OUP, London, 1935.

Joynt, W. D. *Saving the Channel Ports.* Wren, Melbourne, 1975.

Kahan, H. K. *The 28th Battalion.* Imperial Printing Co., Perth, 1968.

Keatinge, M. B. B. *War Book of the Third Pioneer Battalion.* Specialty Press, Melbourne, 1922.

Keown, A. W. *Forward With the Fifth.* Specialty Press, Melbourne, 1921.

Langley, G. F. and E. M. *Sand, Sweat and Camels.* London Publishing Co., London, 1976.

La Nauze, J. A. *Alfred Deakin: a Biography.* 2 vols. Allen & Unwin, London, 1965.

Link, A. S. *The Progressive Era and the Great War.* Appleton-Century Crofts, London, 1969.

Lock, C. B. L. *The Fighting 10th Battalion.* Webb, Adelaide, 1936.

Longmore, A. *Eggs A Cook.* Colortype Press, Perth, 1921.

Macandie, G. L. *The Genesis of the Royal Australian Navy.* NSW Govt Printer, Sydney, 1949.

McCrae, D. *Soldier My Soldier.* G. Robertson, Melbourne, 1916.

McKenzie, K. W. *The Story of the Seventeenth Battalion.* Shipping Newspapers Ltd, Sydney, 1946.

Manning, F. *Her Privates We.* Davies, London, 1930.

Maravigna, P. *Guerra E Vittoria (1915–1918).* Pomba Fratelli, Rome, 1919.

Masefield, J. *Gallipoli.* Heinemann, London, 1916.

Maxwell, J. *Hell's Bells and Mademoiselles.* Angus & Robertson, Sydney, 1932.

Moberly, G. *Experiences of a 'Dinki-Di' R.R.C. Nurse.* Australasian Medical Publishing Co., Sydney, 1933.

Monash, J. *The Australian Victories in France in 1918.* Hutchinson, London, 1920.

Moorehead, A. *Gallipoli.* Hamish Hamilton, London, 1956.

Murdoch, K. (comp.). *'The Day' – and After.* War speeches of the Rt Hon. W. M. Hughes. Cassell, London, 1916.

Newton, L. M. *The Story of the 12th Battalion.* Watch and Sons, Hobart, 1925.

Noble, J. *Port Phillip Pilots and Defences.* Hawthorn Press, Melbourne, 1973.

Norris, G. *The Royal Flying Corps.* Muller, London, 1965.

North, J. *Gallipoli. The Fading Vision.* Faber, London, 1966.

Olden, A. *Westralian Cavalry in the War.* Alexander McCubbin, Melbourne, 1921.

Owen, F. *Tempestuous Journey: Lloyd George, His Times and Life.* Hutchinson, London, 1954.

Reeves, L. C. *Australians in Action.* Australasian News Co., Sydney, 1915.

Returned Soldiers' Assn. *Anzac Memorial.* Returned Soldiers' Association, Sydney, 1916–17.

Richthofen, Manfred Freiherr (trans. J. E. Barket). *The Red Air Fighter.* 'Aeroplane' & General Publishing Co., London, 1918.

Robson, L. L. *The First A.I.F. a Study of its Recruitment 1914–18.* Melbourne University Press, Melbourne, 1970.

Rule, E. J. *Jacka's Mob.* Angus & Robertson, Sydney, 1933.

Schaedel, C. *Men and Machines of the Australian Flying Corps 1914–19.* Kookaburra Technical Publications, Dandenong, 1972.

Skeyhill, T. *Soldier Songs From Anzac.* G. Robertson, Melbourne, 1916.

Stoker, H. G. *Straws in the Wind.* Herbert Jenkins, London, 1925.

Taylor, F. W. and Cusack, T. A. *Nulli Secundus. A History of the Second Battalion A.I.F.* New Century Press, Sydney, 1942.

Tilton, M. *The Grey Battalion.* Angus & Robertson, Sydney, 1933.

Williams, H. R. *The Gallant Company.* Angus & Robertson, Sydney, 1933.

'Vigilant'. *Richthofen, the Red Knight of the Air.* J. Hamilton, London, 1934.

von Mucke, Hellmuth. *The Emden.* Ritter, 1917.

von Sanders, L. *Five Years In Turkey.* United States Naval Institute, Annopolis, 1927.

White, T. A. *Diggers Abroad.* Angus & Robertson, Sydney, 1920.

White, T. W. *Guests of the Unspeakable.* Angus & Robertson, Sydney, 1935.

Wren, E. *Randwick to Hargicourt.* Ronald McDonald, Sydney, 1935.

Articles, Brochures, Bulletins, Magazines, Pamphlets etc.

AIF Education Service Journal. London, January 1919.

AIF Records Section. *Statistics of Casualties to December 1918.* London, 1919.

Anzac Bulletin. Published by authority of the High Commission for Australia. 1916–19.

Aussie. AIF trench magazine. London, 1918.

Australia. *Parliamentary Papers.* 1914, 1915, 1916, 1917, 1918.

Barrak. The Camel Corps Review. Cairo, 1917.

Bean, C. E. W. *The Old AIF.* World Affairs Pamphlet no. 4. 1940.

———. 'Sidelights of the War on Australian Character'. *R.A.H.S. Journal and Proceedings,* Vol. XIII, Part IV, 1927.

British Ministry of Food to Householders. 29 May 1917.

Bystanders' Fragments From France, The. Vols. 1, 2, 3, 4. 1916–1918.

Cacolet, The. Review of the Medical Section of the Camel Corps. Cairo, 1917.

Cole, D. 'The Crimson Thread of Kinship: Ethnic Ideas in Australia 1870–1914'. *Historical Studies,* Vol. 14, no. 56, April 1971.

Commonwealth of Australia. *Yearbook.* 1916.

Gill, G. H. 'The Australian Navy: Origins, Growth and Development'. *R.A.H.S. Journal and Proceedings,* Vol. 45, Part 3, 1959.

HMAS *Sydney.* Ship's Log (18 June 1914–1 December 1915).

Harney, W. 'Harney's War'. *Overland,* no. 13, October 1958.

Illustrated War News, 6 January 1915.

Inglis, K. S. 'The Anzac Tradition'. *Meanjin Quarterly,* Vol. XXIV, no. 1, 1965, pp. 25–44.

Instructions for Control of Invalids by AIF and Australian Expeditionary Force. Government Printer, 1916.

Keating, M. 'Australian Work Force and Employment, 1910–1911 to 1960–1961'. *Australian Economic History Review,* Vol. VII, no. 2, September 1967.

Melbourne Punch, 3 December 1914.

Mother's Answer to a Common Soldier, 14 August 1916, A. Andrew Melrose, London, 1916.

New South Wales Statistical Register, 1914–15.

Order of Procession of the Victory March. London, 3 May 1919.

Order to all Ranks of the Fourth Army, 11 November 1918, signed General Rawlinson.

Owen, G. *Advice to Soldiers and Their Dependants.* Sydney, 1917.

Programme, Peace Thanksgiving Service. London, 6 July 1919.

Rising Sun. AIF trench magazine. France, October 1917.

Robertson, J. R. 'Conscription Issue and the National Movement, Western Australia June 1916–December 1917'. *University Studies in Western Australian History,* Vol. 3, no. 3, October 1959, pp. 5–57.

Robson, L. L. 'The Origin and Character of the First AIF, 1914–1918: Some Statistical Evidence'. *Historical Studies,* Vol. 15, no. 61, October 1973, pp. 737–49.

Roe, M. 'Comments on the Digger Tradition'. *Meanjin Quarterly,* Vol. XXIV, no. 3, 1965.

————. and Ward, R. 'The Australian Legend: an Exchange'. *Meanjin Quarterly,* Vol. XXI, no. 3, 1962.

School Paper, The. Education Department of Victoria. Melbourne, 1890–1917.

Scott, E. 'The Nature of the Issue'. *University of Melbourne War Lectures.* George Robertson, Melbourne, 1915.

Songs of the 7th Battalion. Melbourne, 1915.

Tate, F. *Our Debt to Our Soldiers.* Education Department of Victoria, Melbourne. 20 March 1916.

Tucker, T. G. 'British and German Ideals'. *University of Melbourne War Lectures.* George Robertson, Melbourne, 1915.

Sources of Illustrations

The illustrations in this book have been drawn mainly from the Australian War Memorial, Canberra, and the La Trobe Library, State Library of Victoria, Melbourne. I gratefully acknowledge their permission to reproduce material, as I acknowledge the many men and their families who also provided me with personal photographs.

Much of the material is now lodged in the La Trobe Collection in the State Library of Victoria. The Library are interested in adding to this collection and would be grateful for manuscripts, diaries and letters from any of the wars in which Australians have been involved.

Abbreviations

AAMC	Australian Army Medical Corps
AIF	Australian Imperial Force
ANZAC	Australian and New Zealand Army Corps
AWL	Absent without leave
KIA	Killed in action

Index

Abbot, Capt. 168
Adams, Jack 22, 189
Adams, Steve 189
Advertiser, The 225
Advocate, The 19
AE1 31–7
AE2 32, 83, 319
aerial photography 333
Afric, troopship 42
Age, The 208, 235
AIF *see* Australian Imperial Forces
Air Flying Corps 328–45
Ajax HMS 468
Albany xi, 30, 38, 44
Aleppo Road 312
'All along the crumbling line' 358
Allen, Vic 309
Allenby, Gen. Sir Edmund 305, 313
Amiens 8, 257, 400, 402, 406, 428, 433
Amiens, Bishop of 406, 433
Anti-German feelings in Australia 395–6
Anzac Beach Cemetery xi
The Anzac Book 179
Anzac Cove 9
Anzac Day xi, 5, 17, 302
Anzac Mounted Division 304
Aquitania, SS 118
Arblaster, Capt. C. 238
Archaeological find at Wadi Guzzi 316
Argus, The 11
Argylshire, hospital ship 111
Army pay 43
Ascanius, troopship 42
Asche, Oscar 360
Ashmead-Bartlett, E. 156
'As I was walking down Oxford Street' 275
Ataturk, Kemel 190
Australia, HMAS 19, 20, 32, 35, 36, 323–4; sinking outside Sydney Heads 326–7, 462

'Australia Will Be There' 18
Australian The, poem by W. Ogilvie 231
Australian Army Medical Service 75
Australian Army Nursing Service 43; pay 44
Australian Corps News Sheet 428
Australian Flying Corps 328–45; formed from AIF 329; casualties 342, 473
Australian Imperial Forces 22, 31, 129, 131, 205, 247–8; reinforcing for France 229; Air Flying Corps 328–45; Casualties in France 476; *see also* under names of Battles
Australian Light Horse 23, 30, 100, 125, 302–15, 316
Avenell, Nurse E. 438

Ballarat, troopship 216, 217, 218
Barber, Col. 349
Barnard, Cpl 415
Barnes, Charley 137
Barrett, R. 98
Bartlett, Trooper A. S. 106
Barton, Lieut. 180
Barunga, HMAS 322
Bass, Norman 359
Bath, Mrs A. 396
Battenburg, Lord Louis 38
Bean, C. E. W. 54, 65–6, 67; Lone Pine 114, 126–7; Man with Donkey 163; evacuation 179, 181; Battle of Somme 239, 429; *From Anzac to Amiens* 472–4
Bean, Capt. J. W. B. 25–6, 65–6, 67
Beavis, (Maj.-Gen.) L. E., Red Baron's death 349
Beersheba 8, 305, 306
Bell, Maj.-Gen. A. L. 181

Benalla HMAT 42, 43, 44, 61, 202, 292, 299, 453
Benbow, HMS 468
Bendigo Advertiser 214
Bennett, Brig. 370, 377
Bennett, Ray 98
Bennett, Padre (T.P.) 165–7, 184, 199
Bennie, Dr P. B. 288
Berliner Zeitung am Mittag 351, 395
Berrima 34
Berry, Geoffrey 121
Berry Guy Martin ('Marty') 219–20; grave 352
Berryman, A. 467
Besant (officer *AE1*) 34
Bice, Roy 209
Birch, W. and K. 214
Birdwood, Gen. 90–1, 180, 237, 274, 373, 384; Armistice 436–7
Birtwistle, Pte Ivor T. 208
Blackburn 407
Blighty 271–80, 353
Bock (stretcher-bearer) 373
Boer War 2, 14
Bolton, Col. 61, 78, 98
Bombala SS 23
Bones, Canon 317
Boorara, HMAS 322–3
Bowman, Sister 379
Bowrar, Lieut. F. 172
Boyd, Capt. J. 306
Brazier, Col. 106
Brennan, Christopher 230
Brew, Pte 25
Bridges, Gen. W. T. 22, 100, 104
Brisbane, HMAS 32
British Association for the Advancement of Science 18
Broadmeadows 66, 208
Brookes, Capt. C. A. 339
Brooks, Mrs E. 175
Brooks, Pte G. 171
Brown, Capt. A. R., death of Red Baron 348–9
Browne, Cpl 409
Buchan, John 148
Buchanan, W. 214
Bullecourt 268, 364, 398, 414
Bulletin, The 388, 458
Burke, T. 172
Burn, Lieut. 329
'The Bushrangers' 212
Butler, Pte 180
Butler, Col. A. G. 69, 160
'But of war, when all is torn or rent' 234
Butt, Clara 450
Byrne, Mick 6, 127

cadets' training 11–16
Calder, Robert 'Mac' 94
Camdor Castle, troopship 152
Camel Corps 304, 314–15
Campbell, Alan 155
Canada, hospital ship 116
Carlile, Sister 300
Carr, R. M., bomb-thrower 122
Carrick, Pte G. 'Thoughts of Home' 123
Carroll, H. 414
Carter, M. 424
Castalia, hospital troopship 437
Casualties x, xi, 127, 134, 141–2, 454, 475–6; Somme 236, 240, 248, 255, 260, 269–70, 365; Aust. Flying Corps 342; Ypres 368; Villers Bretonneux 415, 434, 442–4
Cater, Commander 139
Cavalcade 8
Cavell, Nurse Edith 290
Cavell, Pte H. W. 27
Cecelia, hospital ship, 109, 111
cemeteries on Gallipoli 186–92
Ceramic, hospital ship 281
Chalker, E. T. 96
Chapman, Lieut. Duncan 90
Chauvel, Maj.-Gen. H. G. 304–5
Cherry, Lieut. 254
Childers, torpedo boat 32
Churchill, Winston 80
Clan Macgillivray, troopship 221
Clemenceau 351
Close, S. 98
Cocking, Sister A. E. 309
Cole, Lieut. A. T. 332–3
Collum, Sgt Maj. 33
Collum, Lieut. Athel 277, 394
Colour patches 28, 78
'Come cheer up brave Anzacs' 229
Commonwealth SS 225
Conder, Capt. 284
Connor, Capt. J. 423
Conscription 388
referendum figures 390
Conyers, Sister 202
Cook, Mrs A. E. 175
Cook, Rt Hon. J. 21
Coulter, Maj. 98, 204
Countess of Hopetoun, torpedo boat 32
Coward, Noel 8
Craig, Capt. 168, 173
Cranswick, Rev. G. H. 214
Cripps, Lieut. B. A. 33, 221
Crouch, Col. 173
Cunningham, Pte K. S. 253
Curtis, Sister 301
Cutlack, F. M. 343

Dadswell, Sapper Harry 213, 276, 407, 420, 431, 446, 461, 469
Daly, Capt. 73
Darby, L., Surgeon 56
Dardanelles, the 3, 78, 80, 85, 88, 108, 120, 151, 181, 188
Darling, Lieut. 19
Davis, G. E. Miss 387
Davis, J. 409, 416
Dead Man's Ridge 3
death, attitudes to 93, 113
decorations 122
Delville Wood 355
Dennis, C. J. 72, 208, 233, 288
Desert Echo 25
Devanha, troopship 93
Deville (Devil's) Wood 355
Dickenson, Sister 379
Digger becomes common usage 376
Dilman, S. Turkish guide 128, 189–92
'Dinkum Aussies' 208
Divers, W. T. 'Bill' 322–6
Dodds, Will 219, 271
Dominion 18
Doris, HMS 322
Downing, W. H. 256, 261, 279, 374, 459, 470
Drake, –. 410
Drew, Paddy 253
Drummond, Dr 168
Drummond, (Air Marshal Sir) R. M. 333
'Dry Land Sailors' 120
Duigan, Capt. 342
Durack, Fanny 249, 266
Durban's welcome 220–1
Dykes, Sgt-Maj. 245

Ebeling, Maj. 153
Educational Gazette and Teachers' Aid 15
Edwards, Billy 353
Edwards, Harold, disc for Red Baron 350
Egypt ix, 9, 58–62
Elliot, A. J. 171
Elliot, Dale 145
Elliot, W. 224
Elliott, Brig.-Gen. H. E. 'Pompey' 238, 273, 407
Elwell, –. 34
Emden, German cruiser 45–9, 58; ships sunk 47
Emerson, R. W. 11
Encounter HMAS 32
English, Capt. of *Suevic* 456
enlistments 155, 208–20, 475
Entwistle, Capt. T. J. 73

Euripides, troopship 31, 42, 58, 384, 386
evacuation from Gallipoli 178–85
Ewers, W. N. 470

'Fair Dinkums' 208–23
Fanning, Capt. 198, 205, 241–2, 355–7
Fay, Capt. 162
Felmy, Lieut. G. 339–40
Field, H. B. 214
Finlay, Miss 300
Finlay, Mr 61
Fisher, Andrew 30, 155; message to England 17, 21
Fitzgerald, B. 465
flag saluting 14–16
Flers 264–7
Foch, Marshal 406, 432, 451
Fogarty, –. 172
Ford, Sgt F. T. 'Theo' 253, 352, 376, 470
Foreman, Lieut. W. 334–5, 470
'For the man who should loose me is dead' 233, 334–5
Foxcroft, L/Cpl Arthur 251–2
France 9, 204–6, 229–35
Francis, W. W. 'Australia will be there' 18
Franz Joseph, Prince 56
Fraser, Lieut. S. 245
Fromelles 8, 199, 236–48, 355, 473
Fuller, Corp. W. and Elsie 383
Fysh, Sir Hudson 333

Galeka, SS 80, 307
Galibolu Peninsula 186
Gallipoli ix, 8, 9, 77, 83–107, 117–20; evacuation 178, 202
Gamble, Maj. Walter 12
Garland, L/Cpl George 133–4
Garland, Col. Padre 316–17, 389, 439
Garratt, Trooper J. W. 122
Garsia, Lieut. Rupert Clare 18–20, 34, 36–7; sinking of *Emden* 49–58
Gartside, Col. 79, 100, 202
Gas 359, 370–2, 401, 410, 441
Gascon, hospital ship 108, 111, 116, 152, 200, 294, 319
Gayundah, gunboat 32
Gaza, attack on 306, 316
Geelong, troopship 209
George, Lloyd, Vote of Thanks to Flying Service 343, 450
George of Shellal, St, relics 317

Gibbons, Capt. Norman 240
Gilmore, (Dame) Mary 104–5, 231
Giritli, Prof. Ismet 186
Glossop, Capt. 55–7
Gloucester Castle, hospital ship 111
Gneisenau 30, 33, 34, 36–7
'God bless our splendid men' 214
'God send you back to me . . .' 135
Gooch, Sgt Hugh 140
'Goodbye-ee, goodbye-ee' 445
Gorringe, T. 400
Gourlay, A. J. 78
Graham, Vic 229, 234, 249, 252, 355, 470
Grantully Castle, hospital ship 111
Green, –. 172
Grubb, Pte W. E. K. 211–12, 470
Gwalior, Rajah of, presented aircraft 329

Hackett, W. 40–1
Hackney, J. C. 178
'Had he never been born he was mine' 231
Haig, Field Marshal Sir D. 398, 411, 422
Haig, Lieut. F. W. 332
Haig, Paddy 206
Hall, Ray, Glen, Rex, Jack and Roy 28; Brigade Maj. Rex 302–3, 307–9, 313
Hamilton, Gen. Sir Ian 10, 78, 128, 156, 178
Hamilton, Maj. J. W. 80–1
Hamp, Joe and Arthur 224
Hampshire, Kitchener's death 325
Harding, Eric 348
Harding, Richard and William 455
Hardy, HMS 218
Haret el Wasser 71, *see also* Wazzir
Hargreaves, Ethel M. ('Effie') 439
Harney, Bill 24
Harris, Lieut. E. 63
Harris, Lieut. G. W. 136, 363, 364
Harris, Hugh 363
Harvey, Norman 88–9
Health (*see also* casualties) Egypt 66–70; Gallipoli 137–40, 142; illnesses 441–4; casualties 478
Heath, Sister 100
Heathcote, Lieut. L. W. 332
Heney, T. W. 236
Hennay, B. 455
Henry, Lieut.-Col. 14
Herald, The 364
Herbert, Sgt Phillip 257, 274
Herefordshire 384
'Heroes of Anzac' 135

'He's a Young Australian Soldier' 135
Hetherington, Lieut. 416
'He was all I had to give' 232
'He went up to London and straight up he strode' 272
Hicks, Pte G. L. 431, 433, 459
Hill, Cpl 400, 416
Hill, Sgt 276
Hindenberg 432; Red Baron's funeral 350
Hindenburg Line 267, 270, 340, 364, 416, 422, 425, 428
Hindhaugh, Jane and Pte J. W. 176–7
Hinkler, Bert 334
Hitchcock, Pte C. 460
Hodgson, Capt. 98
Holder, –. 276
Hore, Capt. 126, 127
Hororata, troopship 42
Hoskin, Oliver 352, 442
hospital ships 108–12 *see also* under names
Hotham, Pte A. T. 170
Howse, Gen. 442
Hughes, Gen. 106
Hughes, Col. F. G. 74
Hughes, Peter 243
Hughes, William Morris 215, 386, 388
Humphries, –. 407
Humphreys, Pte Angelo 121
Hurley, Maj. 202

Ibuki, Japanese cruiser 42, 44
'If dreams were only true' 358
'If freedom of flight to my soul is given' 359
'If you were the only girl in the world' 335
Ilkington, John 13
Imperial Camel Corps 304, 307, 314–15
Ince, Russell 328; makes parachute 342; Red Baron dead 349
Ionate, hospital ship 116
'It's only an old piece of bunting . . .' 10
'I want to go home' 397

Jackson, Pte B. 104
Jackson, Capt. 153
Jackson, Cpl. 449
James, G. E. 88
James, W. A., reference for E. M. Hargreaves 439

Janssen, Carl and Ernek 23, 41, 57, 64, 65–7, 75–6, 93, 94, 149, 470
Jeffree, E. R. 97
Johnson, Eddie (E.C.) 224–5, 274, 276, 279, 390, 399, 402, 415; and brother Chris 468, 470
Johnson, Maj. 172
Jones, Flight-Commander E. J. 342
Jones, (Air Marshal Sir) George 340
Jones, Moore 147
Jordan xi, 9
'Juliet', patriotic songs 135

Kahn, Sgt Harry 146–7, 183, 274, 353, 407–15, 443
Kanowna SS 33, 451–3
Karoola, troopship 121
'Keep the home fires burning' 388
Kelly, Jim 145
Kemal, Mustapha 91, 190
Kemball, Maj.-Gen. G. V. 330
Keneally, T. *Gossip from the Forest* 435
Kenny, Signaller R. J. 39, 95
Kent-Hughes, (Sir) Wilfred 116
Kerr-Wilson, C. 440
King Edward sunk 118
King, John 215–16, 468
King, Father 298
Kirkpatrick, John Simpson ix, 23, sinking of *Emden* 55, 58; in Egypt 63; Lemnos I. 78–9; Gallipoli 93, 104; death 105; painted by Moore Jones 147; Man with donkey 157–64
Kitchen, sister Alice 44–8, 55; in Egypt 58–62, 79–82, 94, 98–100; Gallipoli 108–12, 116, 151–2, 200–4, 319; London 277, 300–1, 359–63; France 290–302, 451–2; London 376–9, 384, 397, 430–1, 446–51; Australia 453
Kitchener, Field Marshal Earl 178, 293, 325
'Kitchener's Army' 120, 129, 130
Kitto, Sammy, made Red Baron's coffin 350
Kleber 322
Klu, Pte 128
Knight Templar, SS 78
Königsberg 52
Kook, Thorvald 369, 460
Koringal, SS 159
Kyarra 62, 222

Langwarrin Hospital 284–5

'Last night I had a funny dream' 358
Laugher, Bruce, 470
Lawrence of Arabia 311–12
Lawson, Henry 11
Leane, Capt. A. E. 268; Leane family 268
Lemnos Island xi, 77, 111, 116, 118, 123, 138, 153, 183
Liberty, hospital ship 116
Lice 150, 154, 168, 171, 206, 234, 353–4, 444
Light Horsemen 28, 302–15
   see also Australian Light Horse
Lind, Capt. 79
'Lindenow (Gippsland)' 359
Lindsay, Norman 7, 388
Lion, battleship 86
'Lions of War' 230
London Gazette 383
Lone Pine 4, 8, 23, 113–34, 141; V.C.'s awarded 122, 172, 187; evacuated 181; cemetery 189; Logs in War museum 473
Love, Corp. Alfred M. 83–7
Low, David 388
Lowell, Amy 233
Lucan, Lord 228
Lucas Girls' 'Arch of Victory' 393
Ludendorff, Gen. 403
Lutzow, troopship 106

McAllister, Sgt 410
McAuliffe, Father 111, 298
McAuliffe, N. 'Anzac Ghosts' 458
McCallum, Capt. 314
McClure, Pte 120–1
McClure, Pte 120–1
McCarthy, Sister 377
McCrae, Hugh 230
McCrae, J. 'In Flanders Field' 451
MacDonald, Flora 353
McDonald, Sgt Jim 149
McFarlane, Lieut. 74
McGarvie, Pte D. 125
Mack, Lieut. Ernie and Stan 96, 129, 131, 438
Mack, Louise 'Bury it deep' 458
McKay, Maj.-Gen. 199
MacKeller, Dorothea 232
McKenna, Peter 276
McNamara, Lieut. Frank, only airman V.C. 332; Air Vice Marshal RAAF 333
McPhee, Col. 109
McPhee, Jim 79, 92, 138–40, 234, 254, 360, 372, 442, 470
McQueen, L/Cpl Alex 121
McWhae, Col. D. W. 261
'Mademoiselle from Armentières' 445

Madigan, David 166
Maher, M. 172
Mahood, (Rigger) Tom 195, 331, 340, 342
Man and Superman 286
Man with the Donkey *see* Kirkpatrick, John Simpson
Manual of Drill for School Use 13
Masefield, John, *Gallipoli* 358
Mathieson, Lieut. 100
May, Lieut. 347
May, Sgt 252
Medic, troopship 42, 58
Melba, Dame Nellie 450
Melbourne, HMAS 32, 38, 42, 49
Mena House Hospital 62, 69, 363
Menin Road 369, 372 *see also* Ypres
Meranda, Wolla 232
Merz, Lieut. 329
Middleton, C. 155
Millard, Pte John 210
Millear, T. 393
Miller, Sgt 372
Mills, George and Ted 380-1, 427
Mills, Norman 195, 263, 271, 437, 455
Mills, Reg 150-1, 195, 199, 169-70, 271, 279, 340, 456
Mills, Muriel 391
Mills, Roland 153-4, 205, 269, 353, 380, 391, 427, 470; daughter Léonne 380, 470
Minotaur, HMS 38, 42
Monitor 109
Moberly, Matron Gertrude F. 222, 379, 384-5, 437
Monash, Gen. (Sir) John 164, 273, 413-18, 427-9
Monro, Gen. Sir Charles 156, 178
Montauban 261-2
Moods of Ginger Mick 72
Moore, C. L. 34
Moorgate, HMAS 322
Morgan, L/Cpl Roger 252, 423
Morlancourt Ridge 347
Morley, Lieut. C. R. 151, 304, 306
Morris, Lieut. C. 22
Morse, Victor 252
Mortlake, 'Blue' 409
'The Mother' 232
Mouat, Mary J. and Daniel 175-6
Moule, Trooper H. H. 254, 274, 391
Mouquet Farm 234, 251-2, 473
Munro-Ferguson, Sir R. 20
Murdoch, (Sir) Keith 156, 364
Murphy, Barry (B. F.) 24
Murray, Capt. 239
Murray, Gen. Sir Archibald 206, 305, 307

Murray-Jones, Capt. A. 233, 339
'Must you go, need you go . . .' 136
Mutiny 418-22

'Naked Army, The' 148
Naval Bridging Train 120, 183, 257
Navy, Royal Australian *see* Royal Australian Navy
Neale, Lieut. 370, 371
Neuralia, hospital ship 110
Neville, Nurse Alice 435
Newbolt, Sir H. 57
Newcombe, M. 400
Newhand, Pte 171
New Zealand Mounted Rifles 304
Niagara 440
Nicholas, Sgt A. S. 100
Noel, Cpl 371, 372
No Man's Land 290-301
Nurses, army 438, *see also* Australian Army Nursing Service and individual names
N.Z., HMS 19

'O Chalkpit. Can you talk?' 355
O'Gilvie, A. 74
Ogilvie, W. 231
Olden, Lieut.-Col. 106, 311-13
Oliver, Pte T. 113, 119-20
Omrah, SS 30
'On land or sea, wherever you be . . .' 18
Oonah 19
'O, on some morning dateless' 359
'On the trail of the Lonesome Pine' 119
Oram, Miss 108, 111
O'Reilly, Dowell 232
O'Rourke, Alex 242
Orsova, SS 222
Orvieto, SS 41, 42, 46
'O the dalliance and the wit' 280
'Our Boys in Egypt' 135

'Pack up your troubles . . .' 17
'The Padre' 173 *see also* Bennett, Padre
Page, G. 471
Palestine campaign 307-9
Palmer, Herbert E. 276
Palmer, Roger 131
Palmer, Vance 230
Pankhurst, Mrs 450
Parramatta, HMAS 32
Passchendaele 8, 221, 367; *see also* Ypres 368-83
Patriotic songs 135-6
Patriotism 10-16
'Patterns' 233
Pay, army 43; nurses 44

Payne, Charlie 409
Pearce, Jackie 5, 6, 470
Percival, Ernest, Percival Proctor plane 334
Percival, Pte W. S. 122
Pfalz 22
Pincher, destroyer 109
Pinnock, Cliff 131
Pioneer, cruiser 33
'Plum and apple . . .' 136
Plumer, Gen. Sir H. 402
Pockley, Capt. B. C. A. 34, 406
Pockley, Lieut. J. A. 406
Poets, poems 229–34, *see also* individual titles
Ponting, Corp. F. J. 96
Popkin, Cedric, brought down Red Baron 348
Pozières 249–70, 418, 473; casualties 8, 260
Proctor, Capt. 448
Protector, gunboat 32
Purves-Stewart, Col. Sir J. 137, 443

Quartermain, Sister 431
Queen Alexandra Imperial Military Nursing Reserve (QAIMNSR) 43
Queen Elizabeth, HMS 86, 87, 104
Quintal, Corp. F. E. 97

Radio, advent of 56
Rafa, battle of 314
Ralfe, Capt. 342
Rankin, Pte Roy 142–6, 182, 184, 235, 256–7, 393, 470
Recruiting 25–7, 205, 275
'Remember, Lord, Australia's sons tonight' 233
Returned Soldiers' League 231
Rhododendron Ridge 3
Ribble, torpedo boat 93
Richards, Sgt E. R. 'Bill' 147–9
Riddel, A. 40
Robinson, Lieut. 73
Robinson, pilot 22
Robson, Corp. E. R. 63, 94
Roe, Harry 137
Rogers, Sister 301
Rogers, A. 175
'Roll up' 135
Roosevelt, Theodore 14
Rose of No Man's Land 290–301
'Roses are Blooming in Picardy' 5
Ross, Sister 300
Rossell, Dr 424
Royal Australian Navy 33–7; Fleet at Out-break of War 32 *see also* individual ships

Royal Flying Corps 334
Royal George 80
Royal Naval Air Service 334
Rule, Sgt E. J. 250
Russell, Gen. 318
Rutherford, Capt. D. W. 332
Ryan, J. M. 326

Said, Emir, surrenders Damascus 311
Salta 204
Saluting 271–2, 274
Saluting the Flag 14–16
Samsing, Sister 61, 78, 80, 100, 108, 111, 153, 202, 203, 291, 293–4, 297, 360, 379, 430, 446
Samways, Pte W. S. 170
Sanderson, Sgt W. L. 127
Sarafan raid 313
Sargeant, –. 98
Sari Bair 8, 139, 163, 191
Sassoon, Siegfried – 'They' 352
Scarlett, officer *AE1* 34
Scharnhorst 30, 33, 34, 36–7
Scotian 169, 170
Scott, Sgt George 205
Shannon, Chaplain W. F. 328, 354
Shaw, Arnie 154
Shellal Mosaic 316–18
Shepherd, Col. A. E. 443
Sheppard, Sgt 407–8
Sherman, Gen. 286
Ships *see under* individual names; sunk by *Emden* 47
Shrapnel Gully 3, 93, 94, 104, 145, 163, 170
Shuttleworth, A. N. 'If dreams were only true' 358
Simmons, Maj. 202
Simpson, John *see* Kirkpatrick, John Simpson
'Sing us a song of the Northern seas' 326
Skeyhill, Signaller Tom 148
slang 269
Smith, A.B. A. 31
Smith, Charles Kingsford, joined RFC 334
Smith, Capt. George 314–15
Smith, Pte Richard 195–6, 278, 343, 359, 434, 455, 465
Smith, Ronald E. 21–2, 39, 146–7
Smith, (Sir) Ross 333
Smith, Rowan 469
Snee, Lieut.-Col. 13
Snell, Lieut. P. W. 332
'Soldier's Song' 135

Somme, Battle of the xi, 3, 9; Fromelles 236–48, 354; Pozières 249–68, 354–5; Aust. Flying Corps arrive 340; Villers-Bretonneux 404–17, 434
Songs, patriotic 135–6 *see also* individual titles
'Sons of Australia' 38, 135
Southern 42
Southland 142, 169
Souvenirs 382
Sowter, Jimmy 245
Spowers, Dr 448
Springthorpe, Col. 201, 202
Stevens, Sgt J. A. 196, 248, 265–6, 354, 364, 375, 392, 398–403, 419, 425, 467, 470
Stoker, Commander H. G., submarine *AE2* at Gallipoli 320
Stone, –. 407
Stout, Capt. 121
Strange, Ben 389
Sud Australische Zeitung 395
Submarines *see AE1, AE2*
Suevic, troopship 456
Sutton, Sgt-Maj. Harry 265–6
Sutton, Col. 162
Suvla Bay 120, 124, 128–9, 140, 153; evacuation 183
Sydney, HMAS 32, 34, 36, 38, 42, 49; sinks *Emden* 49–58
Sydney Daily Telegraph 14, 18
Sydney Mail 143

'Take me back to dear old Blighty' 271
Tannebring, R. 409
Taplin, Lieut. L. 333
Taylor, Lieut. A. L. D. 342
Taylor, P. J. 342
'Their burial march was the big guns' roar' 179
'There's a long long trail a-winding' 136
'There's a rose that grows, in No Man's Land' 290
'These even as their fathers' 230
'They' — Siegfried Sassoon 352
'They owed their mother such love' 231
'They will never come back' 233
Thomas, Lowell 310
Thompson, Pte R. G. 'Tommy' 120, 129, 183, 257
Times, The 47, 55
Tingira RAN 32
Tivey, Brig. 420
Todd, Maj. 131
To The Last Ridge 261
Towers, Corp. A. C. 163

Trans-Australian Line boys 25
Treherne, Corp. 58
trench feet 353 *see also* casualties and health
troopships' departure 38–48 *see also* names of ships
Triumph, HMS, sunk 107, 137
Tuckwell, Pte 134
Turnbridge, Lieut. J. V. 332

Ulysses, troopship, 42, 281

Vautin, Lieut. C. H. 339
venereal disease viii, 68–76, 278, 281–9
Villers-Bretonneux xi, 8, 221, 401, 404–17; 'adopted' by Melbourne 434, 474
Volkerkreig, Dr 47
von Horn, Count K. 394–5
von Muller 47, 54
von Richthofen, Baron Manfred 340; death, funeral 346–51
von Sanders, Gen. Liman 91
von Spee, Admiral Count 30, 36–7, 327

Wackett, (Sir) Lawrence 333
Wadi Guzzi 316
Walker, Sister 431
Walker, W. H. 171
Waller, Napier 425
Walton, Pte Fred 267
Wanliss, Lieut. Harold 194
War, attitudes to vii, 2, 5, 8–11, 81; 'wholesale murder' 117; butchers' picnic 352–67
War, declaration of 20, 21
War games x
War Loans and Patriotic Funds 390
Warragul Gazette 394
Warrego HMAS 32
Warspite HMS 468
Wazzir, Battle of ix, 71–6, 167, 288
Weigall, Lady G. 396
Weir, 'Ack' 409–15
Weir, Corp. 252
Weindorfer, G. 21
'We know — it is our deathless pride' 231
'We're none of us the same' 352
Westbrook, Frank 359
Western Mail 389
Wemyss, Admiral Sir Rosslyn 183
'What does the World our mother remember?' 232
'What gone! The Australians gone! From Anzac gone?' 178

'What went ye forth to seek?' 230
Wheeler, Sister 430
White, Maj. Cyril Brudenall 22;
    later Lt-Gen. 179, 237
'White Gurkhas' 11
White, Mrs Capt. J. and Capt. E.
    359
White, Hon. Sir Thomas W. 330,
    331
'Who were you with last night?'
    445
Williams, Mr 111
Williams, Lieut. H. R. 197–8,
    240–1, 390
Williams, Brig.-Gen. R. E. 284
Williams, Air Vice-Marshal Sir
    Richard 330, 333
Williams, Lieut. (on the Somme)
    340, 355, 356
Wilson, Lieut. E. G. 125

Wilson, Miss G. M. x
Wilson, Roy 'Bluey' 252
Wiltshire 45
Winn, Capt. R. C. 253
Woods, Rev. Maitland 199–200,
    316–18

Yarra, HMAS 32
Yeddo, SS 159
Young, –. 407
Young, Norman 214–15, 425–7,
    435, 436, 456
Young, Sister 449
Ypres 206, 221, 368–83, 398 *see
    also* Passchendaele

Zambesi 33
Zonnebecke 254
Zwar, Maj. B. T. 69